STP MATHEMATICS
3rd Edition

7

L BOSTOCK S CHANDLER A SHEPHERD

E SMITH I BETTISON

OXFORD
UNIVERSITY PRESS

OXFORD
UNIVERSITY PRESS

Great Clarendon Street, Oxford, OX2 6DP, United Kingdom

Oxford University Press is a department of the University of Oxford. It furthers the University's objective of excellence in research, scholarship, and education by publishing worldwide. Oxford is a registered trade mark of Oxford University Press in the UK and in certain other countries

British Library Cataloguing in Publication Data
Data available

978-1-4085-2378-0

10 9 8 7

Printed in India by Multivista Global Pvt. Ltd

Acknowledgements

Page make-up: Tech-Set Limited, UK
Illustrations: Tech-Set Limited, UK

The publishers would like to thank the following for the permission to reproduce photographs: **Cover**: Antishock/iStockphoto; **p1**: lisafx/iStockphoto; **p8l**: Tony Waltham/Robert Harding World Imagery/Corbis; **p8r**: QiangBa DanZhen/Fotolia; **p10**: Des Willie/Alamy; **p17**: elavuk81See/Fotolia; **p20**: Luis Santos/Fotolia; **p27**: hjschneider/Fotolia; **p34**: Rick Gerharter/Getty Images; **p43**: The National Blood Service 2012; **p44**: volga1971/Fotolia; **p54**: sad/Fotolia; **p68**: Colin Underhill/Alamy; **p74**: Hero Images/Corbis; **p90**: Thomas Francois/Fotolia; **p98**: Mark Bowden/Getty Images; **p102**: Iwanon/photocuisine/Corbis; **p119**: Derek Trask/Getty Images; **p141**: Hedgehog/Fotolia; **p166**: anankkml/Fotolia; **p189l**: Pavel Losevsky/Fotolia; **p189lc**: Ocean/Corbis; **p189rc**: antpkr/Fotolia; **p189r**: Helle: Jochen/Arcaid/Corbis; **p200t**: Omika/Fotolia; **p200b**: Jiang Kehong/Xinhua Press/Corbis; **p226**: Sergiogen/Fotolia; **p230**: nickolae/Fotolia; **p231**: nata789/Fotolia; **p232**: Anyka/Fotolia; **p246l**: Peter Hermes Furian/Fotolia; **p246r**: Accent/Fotolia; **p261l**: Peter Hermes Furian/Fotolia; **p261r**: Accent/Fotolia; **p262**: viperagp/Fotolia; **p282**: mradlgruber/Fotolia; **p301t**: Deyan Georgiev/Fotolia; **p301b**: jacojvr/Fotolia; **p324**: Markus Bormann/Fotolia; **p345**: vector_master/Fotolia; **p358**: Ingram Publishing/Alamy; **p376**: gemphotography/Fotolia; **p392**: Sandra van der Steen/Fotolia; **p395**: Michael Blann/Getty Images. **p399**: contains public sector information licensed under the Open Government Licence v2.0.

Although we have made every effort to trace and contact all copyright holders before publication, this has not been possible in all cases. If notified, the publisher will rectify any errors or omissions at the earliest opportunity.

Contents

Contents

Introduction

To the student

This is the first book of a series that helps you to learn, enjoy and progress through Mathematics in the National Curriculum. As well as a clear and concise text the book offers a wide range of practical, investigational and problem-solving work that is relevant to the mathematics you are learning.

Everyone needs success and satisfaction in getting things right. With this in mind we have provided questions of two types.

The first type are practice questions and problems to help reinforce what you have learnt.

The second type, identified by a blue background, are extension questions and problems for those of you who like a greater challenge.

Questions with this symbol are problems which give you a chance to apply your skills to real-life examples and practise your problem-solving skills.

Each chapter begins with a problem associated with a real-life situation entitled 'Consider'. Although some students will be able to attempt this already, it will prove to be a challenge to most of you. It should therefore act as an introductory stimulus for bringing into play the strategies for problem solving that you are already familiar with. When the problem is reintroduced at the end of the chapter in 'Consider again', you should appreciate how your skills have expanded.

Class discussions may be used by your teacher to promote discussion of key concepts.

Most chapters have a 'Mixed exercise' after the main work of the chapter has been completed. This will help you to revise what you have done, either when you have finished the chapter or at a later date.

All chapters end with some mathematical puzzles ⊕ or practical or investigational work ⊖. For this work you are encouraged to share your ideas with others, to use any mathematics you are familiar with, and to try to solve each problem in different ways, appreciating the advantages and disadvantages of each method.

After every four or five chapters you will find a 'Summary'. This lists the most important points that have been studied in the previous chapters and concludes with revision exercises that test the work you have studied up to that point. This is followed by a mental arithmetic test.

Hints are included throughout to help you avoid common errors and misconceptions.

The first time key words appear, they are highlighted in **bold blue** text. A definition can be found in the 'Key words' section at the back of the book so that you can check the meanings of words.

All of you need to be able to use a calculator accurately but it is unwise to rely on a calculator for work that you should do in your head. By all means use it to check your calculations, but remember, whether you use a calculator or do the working yourself, always estimate your answer and always ask yourself the question, 'Is my answer a sensible one?'

Mathematics is an exciting and enjoyable subject when you understand what is going on. Remember, if you don't understand something, ask someone who can explain it to you. If you still don't understand, ask again. Good luck with your studies.

To the teacher

This is the first book in the STP Mathematics Third Edition. It is based on the ST(P) Mathematics series but has been extensively rewritten and is now firmly based on the 2014 Programme of Study for Key Stage 3.

This series of books aims to prepare students for a high level of achievement at Key Stage 3 leading on to the higher tier at GCSE.

Kerboodle

This textbook is supported by online resources on Kerboodle, including a wide range of assessment activities and teacher-support to help develop problem-solving skills. Kerboodle also includes an online version of this student book for independent use at home.

1 Addition and subtraction of whole numbers

Consider

We use whole numbers all the time in everyday life.

Consider this problem. Jane takes a bar of chocolate costing 75 p, a pen costing £1.23, and a card priced at £1.30 to the cash desk. The cashier asks for £2.56.

What skills does Jane need so that she can quickly check if this is the correct amount?

You should be able to solve this problem after you have worked through this chapter.

Class discussion

Discuss how you would react in each situation, and what you need to know and be able to do so that you feel in control of the situation.

1   Jason needs to get to a cinema by 3 o'clock in the afternoon, and it is vital that he is not late. The journey takes about 35 minutes by bus; he needs to allow 5 minutes to walk to the bus stop and up to 8 minutes to wait for a bus. He is told to start the journey at half-past one.

2   Ethan owes a friend 27 marbles. He gives his friend an unopened bag with 50 marbles in it and gets back 33 marbles.

3   Sara has scored 246 so far in a game of darts. She needs 301 to win the game. Kris says 'You need 52 to finish'.

Discussing these examples should convince you that there are some situations where it is important to be able to add and subtract numbers quickly and accurately. It is also important to be able to judge whether or not a calculation is *roughly* correct. These skills come with practice.

Continuous addition of numbers less than 100

To add a line of numbers, start at the left-hand side:

	Working in your head
$6 + 4 + 3 + 8 = 21$	add the first two numbers ($= 10$)
	then add on the next number ($= 13$)
	then add on the next number ($= 21$)
	Check your answer by starting at the other end.

To add a column of numbers, start at the bottom and, *working in your head,* add up the column:

$$
\begin{array}{r}
8 \\
7 \\
2 \\
+\ 5 \\
\hline
22 \\
\end{array}
$$
$(5 + 2 = 7, 7 + 7 = 14, 14 + 8 = 22)$

Check your answer by starting at the top and add the column *in your head.*

Exercise 1a

Find the value of

1 $2 + 3 + 1 + 4$

2 $1 + 5 + 2 + 3$

3 $5 + 2 + 6 + 1$

4 $3 + 4 + 2 + 6$

5 $5 + 6 + 4 + 2$

6 $2 + 1 + 3 + 5$

7 $7 + 3 + 8 + 6$

8 $5 + 4 + 9 + 1$

9 $7 + 3 + 2 + 8$

10 $6 + 7 + 5 + 9$

11 $2 + 5 + 4 + 1 + 3$

12 $4 + 8 + 2 + 1 + 2$

13 $6 + 7 + 3 + 5 + 6$

14 $4 + 9 + 2 + 8 + 4$

15 $7 + 3 + 9 + 6 + 8$

16 $3 + 2 + 3 + 4 + 1 + 5$

17 $4 + 2 + 5 + 6 + 1 + 7$

18 $8 + 3 + 9 + 2 + 7 + 3$

19 $6 + 9 + 4 + 8 + 7 + 5$

20 $4 + 7 + 8 + 6 + 5 + 2$

21
$$
\begin{array}{r}
3 \\
7 \\
8 \\
+\ 6 \\
\hline
\end{array}
$$

22
$$
\begin{array}{r}
1 \\
9 \\
5 \\
+\ 2 \\
\hline
\end{array}
$$

23
$$
\begin{array}{r}
4 \\
6 \\
7 \\
+\ 3 \\
\hline
\end{array}
$$

24
$$
\begin{array}{r}
9 \\
7 \\
9 \\
+\ 8 \\
\hline
\end{array}
$$

25
$$
\begin{array}{r}
8 \\
7 \\
6 \\
+\ 9 \\
\hline
\end{array}
$$

26
$$
\begin{array}{r}
3 \\
4 \\
5 \\
1 \\
+\ 8 \\
\hline
\end{array}
$$

27
$$
\begin{array}{r}
4 \\
2 \\
3 \\
9 \\
+\ 3 \\
\hline
\end{array}
$$

28
$$
\begin{array}{r}
6 \\
5 \\
3 \\
1 \\
+\ 4 \\
\hline
\end{array}
$$

29
$$
\begin{array}{r}
7 \\
8 \\
2 \\
1 \\
+\ 8 \\
\hline
\end{array}
$$

30
$$
\begin{array}{r}
6 \\
7 \\
3 \\
9 \\
+\ 7 \\
\hline
\end{array}
$$

31
$$
\begin{array}{r}
3 \\
5 \\
2 \\
9 \\
1 \\
+\ 6 \\
\hline
\end{array}
$$

32
$$
\begin{array}{r}
5 \\
7 \\
3 \\
5 \\
4 \\
+\ 2 \\
\hline
\end{array}
$$

33
$$
\begin{array}{r}
8 \\
7 \\
9 \\
2 \\
8 \\
+\ 6 \\
\hline
\end{array}
$$

34
$$
\begin{array}{r}
2 \\
9 \\
5 \\
8 \\
7 \\
+\ 6 \\
\hline
\end{array}
$$

35
$$
\begin{array}{r}
4 \\
8 \\
2 \\
9 \\
9 \\
+\ 7 \\
\hline
\end{array}
$$

36 Find the distance round the edge of this figure.

37 a The following sequence of numbers is formed by starting with 8 and then adding 7 to the previous number: 8, 15, 22, 29, ... Write down the next three numbers.

   b Write down the first five numbers of a sequence formed by starting with 4 and adding 6 each time.

   c Write down the first five numbers of a sequence formed by starting with 6 and adding 9 each time.

38 To score in snooker when there are red balls on the table, a red ball needs to be potted first followed by a colour, then another red followed by another colour, and so on. Each red ball scores 1.
The colours, and their scores are:
black 7,   pink 6,   blue 5,   brown 4,   green 3,   yellow 2
Marco had three visits to the table at which he potted:
   a red, black, red, blue, red, pink, red, black
   b red, black, red, green, red, black, red, pink
   c red, blue, red, yellow, red, pink.
Find Marco's break (i.e. his score) for each visit.

39 In the game of snooker described above, when the last red ball has been potted, there is a free choice of a coloured ball to follow it. Once that ball has been potted, it is put back on the table.
The colours then have to be potted in the order: yellow, green, brown, blue, pink, black.
Kate had a turn when there were just two red balls left and she needed to score 57 to win. Is it possible for her to win, if she pots all the balls?

Place value

The number one thousand, three hundred and forty-two can be written in figures as 1342. The number four thousand, one hundred and twenty-three can be written in figures as 4123.
The same digits are used in both of these, but they are in different places.

   In 1342, the **digit** 4 means 4 tens.
   In 4123, the digit 4 means 4 thousands.

The meaning of a digit in a number is called its *place value*.

We can write a number under place headings:

	thousands	hundreds	tens	units
e.g. 4123 can be written as	4	1	2	3
and 3056 can be written as	3	0	5	6

We can now see that the digit 3 in 4123 represents 3 units, i.e. the place value of 3 is 3 units; whereas the digit 3 in 3056 represents 3 thousands, so the place value of 3 in this number is 3000.

Exercise 1b

1 Write in figures the number
   a two hundred and four   b ten thousand and thirty

2 Write in words the number
   a 1023   b 21 505

3 Write these numbers in order with the smallest first.
   a 207, 89, 1030, 103   b 11 020, 90 110, 370 000, 101 010

4 Write down the value of the 5 in the number
   a 152   b 2506   c 375

5 Make as many different numbers as you can, using each of the digits 2, 6, 7, 0 once in each number.
   Arrange the numbers in order with the largest first.

Addition of whole numbers

Sometimes we need to use pencil and paper to add numbers.
To add a column of numbers, start with the units:

$$\begin{array}{r} 83 \\ 291 \\ +\ 702 \\ \hline 1076 \\ {\scriptstyle 1} \end{array}$$

In the *units* column, $2 + 1 + 3 = 6$ so write 6 in the units column.
In the *tens* column, $0 + 9 + 8 = 17$ tens which is 7 tens and 1 hundred.
Write 7 in the tens column and carry the 1 hundred to the hundreds column to be added to what is there already.
In the *hundreds* column, $1 + 7 + 2 = 10$ hundreds which is 0 hundreds and 1 thousand.

Exercise 1c

Add up the following numbers in your head.

1	28	2	35	3	22	4	103	5	56
	+ 51		+ 62		+ 43		+ 205		+ 203

Use pencil and paper to add up these numbers.

6	101	8	492	10	351	12	9217	14	93
	25		812		1036		824		251
	+ 273		+ 735		+ 915		3216		179
							+ 8572		+ 1312

7	223	9	259	11	87	13	3021	15	6943
	317		28		102		84		278
	+ 342		+ 704		56		926		5419
					+ 304		+ 5041		+ 3604

Worked example

➡ Find   217 + 85 + 976

217 + 85 + 976 = 1278

```
   217
    85
 + 976
 ─────
  1278
   1 1
```

 It is easier to add numbers when they are in a column.

 Make sure you line up the units.

Find

16 28 + 72 + 12

17 56 + 10 + 92

18 83 + 107 + 52

19 256 + 139 + 402

20 1026 + 398 + 542

21 24 + 83 + 76

22 92 + 58 + 27

23 52 + 112 + 38

24 207 + 394 + 651

25 943 + 856 + 984

26 599 + 107 + 2058

27 642 + 321 + 4973

28 555 + 921 + 6049

29 253 + 431 + 1212

30 821 + 903 + 3506

31 727 + 652 + 2716

32 92 + 56 + 109 + 324

33 103 + 72 + 58 + 276

34 329 + 26 + 73 + 429

35 325 + 293 + 502 + 712

36 Darts landing in this ring score double

Darts landing in this ring score single

Darts landing in this ring score triple

Darts landing in this ring score nothing

Find the score on each board.

a   b   c

37 When Lai went to school this morning it took him 4 minutes to walk to the station. He had to wait 12 minutes for the train and the train journey took 26 minutes. He then had an 8 minute walk to his school.

How long did it take Lai to get to school?

38 Find the sum of one thousand and fifty, four hundred and seven and three thousand five hundred.

39 Hannah decided to save some money by an unusual method. She put 1 p in her money box in the first week, 2 p in the second week, 4 p in the third week, 8 p in the fourth week, and so on. Hannah gave up after 10 weeks.

Write down how much she put in her money box each week.

Find the total that she saved.

Why do you think she gave up?

40 Complete the number squares using the numbers 1 to 9 once only in each square to make the total in each row, column and diagonal the same.

a

2		6
9		
4		8

b

8		
	5	
4		2

c

4	9	
	5	
	1	

Subtraction of whole numbers

Exercise 1d

Work out the following subtractions in your head.

1 15
   − 4

2 19
   − 7

3 18
   − 4

4 12
   − 7

5 15
   − 8

6 20 − 8

7 18 − 3

8 17 − 8

9 14 − 6

10 10 − 4

11 15 − 2

12 12 − 9

13 17 − 6

14 16 − 8

15 19 − 9

16 11 − 7

17 13 − 8

18 15 − 9

19 20 − 6

20 15 − 7

Sometimes we need to use pencil and paper for subtraction. You will probably have your own method for subtraction. Use it if you understand it. The worked examples in Exercise 1e show one method.

If you are asked to find the **difference** between two numbers, take the smaller number from the larger one.

Exercise 1e

Worked example

→ Find $642 - 316$

$642 - 316 = 326$

Check: $326 + 316 = 642$

$$\begin{array}{r} 6\,{}^{3}\cancel{4}\,{}^{1}2 \\ -\ 3\ 1\ 6 \\ \hline 3\ 2\ 6 \end{array}$$ Start with the units column: $2 - 6$ is not possible, so take 1 from the number in the tens column. This makes 12 in the units column and leaves 3 in the tens column.

→ Find $907 - 259$

$907 - 259 = 648$

Check: $648 + 259 = 907$

$$\begin{array}{r} {}^{8}9\ {}^{9}\cancel{0}\ {}^{1}7 \\ -\ 2\ 5\ 9 \\ \hline 6\ 4\ 8 \end{array}$$ There are no tens here, so take 1 from the number in the hundreds column. This gives 10 in the tens column, so we can now take 1 from this to give 17 in the units column and leave 9 in the tens column.

Find

1 $526 - 315$	**7** $578 - 291$	**13** $507 - 499$	**19** $4627 - 3924$
2 $526 - 308$	**8** $635 - 457$	**14** $3451 - 623$	**20** $1203 - 527$
3 $564 - 491$	**9** $602 - 415$	**15** $5267 - 444$	**21** $4906 - 829$
4 $495 - 369$	**10** $1237 - 524$	**16** $1027 - 452$	**22** $3506 - 3429$
5 $814 - 344$	**11** $823 - 568$	**17** $3927 - 583$	**23** $7016 - 6824$
6 $592 - 238$	**12** $718 - 439$	**18** $1922 - 398$	**24** $9342 - 5147$

25 A bottle of milk cost me 96 p. I paid with a £5 note (£5 is 500 pence). How much change should I have?

26 In a school there are 856 children. There are 392 girls. How many boys are there?

27 Take two hundred and fifty-one away from three hundred and forty.

28 A shop starts with 750 cans of cola and sells 463. How many cans are left?

29 One shop stocks 129 varieties of sweets and another shop stocks 165 varieties.
What is the difference in the number of varieties of sweets stocked by the two shops?

30 Subtract two thousand and sixty-five from eight thousand, five hundred and forty-eight.

31 Find the difference between the value of the 6 in the number 461 and the value of the 3 in the number 307.

32 The sequence of numbers 100, 93, 86, ... is formed by starting with 100 and subtracting 7 each time.
Write down the next five terms of this sequence.

33 Write down the first five terms of a sequence of numbers formed by starting with 94 as the first term and taking away 12 each time.

34 The diagram shows a simple map with distances between villages.

   a   How far is it from Aston to Barby via Datch?

   b   Ford is 3 km from Barby along the road to Aston. How far is Ford from Aston?

35 The road I live in has 97 houses in it.
The road my friend lives in has 49 houses in it.
How many more houses are there in my road than in my friend's road?

36 Ben Nevis is 1343 m high and is the highest mountain in Great Britain.
Mount Everest is 8843 m high and is the highest mountain in the world.
How much higher than Ben Nevis is Mount Everest?

37 Peter needs a total score of 301 to win a game of darts. On his first turn he scores 58, on his second turn he scores 75.
How many does he still have to score to win?

38 Find the missing digit; it is marked with ☐.

   a   27 + 38 = ☐5   **d**   5☐ + 29 = 83

   b   34 + 5☐ = 89   **e**   ☐4 + 57 = 81

   c   128 + ☐59 = 1087   **f**   1☐7 + 239 = 416

Mixed addition and subtraction

Some problems, like question **37** in the last exercise, can involve a mixture of addition and subtraction.

It is the sign *in front of* a number that tells you what to do with that number.

For example $128 - 56 + 92$ means '128 take away 56 and add on 92'. This can be done in any order, so we could add on 92 and then take away 56, i.e.

$$128 - 56 + 92 = 128 + 92 - 56$$
$$= 220 - 56$$
$$= 164$$

Exercise 1f

Worked example

➤ Find $138 + 76 - 94$

$$\begin{array}{r} 138 \\ + \ 76 \\ \hline 214 \end{array}$$

$$\begin{array}{r} 214 \\ - \ \ 94 \\ \hline 120 \end{array}$$

$$138 + 76 - 94 = 214 - 94$$
$$= 120$$

➤ Find $56 - 72 + 39 - 14$

$$\begin{array}{r} 56 \\ + \ 39 \\ \hline 95 \end{array}$$

$$\begin{array}{r} 95 \\ - \ 72 \\ \hline 23 \end{array}$$

$$56 - 72 + 39 - 14 = 95 - 72 - 14$$
$$= 23 - 14$$
$$= 9$$

Find

1 $25 - 6 + 7 - 9$

2 $14 + 2 - 8 - 3$

3 $7 - 4 + 5 - 6$

4 $23 - 2 + 4 + 5$

5 $46 - 12 + 3 - 9$

6 $27 + 6 - 11 - 9$

7 $2 + 13 - 7 + 3 - 8$

8 $17 + 4 - 9 - 3 - 5$

9 $17 - 9 + 11 - 19$

10 $36 - 24 + 62 - 49$

11 $51 - 27 - 38 + 14$

12 $124 + 51 - 78 - 14$

13 $91 - 50 + 36 - 27$

14 $105 + 23 - 78 - 50$

15 $73 - 42 - 19 + 27$

16 $361 - 200 + 15 - 81$

17 $213 - 307 + 198 - 31$

18 $29 + 108 - 210 + 93$

19 $493 - 1000 + 751 - 140$

20 $612 - 318 + 219 + 84$

21 $95 - 161 + 75 + 10$

22 $952 - 1010 - 251 + 438$

23 Abiola buys a stick of glue costing 280 p and a notebook costing £4.99. He pays with a £10 note.
How much change does he get?

24 Find the sum of eighty-six and fifty-four, and then take away sixty-eight.

25 I have a piece of string 200 cm long. I cut off two pieces, one of length 86 cm and one of length 34 cm. How long is the piece of string that I have left?

26 On Monday 1000 fish fingers were cooked in the school kitchen. At the first sitting 384 fish fingers were served. At the second sitting 298 fish fingers were served.
How many were left?

27 Find the difference between one hundred and ninety, and eighty-three. Then add on thirty-seven.

28 A greengrocer has 38 kg of carrots when he opens on Monday morning. During the day he gets a delivery of 60 kg of carrots and sells 29 kg of carrots.
How many kilograms of carrots are left when he closes for the day?

29 Leo has 30 marbles in his pocket when he goes to school on Monday morning. At first playtime he wins 6 marbles. At second playtime he loses 15 marbles. At third playtime he loses 4 marbles. How many marbles does Leo now have?

30 Sarah gets £10.00 pocket money on Saturday. On Monday she spends 84 p. On Tuesday she is given 50 p for doing a special job at home. On Thursday she spends 47 p.
How much money does she have left?

31 The sequence of numbers 7, 16, 11, 20, 15, … is made by starting with 7, then adding 9 to get the next number. To get the third number, subtract 5. To get the next number, add 9, then the number after that subtract 5, and so on.

  a Write down the next four numbers in the sequence.

  b Starting with 7, write down the third, fifth, seventh numbers, and so on, to make another sequence. What do you think the rule is for generating this sequence?

32 The weekly profit made in a school tuck shop is found by taking away the cost of the items bought for the shop that week from the total takings for the week. (The students run the shop and do not get paid!)
Find the profit when £3699 was spent on items for the shop and the takings were £4980.

33 In question **32**, a general instruction was given for finding the weekly profit and then the profit was found for a particular case. Here is the general instruction for obtaining a sequence of numbers:

'The next number is obtained by adding the previous two numbers.'

a The first number is 3 and the second number is 5. Write down the next six numbers.

b The first number is 4 and the second number is 2. Write down the next six numbers.

34 Write down a general instruction for obtaining the sequence of numbers

    a 1, 3, 5, 7, 9, …   b 50, 42, 34, 26, 18, …

35 Everton is returning from the local farm with an 8-litre can which is full of milk. He meets Amy who is going to the same farm for milk. She has an empty 5-litre can and an empty 3-litre can. Everton knows that there is no more milk left at the farm, so decides to share his milk equally with Amy. How can they do this using only the three containers they have?

Approximation

If you were told that a games machine priced at £147 and a pack of accessories priced at £39 will cost you a total of £205, would you know quickly that the total quoted was wrong?

There are situations when we cannot do a calculation in our heads and when there is not time or opportunity to use pencil and paper. If a calculator is available, we can use that, but we sometimes make mistakes when using them. It is important to know if a result is roughly right. By simplifying numbers it is possible to get a rough answer in our heads.

One way to simplify numbers is to make them into the nearest number of tens. For example

    147 is roughly 15 tens, or 150

and

    39 is roughly 4 tens, or 40

We say that 147 is *rounded up* to 150 and 123 is *rounded down* to 120. In mathematics we say that 147 is approximately equal to 15 tens.

We use the symbol ≈ to mean 'is approximately equal to'.

We would write

    147 ≈ 15 tens

and

    39 ≈ 4 tens

When a number is halfway between tens we always round up. We say

    125 ≈ 13 tens

Exercise 1g

Worked example

➡ Write 56 as an approximate number of tens.

$56 \approx 6$ tens (i.e. 60)

Write each of the following numbers as an approximate number of tens.

1	84	6	37
2	151	7	228
3	46	8	155
4	632	9	73
5	8	10	4

Worked example

➡ Write 1278 as an approximate number of hundreds.

$1278 \approx 13$ hundreds (i.e. 1300)

Write each of the following numbers as an approximate number of hundreds.

11	830	16	450
12	256	17	1560
13	780	18	3780
14	1221	19	972
15	1350	20	1965

Worked example

➡ By writing each number correct to the nearest number of tens, find an approximate answer for $196 + 58 - 84$

$196 \approx 20$ tens
$58 \approx 6$ tens
$84 \approx 8$ tens

Therefore $196 + 58 - 84 \approx 20$ tens $+ 6$ tens $- 8$ tens
$$= 18 \text{ tens} = 180$$

By writing each number correct to the nearest number of tens, find an approximate answer for

21	344 − 87	**31**	137 − 56 + 82
22	95 − 39	**32**	295 + 304 − 451
23	258 − 49	**33**	49 − 25 + 18
24	153 + 181	**34**	68 + 143 + 73
25	89 − 51	**35**	153 + 19 + 57
26	258 + 108	**36**	250 + 31 − 121
27	391 − 127	**37**	127 + 56 + 82 + 95
28	832 − 55	**38**	73 + 21 + 37 + 46 + 29
29	83 + 27 − 52	**39**	83 + 64 + 95 + 51
30	76 − 31 − 29	**40**	63 + 29 + 40 + 37 + 81

Now use your calculator to find the exact answers in questions **21** to **40**. Remember to look at your rough answer to check that your calculator answer is probably right.

In questions **41** to **45**, there are four answers given for each calculation. Three of them are obviously wrong. Without working them out, write down the letter of the answer that *might* be correct.

41	257 − 32:	A	25	B	289	C	225	D	125
42	749 + 412:	A	337	B	1161	C	2550	D	961
43	290 − 181:	A	9	B	89	C	109	D	471
44	682 + 798 − 56:	A	2784	B	424	C	1424	D	882
45	1278 − 569:	A	209	B	709	C	1847	D	967

Consider again

We use whole numbers all the time in everyday life.

Jane takes a bar of chocolate costing 75 p, a pen costing £1.23, and a card priced at £1.30 to the cash desk. The cashier asks for £2.56.

Now write down the skills that Jane needs so that she can quickly check if this is the correct amount.

Number puzzles

1   Each disc shows three digits. Remove one digit from one of the discs and place it on another disc so that the digits on each of the three discs have the same total.

2   Follow these instructions.

   Step 1   Write down any three-digit number in which the number of hundreds differs by at least two from the number of units,
   e.g. 419 or 236 or 973 but not 707 or 514.

   Step 2   Now write down the digits in reverse order,
   e.g. 419 becomes 914.

   Step 3   Subtract the smaller number from the larger number, e.g. 914 − 419 = 495.

   Step 4   Add this number to its reverse,
   i.e. add 495 to 594.

   The result in this case is 1089.

   Now try these four steps with any number of your own choice. Repeat the instructions six times for six different numbers, but do remember that the number of hundreds must differ by at least two from the number of units. What do you notice?

3   Solve the following cross-number puzzle.

   Across **1** 73 − 31
            4 249 + 167
            6 700 − 565
            7 231 − 158

   Down **2** 77 + 166
         3 222 − 136
         5 78 + 79
         6 52 + 106 − 139

4   Use the digits 1, 2, 3, 4, 5, 6, 7, 8 and 9 in order, using each digit once, to make four numbers separated by either a + sign or a − sign so that the answer is 100.

5   Copy this diagram on to a sheet of paper.

   Cut it into three pieces and fit them together to form a magic square.

! Investigations

1. Sonia makes up a pattern starting with 3 and 4. To get the next number in the pattern she adds the previous two numbers together. If the answer is more than 10 she writes down only the number of units.

   Her pattern is   3, 4, 7, 1, 8, 9, 7, ...

   Write down the next ten numbers in this pattern.

   Does the pattern repeat itself?

   If so, how many numbers are there before it starts to repeat?

   Now start with 4 and 3 and see what happens.

   (You need to keep going for a long time!)

   Investigate some other patterns starting with different pairs of numbers.

2. Write down any three-digit number, e.g. 287

   Arrange the digits in order of size; once with the largest digit first and once with the smallest digit first, i.e. 872, 278

   Now find the difference between these two numbers (take the smaller number from the larger number),

   i.e. $872 - 278 = 594$

   Repeat the process for your answer,

   i.e. $954 - 459 = 495$

   Repeat the process again,

   i.e. $954 - 459 = 495$

   These rules give us a chain of numbers. In this example we have
   $$287 \rightarrow 594 \rightarrow 495 \rightarrow 495$$

   Form a similar chain for a three-digit number of your own choice.

   Try a few more.

   What do you notice?

3. A number that reads the same forwards and backwards, e.g. 14241, is called a **palindrome**.

   There is a conjecture (i.e. it has not been proved) that if we take *any* number, reverse the digits and add the numbers together, then do the same with the result, and so on, we will end up with a palindrome,

   e.g. starting with 251,
   $$251 + 152 = 403$$
   $$403 + 304 = 707 \qquad \text{which is a palindrome.}$$

   a Can you find some two-digit numbers for which the palindrome appears after the first sum?

   b If two palindromes are added together, is the result always a palindrome?

4 The Romans did not use symbols for numbers, but used letters of the alphabet. For example, in Roman numerals, X is used for ten, V for five; XV means 'ten and five', i.e. 15.

The numbers one to six are written I, II, III, IV, V, VI.

a Use reference material to find out what the following Roman numbers are.

XIV, CLX, MLII, MMXIV

b Write the following numbers in Roman numerals.

25, 152, 1854, 2002

c Find LXII – XXIV.

d Write down the year in which you were born in Roman numerals.

2 Multiplication and division with whole numbers

Consider

Jake had to collect 27 p from each of the 8 members of his youth group. He didn't keep the money separate from his own so when he needed to hand the total to his group leader, he used his calculator to work out 27×8.

The display read 296, so he handed over £2.96. This is 80 p more than he should have given.

What do you think went wrong? How can Jake avoid this happening to him again?

You should be able to solve this problem after you have worked through this chapter.

Class discussion

Discuss what you need to know, and be able to do, so that you have some control in the following situations.

1   Ali has to order coaches to take 218 children on a school outing. Each coach has 45 seats available. The coach company says it will send 5 coaches.

2   John goes into a shop with £1 to buy some sweets. He chooses 3 sweets costing 21 p each, 4 sweets costing 5 p each, and a lolly costing 36 p. At the cash desk he finds that he does not have enough money to pay for all these things, and has to put some back.

3   Priti needs to buy a ladder that will extend to at least 600 cm in length. The salesman recommends a ladder with three sections, each 250 cm long. When the ladder is fully opened out, there is an overlap of 30 cm between the sections.

These examples show that you need to able to multiply numbers quickly. You also need to know whether or not an answer is roughly correct.

Using the multiplication facts

The basic knowledge that underpins all multiplication and division is knowing the multiplication tables. By 'know' we mean instant recall of the **product** of any pair of numbers from the list 1, 2, 3, 4, 5, 6, 7, 8, 9, 10, 11, 12.

For example 69×4 *can* be found by adding

$69 + 69 + 69 + 69$

but it is quicker to use the multiplications facts if you know them. You will probably have your own methods for multiplying, but here is one way of calculating 69×4.

$69 = 70 - 1$, so 69×4 can be found from $(70 \times 4) - (1 \times 4)$

$69 \times 4 = 280 - 4$

$\qquad = 276$

If you are confident in your ability to multiply and add, you can do this in your head. If you need to use paper, it helps to set the calculation out like this:

$$\begin{array}{r} 69 \\ \times\ 4 \\ \hline 276 \\ {}_{3} \end{array}$$

9 units $\times 4 = 36$ units; write 6 under the units column and 'carry' the 3 by writing it underneath the line in the tens column.

6 tens $\times 4 = 24$ tens; add on the 3 tens carried to give 27 tens, i.e. 2 hundreds and 7 tens.

The next few exercises help you practise the multiplication skills you need.

Exercise 2a

1 a Copy and complete the multiplication table. Time yourself; you should be able to fill in the blank spaces in less than 2 minutes.

   b If you filled in this table by working across the rows, repeat the exercise by working down the columns (or vice-versa).

   c Now choose the squares you fill in at random.

×	3	7	5	2	4	6	9	8	1
4									
1									
6									
2									
9									
3									
5									
8									
7									

Worked example

➔ Find 24×8

$$\begin{array}{r} 24 \\ \times\ 8 \\ \hline 192 \\ {}_{3} \end{array}$$

$24 \times 8 = 192$ $\qquad$ *Check:* $192 \div 8 = 24$

 If you can do this in your head, write the answer down.
If you need to use paper, most people find it easier to set the multiplication in a column.

Do these in your head if you can. If you cannot, use pencil and paper.
Do not use a calculator.
Find

2	23×2	6	58×5	10	72×2	14	21×6
3	42×3	7	31×3	11	83×5	15	84×7
4	13×8	8	25×4	12	47×3	16	73×4
5	76×4	9	16×9	13	54×6	17	2×81

18 67×8	**22** 152×4	**26** 221×9	**30** 876×3
19 73×9	**23** 307×8	**27** 211×4	**31** 312×7
20 8×21	**24** 256×3	**28** 953×3	**32** 142×6
21 7×32	**25** 194×2	**29** 204×8	**33** 513×5

34 Munchy bars cost 62 p each.
How much do 8 of these bars cost?

35 A school day is 7 hours long.
How many minutes is this?

36 One jar of jam weighs 516 g.
What is the weight of 7 jars of jam?

37 Sam can walk up a flight of steps at the rate of 30 steps a minute.
It takes her 3 minutes to reach the top. How many steps are there?

38 Jack bought 6 pads of file paper priced at £3.89 each. He was
asked for £19.57. This is not correct. Without working out
3.89×6, decide if it is too much or too little.
Explain how you decided.

39 A car travelling at 50 miles an hour took 3 hours to travel from
London to Cardiff.
How many miles did the car travel?

40 a The **sequence** of numbers 3, 12, 48, … is formed by
starting with 3 and then multiplying the last number by 4.
Write down the next two numbers in the sequence.

   b Write down the first five numbers of the sequence formed by
starting with 7 and multiplying by 2 each time.

   c Write down, in words, the rule for continuing this sequence:
5, 25, 125, 625, 3125, …

41 Write down the missing **digit** in the following products.

   a $2\square \times 5 = 135$

   b $16 \times \square = 48$

   c $\square 4 \times 7 = 168$

Multiplication by 10, 100, 1000, …

When 85 is multiplied by 10, the 5 units become 5 tens and the 8 tens become 8 hundreds.
So
$$85 \times 10 = 850$$
When 85 is multiplied by 100, the 5 units become 5 hundreds and the 8 tens become
8 thousands. So
$$85 \times 100 = 8500$$
When 85 is multiplied by 20, this is the same as $85 \times 2 \times 10$
So $85 \times 20 = 85 \times 2 \times 10$
$$= 170 \times 10 = 1700$$
In the same way
$$27 \times 4000 = 27 \times 4 \times 1000 = 108 \times 1000 = 108\,000$$

Exercise 2b

Find

1 27×10	**3** 36×10	**5** 256×1000
2 82×100	**4** 108×10	**6** 392×10

Worked example

→ Find 42×900

$$42 \times 900 = 42 \times 9 \times 100$$
$$= 378 \times 100$$
$$= 37\,800 \qquad \textit{Check: } 37\,800 \div 900 = 42$$

 We find 42×9 first and then multiply by 100.

Find

7 21×20	**16** 73×2000	**25** 81×3000
8 42×300	**17** 39×900	**26** 390×90
9 31×40	**18** 157×60	**27** 107×400
10 39×200	**19** 295×80	**28** 240×80
11 52×50	**20** 88×70	**29** 100×88
12 73×400	**21** 350×200	**30** 200×95
13 58×60	**22** 609×80	**31** 856×70
14 221×30	**23** 270×200	
15 121×700	**24** 556×70	

32 How much would you have to pay for 200 tickets costing £28 each?

33 What is the total number of cans in 400 cartons when each carton contains 48 cans?

34 Which of these answers are obviously wrong? $253 \times 2000 =$

A $50\,600$ B $506\,000$ C $5\,060\,000$

35 There are 250 nails in each packet. Alice needed to know the number of nails in 400 packets. Which of these answers are obviously wrong?

A $100\,000$ B $25\,000$ C $10\,000$

36 Jane was asked how many balloons there were in 200 packets, when each packet had 50 balloons in it. She said 1000, which is wrong. She tried to justify her answer by saying '5 times 2 is ten, and then add two noughts for the 200'. What is wrong with her reasoning?

Long multiplication

To multiply 84×26 we use the fact that $84 \times 26 = 84 \times 6 + 84 \times 20$

This can be set out as

```
        84
      × 26
       504    (84 × 6)
    + 1680    (84 × 20)
      2184
```

Exercise 2c

Worked example

→ Find 2813×402

```
        2813
      ×  402
        5626    (2813 × 2)
    + 1125200    (2813 × 400)
      1130826
```

$2813 \times 402 = 1\,130\,826$

Find

1 32×21	**9** 74×106	**17** 487×82	**25** 3060×470
2 43×13	**10** 36×89	**18** 724×98	**26** 385×95
3 86×15	**11** 241×32	**19** 146×259	**27** 750×450
4 27×21	**12** 153×262	**20** 805×703	**28** 605×750
5 34×42	**13** 433×921	**21** 2004×43	**29** 1008×908
6 38×41	**14** 1251×28	**22** 584×97	**30** 1500×802
7 107×26	**15** 3421×33	**23** 187×906	
8 53×82	**16** 512×210	**24** 270×709	

31 It is a curious fact that $12 \times 12 = 144$ and if the digits in the three numbers are reversed you have $21 \times 21 = 441$, which is also true. Find other examples with this property.

32 Using the four digits 2, 3, 6 and 9 once only, you can make several pairs of 2-digit numbers, e.g. 26 and 93. Find 26×93.
Now pair the digits in a different way, e.g. 39 and 62 and find 39×62. What do you notice?
Can you find another four digits with the same property?

Using a calculator for long multiplication

Calculators save a lot of time when used for long multiplication. You do, however, need to be able to estimate the size of answer you expect, as a check on your use of the calculator.

One way to get a rough answer is to **round**

a number between 10 and 100 to the nearest number of tens

a number between 100 and 1000 to the nearest number of hundreds

a number between 1000 and 10 000 to the nearest number of thousands

and so on.

For example $512 \times 78 \approx 500 \times 80 = 40\,000$

and $2752 \times 185 \approx 3000 \times 200 = 600\,000$

The symbol $\approx$ means 'is approximately equal to'.

Exercise 2d

Estimate

1 79×34	**6** 59×18	**11** 159×93
2 29×27	**7** 23×55	**12** 82×309
3 84×36	**8** 62×57	**13** 281×158
4 45×32	**9** 136×29	**14** 631×479
5 87×124	**10** 52×281	**15** 273×784

Worked example

$\rightarrow$ Estimate 2581×39 and then use a calculator to find the exact value.

$2581 \times 39 \approx 3000 \times 40 = 120\,000$ (estimate)

$2581 \times 39 = 100\,659$ (calculator)

 The estimate and calculator answer agree quite well, so the calculator answer is probably correct.

Estimate the answer and then use your calculator to work out the following.

16 258×947	**24** 2501×12	**32** 47×853
17 29×384	**25** 87×76	**33** 94×552
18 182×56	**26** 52×821	**34** 463×87
19 37×925	**27** 89×483	**35** 271×82
20 782×24	**28** 481×97	**36** 753×749
21 78×91	**29** 608×953	**37** 37×634
22 625×14	**30** 4897×61	**38** 541×428
23 33×982	**31** 69×78	**39** 798×583

40 There are three answers given for each calculation. Two of them are obviously wrong.
Write down the letter of the answer that *might* be correct.
   a 521 × 36:   A 1876   B 11 886   C 18 756
   b 63 × 95:   A 5985   B 585   C 10 000

41 Multiply three hundred and fifty-six by twenty-three.

42 One jar of marmalade weighs 454 grams. Find the weight of 124 jars.

43 Find the value of one hundred and fifty multiplied by itself.

44 A car park has 34 rows and each row has 42 parking spaces. How many cars can be parked?

45 A supermarket takes delivery of 54 crates of soft drink cans. Each crate contains 48 cans.
How many cans are delivered?

46 A light bulb was tested by being left on non-stop. It failed after 28 days exactly.
For how many hours was it working?

47 Fill in the missing digits in these calculations.
   a 2☐ × 42 = 966
   b 125 × ☐6 = 7000
   c 157 × 3☐ = 5495

When not to use a calculator

Some people use their calculators for all number calculations. This is silly for two reasons.
- It is quicker to use your head for simple numbers. (The next exercise should convince you that this is true.)
- If you rely on your calculator for all number work, you will forget the number facts. This means you will lose the ability to judge when an answer obtained from a calculator is obviously wrong.

Exercise 2e

Work in pairs. Copy the square once each. One of you should fill it in, working in your head, while being timed by your partner. Now reverse roles but, this time, use a calculator to find each number.

1

×	2	3	4
2			
4			
6			

2

+	5	2	7
9			
8			
4			

3

×	5	10	3
3			
12			
5			

4

+	2	4	6
7			
3			
2			

Division of whole numbers

To find out how many eight-seater mini-buses are needed to take 36 children on an outing, we need to find how many eights there are in 36. $36 \div 8$ means 'how many eights are there in 36?'

We could find out by repeatedly taking 8 away from 36:

$36 - 8 = 28$
$28 - 8 = 20$
$20 - 8 = 12$
$12 - 8 = 4$ So there are 4 eights in 36 with 4 left over.

Therefore $36 \div 8 = 4$, remainder 4.

However, a quicker way uses the multiplication facts.

We know that $32 = 4 \times 8$
therefore $36 \div 8 = 4$, remainder 4

Now we know that we need five mini-buses.

Larger numbers can be divided in a similar way.

To find $534 \div 3$ start with the hundreds:

5 (hundreds) $\div$ 3 = **1 (hundred)**, remainder 2 (hundreds)

Take the remainder, 2 (hundreds), and add to the tens:

23 (tens) $\div$ 3 = **7 (tens)**, remainder 2 (tens)

Take the remainder, 2 (tens), and add to the units:

24 (units) $\div$ 3 = **8 units**

Therefore $534 \div 3 = \mathbf{178}$

This can be set out as $3\overline{)5^23^24}$ with 178 above.

Exercise 2f

Worked example

$\rightarrow$ Calculate $4509 \div 5$, giving the remainder.

$4509 \div 5 = 901, \text{r } 4$

$$5\overline{)4509} \quad 901 \text{ r } 4$$

Check: $901 \times 5 + 4 = 4509$

Calculate, giving the remainder when there is one.

1 $87 \div 3$	14 $21 \div 9$	27 $731 \div 6$
2 $56 \div 4$	15 $78 \div 6$	28 $3501 \div 3$
3 $36 \div 6$	16 $54 \div 2$	29 $1763 \div 4$
4 $57 \div 3$	17 $639 \div 3$	30 $4829 \div 2$
5 $72 \div 4$	18 $548 \div 2$	31 $1758 \div 5$
6 $97 \div 2$	19 $605 \div 3$	32 $6405 \div 6$
7 $73 \div 5$	20 $855 \div 5$	33 $7399 \div 5$
8 $83 \div 4$	21 $693 \div 3$	34 $8772 \div 4$
9 $69 \div 3$	22 $721 \div 7$	35 $9712 \div 8$
10 $82 \div 6$	23 $358 \div 5$	36 $1788 \div 9$
11 $78 \div 8$	24 $294 \div 9$	37 $1098 \div 6$
12 $85 \div 7$	25 $570 \div 7$	38 $2481 \div 7$
13 $39 \div 3$	26 $680 \div 8$	39 $6910 \div 4$

40 How many apples costing 48 p each can I buy for £4?

41 Cara saves the same amount each week. After 7 weeks she has saved £56.
How much does she save each week?

42 A greengrocer bought a sack of potatoes weighing 50 kg.
He divided the potatoes into bags, so that each bag held 3 kg of potatoes.
How many complete bags of potatoes did he get from his sack?

43 Three children are given £4.20 to split equally among them.
How much does each child get?

44 Rajesh is paid £585 for a five-day working week.
How much is he paid for each day?

45 How many times can 5 be taken away from 132?

46 How can you tell, without doing long division or using a calculator, that 153 918 is not divisible exactly by 4?

Division by 10, 100, 1000, ...

$812 \div 10$ means: 'How many tens are there in 812?'
There are 81 tens in 810 so
$$812 \div 10 = 81, r 2$$
$2578 \div 100$ means: 'How many hundreds are there in 2578?'
There are 25 hundreds in 2500 so
$$2578 \div 100 = 25, r 78$$

Exercise 2g

Calculate and give the remainder.

1	$256 \div 10$	5	$4910 \div 1000$	9	$9426 \div 1000$
2	$87 \div 10$	6	$57 \div 10$	10	$8512 \div 100$
3	$196 \div 100$	7	$186 \div 10$	11	$3077 \div 100$
4	$2783 \div 100$	8	$2781 \div 10$	12	$5704 \div 1000$

Long division

To find $2678 \div 21$ we can use the same method as for short division, but we write the working more fully.

```
      127
21)2678
    21↓ |
    57  |
    42 ↓
   158
   147
    11
```

There is **1** twenty-one in 26, r 5 (hundreds).

There are **2** twenty-ones in 57, r 15 (tens).

There are **7** twenty-ones in 158, r 11 (units).

So $2678 \div 21 = 127$, r 11

Exercise 2h

Worked example

→ Find $2606 \div 25$, giving the remainder.

```
      104
25)2606
    25↓↓
    106
    100
      6
```

$2606 \div 25 = 104$, r 6
Check: $104 \times 25 + 6 = 2606$

Calculate and give the remainder.

1	$254 \div 20$	5	$394 \div 19$	9	$389 \div 23$
2	$685 \div 13$	6	$267 \div 32$	10	$298 \div 14$
3	$739 \div 41$	7	$875 \div 25$	11	$433 \div 15$
4	$862 \div 25$	8	$269 \div 16$	12	$614 \div 27$

If you use your calculator to check your answers, it will give the whole number part of the answer but it will not give the remainder as a whole number.

13 2804 ÷ 13   22 5829 ÷ 43   ㉛ 8013 ÷ 40
14 7315 ÷ 21   23 6372 ÷ 27   ㉜ 829 ÷ 106
15 8392 ÷ 34   24 8261 ÷ 38   33 5241 ÷ 201
16 6841 ÷ 15   25 7315 ÷ 24   34 3689 ÷ 151
17 2943 ÷ 23   26 8602 ÷ 15   35 8200 ÷ 250
18 2694 ÷ 31   27 3004 ÷ 31   36 3606 ÷ 300
19 1875 ÷ 25   28 1608 ÷ 25   37 8491 ÷ 150
20 3621 ÷ 30   29 7092 ÷ 35   38 7625 ÷ 302
21 7514 ÷ 34   ㉚ 2694 ÷ 30   39 1092 ÷ 206

40 4000 apples are packed into boxes, each box holding 75 apples.
    How many boxes are required?

41 A vegetable plot is 1000 cm long. Cabbages are planted in a row
    down the length of the plot. The cabbages are planted 30 cm
    apart. The first cabbage is planted 5 cm from the end.
    How many cabbages can be planted in one row?

42 A class is told to work out the odd-numbered questions in an
    exercise containing 29 questions.
    How many questions do they have to do?

43 Find the missing digits in the following calculations.
    a   256 ÷ 1☐ = 16
    b   86☐ ÷ 24 = 36
    c   105☐ ÷ 25 = 42, r 2

Mixed operations of +, −, ×, ÷

When a calculation involves a mixture of the operations +, −, ×, ÷, we always do
multiplication and division first.

For example

$$2 \times 4 + 3 \times 6 = 8 + 18$$
$$= 26$$

 Do the multiplication first,
i.e. 2×4 and 3×6 first.

Exercise 2i

Worked example

→ Find $2 + 3 \times 6 - 8 \div 2$

$$2 + 3 \times 6 - 8 \div 2 = 2 + 18 - 4$$
$$= 16$$

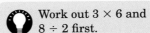 Work out 3×6 and
$8 \div 2$ first.

→ Find $5 - 10 \times 2 \div 5 + 3$

$$5 - 10 \times 2 \div 5 + 3 = 5 - 20 \div 5 + 3$$
$$= 5 - 4 + 3$$
$$= 4$$

 Do the multiplication first.
Now do the division.

Find

1 $2 + 4 \times 6 - 8$

2 $24 \div 8 - 3$

3 $6 + 3 \times 2$

4 $7 \times 2 + 6 - 1$

5 $18 \div 3 - 3 \times 2$

6 $7 + 4 - 3 \times 2$

7 $8 \div 2 + 6 \times 3$

8 $14 \times 2 \div 7 - 3 + 6$

9 $6 - 2 \times 3 + 7$

10 $5 + 4 \times 3 + 8 \div 2$

11 $7 + 3 \times 2 - 8 \div 2$

12 $5 \times 4 \div 2 + 7 \times 2$

13 $6 \times 3 - 8 \times 2$

14 $9 \div 3 + 12 \div 6$

15 $12 \div 3 - 15 \div 5$

16 $9 + 3 - 6 \div 2 + 1$

17 $6 - 3 \times 2 + 9 \div 3$

18 $7 + 2 \times 4 - 8 \div 4$

19 $7 \times 2 + 8 \times 3 - 2 \times 6$

20 $5 \times 3 \times 2 - 4 \times 3 \div 2$

21 $19 + 3 \times 2 - 8 \div 2$

22 $7 \times 2 - 3 + 6 \div 2$

23 $8 + 3 \times 2 - 4 \div 2$

24 $7 \times 2 - 4 \div 2 + 1$

25 $6 + 8 \div 4 + 6 \times 3 \div 2$

26 $5 \times 3 \times 4 \div 12 + 6 - 2$

27 $5 + 6 \times 2 - 8 \div 2 + 9 \div 3$

28 $7 - 9 \div 3 + 6 \times 2 - 4 \div 2$

29 $9 \div 3 - 2 + 1 + 6 \times 2$

30 $4 \times 2 - 6 \div 3 + 3 \times 2 \times 4$

Worked example

→ In the greengrocers, I bought 3 oranges that cost 50 p each and one cabbage that cost 96 p. I paid with two £2 coins.
How much change did I get?

Cost of the oranges = 150 p
Cost of the cabbage = 96 p
Total cost = 246 p
Change from £4 = 400 p − 246 p
= 154 p, i.e. £1.54

31 I bought 5 oranges that cost 45 p each and 2 lemons that cost 36 p each. How much did I spend?

32 Three children went into a sweet shop. Anna bought three sweets costing 10 p each, Amjad bought three sweets costing 15 p each, and Clara bought three sweets costing 12 p each. How much money did they spend altogether?

33 A club started the year with 82 members. During the year 36 people left and 28 people joined.
How many people belonged to the club at the end of the year?

34 One money box has five 5 p pieces and four 10 p pieces in it.
Another money box has six 10 p pieces and ten 2 p pieces in it.
a   What is the total sum of money in the two money boxes?
b   Which box has more money in it? How much more is there in this box than the other box?

35 In a school election one candidate got 26 votes. The other candidate got 35 votes. 10 voting papers were spoiled and 5 students did not vote.
How many students altogether could have voted?

36 An extension ladder is made of three separate parts, each 300 cm long. When it is fully extended, there is an overlap of 30 cm at each junction.
How long is the extended ladder?

37 Anjie, Jeng and Dan come to school with £2.20 each. Anjie owes Jeng 40 p and she also owes Dan 85 p. Jeng owes Anjie 40 p and he also owes Dan 85 p.
When all their debts are settled, how much money does each person have?

38 The total number of students in the first year of a school is 500. There are 50 more girls than boys. How many of each are there?

39 In a book of street plans of a town, the street plans start on page 6 and end on page 72. How many pages of street plans are there?

40 Sam said that $25 + 5 \times 5$ was equal to 150.
Explain his mistake and give the correct answer.

41 A mountaineer starts from a point which is 150 m above sea level. He climbs 200 m and then descends 50 m before climbing another 300 m. How far is he now above sea level?

42 The calculation for the worked example above question **31** can be set out using the numbers given, as $400 - 3 \times 50 - 96$
Set out the calculations for questions **31** to **36** in the same way, using only the numbers given in the questions.

43 My great-grandmother died in 1975, aged 62. In which year was she born?

44 An oak tree was planted in the year in which Lord Swell was born. He died in 1940, aged 80. How old was the oak tree in 2014?

45 A bus leaves the bus station at 9.30 a.m. It reaches the Town Hall at 9.40 a.m. and gets to the railway station at 9.52 a.m.
a   How long does it take to go from the Town Hall to the railway station?
b   Which piece of information given in the question is not needed to answer part **a**?

46 Four married couples went to a party. Everyone shook hands with everyone else except each husband with his own wife.
How many handshakes were there?

Mixed operations using a calculator

A scientific calculator obeys the rule 'multiplication and division before addition and subtraction'.

When $2 + 3 \times 6$ is keyed in as $\boxed{2}\ \boxed{+}\ \boxed{3}\ \boxed{\times}\ \boxed{6}$, the calculator will work out 3×6 first.

If we need to do addition or subtraction first, we can use brackets to show this, i.e. $(2 + 3) \times 6$ means 'add 2 and 3 first'.

We can use the bracket keys on a calculator to find this in one operation, i.e. press $\boxed{(}\ \boxed{2}\ \boxed{+}\ \boxed{3}\ \boxed{)}\ \boxed{\times}\ \boxed{6}\ \boxed{=}$

We can also do this on a calculator by pressing the $\boxed{=}$ key after entering $2 + 3$, then we carry on with $\times\ 6$, i.e. press $\boxed{2}\ \boxed{+}\ \boxed{3}\ \boxed{=}\ \boxed{\times}\ \boxed{6}\ \boxed{=}$

Exercise 2j

Worked example

→ Use your calculator to find $2578 - (36 + 24) \times 13$

Estimate: $2578 - (36 + 24) \times 13 \approx 3000 - (40 + 20) \times 10$
$$= 3000 - 600 = 2400$$
$$2578 - (36 + 24) \times 13 = 1798$$

 Notice that 3000 is a big overestimate for 2578 and 600 is a large underestimate for $(36 + 24) \times 13$. This means that 2400 is a *very rough* estimate, but if the calculator result is over 10 000 or under 1000 we should be suspicious.

Use your calculator to find the answers. Do not forget to estimate the answer first.

1 $25 + 52 \times 26$

2 $279 \times (32 + 27)$

3 $(25 + 52) \times 26$

4 $398 \times 24 - 2560$

5 $579 + (46 - 37) \times 16$

6 $2965 \times 36 - 293 \times 178$

7 $36 - 216 \div (33 - 21)$

8 $4088 \div 73 - 29$

9 $27 + (1201 + 17) \div 58$

10 $1380 - (120 \times 18) \div 15$

Mixed exercises

Exercise 2k

Find

1 $126 + 501 + 378$

2 $153 - 136$

3 76×9

4 $84 \div 3$

5 $350 + 8796 - 2538$

6 $8 \times 321 - 1550$

7 $35 + 86 + 94 + 27$

8 $20 \div (9 - 4) + 3$

9 $2 + 3 \times 4 \div 6 - 3$

10 How many packets of popcorn costing 65 p each can I buy with £5?

11 I buy three bars of chocolate costing 95 p each.
How much change do I get from £5?

12 You are asked to read pages 12 to 24 of a book for homework.
How many pages is this?

Exercise 2l

Find

1 $92 + 625 + 153$

2 $247 - 193$

3 84×8

4 $79 \div 8$

5 $(7 + 30) \times 2 - 45$

6 $382 - 792 \div 3$

7 $68 - 42 + 12 \times 2$

8 $79 - 35 + 56 - 63$

9 $4 + 16 \times 5 \div 10 + 3$

10 How many times can 6 be taken away from 45?

11 The contents of a tin of sweets weigh 2500 grams. The sweets are
divided into packets each weighing 500 grams.
How many packets of sweets can be made up?

12 John bought 3 ice lollies at 65 p each, one bar of chocolate at 75 p,
and a drink at £1.30.
How much change did he get from a £5 note?

Consider again

Jake used his calculator to work out 27×8.
The display read 296, so he handed over £2.96.
This is 80 p more than he should have given.

Can you now write down what you think went wrong?
How can Jake avoid this happening to him again?

🧩 Number puzzles

1 Copy the following sets of numbers. Put $+$, $-$, $\times$, or
$\div$ in each space so that the calculations are correct.

   a   9 ☐ 4 = 5

   b   7 ☐ 3 = 21

   c   28 ☐ 4 = 7

   d   8 ☐ 2 = 4

   e   5 ☐ 4 ☐ 6 = 3

   f   8 ☐ 3 ☐ 4 = 1

   g   3 ☐ 4 ☐ 2 = 9

   h   2 ☐ 1 ☐ 3 = 6

2 My calculator has an odd fault. The $+$ button multiplies
and the $\times$ button adds.

   a   When I press $7 + 5$, what number shows on the
display?

   b   Before I realised what the fault was, I got 21 when
I tried to add two numbers.
What were the two numbers?

   c   I pressed $2 + 8 \times 5$. What number showed in the
display?

   d   Find a calculation, using three or four numbers, for
which my calculator will give the correct answer.

3 Solve this cross-number puzzle.

Across	1	$127 - 64$
	3	$44 + 73 - 58$
	4	6×53
	8	330×41
	11	$9 \times 10 - 9$
	12	The next number after 40
Down	2	$3 \times 13 - 6$
	3	$464 \div 8$
	5	$625 \div 5$
	6	74×7
	7	9×89
	9	$5 \times 8 - 27 \div 3$
	10	$2 \times 19 - 4$

> ### ! Investigation
>
> 1 Elsie has some tennis balls and some bags to keep them in. If 9 balls are put into each bag, one ball is left over. If 11 balls are put into each bag, one bag is empty.
> How many tennis balls and how many bags are there?
> Explain your thinking.
>
> 2 a Multiply 123 456 789 by 3 and then multiply the result by 9. What do you notice?
>
> b Repeat part **a**, multiplying the first number by a different number less than 9 and then multiplying the result by 9.
> Do this twice, without using a calculator.
>
> c Is there a rule for predicting the answer when 123 456 789 is multiplied by one of the numbers 2, 3, 4, 5, 6, 7 or 8, and the result is multiplied by 9? If you find one, write it down and test it.
>
> d Now try using your calculator. What do you notice?

3 Collecting and displaying data

Consider

The news and advertising media bombard us with information. For example:

- 'Two in every five students do not have anything to eat before they go to school.'
- 'Children between the ages of 8 and 12 spend an average of 10 hours a week playing computer games.'
- 'Air pollution in town centres is up to six times the recommended levels.'

Statements like these are the result of a process that involves collecting information and organising it. The process starts with someone asking a question.

The first example probably started with the question 'How many children arrive at school without having had anything to eat?' How would you go about checking whether the first statement was true for

a   children in your own class

b   children in your school

c   children across the country?

You should be able to solve this problem after you have worked through this chapter.

Class discussion

Discuss what information is needed to answer these questions.

1   How much money do the students in my class have each week to spend as they wish?

2   Do tubes of Smarties have more red Smarties in them than any other colour?

3   In which months are most students in my year born?

4   Does this dice give more sixes than any other score?

5   What pets do the other members of my class have?

6   Are left-handed people taller than right-handed people?

7   Do people with large feet also have large hands?

8   How many books do my class-mates read each week?

9   Are people who do not eat green vegetables less healthy than those who do?

10 Decide on a question you would like to ask and state what information you need to collect.

11 The third example involved collecting measurements of air pollution. But what is air pollution? Where was it measured? How often was it measured?

Making lists

If we want to know how many brothers and sisters each member of a class has, we could ask each student and write the information down in a list.

This is a list of the number of brothers and sisters of the 30 students in Class 7D.

Each figure represents the number of brothers and sisters of one member of the class.

```
0   1   1   3   0   1   2   1   0   1
1   3   1   0   1   2   3   1   1   0
1   0   2   0   1   1   1   2   4   1
```

Making a frequency table

To make sense of the numbers that we have collected we need to put them in order.

One way of doing this is to make a **frequency table**. The **frequency** tells us how many of each type of item there are.

There are five different items in our list: 0, 1, 2, 3 and 4.

We start by making a table like the one below. Then we work down the columns in the list, making a tally mark, *l*, in the tally column next to the appropriate item.

Number of brothers and sisters	Tally	Frequency
0	卌	
1	卌 ll	
2	ll	
3	ll	
4		
	Total	

> Do not go through the list looking for all the zeros etc. You may miss some.

Next we count up the tally marks and write the total in the frequency column.

Lastly, we total the frequency column to check that the total number of items recorded in the table is the same as the number of items in the list.

Exercise 3a

1   The table above is incomplete; copy it without the tally marks. Now make the tally marks afresh from the original information and complete the table.

2   A box contains bags of crisps. Some are plain salted (S), some are salt and vinegar (V), some are cheese and onion (C), and some are prawn cocktail (P). The bags are taken out of the box one at a time and the flavour of each bag is written down in a list.

```
P   S   S   V   C   S   P   P   S
S   P   V   S   C   C   P   V   S
P   S   V   C   C   C   V   P   V
V   S   S   C   S   S   P   S   S
```

Make a frequency table for this list like the one above.

3   This is a list of the favourite colours of some children, chosen
    from red (R), green (G), blue (B), yellow (Y) and pink (P).

R	R	P	Y	R	Y	P	G	R	B	R
P	Y	Y	R	B	Y	R	R	R	Y	Y
R	Y	B	G	Y	R	P	P	R	R	Y
Y	R	R	R	P	Y	Y	B	Y	G	R

Make a frequency table for this list.

4   This is a list of the shoe sizes of a group of children.

26	25	27	25	23	26	24	24	27	24	25
24	23	25	24	24	23	26	23	24	25	25
23	24	25	25	24	23	24	26	25	24	23
22	24	23	27	23	25	24	24	25	23	24

Make a frequency table for this list.

Observation sheets

We can sometimes avoid having to sort information afterwards by collecting it straight
onto a specially designed sheet that sorts the information as we collect it. This is called an
observation sheet. The simplest observation sheet is a tally chart.

Exercise 3b

1   Copy the tally chart below and use it to record the number of
    heads that show when two coins are tossed 20 times.

Number of heads	Tally	Frequency
0		
1		
2		

2   This observation sheet can be used to collect information so that
    we can compare shoe size and hand span of several people.

Name	Shoe size	Hand span (cm)
John		
Rajan		
Shona		

Explain why a tally chart would not be a suitable observation
sheet for gathering this information.

3   Mrs Edwards wants to know what games equipment each member
    of her class has in school. She uses a sheet like the one below.

Name	Trainers	Games shirt	Tracksuit trousers	Tracksuit top
Ben	✓	✗	✓	✓

a   Design a sheet on which similar information about your class could be gathered.

b   Mrs Edwards just wants to know how many students in her class have each item in school that day. Design an appropriate sheet for just this purpose.

4   Jack wants to record the number of people in each car passing the bus stop while he waits for the bus to school each morning. Use your personal experience to decide whether it is sensible to use a tally sheet or to write down the numbers in an unordered list and sort them later.
   Give reasons for and against each option.

5   Design an observation sheet to record
   a   the number of letters in each word on this page
   b   the different types of book that are in each student's bag when they arrive at school tomorrow morning
   c   the number of pencils, rubbers, rulers, calculators, and pens brought by all the students to your next maths class
   d   the number of red cars passing a bus stop each minute.

Making a bar chart

A **bar chart** shows frequencies very clearly.

This bar chart uses the frequency table in question **1** of Exercise 3a, and shows the frequencies of the numbers of brothers and sisters of the students in a class.

Notice that the vertical axis is used for frequency. The different kinds of item are on the horizontal axis.

Notice also that the bars are all the same width. It does not matter what width you choose to make the bars, provided that all bars are the same width. In this diagram there is a space between the bars, but the bars can touch if we want them to.

Exercise 3c

1   Mo and Rachel did a survey of the types of vehicle passing the school gate one lunch hour and produced the following frequency table.

Type of vehicle	Bicycle	Motorbike	Car	Lorry
Frequency	4	10	25	16

   a   How many vehicles passed the school gate altogether?
   b   Which was the most common type of vehicle?
   c   Draw a bar chart to show the information.

2 This frequency table shows the results of a survey on people's opinions about the quality of school dinners.

Opinion	Very good	Good	Satisfactory	Poor	Very poor
Frequency	2	12	20	10	8

   a How many people were asked their opinion on school dinners?

   b Draw a bar chart to show the information.

3 Use the frequency table that you made for question **2** of Exercise 3a for this question.

   a Which is the most common type of crisp in the box?

   b Draw a bar chart to show the information.

4 Use the frequency table that you made for question **3** of Exercise 3a for this question.

   a Which was the most commonly chosen colour?

   b Draw a bar chart to show the information.

Using bar charts

Bar charts can come in other forms. Sometimes the bars are lines (these are called bar line graphs). Sometimes the bars are horizontal.

 When you look at a bar chart to find information from it, always read the labels on the axes carefully.

Exercise 3d

1 Use the bar chart to answer the following questions.

   a What is the most popular pet?

   b How many dogs were counted?

   c What is the total number of pets owned by members of Class 7D?

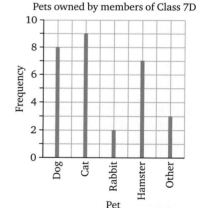

Pets owned by members of Class 7D

2

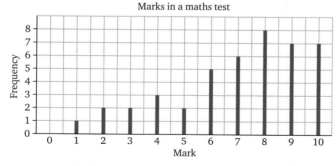

Marks in a maths test

   a How many students had a mark of 8?

   b What was the lowest mark given and how many students got it?

   c What was the most common mark?

   d How many students had a mark of 7 or more?

3

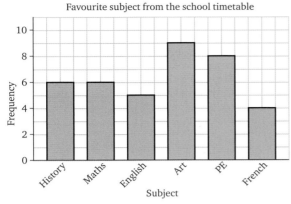

Favourite subject from the school timetable

a   How many children chose history as their favourite subject?

b   What was the most popular subject?

c   What was the least popular subject?

4

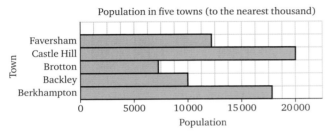

Population in five towns (to the nearest thousand)

a   Which town has the largest population?

b   What is the population of Backley?

c   Which town has the smallest population?
    What is the population of this town?

Reading bar charts

Bar charts can be used for information other than frequencies. When you look at a bar chart, read the labels on the axes.

The bars are usually vertical but can be horizontal.

Exercise 3e

1   This bar chart gives rough guide-lines on the distances that should be allowed between moving cars.

a   Roughly how far should a car travelling at 70 mph keep from the car in front?

b   Write two sentences on why this rule is only a rough guide.

3 car lengths
At 30 mph

13 car lengths
At 50 mph

24 car lengths
At 70 mph

2 No numbers are given but we can get an idea about the relative costs.

Cost of fuel in an average home with central heating

a Which is the most expensive method overall?

b Which is the cheapest?

c Which is the most expensive method of producing hot water?

d Which is the cheapest method of cooking?

3

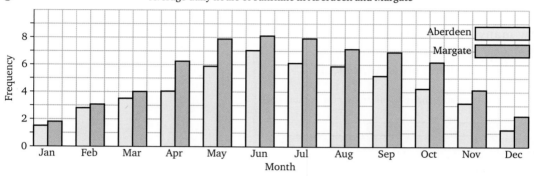

Average daily hours of sunshine in Aberdeen and Margate

a Is there more sunshine in Margate than in Aberdeen?

b Which month is the sunniest in both towns?

c Which month has the least sunshine in each town?

4 This graph shows the number of women elected to parliament at general elections.

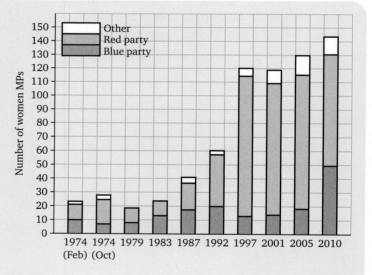

a How many women Blue Party MPs were elected in 1983?

b Were there more Red Party or Blue Party women MPs elected in 1987?

c In which general election were the highest number of women Red Party MPs elected?

d Redraw this bar chart so that it looks similar to the bar chart for question **3**.
There will be three columns for each year.

e You now have two graphs showing the same information but in different ways. Which would you find more useful if

  i you wanted to see how the total numbers of women in parliament varied since 1974

  ii you wanted to compare the numbers of Blue Party and Red Party women MPs?

Pictograms

To attract attention, pictograms are often used on posters and in newspapers and magazines. The best pictograms give numerical information as well; the worst give the wrong impression.

Exercise 3f

1 Road deaths in the past four years at an accident black spot

a Give an estimate of the number of deaths in each year.

b What message is the poster trying to convey?

c How effective do you think it is?

2

a Which is the most popular subject?

b How many students chose each subject and how many were asked altogether?

c Is this a good way of presenting the information? Give a reason for your answer.

3 This bar chart comes from an advertisement showing the consumption of Fizz lemonade.

a What does this show about the consumption of lemonade? What does it not show?

It was decided to change from a bar chart to a pictograph for the next advertisement.

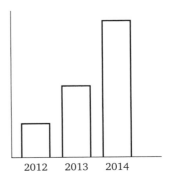

b This looks impressive, but it could be misleading. Why?

Consider again

- 'Two in every five students do not have anything to eat before they go to school.'
- 'Children between the ages of 8 and 12 spend an average of 10 hours a week playing computer games.'
- 'Air pollution in town centres is up to six times the recommended levels.'

How would you go about checking whether the first statement was true for

a children in your own class

b children in your school

c children across the country?

What questions need to be asked and how much information needs to be collected to answer these questions?

The third example involved collecting measurements of air pollution. But what is air pollution? Where was it measured? How often was it measured?

! Practical work

1   This is an individual activity.

1.6 million people donated blood in 2012.

Although that sounds a lot, that's only 4% of the population giving two or three times a year.

This amounts to 2.1 million donations. Anyone who is in good health, aged 17 to 65 can donate.

A regular supply of blood is vital. Red blood cells, which carry blood around the body, last only 35 days. Platelets, the vital cells that help your blood to clot, only survive for 5 days.

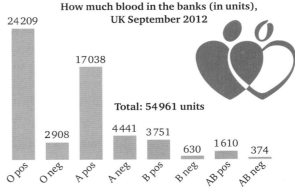

How much blood in the banks (in units), UK September 2012

24 209, 17 038, 2908, 4441, 3751, 630, 1610, 374

O pos, O neg, A pos, A neg, B pos, B neg, AB pos, AB neg

Total: 54 961 units

(Source: NHS Blood and Transplant)

    a   Which blood group is
      i   the most common
      ii   the least common?

    b   For which group would the stock last longest?

    c   How many more units of blood were there in the blood bank for the A positive group than for the A negative group?

    d   What is the maximum period that blood should be kept before it is used? What is the reason for this?

How many days the stock would last, UK 2012

10.98, 4.71, 9.00, 9.72, 8.30, 5.21, 12.58, 8.50

O pos, O neg, A pos, A neg, B pos, B neg, AB pos, AB neg

    e   Clarrie said that the total amount of blood in the bank for people with group O blood was more than for the rest of the groups put together. Is this true? Justify your answer.

2   This is a group activity that can be done with the whole class.

This chapter starts with a statement that 'two in every five children do not have anything to eat before they go to school'. Is this true of your class?

Your answer should include

    a   the question that you ask the members of your class

    b   the observation sheet that you collect replies on

    c   a bar chart illustrating the results

    d   a conclusion

    e   a report of any difficulties encountered and suggestions as to how these could be overcome.

4 Number and patterns

Consider

A manufacturer has three customers who want large weekly deliveries of his packs of paper plates. The first customer wants 480 packs a week, the second wants 960 and the third wants 288. The manufacturer would like to make up sealed cartons, each with the same number of packs, so that these orders can each be fulfilled by delivering a whole number of sealed cartons. How can he find out the best way of doing this?

The church at Bracksford has four bells. Bell 1 rings every 5 seconds, bell 2 rings every 6 seconds, bell 3 rings every 7 seconds, and bell 4 rings every 8 seconds. They are first rung together. How can we find out how long it will be before they all ring together again?

These and similar problems can be solved quite easily if we understand the properties of different types of number.

You should be able to solve these problems after you have worked through this chapter.

Class discussion

Discuss how you might solve the following problems.

1   Sandra wants to choose a group of players for a marching band competition. At certain times she wants them to march in equal rows of 5, and at other times in equal rows of 6. She has 65 players altogether.
    What is the smallest number of players she could choose?
    What is the largest number she can use?
    Could she use all of them?

2   A plant breeding station wishes to divide a rectangular field measuring 558 m by 450 m into squares so that different varieties of plants can be grown under different conditions.
    How can they decide on the size of the largest possible square?

To solve these problems, you have probably realised that we need to look for numbers that divide exactly into other numbers.

Factors

The number 2 is a **factor** of 12 because 2 will divide exactly into 12, i.e. without a remainder.

The number 12 may be expressed as the **product** of two factors in several different ways:

$$1 \times 12, \quad 2 \times 6 \quad \text{or} \quad 3 \times 4$$

Exercise 4a

Express each of the following numbers as the product of two different factors in as many ways as you can.

1	18	5	30	9	48	13	80
2	20	6	36	10	60	14	96
3	24	7	40	11	64	15	144
4	27	8	45	12	72	16	160

Multiples

12 is a **multiple** of 2 because 12 contains the number 2 a whole number of times. Any number that 2 divides into exactly is a multiple of 2, e.g. 2, 4, 6, 8, ... are all multiples of 2.

Exercise 4b

1 Write down all the multiples of 3 between 20 and 40.

2 Write down all the multiples of 5 between 19 and 49.

3 Write down all the multiples of 7 between 25 and 60.

4 Write down all the multiples of 11 between 50 and 100.

5 Write down all the multiples of 13 between 25 and 70.

Prime numbers

Some numbers can be expressed as the product of two different factors in one way only. For example, the only factors of 3 are 1 and 3 and the only factors of 5 are 1 and 5. Any number bigger than 1 that is of this type is called a **prime number**. Note that 1 is not a prime number because it does not have two different factors.

Exercise 4c

1 Which of the following numbers are prime numbers?

2, 3, 4, 5, 6, 7, 8, 9, 10, 11, 12

2 Write down all the prime numbers between 20 and 30.

3 a Write all the numbers from 1 to 100 in a table as shown below.

1	2	3	4	5	6	7	8	9	10
11	12	13	14	15	16	17	18	19	20
21	22	23	24	25	26	27	28	29	30
31	32	33	34	35	36	37	38	39	40
41	42	43	44	45	46	47	48	49	50
51	52	53	54	55	56	57	58	59	60
61	62	63	64	65	66	67	68	69	70
71	72	73	74	75	76	77	78	79	80
81	82	83	84	85	86	87	88	89	90
91	92	93	94	95	96	97	98	99	100

b Cross out 1, which is not a prime number.

c Do not cross out 2, because it is a prime number, but cross out all the multiples of 2.

d Do not cross out 3, because it is a prime number, but cross out all the multiples of 3.

e Do the same for 5, and repeat what you have been doing with multiples of all prime numbers from 7 onwards until there are no further multiples left to be crossed out.

f List the numbers that have not been crossed out. These are the prime numbers less than 100.

4 Which of the following numbers are prime numbers?

41, 57, 91, 101, 127

5 Find as many prime numbers as you can between 100 and 200.

6 Write each even number from 8 to 20 as the sum of two odd primes.

7 Write each odd number between 10 and 30 as the sum of three odd primes.

8 Are the following statements true or false? Give reasons for your answers.

a All the prime numbers are odd numbers.

b All odd numbers are prime numbers.

c All prime numbers between 10 and 100 are odd numbers.

d The only even prime number is 2.

e There are six prime numbers less than 10.

9 a List all the prime numbers less than 50.

b

```
                    1
                 2    5
              8    9    19
           11   5   17   12
         7    3    9   13   14
      38   13   33   7   28   36
    15   10   19   5   9   11   18
  5   47   8   23   14   11   26   13
```

Begin at the top and move down through the pyramid until you get to the bottom row. You must go through one number in each row but, apart from 1, this number must be a prime and must be next to the number you have just passed through. For example, if you are at 5 in the second row from the top, the only choice you have next is 9 or 19.

Is there more than one route?

10

```
                      7
                   3    5
                4    12    2
             5    8    13    46
          2    24   42    41    34
       19   43   37   45   31   21
     18   28   3   32   11   27   17
   7   11   16   5   28   47   19   5
 12   31   17   7   19   36   11   21   43
9   5   15   11   12   13   14   19   6   19
```

Begin in the bottom row and move up, one row at a time, until you get to the top. You can pass through one number only in each row but this number must be a prime. As you go from one row to the next you must go to an adjacent number. For example, if you start at 13 in the bottom row you must go next to 19 or 36.

Is there more than one route?

Index numbers

The accepted shorthand way of writing $2 \times 2 \times 2 \times 2$ is 2^4. We read this as '2 to the **power** 4' or '2 to the four'. The 4 is called the **index**.

Hence $16 = 2 \times 2 \times 2 \times 2 = 2^4$ and similarly $3^3 = 3 \times 3 \times 3 = 27$.

Numbers to the power 2 are called **square numbers**, e.g. 3 squared is 3^2.

Numbers to the power 3 are called **cube numbers**, e.g. 5 cubed is 5^3.

Exercise 4d

Write the following products in index form.

1 $2 \times 2 \times 2$ 6 $3 \times 3 \times 3 \times 3 \times 3 \times 3$

2 $3 \times 3 \times 3 \times 3$ 7 $13 \times 13 \times 13$

3 $5 \times 5 \times 5 \times 5$ 8 19×19

4 $7 \times 7 \times 7 \times 7 \times 7$ 9 $2 \times 2 \times 2 \times 2 \times 2 \times 2 \times 2$

5 $2 \times 2 \times 2 \times 2 \times 2$ 10 $6 \times 6 \times 6 \times 6$

Worked example

⟶ Find the value of 3^5.

$3^5 = 3 \times 3 \times 3 \times 3 \times 3$
$\quad = 243$

$3 \times 3 \times 3 \times 3 \times 3 = 9 \times 3 \times 3 \times 3$
$\qquad\qquad\qquad\quad = 27 \times 3 \times 3$
$\qquad\qquad\qquad\quad = 81 \times 3$
$\qquad\qquad\qquad\quad = 243$

Find the value of

11 2^5 13 5^2 15 3^2 17 3^4

12 3^3 14 2^3 16 7^2 18 2^4

Worked example

⟶ Express 125 in index form.

$125 = 5 \times 25$
$\quad\ = 5 \times 5 \times 5$
$\quad\ = 5^3$

Express the following numbers as powers of prime numbers.

19 4   21 8   23 49   25 32

20 9   22 27   24 25   26 64

Products of prime numbers

We can now write numbers as the product of prime numbers in index form.
Consider the number 108.

$\qquad 108 = 12 \times 9$
$\qquad\qquad = 4 \times 3 \times 9$
$\qquad\qquad = 2 \times 2 \times 3 \times 3 \times 3$
$\qquad 108 = 2^2 \times 3^3$

Therefore 108 expressed as the product of prime numbers or factors in index form is $2^2 \times 3^3$.
Similarly $\qquad 441 = 9 \times 49$
$\qquad\qquad\qquad = 3 \times 3 \times 7 \times 7$
$\qquad\qquad\qquad = 3^2 \times 7^2$

Exercise 4e

Worked example

➡ Write the product $2 \times 3 \times 3 \times 3 \times 2$ in index form.

Remember that we can multiply a string of numbers in any order so we can arrange these to bring the 2s together.

$2 \times 3 \times 3 \times 3 \times 2 = 2 \times 2 \times 3 \times 3 \times 3$
$\qquad\qquad\qquad\qquad\quad = 2^2 \times 3^3$

Write the following products in index form.

1 $2 \times 2 \times 7 \times 7$
2 $3 \times 3 \times 3 \times 5 \times 5$
3 $5 \times 5 \times 5 \times 13 \times 13$
4 $2 \times 3 \times 3 \times 5 \times 2 \times 5$
5 $2 \times 2 \times 3 \times 2 \times 3 \times 5 \times 5$
6 $3 \times 11 \times 11 \times 2 \times 2$
7 $7 \times 7 \times 7 \times 3 \times 5 \times 7 \times 3$
8 $13 \times 5 \times 13 \times 5 \times 13$
9 $3 \times 5 \times 5 \times 3 \times 7 \times 3 \times 7$
10 $2 \times 3 \times 2 \times 5 \times 3 \times 5$

Worked example

➡ Find the value of $2^3 \times 3^2$

$2^3 \times 3^2 = 2 \times 2 \times 2 \times 3 \times 3 = 72$

Find the value of

11 $2^2 \times 3^3$ 13 $2^4 \times 7$ 15 $2^2 \times 3^2 \times 5$
12 $3^2 \times 5^2$ 14 $2^2 \times 3^2$ 16 $2 \times 3^2 \times 7$

Finding prime factors

The following rules may help us to decide whether a given number has certain prime numbers as factors.

A number is divisible

by 2 if the last digit is even
by 3 if the sum of the digits is divisible by 3
by 5 if the last digit is 0 or 5.

Exercise 4f

Worked example

→ Is 446 divisible by 2?

Since the last figure is even, 446 is divisible by 2.

→ Is 1683 divisible by 3?

The sum of the digits is $1 + 6 + 8 + 3 = 18$, which is divisible by 3. Therefore 1683 is divisible by 3.

→ Is 7235 divisible by 5?

Since the last digit is 5, 7235 is divisible by 5.

1 Is 525 divisible by 3?

2 Is 747 divisible by 5?

3 Is 2931 divisible by 3?

4 Is 740 divisible by 5?

5 Is 543 divisible by 5?

6 Is 1424 divisible by 2?

7 Is 9471 divisible by 3?

8 Is 2731 divisible by 2?

Worked example

→ Is 8820 divisible by 15?

8820 is divisible by 5 since it ends in 0.
8820 is divisible by 3 since $8 + 8 + 2 = 18$, which is divisible by 3.
8820 is therefore divisible by both 5 and 3,
∴ it is divisible by 5×3, i.e. 15.

9 Is 10 752 divisible by 6?

10 Is 21 168 divisible by 6?

11 Is 30 870 divisible by 15?

12 Is 6540 divisible by 20? Explain your reasoning.

Expressing a number as a product of prime numbers

We can find the prime factors of small numbers like 12 and 18 easily, but bigger numbers need to be dealt with in a more orderly way.

To express a number in prime factors start by trying to divide by 2, and keep on until you can no longer divide exactly by 2. Next try 3 in the same way, then 5 and so on for each prime number until you are left with 1.

Exercise 4g

Worked example

→ Express   720 in prime factors.

$720 = 2 \times 360$
$ = 2 \times 2 \times 180$
$ = 2 \times 2 \times 2 \times 90$
$ = 2 \times 2 \times 2 \times 2 \times 45$
$ = 2 \times 2 \times 2 \times 2 \times 3 \times 15$
$ = 2 \times 2 \times 2 \times 2 \times 3 \times 3 \times 5$

 Test for the prime factors in order, 2 first, then 3, and so on.

Therefore $720 = 2 \times 2 \times 2 \times 2 \times 3 \times 3 \times 5$
i.e. $720 = 2^4 \times 3^2 \times 5$

Express each of the following numbers in prime factors.

1   24
2   28
3   63
4   72
5   136

6 84
7 216
8 528
9 405
10 784

Common factors

Two or more numbers may have the same factor. This is called a **common factor**.

For example, 7 is a factor of 14, 28 and 42. Sometimes it is useful to find the highest factor that is common to a set of numbers. This is called the **highest common factor (HCF)**. In this case the highest factor that will divide exactly into 14, 28 and 42 is 14.

Exercise 4h

Find the largest whole number that will divide exactly into all the given numbers.

1   9, 12
2   8, 16
3   12, 24
4   25, 50, 75
5   22, 33, 44

Common multiples

A **common multiple** is a multiple of two or more numbers. The **least common multiple (LCM)** of two or more numbers is the smallest number that the numbers divide into exactly. The smallest number that 5 and 12 will divide into is 60 and the smallest number that 3, 6 and 5 will divide into is 30. (Notice that 3 divides exactly into 6, so we need not worry about the 3.)

Exercise 4i

Worked example

$\longrightarrow$ Find the smallest number that can be divided exactly by 15 and by 20.

When the required number is not obvious, we try multiples of 15 until we find one that 20 divides into exactly, i.e. 15, 30, 45, <u>60</u>.

60 is the smallest number that 15 and 20 divide into exactly.

Check: $60 \div 15 = 4$ and $60 \div 20 = 3$

Find the smallest number that all the given numbers will divide into exactly.

1	3, 5	**4**	3, 9, 12
2	6, 8	**5**	12, 16, 24
3	5, 15	**6**	4, 5, 6

Common factors and common multiples

When either the HCF or the LCM is not easy to see, we can find it by expressing each number as the product of its prime factors.

Consider for example the numbers 36, 54 and 60.

$$36 = 2^2 \times 3^2, \quad 54 = 2 \times 3^3 \quad \text{and} \quad 60 = 2^2 \times 3 \times 5$$

The HCF of these numbers must divide exactly into each of them.

Therefore the HCF is the product of the lowest powers of the prime factors common to 36, 54 and 60, i.e 2×3. Therefore the HCF of 36, 54 and 60 is 6.

The LCM of these numbers must be divisible by all the prime factors of 36, 54 and 60. Therefore the LCM is the product of the highest powers of all the prime factors, i.e $2^2 \times 3^3 \times 5$. So the LCM of 26, 54 and 60 is 540.

> **The HCF of a set of numbers is the product of the lowest powers of prime factors common to each number in the set.**
>
> **The LCM of a set of numbers is the product of the highest powers of the prime factors of each number in the set.**

Exercise 4j

Find the highest common factor of each set of numbers.

1	20, 45	7	25, 35, 50, 60
2	9, 15	8	36, 44, 52, 56
3	18, 24	9	14, 42
4	6, 45	10	39, 13, 26
5	24, 36	11	15, 30, 45, 60
6	21, 42, 84	12	10, 18, 20, 36

Find the lowest common multiple of each set of numbers.

13	20, 45	19	9, 12, 18
14	9, 12	20	18, 27, 36
15	18, 24	21	14, 45, 84
16	6, 45	22	10, 15, 20
17	6, 15	23	9, 12, 36
18	6, 12, 15	24	6, 7, 8

Exercise 4k

Some problems in this exercise can be solved by finding factors, others by finding multiples.

1 What is the smallest sum of money that can be made up of an exact number of 20 p pieces or of 50 p pieces?

2 Find the least sum of money into which 24 p, 30 p and 54 p will divide exactly.

3 Find the smallest length that can be divided exactly into equal sections of length 5 m or 8 m or 12 m.

4 The light at one lighthouse flashes every 8 seconds, while the light at another lighthouse flashes every 15 seconds.
They flash together at midnight.
What is the time when they next flash together?

5 If I go up a flight of stairs two at a time I get to the top without any being left over. If I then try three at a time and again five at a time, I still get to the top without any being left over.
Find the shortest flight of stairs for which this is possible.
How many would remain if I were to go up this flight seven at a time?

6 A room measures 450 cm by 350 cm.
Find the side of the largest square tile that can be used to tile the floor without any cutting.

7 Two toy cars travel around a race track, one completing the circuit in 6 seconds and the other in $6\frac{1}{2}$ seconds.
If they leave the starting line together, how long will it be before they are again side by side?

8 Find the largest number of children who can share equally 126 oranges and 147 bananas.

9 A gear wheel with 30 teeth drives another wheel with 65 teeth. A certain pair of teeth are touching when the wheels start. How many times must each wheel turn before the same two teeth touch each other again?

10 In Year 7 of a large comprehensive school it is possible to divide the pupils into equal-sized classes of either 24 or 30 or 32 and have no pupils left over.
Find the size of the smallest entry that makes this possible.
How many classes will there be if each class is to have 24 pupils?

11 Lance wrote down a lot of plus sevens and minus fours.
Altogether he wrote 22 digits.
When he came to add them all up the total was zero.
How many plus sevens were there?

Consider again

The first customer wants 480 packs of paper plates a week, the second wants 960 and the third wants 288. How can the manufacturer find the best way of making up cartons with the same number of packs, to fulfil these orders with sealed cartons?

The church at Bracksford has four bells. Bell 1 rings every 5 seconds, bell 2 bell rings every 6 seconds, bell 3 rings every 7 seconds, and bell 4 rings every 8 seconds. They are first rung together. How can we find out how long it will be before they all ring together again?

Try to solve these two problems.

Number patterns

Consider

At the end of each hour, the number of bacteria growing in a Petri dish is twice the number at the start of the hour. There were 20 bacteria at 9 a.m. How many will there be at 4 p.m.?

You should be able to solve this problem after you have worked through the rest of this chapter.

Patterns of numbers where there is a rule to continue the pattern are called **sequences**. Two very simple sequences are: 1, 3, 5, 7, 9, ... and 2, 4, 6, 8, ... These are: the pattern of odd numbers and the pattern of even numbers.

These sequences are continued by adding a fixed amount (2) to each term to get the next term.

Any sequence that can be continued by adding or subtracting a fixed amount to each term to get the next term is called an **arithmetic progression**.

Exercise 41

In questions **1** to **6** each pattern is formed either by adding a fixed amount to, or by subtracting a fixed amount from, each term to get the next one. Write down this difference, stating clearly whether the quantity is added or subtracted.

1	2, 6, 10, 14	4	6, 17, 28, 39
2	5, 10, 15, 20	5	20, 17, 14, 11
3	4, 11, 18, 25	6	62, 57, 52, 47

In questions **7–12** find the difference between consecutive terms in the pattern, and hence write down the next three terms of each pattern.

7	1, 5, 9, 13	10	43, 36, 29, 22
8	10, 20, 30, 40	11	5, 13, 21, 29
9	60, 55, 50, 45	12	6, 18, 30, 42

Worked example

→ You want Shelley to write down the sequence of numbers 4, 11, 18, 25, 32 ... by giving her the first term followed by an instruction. What would you tell Shelley to do?

I would tell Shelley 'Write down the sequence of numbers you get by starting with 4 and then adding 7 each time'.

Check: **4**, 4 + 7 = **11**, 11 + 7 = **18**, 18 + 7 = **25**, 25 + 7 = **32**

You note that each term is found by adding 7 to the previous term.

In questions **13** to **18** write down a general instruction that would give the pattern.

13 10, 25, 40, 55

14 7, 10, 13, 16

15 8, 15, 22, 29

16 100, 91, 82, 73

17 63, 55, 47, 39

18 8, 21, 34, 47

Rectangular numbers

Any number that can be shown as a rectangular pattern of dots is called a **rectangular number**.

24 is a rectangular number e.g.:

⬤ ⬤ ⬤ ⬤ ⬤ ⬤
⬤ ⬤ ⬤ ⬤ ⬤ ⬤   or   ⬤ ⬤ ⬤ ⬤ ⬤ ⬤ ⬤ ⬤ ⬤ ⬤ ⬤ ⬤
⬤ ⬤ ⬤ ⬤ ⬤ ⬤   ⬤ ⬤ ⬤ ⬤ ⬤ ⬤ ⬤ ⬤ ⬤ ⬤ ⬤ ⬤
⬤ ⬤ ⬤ ⬤ ⬤ ⬤

5 is not a rectangular number since a line of dots is not a rectangle, i.e. ⬤ ⬤ ⬤ ⬤ ⬤

Exercise 4m

In questions **1** to **5** draw dot patterns for any of the following numbers that are rectangular numbers.

1 8

2 15

3 23

4 27

5 35

6 Show in two different ways that 12 is a rectangular number.

7 Which of the numbers between 2 and 20 are not rectangular numbers? What special name do we give to these numbers?

Square numbers

If the number of dots representing a number can be arranged as a square the number is called a **square number**.

For example, 9 and 25 are square numbers.

Note that 1 is also a square number.

Square numbers can be written in index form. For example, 3^2 and 5^2.

Exercise 4n

1 **a** Write down the first six square numbers.
  b What is **i** the tenth square number
               ii the twelfth square number?

2 Look at the pattern.
What total do you get for each line in
this pattern?
Are all these totals rectangular numbers
and/or square numbers?

$$1$$
$$1\ 2\ 1$$
$$1\ 2\ 3\ 2\ 1$$
$$1\ 2\ 3\ 4\ 3\ 2\ 1$$

3 Repeat question **2** for the pattern formed
by adding the odd numbers.

$$1$$
$$1 + 3$$
$$1 + 3 + 5$$
$$1 + 3 + 5 + 7$$

Triangular numbers

If the dots are arranged in rows so that
each row is one dot longer than the row
above, we have a pattern of
triangular numbers.

1: 3:   6: 10:

Exercise 4p

1 Draw a dot pattern for the next three triangular numbers after 10.

2 Without drawing a dot pattern, write down the next three
triangular numbers after 28.

3 What pattern do you get if you sum the
numbers in each line of this pattern?

$$1$$
$$1 + 2$$
$$1 + 2 + 3$$
$$1 + 2 + 3 + 4$$
$$1 + 2 + 3 + 4 + 5$$

4 Using the text and your answers for questions **1** and **2**, write
down the first 10 triangular numbers in order. Now follow these
instructions.
  Step 1   Choose any triangular number other than 1.
  Step 2   Multiply your chosen number by the next but one
              triangular number. Note your answer.
  Step 3   Write down the triangular number that was between
              the two numbers you chose.
  Step 4   Multiply this number by the number that is 1 smaller.
  Step 5   Compare your Step 2 and Step 4 answers.
  Step 6   Repeat the previous steps for a different number.

Other patterns

Lots of other patterns are possible apart from those we have already considered.

Exercise 4q

In questions **1** to **10** write down the next three terms for each pattern.

1 1, 2, 4, 8, 16,

2 5, 25, 125, 625,

3 2, 6, 18, 54,

4 1, 2, 4, 7, 11,

5 5, 7, 11, 17, 25,

6 2, 3, 5, 7, 11, 13,

In some patterns the next number is found by adding the previous pair.
For example 2, 4, 6, 10, 16, …

7 4, 2, 6, 8,

8 1, 2, 3, 5, 8,

9 2, 1, 3, 4, 7,

10 1, 1, 2, 3, 5,

A sequence of patterns can also be formed from shapes.
Give the next two shapes for the following patterns.

11

12

13

14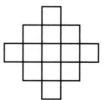

Consider again

At the end of each hour, the number of bacteria growing in a Petri dish is twice the number at the start of the hour. There were 20 bacteria at 9 a.m. How many will there be at 4 p.m.? Now answer this question.

Mixed exercise

Exercise 4r

1 Write $3 \times 3 \times 3 \times 3 \times 3$ in index form.

2 Find the value of **a** 4^3 **b** $3^2 \times 4^3$

3 Express 216 as the product of prime numbers in index form.

4 Is 1273 divisible by 3?

5 Find the largest whole number that will divide exactly into 21, 42 and 63.

6 Find the smallest whole number that 6, 8 and 12 will divide into exactly.

7 Find the largest number of children that can share equally 72 sweets and 54 chocolates.

8 Write down the next three terms in the pattern.

    a 20, 26, 32, 38, ...   **b** 1, 3, 7, 13, 21, ...

! Investigation

1

The diagrams show a pattern that starts with 1 purple square surrounded by white squares. As the row of purple squares increases, so does the number of white squares needed to enclose it.

a Copy and complete the fourth diagram, and draw the fifth and sixth diagrams.
Copy and complete the following table.

Position of diagram	Number of purple squares	Number of white squares needed to surround the purple squares
1	1	8
2	2	
3	3	
4	4	
5	5	
6		

b Without drawing diagrams, can you say how many white squares are needed if the number of purple squares is
    i 10   **ii** 20?

c Write, in words, the connection between the number of white squares and the number of purple squares in each diagram.

d Is there a connection between the number of purple squares and the number of white squares if you arrange the purple squares as nearly as possible in the shape of a square instead of a row? For example

2 a Write down the next three steps for the pattern.

$$4 \times 9 = 36$$
$$44 \times 9 = 396$$
$$444 \times 9 = 3996$$

b Does your method work when other similar patterns of a different digit are multiplied by 9?

Try, for example 7×9, 77×9, $777 \times 9, \ldots$
and then 8×9, 88×9, $888 \times 9, \ldots$

Without multiplying, write down the pattern you get when $5, 55, 555, 5555$, and so on are multiplied by 9.

Check your values by doing the multiplication.

Does this pattern always follow?

Can you justify your answer?

3 a If the digits of a number are added together we have a reduced number. For example 26 reduces to 8, 167 reduces to 14 which further reduces to 5.

Investigate the reduced numbers for the numbers in the pattern.

$$1, 1, 2, 3, 5, 8, 13, 21, 34, \ldots$$

Add more numbers to the original pattern. If you go far enough the pattern of reduced numbers starts to repeat itself. Why does this happen?

Can you be certain that it will continue to happen as you add more numbers to the pattern?

b Investigate the pattern of reduced numbers for the numbers.

$$1, 3, 4, 7, 11, 18, 29, \ldots$$

What happens when you write down alternate numbers from the pattern of reduced numbers? Do not give up too soon!

What happens if you start the pattern with the numbers 3, 1 instead of 1, 3?

c Try making up some similar patterns of your own.

Find the reduced numbers for your pattern.

Do they have a pattern?

Summary 1

Mixed addition and subtraction

The sign in front of a number refers to that number only.
The order in which you add or subtract does not matter, so
$1 - 5 + 8$ can be calculated in the order $1 + 8 - 5$, i.e. $9 - 5 = 4$

Rounding numbers

To round a number to the nearest 10, look at the units; if there are 5 or
more units, add one to the number of tens, otherwise leave it untouched.
To round a number to the nearest hundred, look at the tens; add one to
the hundreds if there are 5 or more tens, otherwise leave it untouched,
e.g. $137 = 140$ to the nearest 10
and $137 = 100$ to the nearest 100

Mixed operations of $\times, \div, +, -$

When a calculation involves a mixture of operations, start by
calculating anything inside brackets, then follow the rule 'do the
multiplication and division first',

e.g. $2 + 3 \times 2 = 2 + 6$ and $(2 + 3) \times 2 = 5 \times 2$
$$= 8 \qquad\qquad\qquad\qquad = 10$$

Factors and multiples

A factor of a number will divide into the number exactly.
When two or more numbers have the same factor, it is called a common
factor. The highest common factor of a set of numbers is the product of
the lowest powers of prime factors common to each number in the set.
A multiple of a number has that number as a factor,
e.g.   3 is a factor of 12   and   12 is a multiple of 3
A common multiple of two or more numbers can be divided exactly by
each of those numbers. The lowest common multiple of a set of numbers
is the product of the highest powers of the prime factors of each number
in the set.

Types of number

Even numbers divide exactly by 2, e.g. 6, 10, ...
Odd numbers do not divide exactly by 2, e.g. 3, 7, ...
A prime number has only 1 and itself as factors, e.g. 7.
Remember that 1 is *not* a prime number.

Square numbers can be drawn as a square grid of dots,
e.g. 9:

Rectangular numbers can be drawn as a rectangular
grid of dots, e.g. 6:

Triangular numbers can be drawn as a triangular grid of dots, e.g. 6:

Index numbers

The small superscript 2 in 3^2 is called an index and it tells you how many 3s are multiplied together,

e.g. 3^2 means 3×3 and 3^5 means $3 \times 3 \times 3 \times 3 \times 3$

REVISION EXERCISE 1.1 (Chapters 1 and 2)

1 Write the number
   a three hundred and seventy-two in figures
   b 4076 in words

2 Find, without using a calculator
   a 56 + 31   **b** 199 − 48   **c** 114 + 58 + 47

3 Find, without using a calculator
   a 496 + 265   **b** 608 − 399

4 Find the distance round the edge of this template.

5 Helen was due to have a history lesson that lasted 55 minutes.
   She arrived 7 minutes late, and had to leave 15 minutes early to go
   for a dental appointment.
   How long was she in the lesson?

6 Find, without using a calculator
   a 574 × 3   **b** 76 × 25   **c** 1300 × 360

7 a Find, giving the remainder if there is one
      i 427 ÷ 5   **ii** 1035 ÷ 23   **iii** 1624 ÷ 36
   b Find 10 + 4 × 3 − 12 + 2

8 In a concert hall there are 24 rows in tier 2 with 18 seats in each row.
   How many people can be seated in tier 2?

9 Estimate the value of 197 × 38, and then use a calculator to find
   the exact value.

10 How many 13-seater mini-buses are needed to transport
   50 children to a match? How many spare seats are there?

REVISION EXERCISE 1.2 (Chapters 3 and 4)

1 Gemma counted the numbers of people in the cars that passed her home one lunch time. The numbers she recorded were

$$
\begin{array}{llllllll}
1 & 1 & 1 & 1 & 4 & 1 & 1 & 1 \\
2 & 4 & 2 & 2 & 1 & 3 & 2 & 1 \\
1 & 1 & 3 & 1 & 1 & 1 & 1 & 2 \\
1 & 2 & 1 & 1 & 2 & 1 & 1 & 3
\end{array}
$$

  a How many cars did she count?

  b How many people did she count altogether?

  c Make a frequency table for this list.

2 The bar chart shows the number of letters delivered by a postman to each house in a street one morning.

  a What was the most common number of letters delivered?

  b How many houses received 4 letters?

  c How many houses received 4 letters or more?

  d How many houses were there in the street?

  e How many houses did not have a letter delivered?

  f How many letters were delivered altogether?

3 Write down all the multiples of 7 between 30 and 50.

4 Write in index form

  a $5 \times 5 \times 5$

  b $3 \times 3 \times 3 \times 3 \times 3 \times 3$

5 Find the largest whole number that will divide exactly into

  a 14 and 21

  b 52, 13 and 39

  c 15, 40 and 65

6 Express as products of prime numbers in index form.

  a 81

  b 64

  c 48

7 Write down the next three terms in the pattern.

  a 10, 25, 40, 55

  b 4, 12, 20, 28

8 Explain how you can find out whether 2493 is divisible by 3 without doing the division.

9 A gear wheel with 35 teeth drives another wheel with 55 teeth. When the wheels begin to turn two particular teeth are touching. How many turns must each wheel make before the same two teeth touch each other again?

10 6, 7, 8, 12, 15, 16, 17, 19, 20, 21, 23, 25
Which of the numbers in this list are
  a prime numbers   **c** triangular numbers
  b square numbers   **d** rectangular numbers?

11 Find the prime factors of 30 and 220.
Hence find
  a the HCF of 30 and 220   **b** the LCM of 30 and 220.

REVISION EXERCISE 1.3 (Chapters 1 to 4)

1 Find the sum of one thousand and forty-two, sixty-nine and five hundred and thirty-six.

2 A machine produced 7294 components in one hour.
If 149 were found to be faulty, how many were satisfactory?

3 Find, without using a calculator
  a $460 \div 20$ **b** 504×60 **c** $12 \div 3 - 6 \div 2 + 1$

4 A can of tomatoes weighs 458 grams.
What is the weight of 56 cans?

5 By writing each number correct to the nearest 10, find an approximate value for
  a $163 + 191$ **b** $732 - 65$ **c** $53 + 78 + 82$

6 What is the cost of 4 cream cakes at 96 p each?

7 Express in prime factors
  a 56   **b** 540   **c** 3087

8 Write down the next three terms in the pattern.
  a 2, 4, 6, 8, ...   **b** 2, 4, 8, 16, ...   **c** 2, 4, 6, 10, ...

9 A sequence of numbers is formed by starting with 5, and then multiplying the last number by 6.
Write down the first four numbers in the sequence.

10 The customers at a greengrocer were placed in one of four categories man (M), woman (W), boy (under 18) (B), girl (under 18) (G). The list shows the information as it was collected.

           G B G M G G B G B
           B W W G G G W M G
           M W B B M W B M W
           G W G B W W W B W

  a Make a frequency table for this information.
  b Draw a bar chart to illustrate the information.
  c How many of the customers were boys and how many were girls?

d How many more women customers than men customers were there?

e How many customers were there altogether?

REVISION EXERCISE 1.4 (Chapters 1 to 4)

1 Find, without using a calculator.
 a $314 - 169 + 249 - 73$
 b $64 - 184 - 47 + 206$
 c $12 + 4 \times 3 \div 2 + 24 \div 3$

2 Bella needs to score 301 to win a game of darts. She scores 83 on her first turn and 39 on her second turn.
 How many does she still have to score to win?

3 Fill in the blanks (marked with $\square$) in the following calculations.
 a $35 \times 49 = 171\square$
 b $4\square \times 57 = 2394$
 c $63 \times \square 2 = 4536$
 d $54 \times 78 = 4\square 12$

4 Use a calculator to find
 a 83×37
 b $416 \div 32$
 c 517×429
 d $435 - (56 - 37) \times 14$

5 Sanjay did a survey of the main hobby of each student in his class, including himself, and produced the following frequency table.

Type of hobby	Computers	Playing a sport	Reading	Music	Collecting stamps
Frequency	10	9	2	3	4

 a How many students are there in Sanjay's class?
 b Which hobby is the most popular?
 c Draw a bar chart to show this information.

6 Write each even number from 31 to 39 as the sum of two primes.

7 Find the smallest whole number that 8, 10 and 16 will divide into exactly.

8 A number 9 bus is due every 8 minutes, and a number 64 is due at the same bus stop every 10 minutes. Both buses are due at 8.30 a.m. At what time are a number 9 bus and a number 64 bus next due to arrive at this bus stop together?

Mental arithmetic practice 1

Answer these questions without using a calculator or pen and paper.

1   Write down the number ten thousand and twenty.

2   Add 205 and 98.

3   Write down the value of the digit 6 in the number 2060.

4   Find $5 + 4 + 7 + 9$

5   Write down two pairs of whole numbers whose sum is 5.

6   Add 168 and 107.

7   To get to school, Adam walked for 10 minutes, waited 6 minutes for a bus, and then spent 15 minutes on the bus. How long did his journey take?

8   Add 12, 6 and 15.

9   What needs to be added to 14 to make 20?

10   $7 + ? = 20$

11   Mike bought 2 apples costing 38 p each, and paid with a £1 coin. How much change should he get?

12   Find $20 - 9$

13   Find $258 + 82$

14   Subtract 56 from 125.

15   A sequence starts with 1, then 6 is added to get the next number, and so on. What are the third and fourth numbers?

16   Find 6×8

17   Find $59 - 36$

18   Find $15 + 6 + 2$

19   What multiplied by 8 gives 56?

20   Find 25×3

21   Find 253×2

22   Find 253×100

23   Find $253 + 150$

24   Ahmed bought five 60 p stamps. How much did they cost him?

25   Find $2 \times 4 \times 6$

26   A sequence starts with 3 and continues as '7 $\times$ the last term'. Find the second and third terms.

27   Find 305×500

28   Find $305 + 500$

29   Find $305 - 120$

30 26 + ? makes 52

31 Find the remainder when 86 is divided by 8.

32 How many sweets costing 9 p each can be bought for 80 p?

33 Find 4000 × 47

34 Add 97 and 155

35 Subtract 37 from 200

36 Estimate the cost of 27 tickets at £18 each.

37 Add 3, 8, 5 and 4

38 140 ÷ ? = 35

39 Find 4 + 3 × 2

40 How many pages are there in Chapter 2 which starts on page 17 and ends on page 33?

41 Find 293 × 200

42 Estimate 4107 × 504

43 Find 309 − 87

44 Stamps cost 60p each. How much do 40 stamps cost?

45 Add 12, 9 and 22

46 Find 7 × 8

47 Write down the prime numbers between 20 and 30.

48 Find 97 × 400

49 Write down all the different factors of 24.

50 Find 308 + 2558

51 Write 30 as the sum of two prime numbers.

52 Find 8 × 9

53 16 + ? = 20

54 Find 2 + 7 + 3 − 4

55 Find the value of 2 cubed.

56 Find 3 × 4 × 7

57 Find the value of 4 squared divided by 2.

58 What is the smallest whole number that 4 and 5 will divide into exactly?

59 What is the total weight of a television set that weighs 56 kg together with its stand which weighs 18 kg?

60 What is the value of 15 squared?

5 Sets

Consider

Thirty students wrote down what kind of transport they used one day to get to school.

- 15 used a bus. 18 used a car.
- 6 used both a bus and a car.

How can you find the number that used neither a bus nor a car?

You should be able to solve this problem after you have worked through this chapter.

Class discussion

Thirty students were asked if they had a pencil with them. They were then asked if they had a pen with them.

- 25 students said they had a pencil.
- 21 students said they had a pen.

These two numbers add up to more than the number of students in the class.

Why do you think this is the case?

Set notation

A **set** is a clearly defined collection of things that have something in common, for example, a set of drawing instruments, a set of books.

Things that belong to a set are called **members** or **elements of a set**. These members are usually written down separated by commas and enclosed in curly brackets.

For example, the set of prime numbers between 0 and 10 can be written as {2, 3, 5, 7}.

We do not have to list all the members of a set when we can use words to describe them. For example, instead of {1, 2, 3, 4, 5, ..., 19, 20} we can write {whole numbers from 1 to 20 inclusive}.

Exercise 5a

Worked example

→ Write {the prime factors of 30} as a list of members.

$30 = 2 \times 15$
$\quad = 2 \times 3 \times 5$

Therefore {the prime factors of 30} = {2, 3, 5}

Write each of the following sets as a list of members.

1 {the days of the week}
2 {the even numbers between 1 and 11}
3 {the prime numbers between 10 and 20}
4 {the multiples of 3 between 1 and 20}
5 {the last four letters of the Roman alphabet}
6 {multiples of 5 between 20 and 50 inclusive}
7 {the prime factors of 70}
8 {the square numbers between 1 and 100 inclusive}
9 {the triangular numbers between 1 and 50 inclusive}
10 {the different factors of 12}

Finite and infinite sets

When we need to refer to a set several times, we can use a capital letter to label that set. For example

A = {months of the year beginning with J}

or A = {January, June, July}

In many cases it is not possible to list all the members of a set. For example, if

N = {positive whole numbers}

we can write

$N = \{1, 2, 3, 4, 5, ...\}$

where the dots show that the list continues indefinitely.

N is an example of an **infinite set**, whereas A is an example of a **finite set**.

Exercise 5b

State whether the following sets are finite or infinite.

1 A = {vowels of the Roman alphabet}
2 B = {the factors of 30}
3 C = {even numbers}
4 D = {even numbers between 3 and 9}
5 E = {students taking violin lessons}
6 F = {odd numbers}
7 G = {grains of sand on the Earth}
8 H = {multiples of 3}
9 I = {different shapes of triangle}
10 J = {different languages spoken in the world}

Universal sets

Consider the set X = {whole numbers less than 16}.

Now consider the sets A and B whose members are in X where

A = {prime numbers less than 16} = {2, 3, 5, 7, 11, 13}

and

B = {multiples of 5 less than 16} = {5, 10, 15}

The set X is called a **universal set** for the sets A and B. It is a set that contains all the members of the sets A and B, together with other members that are not in A or in B. The universal set could also be any set of whole numbers that includes the members of A and B, for example {whole numbers less than 20}. The universal set is usually labelled U.

Exercise 5c

Worked example

$\rightarrow$ Suggest a universal set for the sets
A = {students in my class who have piano lessons}
B = {students in my class who have guitar lessons}

U = {all the students in my class}
(The universal set could be any other set that includes the students in A and B.)

Suggest a universal set for

1 {2, 4, 6, 8, 10} and {4, 8, 12}

2 {1, 3, 5, 7, 11} and {3, 6, 9, 12, 15}

3 {knives} and {forks}

4 {odd whole numbers} and {multiples of 3}

5 {students in my class who play football} and {students in my class who play tennis}

6 {cups and saucers} and {plates}.

Venn diagrams

Venn diagrams are a way of representing sets. A **Venn diagram** consists of a rectangle with circles inside, representing sets.

The rectangle represents a universal set. The members of a universal set are all the members of the given sets together with possible other members.

For example, if A = {the odd numbers between 0 and 10} = {1, 3, 5, 7, 9} and B = {multiples of 3 between 1 and 20} = {3, 6, 9, 12, 15, 18}, the universal set could be {all whole numbers between 1 and 20 inclusive}.

This is the Venn diagram representing the sets A and B and $U = \{1, 2, 3, \ldots 19, 20\}$.

There is nothing special about circles, you can use any enclosed shape.

- The numbers 3 and 9 are in both sets, so they go in the overlapping part.
- The numbers 1, 5 and 7 are only in A, so they go in the left-hand part of the circle marked A.
- The numbers 6, 12, 15 and 18 go in the right-hand side of the circle marked B.

The union of two sets

The **union of sets** A and B is the set of members that are in either A or in B. This includes the members that are in both A and B.

For example, if $A = \{1, 3, 5, 7, 9\}$ and $B = \{3, 6, 9, 12, 15, 18\}$, the union of the sets A and B is the set $\{1, 3, 5, 6, 7, 9, 12, 15, 18\}$.

The union of the sets A and B is written as $A \cup B$.
This is represented in the Venn diagram above by the region enclosed by both circles.

When two sets have no members in common the circles are drawn without an overlap, for example:

Exercise 5d

Draw Venn diagrams to show the union of the following sets.

1   $P = \{a, b, c, d, e\}$, $Q = \{a, e, i, o, u\}$

2   $X = \{2, 4, 6, 8, 10\}$, $Y = \{4, 8, 12, 16\}$

3   $A = \{$letters in the word 'Bernado'$\}$,
    $B = \{$letters in the word 'Bashira'$\}$

4   $F = \{4, 8, 12, 16, 20\}$, $G = \{3, 6, 9, 12, 15\}$

5   $P = \{2, 3, 5\}$, $Q = \{2, 3, 7\}$

6   $X = \{$prime numbers less than 10$\}$,
    $Y = \{$even numbers less than 10$\}$

7 F = {square numbers less than 50},
   G = {triangular numbers less than 50}

8 M = {square numbers less than 100},
   N = {cube numbers less than 100}

9 A = {capital letters in the alphabet that can be written using only straight lines},

   B = {capital letters in the alphabet that cannot be written using only straight lines}

10 P = {letters in the word ALGEBRA},
   Q = {letters in the word GEOMETRY}

Intersection of sets

The **intersection of sets** A and B is the set of members that is in both A and B.
Consider again the sets A = {1, 3, 5, 7, 9} and B = {3, 6, 9, 12, 15, 18}

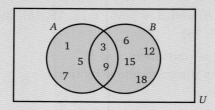

From the Venn diagram we can see that the members {3, 9} are in both A and B.
The intersection of A and B is written as $A \cap B$.
Therefore $A \cap B$ = {3, 9}

Exercise 5e

Use the diagrams that you drew for Exercise 5d, questions **1** to **6** to write down the intersection of each pair of sets.

7 Draw a Venn diagram to illustrate the sets A = {2, 4, 6, 8, 10, 12} and B = {3, 6, 9, 12} with U = {whole numbers from 1 to 12 inclusive}. Hence write down the set of numbers that are in U but not in either A or B.

8 Draw a Venn diagram to illustrate the sets A = {factors of 6} and B = {factors of 10} with U = {whole numbers from 1 to 10 inclusive}. Hence write down the set of numbers that are in U but not in either A or B.

9 Given F = {square numbers less than 50}, G = {triangular numbers less than 50} and U = {whole numbers from 1 to 50 inclusive}

   a list the members of $F \cap G$

   b find the number of members of the set that are not members of F or G.

10 Given M = {square numbers less than 100}, N = {cube numbers less than 100} and U = {whole numbers from 1 to 100 inclusive}

    a list the members of $M \cap N$

    b find the number of members of the set that are not members of M or N.

Consider again

Thirty students wrote down what kind of transport they used one day to get to school.

- 15 used a bus. 18 used a car.
- 6 used both a bus and a car.

Now can you find the number that used neither a bus nor a car?

! Investigation

Consider the following sets X and Y.

X = {0, 2, 4, 6, 8, 10, ...}, Y = {1, 3, 5, 7, 9, 11, ...}

a Describe X and Y in words.

b Write down the next three numbers in X. Write down the next three numbers in Y.

c Choose two numbers from X and find their sum. Is this sum a member of X? Is this always true?

d Choose two numbers from Y and find their sum. Which set contains this sum? Is this always true?

e What can you say about two numbers so that their sum is in Y?

6 Parts of a whole

Consider

There are 30 students in class 7G: $\frac{2}{5}$ of them are girls; 10% of them are absent; 0.3 of them did not hand in homework on time.

Parts of class 7G are described in different ways. Can you compare them? How can you find the number of students that are absent? How many handed in the homework on time?

You should be able to solve this problem after you have worked through this chapter.

The meaning of fractions

Think of cutting a cake right through the middle into two equal pieces. Each piece is one half of the cake. One half is a **fraction**, written as $\frac{1}{2}$.

If we cut the cake into four equal pieces, each piece is one quarter, written $\frac{1}{4}$, of the cake. When one piece is taken away there are three pieces left, so the fraction that is left is three quarters, or $\frac{3}{4}$.

When the cake is divided into five equal slices, one slice is $\frac{1}{5}$, two slices is $\frac{2}{5}$, three slices is $\frac{3}{5}$ and four slices is $\frac{4}{5}$ of the cake.

Notice that the top number in each fraction (called the **numerator**) tells you *how many* slices and the bottom number (called the **denominator**) tells you about the size of the slices.

Exercise 6a

Write down the fraction that is shaded in each of the following diagrams.

1

3

5

2

4

6

It is not only cakes that can be divided into fractions. Anything that can be split up can be divided into fractions.

Write down the fraction that is shaded in each of the following diagrams.

7

8

9

10

11

12

13

14

15

16

Mixed numbers

So far we have considered **proper fractions** i.e. fractions that are less than 1, but some fractions are bigger than 1.

Suppose we have one and a half bars of chocolate. We write this as $1\frac{1}{2}$ bars, and $1\frac{1}{2}$ is called a **mixed number**.

Other examples of mixed numbers are $1\frac{7}{10}$, $12\frac{3}{4}$ and $24\frac{2}{5}$.

Equivalent fractions

In A, a cake is cut into four equal pieces. One slice is $\frac{1}{4}$ of the cake.

In B, the cake is cut into eight equal pieces. Two slices is $\frac{2}{8}$ of the cake.

In C, the cake is cut into sixteen equal slices. Four slices is $\frac{4}{16}$ of the cake.

But the same amount of cake has been taken each time.

Therefore $\frac{1}{4} = \frac{2}{8} = \frac{4}{16}$

and we say that $\frac{1}{4}$, $\frac{2}{8}$ and $\frac{4}{16}$ are **equivalent fractions**.

Now $\frac{1}{4} = \frac{1 \times 2}{4 \times 2} = \frac{2}{8}$ and $\frac{1}{4} = \frac{1 \times 4}{4 \times 4} = \frac{4}{16}$

So all we have to do to find equivalent fractions is to multiply the numerator and the denominator by the same number. For example

$$\frac{1}{4} = \frac{1 \times 3}{4 \times 3} = \frac{3}{12}$$

and $\frac{1}{4} = \frac{1 \times 5}{4 \times 5} = \frac{5}{20}$

Any fraction can be treated in this way.

Exercise 6b

In questions **1** to **6**, draw cake diagrams to show that

1 $\quad \frac{1}{3} = \frac{2}{6}$ **3** $\quad \frac{1}{5} = \frac{2}{10}$ **5** $\quad \frac{2}{3} = \frac{6}{9}$

2 $\quad \frac{1}{2} = \frac{3}{6}$ **4** $\quad \frac{3}{4} = \frac{9}{12}$ **6** $\quad \frac{2}{3} = \frac{8}{12}$

Worked example

Fill in the missing numbers to make equivalent fractions.

$\rightarrow \quad \dfrac{1}{5} = \dfrac{3}{}$

$\dfrac{1}{5} = \dfrac{1 \times 3}{5 \times 3} = \dfrac{3}{15}$

💡 If $\frac{1}{5} = \frac{3}{}$ the numerator has been multiplied by 3.

$\rightarrow \quad \dfrac{1}{5} = \dfrac{}{20}$

$\dfrac{1}{5} = \dfrac{1 \times 4}{5 \times 4} = \dfrac{4}{20}$

💡 If $\frac{1}{5} = \frac{}{20}$ the denominator has been multiplied by 4.

In questions **7** to **30**, copy the fractions and fill in the missing numbers to make equivalent fractions.

7 $\dfrac{1}{3} = \dfrac{2}{}$

8 $\dfrac{2}{5} = \dfrac{}{10}$

9 $\dfrac{3}{7} = \dfrac{9}{}$

10 $\dfrac{9}{10} = \dfrac{}{40}$

11 $\dfrac{2}{9} = \dfrac{4}{}$

12 $\dfrac{3}{8} = \dfrac{}{80}$

13 $\dfrac{5}{11} = \dfrac{}{22}$

14 $\dfrac{4}{5} = \dfrac{8}{}$

15 $\dfrac{1}{10} = \dfrac{10}{}$

16 $\dfrac{1}{6} = \dfrac{3}{}$

17 $\dfrac{1}{3} = \dfrac{}{12}$

18 $\dfrac{2}{5} = \dfrac{6}{}$

19 $\dfrac{3}{7} = \dfrac{}{28}$

20 $\dfrac{2}{9} = \dfrac{}{36}$

21 $\dfrac{3}{8} = \dfrac{}{800}$

22 $\dfrac{5}{11} = \dfrac{50}{}$

23 $\dfrac{4}{5} = \dfrac{}{50}$

24 $\dfrac{1}{10} = \dfrac{100}{}$

25 $\dfrac{9}{10} = \dfrac{90}{}$

26 $\dfrac{1}{6} = \dfrac{}{36}$

27 $\dfrac{4}{5} = \dfrac{}{20}$

28 $\dfrac{2}{3} = \dfrac{12}{}$

29 $\dfrac{2}{9} = \dfrac{20}{}$

30 $\dfrac{3}{8} = \dfrac{3000}{}$

Worked example

$\rightarrow$ Write $\dfrac{2}{3}$ as an equivalent fraction with denominator 24.

$\dfrac{2}{3} = \dfrac{2 \times 8}{3 \times 8} = \dfrac{16}{24}$

💡 To change 3 to 24, we need to multiply 3 by 8, but if we multiply the denominator by 8 we must also multiply the numerator by 8.

31 Write each of the following fractions as an equivalent fraction with denominator 24.

    a $\dfrac{1}{2}$ c $\dfrac{1}{6}$ e $\dfrac{5}{12}$

    b $\dfrac{1}{3}$ d $\dfrac{3}{4}$ f $\dfrac{3}{8}$

32 Write each of the following fractions in equivalent form with denominator 45.

    a $\dfrac{2}{15}$ b $\dfrac{4}{9}$ c $\dfrac{3}{5}$

d $\frac{1}{3}$ e $\frac{14}{15}$ f $\frac{1}{5}$

33 Find an equivalent fraction with denominator 36 for each of the following fractions.

a $\frac{3}{4}$ c $\frac{1}{6}$ e $\frac{7}{12}$

b $\frac{5}{9}$ d $\frac{5}{18}$ f $\frac{2}{3}$

34 Change each of the following fractions into an equivalent fraction with numerator 12.

a $\frac{1}{6}$ c $\frac{6}{7}$ e $\frac{2}{3}$

b $\frac{3}{4}$ d $\frac{4}{5}$ f $\frac{1}{2}$

35 Some of the following equivalent fractions are correct, but two of them are wrong. Find the wrong ones and explain why they are wrong.

a $\frac{2}{5} = \frac{6}{15}$ c $\frac{3}{7} = \frac{6}{14}$ e $\frac{7}{10} = \frac{77}{100}$

b $\frac{2}{3} = \frac{4}{9}$ d $\frac{4}{9} = \frac{12}{27}$ f $\frac{9}{13} = \frac{18}{26}$

Simplifying fractions

Think of the way you find equivalent fractions.

For example, $\frac{2}{5} = \frac{2 \times 7}{5 \times 7} = \frac{14}{35}$

Looking at this the other way round, we see that

$$\frac{14}{35} = \frac{{}^1\cancel{7} \times 2}{{}^1\cancel{7} \times 5} = \frac{2}{5}$$

In the middle step, 7 is a factor of both the numerator and the denominator and it is called a common factor. To get the final value of $\frac{2}{5}$ we have 'crossed out' the common factor and this is called **cancelling**. What we have really done is to divide the top and the bottom by 7 and this **simplifies** the fraction.

When all the simplifying is finished we say that the fraction is in its *lowest terms*.

Any fraction whose numerator and denominator have a common factor (perhaps more than one) can be simplified in this way. Suppose, for example, that we want to simplify $\frac{24}{27}$. As 3 is a factor of 24 and of 27, we say

$$\frac{24}{27} = \frac{3 \times 8}{3 \times 9} = \frac{8}{9}$$

A quicker way to write this down is to divide the numerator and the denominator mentally by the common factor, crossing them out and writing the new numbers beside them (it is a good idea to write the new numbers smaller so that you can see that you have simplified the fraction), i.e.

$$\frac{\cancel{24}^{\,8}}{\cancel{27}^{\,9}} = \frac{8}{9}$$

Exercise 6c

Worked example

→ Simplify $\dfrac{66}{176}$

$$\dfrac{\cancel{66}^{\cancel{33}\ 3}}{\cancel{176}_{\cancel{88}\ 8}} = \dfrac{3}{8}$$

 We divided top and bottom by 2, and then by 11.

Simplify the following fractions.

① $\dfrac{2}{6}$

6 $\dfrac{4}{8}$

11 $\dfrac{8}{28}$

16 $\dfrac{10}{30}$

2 $\dfrac{30}{50}$

7 $\dfrac{5}{15}$

12 $\dfrac{27}{90}$

17 $\dfrac{36}{72}$

3 $\dfrac{3}{9}$

8 $\dfrac{12}{18}$

13 $\dfrac{14}{70}$

18 $\dfrac{15}{75}$

4 $\dfrac{6}{12}$

9 $\dfrac{10}{20}$

14 $\dfrac{24}{60}$

19 $\dfrac{60}{100}$

5 $\dfrac{9}{27}$

10 $\dfrac{8}{32}$

15 $\dfrac{16}{56}$

20 $\dfrac{36}{90}$

Introducing decimals

This bolt is being measured using a ruler marked in centimetres and tenths of a centimetre. The length of the bolt is $\frac{8}{10}$ of a centimetre. Other instruments have scales that are divided into tenths or hundredths, as you will see if you look at a set of kitchen scales or a thermometer. Many quantities are divided into tenths or hundredths.

- £1 is divided into 100 pence.
- 1 metre is divided into 100 centimetres.

Instead of writing $\frac{1}{10}$ths, $\frac{1}{100}$ths and $\frac{1}{1000}$ths, we use decimal notation which is much simpler.

The meaning of decimals

Consider the number 426. The position of the digits indicates what each digit represents. We can write:

hundreds	tens	units
4	2	6

Each quantity in the heading is $\frac{1}{10}$ of the quantity to its left: ten is $\frac{1}{10}$ of a hundred, a unit is $\frac{1}{10}$ of ten. Moving further to the right we can have further headings: tenths of a unit, hundredths of a unit and so on (a hundredth of a unit is $\frac{1}{10}$ of a tenth of a unit).

For example:

tens	units		tenths	hundredths
1	6	.	0	2

To mark where the units come we put a point after the units' position. 16.02 is 1 ten, 6 units and 2 hundredths, i.e. $16\frac{2}{100}$.

0.004 is 4 thousandths or $\frac{4}{1000}$. In this case, 0 is written before the point to help make it clear that there are no units, and so that the point doesn't get lost.

units		tenths	hundredths	thousandths
0	.	0	0	4

Numbers written this way are called decimal fractions, or simply decimals.

Exercise 6d

Worked example

➤ Write 34.62, in headed columns.

	tens	units		tenths	hundredths
34.62 =	3	4	.	6	2

➤ Write 0.207, in headed columns.

	units		tenths	hundredths	thousandths
0.207 =	0	.	2	0	7

Write the following numbers in headed columns.

1	2.6	5	101.3	9	6.34
2	32.1	6	0.007	10	0.604
3	6.03	7	1.046	11	15.045
4	0.09	8	12.001	12	0.092

Worked example

Express as a decimal

➤ $\frac{3}{10}$

$\frac{3}{10} = 0.3$

 The first place after the decimal point is 'tenths', so $\frac{3}{10}$ is 0.3.

➤ $\frac{13}{100}$

$\frac{13}{100} = 0.13$

 $\frac{13}{100} = \frac{10}{100} + \frac{3}{100}$, and $\frac{10}{100} = \frac{1}{10}$, so 1 goes in the first decimal place and 3 goes in the second decimal place.

Express as decimals.

13 $\frac{1}{10}$ 17 $\frac{15}{100}$ 21 $\frac{2}{10}$

14 $\frac{3}{100}$ 18 $\frac{81}{100}$ 22 $\frac{5}{100}$

15 $\frac{7}{10}$ 19 $\frac{37}{100}$ 23 $\frac{17}{100}$

16 $\frac{9}{100}$ 20 $\frac{4}{10}$ 24 $\frac{38}{100}$

25 Express $\frac{2}{5}$ as a decimal. Explain your reasoning.

The idea of a percentage

The shaded part of the cake is $\frac{10}{100}$ of the cake, or 0.1 of the cake.

Another way to describe this part of a whole is to say that 10% of the cake is shaded.

10% means '10 out of 100' and we say '10 **per cent**'.

(Cent comes from the Latin word for 100.)

30% means '30 out of 100' or $\frac{30}{100}$.

Exercise 6e

Worked example

Express the shaded part of the cake as

→ a percentage

The shaded part of the cake is 25 parts out of 100, i.e. 25%

→ a decimal

As a decimal $\frac{25}{100} = 0.25$

→ a fraction.

As a fraction $\frac{25}{100}$ simplifies to $\frac{1}{4}$.

In questions **1** to **12**, write down the part of the circle that is shaded as
a a percentage   **b** a decimal   **c** a fraction.

1

2

3

4

5

6

7

8

9

10

11

12

In questions **13** to **15**, estimate the part of the circle that is shaded.
Give your answer as
a a percentage   **b** a decimal   **c** a fraction.

13   14   15

For questions **16** to **20**, draw a circle and calibrate it like the circles opposite. Shade the part of the circle asked for.

16 $\frac{3}{10}$ 19 0.4

17 0.6   20 $\frac{7}{10}$

18 60%

Changing between percentages and fractions

We know that 20% of the cars in a car-park means $\frac{20}{100}$ of the cars there.

$\frac{20}{100}$ can be simplified to the equivalent fraction $\frac{1}{5}$,

i.e. $20\% = \frac{1}{5}$

Similarly 45% of the sweets in a bag means the same as $\frac{45}{100}$ of them and $\frac{45}{100} = \frac{9}{20}$,

i.e. $45\% = \frac{9}{20}$

Exercise 6f

Worked example

→ Ninety per cent of the students who sat a test passed.
   What fraction was this?

$90\% = \dfrac{90}{100}$

$ = \dfrac{9}{10}$

For questions **1** to **10**, express the given percentage as a fraction in its lowest terms.

1   Last summer 60% of the students in my class went on holiday.

2   Luka took a lot of geranium cuttings and had an 80% success rate.

3   At my youth club only 35% of the members are boys.

4 The rate of inflation is about 5%.

5 Only 15% of the people who have played for the club have scored a goal.

6 The Post Office claims that 95% of the letters posted by first class post arrive the following day.

7 A shoe inspection showed that 48% of the students were wearing brown shoes.

8 When value added tax was first introduced the rate was 8%.

9 In a cricket match Peter Jones scored 68% of all the runs scored by the team.

10 A survey showed that 32% of the students in Year 7 needed to wear glasses.

Worked example

→ Three-fifths of the spectators at a match were women.
What percentage is this?

$$\frac{3}{5} = \frac{3 \times 20}{5 \times 20}$$

$$= \frac{60}{100}$$

$$= 60\%$$

 We need to express $\frac{3}{5}$ as a number of hundredths. We can do this by making $\frac{3}{5}$ into an equivalent fraction with denominator 100.

In each of questions 11 to 15, express the fraction as a percentage.

11 Recently, at the local garage, $\frac{1}{5}$ of the cars tested failed to get an MOT test certificate.

12 At a youth club, $\frac{17}{20}$ of those present took part in at least one sporting activity.

13 About $\frac{17}{50}$ of Year 7 students watch more than 20 hours of television a week.

14 Approximately $\frac{3}{5}$ of Year 11 students have a Saturday job.

15 In one day, $\frac{24}{25}$ of the components produced by a machine were satisfactory.

Changing between percentages and decimals

Consider 20% of the cars in a car-park again.

20% of the cars = $\frac{20}{100}$ of the cars

But $\frac{20}{100} = 0.20$

i.e. $20\% = 0.20 = 0.2$

Exercise 6g

Worked example

→ Gail gave 46% of her CDs to her sister.
What decimal part of the CDs did she give to her sister?

$46\% = \dfrac{46}{100} = 0.46$

For statements **1** to **8**, express the given percentage as a decimal.

1 At the beginning of term, 65% of the students in the class needed a new exercise book.

2 When all the textbooks had been handed in, it was discovered that 15% of them needed replacing.

3 A survey of the whole school revealed that 45% of the students had no brothers or sisters.

4 The police stopped all the vehicles on an approach road to a motorway and found that 6% of these vehicles had defective tyres.

5 A travel agent reported that 37% of all the holidays they arranged were to Spain.

6 In the school orchestra about 55% of the members play stringed instruments.

7 A consignment of oranges was delayed at the docks. As a result, 24% of the oranges had to be destroyed.

8 A double glazing firm claimed that if their windows were installed there would be a 12% reduction in Mr Symes' heating bills.

Worked example

→ A close inspection of the components produced by the night shift showed that 0.12 of them were faulty.
What percentage is this?

 0.12 means 12 hundredths, and 12 out of a hundred is 12%, so 0.12 = 12%.

$0.12 = 12\%$

For statements **9** to **12**, express each decimal as a percentage.

9 At Berkley it rained on 0.33 of the days in the year.

10 A large number of new car buyers were interviewed. Red was the car colour chosen by 0.28 of them.

11 An opinion poll suggested that 0.78 of the population have a good idea now as to how they will vote in the next general election.

12 When a large number of electric light bulbs were tested, 0.92 of them burned for more than 100 hours.

Interchanging decimals and fractions

Exercise 6h

Worked example

Write as a fraction, or as a mixed number, in its lowest terms.

→ 0.6

	units	tenths

$0.6 = 0 \,.\, 6 = \dfrac{6}{10}$

$= \dfrac{3}{5}$

→ 12.04

	tens	units	tenths	hundredths

$12.04 = 1 \quad 2 \,.\, 0 \qquad 4 = 12\dfrac{4}{100}$

$= 12\dfrac{1}{25}$

In questions **1** to **8**, write each decimal as a fraction in its lowest terms, using mixed numbers where necessary.

1	0.2	**3**	0.001	**5**	1.8	**7**	15.5
2	0.06	**4**	1.7	**6**	0.007	**8**	2.01

For each statement from **9** to **12**, write the decimal as a fraction in its lowest terms.

9 It is estimated that 0.86 of the families in Northgate Street own a car.

10 In a wood, 0.68 of the trees lose their leaves in the winter.

11 George observed that 0.48 of the cars that passed him carried only the driver.

12 There were 360 seats on the aircraft and only 0.05 of them were vacant.

Worked example

→ At a political meeting $\dfrac{3}{5}$ of the audience left before the end. Express this fraction as a decimal.

$\dfrac{3}{5} = \dfrac{3 \times 2}{5 \times 2}$

$= \dfrac{6}{10}$

$= 0.6$

 We need to write $\dfrac{3}{5}$ as an equivalent fraction with denominator 10 or 100 or 1000, then we can write it as a decimal.

In questions **13** to **23**, express each fraction as a decimal.

13 $\frac{13}{100}$ **15** $\frac{4}{10}$ **17** $\frac{3}{20}$ **19** $\frac{23}{50}$

14 $\frac{7}{10}$ **16** $4\frac{7}{10}$ **18** $12\frac{1}{2}$ **20** $7\frac{9}{10}$

21 At a wedding reception, $\frac{2}{5}$ of the guests did not drink sherry.

22 For an afternoon performance of Cinderella, $\frac{13}{20}$ of the audience were children.

23 In a multi-storey car-park, $\frac{3}{8}$ of the parked cars were at ground level.

Expressing parts of a whole in different ways

Now we can express a part of a whole as either a fraction, a decimal or a percentage.

A bookseller is offering a book you would like to have at 15% below the list price. You would like to know by what fraction the price of the book is reduced.

To find this fraction you must convert 15% into a fraction,

i.e. $15\% = \frac{15}{100} = \frac{3}{20}$

The price of the book is reduced by $\frac{3}{20}$.

Exercise 6i

Worked example

➤ Express $\frac{4}{5}$ of the people at a concert as the percentage of people at the concert.

$$\frac{4}{5} = \frac{4 \times 20}{5 \times 20}$$
$$= \frac{80}{100}$$
$$= 80\%$$

1 At a dancing class, $\frac{13}{20}$ of those present were boys.
    a What percentage is this?
    b Express the fraction as a decimal.

2 When Hetty went to a car boot sale, she found that $\frac{3}{10}$ of the vehicles were vans. What percentage was this?

3 The registers showed that only 0.05 of the students in Year 7 had 100% attendance last term.
    a What fraction is this?
    b What percentage of Year 7 students had 100% attendance last term?

4 Jo is given an 8% wage increase.
By what fraction will her wage increase?

5 Nardia spends $\frac{21}{50}$ of her income on food and lodgings.
   a What percentage is this?
   b As a decimal, what part of her total income does she spend on food and lodgings?

6 Marmalade consists of 28% fruit, $\frac{29}{50}$ sugar and the remainder water.
   a What fraction of the marmalade is fruit?
   b What percentage of the marmalade is sugar?
   c What percentage is water?

7 The value of a house increased by 90% over a 10-year period.
By what fraction did the value of the house increase?

8

One tablespoon of orange concentrate is added to 9 tablespoons of water to make a drink.
   a What fraction of the drink is water?
   b What percentage of the drink is concentrate?

(When we mix two quantities together to make a whole, we can use the word 'ratio' to describe how much of each we use. In this case concentrate and water are mixed in the ratio 1 to 9. We write this as 1 : 9)

9 An alloy is 60% copper, $\frac{1}{5}$ is nickel and the remainder is tin.
   a What fraction is copper?
   b What percentage is
      i nickel
      ii either nickel or copper?
   c Express the part that is tin as a decimal.

Exercise 6j

1 Express as a fraction in its lowest terms.
   a 30%   **b** 85%   **c** 42%   **d** 5%

2 Express as a decimal.
   a 44%   **b** 68%   **c** 170%   **d** 16%

3 Express as a percentage.
   a $\frac{2}{5}$ **b** $\frac{17}{20}$ **c** $\frac{1}{4}$ **d** $\frac{17}{25}$

4 Express as a percentage.

    a   0.2   **c**   0.84

    b   0.62   **d**   0.78

Copy and complete the following table. Number **5** is done for you.

	Fraction	**Percentage**	**Decimal**
5	$\frac{3}{4}$	75%	0.75
6	$\frac{4}{5}$		
7		60%	
8			0.7
9	$\frac{11}{20}$		
10		44%	

Fractions of a quantity

Margot was given £60 in cash for her birthday. She was persuaded to put $\frac{3}{5}$ of it into a savings account. How much should she put in?

To find out how much she should put in a savings account Margot needs to know that $\frac{3}{5}$ means 3 parts out of 5 equal parts.

To find $\frac{3}{5}$ of £60 we first divide 60 by 5 to find the size of one of the equal parts.

$$60 \div 5 = 12 \qquad \text{so } \tfrac{1}{5} \text{ of £60} = £12$$

then $\frac{3}{5}$ of £60 = £12 $\times$ 3 = £36

Exercise 6k

Worked example

$\rightarrow$ Find $\frac{3}{5}$ of 95 metres.

$\frac{1}{5}$ of 95 = 95 $\div$ 5 = 19

$\therefore$ $\frac{3}{5}$ of 95 = 3 $\times$ 19 = 57

i.e. $\frac{3}{5}$ of 95 metres is 57 metres.

Check: 57 $\div$ 3 = 19

            19 $\times$ 5 = 95

$\rightarrow$ Find $\frac{3}{4}$ of £1.

£1 = 100 pence

$\frac{1}{4}$ of 100 = 100 $\div$ 4 = 25

$\therefore$ $\frac{3}{4}$ of 100 = 25 $\times$ 3 = 75

i.e. $\frac{3}{4}$ of £1 is 75 pence.

Check: 75 $\div$ 3 = 25

            25 $\times$ 4 = 100

Find

1    $\frac{3}{5}$ of 45 p

2    $\frac{9}{10}$ of 50 litres

3    $\frac{3}{8}$ of 88 miles

4    $\frac{7}{16}$ of 48 kilograms

5    $\frac{4}{5}$ of 1 year of 365 days

6    $\frac{5}{8}$ of 16 dollars

7    $\frac{3}{7}$ of 35 miles

8    $\frac{4}{9}$ of 63 kilometres

9    $\frac{1}{7}$ of 1 week

10   $\frac{7}{8}$ of 1 day (24 hours)

11 In an election for club secretary, Peter got $\frac{5}{12}$ of the votes and Sue got $\frac{2}{5}$. If 60 people were entitled to vote,

   a   how many voted for
      i   Peter
     ii   Sue?

   b   how many people did not vote?

12 Sally has a 60 metre ball of string. She used $\frac{3}{5}$ of it on Monday and $\frac{1}{4}$ of it on Tuesday.

   a   What length of string did she use
      i   on Monday
     ii   on Tuesday?

   b   What length remained?

We can find the percentages of quantities in a similar way.

Worked example

➡   A joint of meat, weighing 1600 grams, contains 15% fat.
    What weight of fat is there in the joint?

The weight of fat is 15% of 1600 g.

But $15\% = \dfrac{15}{100}$

    $\dfrac{1}{100}$ of $1600 = 1600 \div 100 = 16$

so $\dfrac{15}{100}$ of $1600 = 16 \times 15 = 240\,g$

∴   the amount of fat in the meat is 240 g.

Check: $240 \div 15 = 16$
        $16 \times 100 = 1600$

Find the value of

13 40% of £800

14 15% of 100 metres

15 33% of 600 kilograms

16 74% of 200 litres

17 40% of £48

20 86% of 1100 grams

18 6% of 3500 millimetres

21 30% of £4200

19 30% of 500 litres

22 25% of £60

23 Tim gets £12 a week and saves 25% of it.
   a How much does he save?
   b How much does he spend?

24 In a choir, 55% of the 80 choristers wear spectacles.
   How many choristers
   a wear spectacles
   b do not wear spectacles?

25 The audience for a performance of *Les Miserables* totalled 840.
   $\frac{1}{10}$ of the audience were men, 45% were women and the remainder
   were children.
   a How many in the audience were
      i men   **ii** women?
   b How many children were there?

26 There are 250 Year 7 students in a school. 26% of these students
   walk to school, $\frac{3}{5}$ of them come by bus and the remainder are
   brought by car. How many Year 7 students
   a walk to school
   b come by bus
   c come by car?

Comparing the sizes of fractions

Alec has one box of milk chocolates and one box of dark chocolates. Each box contains the
same number of chocolates. He gives $\frac{5}{7}$ of the milk chocolates to Bernard and $\frac{2}{3}$ of the dark
chocolates to Aya. Does he give more chocolates to Bernard than to Aya, or does Aya get the
greater number?

Before we can compare these two fractions we must change them into the *same kind* of
fraction. That means we must find equivalent fractions that have the same denominator.
This denominator must be a number that both 7 and 3 divide into. So our new denominator
is 21. Now

$$\frac{5}{7} = \frac{15}{21} \quad \text{and} \quad \frac{2}{3} = \frac{14}{21}$$

We can see that $\frac{15}{21}$ is bigger than $\frac{14}{21}$, i.e. $\frac{5}{7}$ is bigger than $\frac{2}{3}$, so Bernard gets more chocolates.

We often use the symbol > instead of writing 'is bigger than'. Using this symbol we could
write

$$\frac{15}{21} > \frac{14}{21}, \quad \text{so} \quad \frac{5}{7} > \frac{2}{3}$$

Similarly we use < instead of writing 'is less than'.

Exercise 6l

Worked example

➔ Which is the bigger fraction, $\frac{3}{5}$ or $\frac{7}{11}$?

$\frac{3}{5} = \frac{33}{55}$ and $\frac{7}{11} = \frac{35}{55}$

 55 divides by 5 and by 11.

So $\frac{7}{11}$ is the bigger fraction.

In questions **1** to **10**, find which is the bigger fraction.

1 $\frac{1}{2}$ or $\frac{1}{3}$ **3** $\frac{2}{3}$ or $\frac{4}{5}$ **5** $\frac{2}{7}$ or $\frac{3}{8}$

2 $\frac{3}{4}$ or $\frac{5}{6}$ **4** $\frac{2}{9}$ or $\frac{1}{7}$ **6** $\frac{2}{3}$ or $\frac{3}{4}$

7 $\frac{2}{5}$ of a field or $\frac{3}{7}$ of the field

8 $\frac{4}{5}$ of an audience or $\frac{6}{7}$ of the audience

9 $\frac{4}{7}$ of a bag of potatoes or $\frac{3}{5}$ of the bag

10 $\frac{2}{9}$ of the cars sold or $\frac{3}{11}$ of them.

In questions **11** to **20**, put either > or < between the fractions.

11 $\frac{1}{4}$ $\frac{2}{7}$ **16** $\frac{8}{11}$ $\frac{3}{4}$

12 $\frac{2}{3}$ $\frac{5}{6}$ **17** $\frac{3}{5}$ $\frac{2}{3}$

13 $\frac{5}{8}$ $\frac{7}{10}$ **18** $\frac{2}{9}$ $\frac{3}{7}$

14 $\frac{1}{3}$ $\frac{2}{5}$ **19** $\frac{5}{8}$ $\frac{4}{5}$

15 $\frac{2}{9}$ $\frac{1}{5}$ **20** $\frac{1}{3}$ $\frac{2}{7}$

Worked example

➔ Arrange the following fractions in order of size with the smallest first.

$\frac{3}{4}, \frac{7}{10}, \frac{1}{2}, \frac{4}{5}$

$\frac{3}{4} = \frac{15}{20}$

$\frac{7}{10} = \frac{14}{20}$

$\frac{1}{2} = \frac{10}{20}$

Since 20 is the lowest number that denominators 4, 10, 2 and 5 will all go into exactly, we express every fraction in twentieths.

$\frac{4}{5} = \frac{16}{20}$

In ascending order the fractions are $\frac{1}{2}, \frac{7}{10}, \frac{3}{4}, \frac{4}{5}$.

In questions **21** to **23**, arrange the fractions in order of size with the smallest first.

21 $\frac{2}{3}, \frac{1}{2}, \frac{3}{5}, \frac{7}{10}$

22 $\frac{13}{20}, \frac{3}{4}, \frac{4}{10}, \frac{5}{8}$

23 $\frac{2}{5}, \frac{3}{8}, \frac{17}{20}, \frac{1}{2}, \frac{7}{10}$

24 The lengths of five small panel pins are

$\frac{7}{10}$ inch, $\frac{2}{5}$ inch, $\frac{3}{5}$ inch, $\frac{14}{25}$ inch, $\frac{1}{2}$ inch

Arrange these pins in order of size with the smallest first.

In questions **25** and **26**, arrange the fractions in order of size with the largest first.

25 $\frac{5}{6}, \frac{1}{2}, \frac{7}{9}, \frac{11}{18}, \frac{2}{3}$

26 $\frac{13}{20}, \frac{3}{5}, \frac{1}{2}, \frac{3}{4}, \frac{7}{10}$

27 Daisy has 5 drills. Their sizes are

$\frac{7}{16}$ inch, $\frac{1}{2}$ inch, $\frac{5}{8}$ inch, $\frac{19}{32}$ inch, $\frac{3}{4}$ inch

Arrange these drills in order of size with the smallest first.

Comparing the sizes of decimals

To decide which of the decimals 4.67 or 4.63 is the larger:
- Look first at the number of units – they are the same.
- Next look at the number of tenths – they are also the same.
- Finally look at the number of hundredths – 7 is bigger than 3, so 4.67 is larger than 4.63.

Exercise 6m

Worked example

$\rightarrow$ Which is the larger, 1.5 or 1.55?

To compare these decimals, we write 1.5 as 1.50 showing that 1.55 is larger than 1.5

Which is the larger?

1 3.57 or 3.59   **2** 25.64 or 25.46   **3** 5 or 4.88

Put these numbers in ascending order.

4 6.76, 4.83, 6.29   **6** 9.07, 9.51, 9.18, 9.03

5 12.6, 14.09, 12.55, 13.75   **7** 7.555, 7.5, 7.05, 7.55

Put these numbers in descending order.

8 4.07, 4.87, 4.76, 4.69   **9** 9.88, 10.1, 7.06, 10.05

It is often easier to put fractions in order of size by converting them into decimals.

Worked example

→ Convert the fractions $\frac{3}{4}, \frac{4}{5}, \frac{17}{20}, \frac{7}{10}, \frac{17}{25}$ into decimals and use your answers to put the fractions in ascending order.

$$\frac{3}{4} = 0.75$$

$$\frac{4}{5} = 0.8$$

$$\frac{17}{20} = 0.85$$

$$\frac{7}{10} = 0.7$$

$$\frac{17}{25} = 0.68$$

In ascending order the decimals are 0.68, 0.7, 0.75, 0.8 and 0.85. Therefore the fractions in ascending order are

$\frac{17}{25}, \frac{7}{10}, \frac{3}{4}, \frac{4}{5}$ and $\frac{17}{20}$

In questions **10** and **11**, use decimals to put the fractions in ascending order.

10 $\frac{3}{5}, \frac{6}{25}, \frac{7}{10}, \frac{13}{20}, \frac{3}{4}$ **11** $\frac{1}{2}, \frac{11}{25}, \frac{11}{20}, \frac{4}{5}, \frac{9}{10}$

12 The thicknesses of four sheets of metal are $\frac{35}{1000}$ inch, $\frac{13}{100}$ inch, $\frac{97}{1000}$ inch and $\frac{1}{10}$ inch. Arrange these sheets in ascending order of thickness.

Mixed exercise

Exercise 6n

1 Fill in the missing numbers to make equivalent fractions.

     a $\frac{5}{7} = \frac{}{28}$ **c** $\frac{19}{20} = \frac{57}{}$

     b $\frac{7}{15} = \frac{}{60}$ **d** $\frac{5}{12} = \frac{}{144}$

2   Part of this circle is shaded. Express the shaded part as
    a   a percentage
    b   a decimal
    c   a fraction in its lowest terms.

3   Express
    a   65% as a fraction in its lowest terms
    b   78% as a decimal
    c $\frac{27}{50}$ as a percentage
    d $\frac{19}{20}$ as a decimal
    e   0.41 as a percentage
    f   0.44 as a fraction in its lowest terms.

4   Find
    a $\frac{7}{12}$ of 84 m
    b   35% of 440 kg
    c   0.76 of 550 cm

5   Which is the larger
    a   2.54 or 2.6
    b $\frac{5}{7}$ or $\frac{7}{10}$?

6   The thicknesses of four sheets of plastic are

    $\frac{7}{20}$ mm, $\frac{1}{2}$ mm, $\frac{31}{50}$ mm and $\frac{4}{10}$ mm

    By converting these fractions into decimals, or otherwise, put
    them in ascending order.

Consider again

There are 30 students in class 7G: $\frac{2}{5}$ of them are girls; 10% of them
are absent; 0.3 of them did not hand in homework on time.

Parts of class 7G are described in different ways. Can you compare
them? How can you find the number of students that are absent?
How many handed in the homework on time?

Now answer these questions.

Practical work

You are invited to my...

13th Birthday Party

You need 12 of 2 p coins for this work, together with an exact copy of the outside edge of the rectangular ticket shown above.

Place the coins on the rectangle so that they all fit on it. The coins should touch one another without overlapping and the outer coins of the arrangement must touch the edges of the ticket.

1 How many coins touch the edges of the ticket?
What fraction of the total number of coins is this?

2 How many coins touch exactly two other coins?
What fraction of the total number of coins is this?

3 What fraction of the total number of coins touch
   a 3 other coins
   b 4 other coins?

(All answers in fractions should be given in their lowest terms.)

Investigation

Using the numbers 1, 2, 4 and 8, write down all the fractions you can think of that are equal to or smaller than 1. Use a single digit for the numerator and a single digit for the denominator. You are allowed to use a digit more than once in the same fraction.

a **i** How many different fractions can you find?
   ii Which fractions are equivalent fractions?
   iii Which fraction does not have an equivalent fraction in the list you have written?

b Add 16 to the list of numbers 1, 2, 4, 8, and repeat part **a**.

c Two-digit numbers, such as 14 and 82, can be made from the digits 1, 2, 4 and 8. Use such numbers to repeat part **a**.

7 Addition and subtraction of fractions and decimals

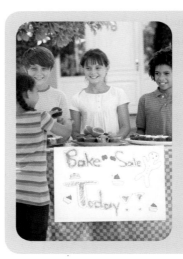

Consider

Class 7W collected £252 for charity. They decided to give $\frac{1}{4}$ of the sum collected to the NSPCC, $\frac{1}{3}$ to the local hospice and the remainder to OXFAM.

Anna commented, 'That leaves more than half for OXFAM!'

Hasib replied, 'No, it doesn't'.

Do you know who is right and why?

Sam joined in the argument with: 'But $\frac{1}{3}$ is more than $\frac{1}{4}$, so the two together must be more than $\frac{1}{2}$.'

Is this a sensible statement? Give a reason for your answer.

You should be able to solve this problem after you have worked through this chapter.

Class discussion

1   Think of problems where fractions are involved.

2   Discuss what you need to be able to do with fractions to solve these problems.

For example, in an audience $\frac{1}{15}$ are men, $\frac{7}{15}$ are women, $\frac{1}{5}$ are boys and the remainder are girls.

To find out what fraction are males, we need to be able to add $\frac{1}{15}$ and $\frac{1}{5}$. To find out what fraction are girls, we must be able to add $\frac{1}{15}, \frac{7}{15}$ and $\frac{1}{5}$, and subtract the total from 1.

This example together with your discussions should convince you of the need to be able to add and subtract fractions, and to have an idea whether your answers are roughly correct.

Adding fractions

Suppose there is a bowl of oranges and apples. You take first three oranges and then two more oranges. You then have five oranges; we can add the 3 and the 2 together because they are the same kind of fruit. But three oranges and two apples cannot be added together because they are different kinds of fruit.

For fractions it is the denominator that tells us the kind of fraction, so we can add fractions together if they have the same denominator but not while their denominators are different.

Exercise 7a

Worked example

Add the fractions, simplifying the answers where you can.

➡ $\dfrac{2}{7} + \dfrac{3}{7}$

➡ $\dfrac{9}{22} + \dfrac{5}{22}$

$$\dfrac{2}{7} + \dfrac{3}{7} = \dfrac{2+3}{7}$$

$$= \dfrac{5}{7}$$

$$\dfrac{9}{22} + \dfrac{5}{22} = \dfrac{9+5}{22}$$

$$= \dfrac{\cancel{14}^{7}}{\cancel{22}_{11}}$$

$$= \dfrac{7}{11}$$

 We divide the top and bottom by 2 to get a simpler fraction.

Add the fractions given in questions **1** to **18**, simplifying the answers where you can.

1 $\dfrac{1}{4} + \dfrac{2}{4}$

2 $\dfrac{1}{8} + \dfrac{3}{8}$

3 $\dfrac{3}{11} + \dfrac{2}{11}$

4 $\dfrac{3}{13} + \dfrac{7}{13}$

5 $\dfrac{2}{7} + \dfrac{4}{7}$

6 $\dfrac{8}{30} + \dfrac{19}{30}$

7 $\dfrac{11}{23} + \dfrac{8}{23}$

8 $\dfrac{1}{7} + \dfrac{2}{7}$

9 $\dfrac{2}{5} + \dfrac{1}{5}$

10 $\dfrac{3}{10} + \dfrac{1}{10}$

11 $\dfrac{5}{16} + \dfrac{7}{16}$

12 $\dfrac{21}{100} + \dfrac{19}{100}$

13 $\dfrac{2}{21} + \dfrac{9}{21}$

14 $\dfrac{7}{30} + \dfrac{8}{30}$

15 $\dfrac{6}{13} + \dfrac{5}{13}$

16 $\dfrac{1}{10} + \dfrac{7}{10}$

17 $\dfrac{4}{11} + \dfrac{2}{11}$

18 $\dfrac{7}{15} + \dfrac{3}{15}$

We can add more than two fractions in the same way.

Worked example

Add the fractions

➡ $\dfrac{3}{17} + \dfrac{5}{17} + \dfrac{8}{17}$

$$\dfrac{3}{17} + \dfrac{5}{17} + \dfrac{8}{17} = \dfrac{3+5+8}{17}$$

$$= \dfrac{16}{17}$$

Add the fractions given in questions **19** to **24**.

19 $\dfrac{2}{15} + \dfrac{4}{15} + \dfrac{6}{15}$

20 $\dfrac{8}{100} + \dfrac{21}{100} + \dfrac{11}{100}$

21 $\dfrac{4}{45} + \dfrac{11}{45} + \dfrac{8}{45} + \dfrac{2}{45}$

22 $\dfrac{1}{14} + \dfrac{3}{14} + \dfrac{5}{14} + \dfrac{2}{14}$

23 $\dfrac{2}{51} + \dfrac{4}{51} + \dfrac{6}{51} + \dfrac{8}{51} + \dfrac{7}{51}$

24 $\dfrac{3}{99} + \dfrac{11}{99} + \dfrac{4}{99} + \dfrac{7}{99}$

25 If $\dfrac{5}{8}$ of the spectators at a match are men and $\dfrac{1}{8}$ are women, what fraction of the spectators are adults?

26 In a shop $\dfrac{1}{10}$ of the DVDs are films, $\dfrac{3}{10}$ are sport and $\dfrac{3}{10}$ are documentaries.

What fraction of the DVDs are either films, sport or documentaries?

Fractions with different denominators

To add fractions with different denominators, we must first change the fractions into equivalent fractions with the same denominator. This new denominator must be a number that both original denominators divide into.

For example, if we want to add $\dfrac{2}{5}$ and $\dfrac{3}{7}$ we choose 35 for our new denominator because 35 can be divided by both 5 and 7:

$$\frac{2}{5} = \frac{14}{35}$$

$$\frac{3}{7} = \frac{15}{35}$$

So $\quad \dfrac{2}{5} + \dfrac{3}{7} = \dfrac{14}{35} + \dfrac{15}{35} = \dfrac{29}{35}$

Exercise 7b

Worked example

→ Find $\dfrac{2}{7} + \dfrac{3}{8}$

$\dfrac{2}{7} + \dfrac{3}{8} = \dfrac{16}{56} + \dfrac{21}{56} = \dfrac{37}{56}$

 7 and 8 both divide into 56, so we use 56 as the new denominator.

Find

1 $\dfrac{2}{3} + \dfrac{1}{5}$

2 $\dfrac{1}{5} + \dfrac{3}{8}$

3 $\dfrac{1}{5} + \dfrac{1}{6}$

4 $\dfrac{2}{5} + \dfrac{4}{7}$

5 $\dfrac{3}{10} + \dfrac{2}{3}$

6 $\dfrac{4}{7} + \dfrac{1}{8}$

7 $\dfrac{3}{7} + \dfrac{1}{6}$

8 $\dfrac{2}{3} + \dfrac{2}{7}$

9 $\dfrac{1}{6} + \dfrac{2}{7}$

10 $\dfrac{5}{6} + \dfrac{1}{7}$

11 $\dfrac{3}{11} + \dfrac{5}{9}$

12 $\dfrac{2}{9} + \dfrac{3}{10}$

The new denominator, which is called the **common denominator**, is not always as big as you might first think. For example, if we want to add $\frac{3}{4}$ and $\frac{1}{12}$, the common denominator is 12 because it can be divided exactly by 4 and by 12.

Worked example

➤ Find $\frac{3}{4} + \frac{1}{12}$

$$\frac{3}{4} + \frac{1}{12} = \frac{9}{12} + \frac{1}{12}$$

$$= \frac{\cancel{10}^{5}}{\cancel{12}^{6}}$$

$$= \frac{5}{6}$$

Find

13 $\frac{2}{5} + \frac{3}{10}$ 17 $\frac{1}{5} + \frac{7}{10}$ 21 $\frac{1}{20} + \frac{3}{5}$

14 $\frac{3}{8} + \frac{7}{16}$ 18 $\frac{1}{4} + \frac{3}{8}$ 22 $\frac{4}{11} + \frac{5}{22}$

15 $\frac{3}{7} + \frac{8}{21}$ 19 $\frac{2}{3} + \frac{2}{9}$ 23 $\frac{2}{5} + \frac{7}{15}$

16 $\frac{3}{10} + \frac{3}{100}$ 20 $\frac{4}{9} + \frac{5}{18}$ 24 $\frac{7}{12} + \frac{1}{6}$

More than two fractions can be added in this way. The common denominator must be divisible by *all* of the original denominators.

Worked example

➤ Find $\frac{1}{8} + \frac{1}{2} + \frac{1}{3}$

$$\frac{1}{8} + \frac{1}{2} + \frac{1}{3} = \frac{3}{24} + \frac{12}{24} + \frac{8}{24}$$

$$= \frac{3 + 12 + 8}{24}$$

$$= \frac{23}{24}$$

 8, 2 and 3 all divide into 24, so 24 is the new denominator.

Find

25 $\frac{1}{5} + \frac{1}{4} + \frac{1}{2}$ 28 $\frac{5}{12} + \frac{1}{6} + \frac{1}{3}$ 31 $\frac{1}{3} + \frac{2}{9} + \frac{1}{6}$

26 $\frac{1}{8} + \frac{1}{4} + \frac{1}{3}$ 29 $\frac{1}{3} + \frac{1}{6} + \frac{1}{2}$ 32 $\frac{2}{15} + \frac{1}{10} + \frac{2}{5}$

27 $\frac{3}{10} + \frac{2}{5} + \frac{1}{4}$ 30 $\frac{1}{2} + \frac{3}{8} + \frac{1}{10}$ 33 $\frac{1}{4} + \frac{1}{12} + \frac{1}{3}$

34 In a car-park, $\frac{3}{7}$ of the cars were manufactured in the UK and $\frac{5}{14}$ in mainland Europe. What fraction were made in Europe?

35 In a class, $\frac{1}{5}$ of the students are less than 120 cm in height and $\frac{3}{10}$ are between 120 cm and 130 cm. No student is exactly 120 cm or 130 cm.
What fraction of the class is less than 130 cm in height?

36 When Kirsty comes home from shopping, $\frac{1}{12}$ of the weight in her basket is green vegetables, $\frac{1}{3}$ is fruit and $\frac{1}{4}$ is root vegetables. What fraction of the weight she carries is fruit and vegetables?

37 Decide, without adding the fractions, whether $\frac{1}{4} + \frac{1}{5}$ is more than or less than $\frac{1}{2}$.
Give reasons for your answer.

38 Three possible answers are given for each addition. Two of them are obviously wrong. Without working out the addition, decide which answer is most likely to be correct.

    a $\frac{1}{5} + \frac{1}{7} =$ A $\frac{1}{4}$ B $\frac{1}{35}$ C $\frac{12}{35}$

    b $\frac{2}{7} + \frac{1}{3} =$ A $\frac{3}{10}$ B $\frac{13}{21}$ C $\frac{2}{21}$

    c $\frac{5}{18} + \frac{2}{9} =$ A $\frac{1}{2}$ B $\frac{10}{27}$ C $\frac{7}{27}$

39 Lyn adds two fractions and writes down

$$\frac{1}{4} + \frac{2}{5} = \frac{5}{20} + \frac{4}{20} = \frac{9}{40}$$

How many mistakes are there? Explain why they are mistakes.

Subtracting fractions

Exactly the same method is used for subtracting fractions as for adding them. To work out the value of $\frac{7}{8} - \frac{3}{8}$ we notice that the denominators are the same, so

$$\frac{7}{8} - \frac{3}{8} = \frac{7 - 3}{8}$$

$$= \frac{\cancel{4}^1}{\cancel{8}^2}$$

$$= \frac{1}{2}$$

Exercise 7c

Worked example

→ Find $\dfrac{7}{9} - \dfrac{1}{4}$

 The denominators are not the same, so we use equivalent fractions with denominator 36.

$$\dfrac{7}{9} - \dfrac{1}{4} = \dfrac{28}{36} - \dfrac{9}{36}$$
$$= \dfrac{28 - 9}{36}$$
$$= \dfrac{19}{36}$$

Find

1. $\dfrac{8}{9} - \dfrac{2}{9}$

2. $\dfrac{7}{10} - \dfrac{2}{10}$

3. $\dfrac{3}{4} - \dfrac{1}{5}$

4. $\dfrac{9}{10} - \dfrac{1}{2}$

5. $\dfrac{2}{3} - \dfrac{3}{7}$

6. $\dfrac{11}{15} - \dfrac{4}{15}$

7. $\dfrac{8}{11} - \dfrac{2}{5}$

8. $\dfrac{7}{9} - \dfrac{2}{3}$

9. $\dfrac{8}{13} - \dfrac{1}{2}$

10. $\dfrac{11}{12} - \dfrac{5}{6}$

11. $\dfrac{19}{100} - \dfrac{1}{10}$

12. $\dfrac{5}{8} - \dfrac{2}{7}$

13. $\dfrac{15}{16} - \dfrac{3}{4}$

14. $\dfrac{7}{15} - \dfrac{1}{5}$

15. $\dfrac{3}{4} - \dfrac{5}{8}$

16. $\dfrac{7}{12} - \dfrac{1}{3}$

17. $\dfrac{13}{18} - \dfrac{5}{9}$

18. $\dfrac{13}{15} - \dfrac{3}{5}$

19. In the supermarket, $\dfrac{7}{12}$ of Marco's bill is for fruit and vegetables. If $\dfrac{1}{8}$ is for fruit, what fraction is for vegetables?

20. Decide, without subtracting the fractions, if $\dfrac{3}{4} - \dfrac{1}{3}$ is less than or more than $\dfrac{1}{2}$. Give reasons for your answer.

21. In a class, $\dfrac{2}{5}$ of the students are less than 115 cm in height and $\dfrac{7}{10}$ are less than 130 cm. No student is exactly 115 cm. What fraction of the class is more than 115 cm but less than 130 cm in height?

22. Three possible answers are given for each of the following subtractions. Without working them out, choose the answer you think is most likely to be correct.

    a $\dfrac{5}{9} - \dfrac{1}{3} =$ A $\dfrac{2}{9}$ B $\dfrac{5}{6}$ C $\dfrac{2}{3}$

    b $\dfrac{14}{15} - \dfrac{4}{5} =$ A 1 B $\dfrac{2}{3}$ C $\dfrac{2}{15}$

    c $\dfrac{19}{21} - \dfrac{3}{7} =$ A $\dfrac{16}{21}$ B $\dfrac{10}{21}$ C $\dfrac{4}{7}$

23. The following calculation contains at least one mistake. Point out any mistake and give a reason why you think it is a mistake.

    $$\dfrac{11}{12} - \dfrac{7}{9} = \dfrac{33}{36} - \dfrac{27}{36} = \dfrac{6}{36} = \dfrac{1}{3}$$

Adding and subtracting fractions

Fractions can be added and subtracted in a similar way. For example

$$\frac{7}{9} + \frac{1}{18} - \frac{1}{6} = \frac{14}{18} + \frac{1}{18} - \frac{3}{18}$$
$$= \frac{14 + 1 - 3}{18}$$
$$= \frac{12}{18}$$
$$= \frac{2}{3}$$

It is not always possible to work from left to right in order because we might have to subtract too much too soon. In this case we can do the adding first.

Remember that it is the sign *in front* of a number that tells you what to do with that number.

Exercise 7d

Worked example

→ Find $\frac{1}{8} - \frac{3}{4} + \frac{11}{16}$

$$\frac{1}{8} - \frac{3}{4} + \frac{11}{16} = \frac{2}{16} - \frac{12}{16} + \frac{11}{16}$$
$$= \frac{13 - 12}{16}$$
$$= \frac{1}{16}$$

 Find 2 + 11 first.

Find

1. $\frac{3}{4} + \frac{1}{2} - \frac{7}{8}$

2. $\frac{6}{7} - \frac{9}{14} + \frac{1}{2}$

3. $\frac{3}{8} + \frac{7}{16} - \frac{3}{4}$

4. $\frac{3}{5} + \frac{3}{25} - \frac{27}{50}$

5. $\frac{2}{3} + \frac{1}{6} - \frac{5}{12}$

6. $\frac{4}{5} - \frac{7}{10} + \frac{1}{2}$

7. $\frac{7}{10} - \frac{41}{100} + \frac{1}{20}$

8. $\frac{5}{8} - \frac{21}{40} + \frac{2}{5}$

9. $\frac{7}{12} - \frac{1}{6} + \frac{1}{3}$

10. $\frac{2}{9} - \frac{1}{3} + \frac{1}{6}$

11. $\frac{1}{6} - \frac{2}{3} + \frac{7}{12}$

12. $\frac{1}{8} - \frac{13}{16} + \frac{3}{4}$

13. $\frac{1}{6} - \frac{5}{18} + \frac{1}{3}$

14. $\frac{1}{5} - \frac{7}{10} + \frac{17}{20}$

15. $\frac{2}{3} - \frac{5}{6} + \frac{1}{2}$

16. $\frac{3}{10} - \frac{61}{100} + \frac{1}{2}$

17. $\frac{1}{8} + \frac{7}{24} - \frac{2}{15}$

18. $\frac{3}{10} + \frac{2}{15} - \frac{2}{5}$

19. Some scientific calculators will work in fractions.
    Use your calculator, if it will work in fractions, to check your answers to questions **1** to **18**.

Worked example

In a class of school children, $\frac{1}{3}$ of the children come to school by bus, $\frac{1}{4}$ come to school on bicycles and the rest walk to school.

→ What fraction of the children come to school on a bicycle or by bus?

The fraction who come to school on bicycle and bus $= \frac{1}{3} + \frac{1}{4}$

$$= \frac{4 + 3}{12}$$

$$= \frac{7}{12}$$

→ What fraction do not come to school by bus?

The complete class of children is a whole unit, i.e. 1.
The fraction of children who do not use a bus is found by taking the bus-users from the complete class, i.e.

$$\frac{1}{1} - \frac{1}{3} = \frac{3 - 1}{3} = \frac{2}{3}$$

20 Juanita spends $\frac{1}{5}$ of her pocket money on sweets and $\frac{2}{3}$ on CDs.
   a   What fraction has she spent?
   b   What fraction has she left?

21 A group of friends went to a hamburger bar; $\frac{2}{5}$ of them bought a hamburger, $\frac{1}{3}$ of them just bought chips. The rest bought cola.
   a   What fraction of the group bought food?
   b   What fraction bought a drink?

22 At a music festival, $\frac{2}{3}$ of the groups were all male, $\frac{1}{4}$ of the groups included one girl and the rest included more than one girl.
   What fraction of the groups
   a   were not all male   b   contained more than one girl?

23 At a youth club, $\frac{1}{2}$ of the meetings are for playing table tennis, $\frac{1}{8}$ of the meetings are for discussions, and the rest are music sessions. What fraction of the meetings are
   a   music sessions   b   not for discussions?

24 George Bentley had 3 sons and 1 daughter. When he died, he left $\frac{3}{8}$ of his estate to his wife, $\frac{3}{32}$ to the youngest son, twice as much to his next son and three times as much to the eldest son as he had left to the youngest son. The remainder went to the daughter. What fraction did the daughter get?

25 Maria can dig a plot of ground in 5 hours and James can dig it in 6 hours.
   a   What fraction of the plot can each of them dig in 1 hour?
   b   If they work together, what fraction can they dig in 1 hour?
   c   What fraction remains to be dug after 2 hours?

26 Fred is an elderly man. He lived one-eighth of his life as a boy,
one-twelfth as a youth, one-half as a man and he spent 28 years
in his old age. How old is Fred now?

Mixed numbers and improper fractions

Most of the fractions we have met so far have been less than a whole unit.
These are called **proper fractions**. But we often
have more than a whole unit. Suppose, for example,
that we have one and a quarter bars of chocolate:

We have $1\frac{1}{4}$ bars, and $1\frac{1}{4}$ is called a mixed number.
Another way of describing the amount of
chocolate is to say that we have five
quarter bars.

We have $\frac{5}{4}$ bars and $\frac{5}{4}$ is called an **improper fraction**, because the numerator is bigger
than the denominator.

But the amount of chocolate in the two examples is the same, so

$$\frac{5}{4} = 1\frac{1}{4}$$

Improper fractions can be changed into mixed numbers by finding out how many whole
units there are. For example, to change $\frac{8}{3}$ into a mixed number we look for the biggest
number below 8 that divides by 3, i.e. 6. Then

$$\frac{8}{3} = \frac{6+2}{3} = \frac{6}{3} + \frac{2}{3} = 2 + \frac{2}{3} = 2\frac{2}{3}$$

We can also change mixed numbers into improper fractions. For example, in $2\frac{4}{5}$ we have two
whole units and $\frac{4}{5}$. In each whole unit there are five fifths, so in $2\frac{4}{5}$ we have ten fifths and
four fifths, i.e.

$$2\frac{4}{5} = \frac{10}{5} + \frac{4}{5} = \frac{14}{5}$$

Exercise 7e

Worked example

→ Change $\frac{15}{4}$ into a mixed number.

$$\frac{15}{4} = \frac{12+3}{4}$$

$$= \frac{12}{4} + \frac{3}{4}$$

$$= 3\frac{3}{4}$$

 12 is the biggest number below
15 that divides exactly by 4.

In questions **1** to **15**, change the improper fractions into mixed numbers.

1 $\frac{9}{4}$ 5 $\frac{88}{9}$ 9 $\frac{127}{5}$ 13 $\frac{41}{3}$

2 $\frac{19}{4}$ 6 $\frac{7}{2}$ 10 $\frac{114}{11}$ 14 $\frac{67}{5}$

3 $\frac{37}{6}$ 7 $\frac{27}{4}$ 11 $\frac{83}{7}$ 15 $\frac{49}{10}$

4 $\frac{53}{10}$ 8 $\frac{41}{8}$ 12 $\frac{91}{6}$

Worked example

➡ Change $3\frac{1}{7}$ into an improper fraction.

$3\frac{1}{7} = 3 + \frac{1}{7}$

$\qquad = \frac{21}{7} + \frac{1}{7}$

$\qquad = \frac{22}{7}$

 There are 7 sevenths in 1, so there are 7 × 3, i.e. 21, sevenths in 3.

In questions **16** to **30**, change the mixed numbers into improper fractions.

16 $4\frac{1}{3}$ 20 $8\frac{1}{7}$ 24 $3\frac{2}{3}$ 28 $8\frac{3}{4}$

17 $8\frac{1}{4}$ 21 $6\frac{3}{5}$ 25 $5\frac{1}{2}$ 29 $1\frac{9}{10}$

18 $1\frac{7}{10}$ 22 $2\frac{6}{7}$ 26 $7\frac{2}{5}$ 30 $7\frac{3}{8}$

19 $10\frac{8}{9}$ 23 $4\frac{1}{6}$ 27 $3\frac{4}{5}$

The meaning of 15 ÷ 4

15 ÷ 4 means 'how many fours are there in 15?'

There are 3 fours in 15 with 3 left over, so 15 ÷ 4 = 3, remainder 3.

The remainder, 3, is $\frac{3}{4}$ of 4. So we can say that there are $3\frac{3}{4}$ fours in 15

$\qquad$ i.e. $\qquad 15 \div 4 = 3\frac{3}{4}$

$\qquad$ and $\qquad \frac{15}{4} = 3\frac{3}{4}$

Therefore 15 ÷ 4 and $\frac{15}{4}$ mean the same thing.

Exercise 7f

Worked example

→ Calculate $27 \div 8$, giving your answer as a mixed number.

$$27 \div 8 = \frac{27}{8}$$
$$= 3\frac{3}{8}$$

Calculate the following divisions, giving your answers as mixed numbers.

1	$36 \div 7$	5	$82 \div 5$	9	$98 \div 12$
2	$59 \div 6$	6	$29 \div 4$	10	$107 \div 10$
3	$52 \div 11$	7	$41 \div 3$	11	$37 \div 5$
4	$20 \div 8$	8	$64 \div 9$	12	$52 \div 8$

Adding mixed numbers

If we want to find the value of $2\frac{1}{3} + 3\frac{1}{4}$, we add the whole numbers and then the fractions, i.e.

$$2\frac{1}{3} + 3\frac{1}{4} = 2 + 3 + \frac{1}{3} + \frac{1}{4}$$
$$= 5 + \frac{4+3}{12}$$
$$= 5 + \frac{7}{12}$$
$$= 5\frac{7}{12}$$

Sometimes there is an extra step in the calculation. For example

$$3\frac{1}{2} + 2\frac{3}{8} + 5\frac{1}{4} = 3 + 2 + 5 + \frac{1}{2} + \frac{3}{8} + \frac{1}{4}$$
$$= 10 + \frac{4+3+2}{8}$$
$$= 10 + \frac{9}{8}$$

But $\frac{9}{8}$ is an improper fraction, so we change it into a mixed number,

i.e. $$3\frac{1}{2} + 2\frac{3}{8} + 5\frac{1}{4} = 10 + \frac{8+1}{8}$$
$$= 10 + 1 + \frac{1}{8}$$
$$= 11\frac{1}{8}$$

Exercise 7g

Worked example

→ Find $2\frac{1}{2} + 4\frac{3}{4} + 1\frac{1}{6}$

$$2\frac{1}{2} + 4\frac{3}{4} + 1\frac{1}{6} = 7\frac{6+9+2}{12}$$

$$= 7\frac{17}{12}$$

$$= 8\frac{5}{12}$$

 Add the whole numbers. Then add the fractions. Split $\frac{17}{12}$ into $1 + \frac{5}{12}$.

Find

1 $2\frac{1}{4} + 3\frac{1}{2}$

2 $1\frac{1}{2} + 2\frac{1}{3}$

3 $4\frac{1}{5} + 1\frac{3}{8}$

4 $5\frac{1}{9} + 4\frac{1}{3}$

5 $3\frac{1}{4} + 2\frac{5}{9}$

6 $1\frac{1}{3} + 2\frac{5}{6}$

7 $3\frac{1}{4} + 1\frac{1}{5}$

8 $2\frac{1}{7} + 1\frac{1}{14}$

9 $6\frac{3}{10} + 1\frac{2}{5}$

10 $8\frac{1}{7} + 5\frac{2}{3}$

11 $7\frac{3}{8} + 3\frac{7}{16}$

12 $1\frac{3}{4} + 4\frac{7}{12}$

13 $3\frac{5}{7} + 7\frac{1}{2}$

14 $6\frac{1}{2} + 1\frac{9}{16}$

15 $8\frac{7}{8} + 3\frac{3}{16}$

16 $2\frac{7}{10} + 9\frac{1}{5}$

17 $5\frac{7}{10} + 2\frac{3}{5}$

18 $9\frac{2}{3} + 8\frac{5}{6}$

19 $2\frac{4}{5} + 7\frac{3}{10}$

20 $6\frac{3}{10} + 4\frac{4}{5}$

21 $1\frac{1}{4} + 3\frac{2}{3} + 6\frac{7}{12}$

22 $5\frac{1}{7} + 4\frac{1}{2} + 7\frac{11}{14}$

23 $3\frac{3}{4} + 5\frac{1}{8} + 8\frac{5}{16}$

24 $10\frac{2}{3} + 3\frac{1}{6} + 7\frac{2}{9}$

25 Johan wanted to raise his front gate because it was dragging on the ground when it opened. He put three washers on each support: one $\frac{1}{8}$ inch thick, one $\frac{3}{16}$ inch thick and one $\frac{1}{16}$ inch thick. How much higher did this make the gate?

26 George has three pieces of wood. One is $10\frac{1}{8}$ m long, another is $6\frac{1}{2}$ m long and the third is $5\frac{7}{8}$ m long. How far do they stretch if they are laid end to end?

27 A recipe for sugar crisps requires $\frac{1}{2}$ cup fat, $\frac{3}{4}$ cup sugar, $\frac{2}{3}$ cup syrup and $2\frac{1}{2}$ cups flour. How many cups of ingredients is this altogether?

28 Is $6\frac{1}{4}$ bigger or smaller than the sum of $3\frac{1}{3}$ and $2\frac{7}{8}$?

29 Hank has a length of timber that is $9\frac{1}{2}$ ft long. He wants to cut off three pieces, one $1\frac{5}{8}$ ft long, a second twice as long, and a third three times as long as the first. Does he have enough wood?

Subtracting mixed numbers

If we want to find the value of $5\frac{3}{4} - 2\frac{2}{5}$ we can use the same method as for adding.

$$5\frac{3}{4} - 2\frac{2}{5} = 5 - 2 + \frac{3}{4} - \frac{2}{5}$$
$$= 3 + \frac{15 - 8}{20}$$
$$= 3 + \frac{7}{20}$$
$$= 3\frac{7}{20}$$

But when we find the value of $6\frac{1}{4} - 2\frac{4}{5}$ we get

$$6\frac{1}{4} - 2\frac{4}{5} = 6 - 2 + \frac{1}{4} - \frac{4}{5}$$
$$= 4 + \frac{1}{4} - \frac{4}{5}$$

This time it is not so easy to deal with the fractions because $\frac{4}{5}$ is bigger than $\frac{1}{4}$. So we take one of the whole units and change it into a fraction, giving

$$3 + 1 + \frac{1}{4} - \frac{4}{5}$$
$$= 3 + \frac{20 + 5 - 16}{20}$$
$$= 3 + \frac{9}{20}$$
$$= 3\frac{9}{20}$$

Exercise 7h

Find

1 $2\frac{3}{4} - 1\frac{1}{8}$

2 $3\frac{2}{3} - 1\frac{4}{5}$

3 $1\frac{5}{6} - \frac{2}{3}$

4 $3\frac{1}{4} - 2\frac{1}{2}$

5 $7\frac{3}{4} - 2\frac{1}{3}$

6 $3\frac{5}{6} - 2\frac{1}{3}$

7 $2\frac{6}{7} - 1\frac{1}{2}$

8 $4\frac{1}{2} - 2\frac{1}{5}$

9 $4\frac{4}{5} - 3\frac{1}{10}$

10 $6\frac{5}{7} - 3\frac{2}{5}$

11 $3\frac{1}{3} - 1\frac{1}{5}$

12 $5\frac{3}{4} - 2\frac{1}{2}$

13 $8\frac{4}{5} - 5\frac{1}{2}$

14 $5\frac{7}{9} - 3\frac{5}{7}$

15 $4\frac{5}{8} - 1\frac{1}{3}$

16 $6\frac{3}{4} - 3\frac{6}{7}$

17 $7\frac{1}{2} - 5\frac{3}{4}$

18 $4\frac{3}{5} - 1\frac{1}{4}$

19 $7\frac{6}{7} - 4\frac{3}{5}$

20 $8\frac{8}{11} - 2\frac{2}{3}$

21 $8\frac{6}{7} - 5\frac{3}{4}$

22 $3\frac{1}{2} - 1\frac{7}{8}$

23 $2\frac{1}{2} - 1\frac{3}{4}$

24 $5\frac{4}{7} - 3\frac{4}{5}$

25 $3\frac{1}{4} - 1\frac{7}{8}$

26 $5\frac{3}{5} - 2\frac{9}{10}$

27 $8\frac{2}{3} - 7\frac{8}{9}$

28 $4\frac{1}{6} - 2\frac{2}{3}$

29 $9\frac{7}{10} - 5\frac{4}{5}$

30 $2\frac{5}{12} - 1\frac{3}{4}$

31 Lily cuts a piece of metal $5\frac{1}{2}$ cm long from a bar $27\frac{7}{10}$ cm long. What length remains?

32 A recipe for frozen Christmas puddings lists the main ingredients as: $1\frac{1}{2}$ cups of vanilla wafer crumbs, $\frac{1}{2}$ cup chopped nuts, $\frac{1}{2}$ cup chopped dates, $\frac{1}{2}$ cup chopped fruit peel, $\frac{1}{4}$ cup hot orange juice, $\frac{1}{3}$ cup sugar and 1 cup whipped cream.
If all the ingredients total $4\frac{3}{4}$ cups, how many cups of unlisted ingredients are there?

33 How much less than 1 is the difference between $5\frac{2}{3}$ and $4\frac{7}{8}$?

34 How much more than 2 is the difference between $3\frac{4}{5}$ and $6\frac{3}{4}$?

35 Which is the greater and by how much: the difference between $4\frac{7}{8}$ and $9\frac{1}{3}$ or the sum of $1\frac{3}{4}$ and $2\frac{3}{10}$?

Adding and subtracting decimals

A dealer in animal foods has a stock of 21.8 tonnes of cattle food.
That day he takes delivery of 10.75 tonnes and sells 15.5 tonnes.
To find how much feed he has at the end of the day, we must be able to subtract 15.5 from the sum of 21.8 and 10.75.

Addition of decimals

To add decimals, we add in the usual way.

$4.2 + 13.1 = 17.3$

tens	units		tenths
	4	.	2
+ 1	3	.	1
1	7	.	3

 2 tenths + 1 tenth = 3 tenths

$5.3 + 6.8 = 12.1$

tens	units		tenths
	5	.	3
+	6	.	8
_1_	_1_		
1	2	.	1

 3 tenths + 8 tenths = 11 tenths = 1 unit and 1 tenth

 The headings above the figures need not be written as long as we know what they are and the decimal points are in line (including the invisible point after a whole number, e.g. 4 = 4.0).

Exercise 7i

Worked example

→ Find 32.6 + 1.7

32.6 + 1.7 = 34.3

```
  32.6
+  1.7
  34.3
```

→ Find 3 + 1.6 + 0.032 + 2.0066

3 + 1.6 + 0.032 + 2.0066 = 6.6386

```
  3.0
  1.6
  0.032
+ 2.0066
  6.6386
```

In questions **1** to **20**, find

1 7.2 + 3.6

2 6.21 + 1.34

3 0.013 + 0.026

4 3.87 + 0.11

5 4.6 + 1.23

6 13.14 + 0.9

7 4 + 3.6

8 9.24 + 3

9 3.6 + 0.08

10 7.2 + 0.32 + 1.6

11 0.0043 + 0.263

12 0.002 + 2.1

13 0.00052 + 0.00124

14 0.068 + 0.003 + 0.06

15 4.62 + 0.078

16 0.32 + 0.032 + 0.0032

17 4.6 + 0.0005

18 16.8 + 3.9

19 1.62 + 2.078 + 3.1

20 7.34 + 6 + 14.034

21 Add 0.68 to 1.7

22 Find the sum of 3.28 and 14.021

23 To 7.9 add 4 and 3.72

24 Evaluate 7.9 + 0.62 + 5

25 Find the sum of 8.6, 5 and 3.21

Worked example

→ Find the **perimeter** of the triangle (the perimeter is the distance all round).

Perimeter = 1.6 + 2.3 + 2.6 cm
        = 6.5 cm

```
  1.6
  2.3
+ 2.6
  6.5
```

26 Find the perimeter of the rectangle.

27 Find the total bill for three articles costing £5, £6.52 and £13.25.

28 Find the perimeter of the quadrilateral.

Subtraction of decimals

Subtraction may also be done in the usual way, making sure that the decimal points are in line.

Exercise 7j

Worked example

→ Find   24.2 − 13.7

24.2 − 13.7 = 10.5

$$\begin{array}{r} 24.2 \\ -\ 13.7 \\ \hline 10.5 \end{array}$$

Find

1 6.8 − 4.3

2 9.6 − 1.8

3 32.7 − 14.2

4 0.62 − 0.21

5 0.0342 − 0.0021

6 17.23 − 0.36

7 3.273 − 1.032

8 0.262 − 0.071

9 102.6 − 31.2

10 7.32 − 0.67

11 54.07 − 12.62

12 7.063 − 0.124

It may be necessary to add zeros so that there are the same number of digits after the point in both numbers.

Worked example

→ Find 4.623 − 1.7

4.623 − 1.7 = 2.923

```
  4.623
− 1.700
  2.923
```

→ Find 4.63 − 1.0342

4.63 − 1.0342 = 3.5958

```
  4.6300
− 1.0342
  3.5958
```

→ Find 2 − 1.4

2 − 1.4 = 0.6

```
  2.0
− 1.4
  0.6
```

In questions **13** to **32**, find

13 3.26 − 0.2

14 3.2 − 0.26

15 14.23 − 11.11

16 6.8 − 4.14

17 11 − 8.6

18 7.98 − 0.098

19 7.098 − 0.98

20 3.2 − 0.428

21 11.2 − 0.0026

22 0.000 32 − 0.000 123

23 0.0073 − 0.0006

24 0.0073 − 0.006

25 0.006 − 0.000 73

26 0.06 − 0.000 73

27 6 − 0.73

28 6 − 0.073

29 7.3 − 0.06

30 730 − 0.6

31 0.73 − 0.000 06

32 0.73 − 0.6

33 Take 19.2 from 76.8

34 Subtract 1.9 from 10.2

35 From 0.168 subtract 0.019

36 Evaluate 7.62 − 0.81

37 A piece of fabric is 7.6 m long. If 2.3 m is cut off, how much is left?

38 The bill for two books came to £14.24. One book cost £3.72. What was the cost of the other one?

39 Add 2.32 and 0.68, and subtract the result from 4.

40 To answer the question 'What length is left when I cut 2.5 cm and then 7 cm of tape from a roll 150 cm long?' Janet wrote

2.5 cm + 7 cm = 3.2 cm
150 cm − 3.2 cm = 147.8 cm

Her answer is wrong.

a Without checking her working, how do you know that her answer is obviously wrong?

b Find her mistakes. Explain how you know they were mistakes.

Exercise 7k

Find the value of

1 8.62 + 1.7

2 8.62 − 1.7

3 3.8 − 0.82

4 0.08 + 0.32 + 6.2

5 5 − 0.6

6 100 + 0.28

7 100 − 0.28

8 0.26 + 0.026

9 0.26 − 0.026

10 78.42 − 0.8

11 38.2 + 1.68

12 38.2 − 1.68

13 0.84 + 2 + 200

14 16 + 1.6 + 0.16

15 1.4 − 0.81

16 0.02 − 0.013

17 0.062 + 0.32

18 6.83 − 0.19

19 17.2 + 20 + 1.62

20 9.2 + 13.21 − 14.6

21 The perimeter of the quadrilateral is 19 cm.
What is the length of the fourth side?

22 The bill for three meals was £36.
The first meal cost £9.72 and the second £14.88.
What was the cost of the third?

23 Kane bought 3 magazines and a newspaper. The first magazine
cost £4.75, the second cost 70 p more than the first, and the third
magazine cost 56 p more than the second.
If he received £1.20 change when he paid with a £20 note, how
much did the newspaper cost?

24 A quadrilateral, like the one shown in question **21**, has a
perimeter of 27 cm. The shortest side is 5.2 cm long, the next
shortest side is 1.36 cm longer than this, and the length of the
longest side is 50% more than the length of the shortest side.
How long is the fourth side?

Mixed exercises

Exercise 7l

1 Add   **a** $\frac{3}{5} + \frac{1}{5}$ **b** $\frac{1}{3} + \frac{1}{4} + \frac{7}{24}$

2 Find   **a** $\frac{9}{16} - \frac{7}{16}$ **b** $\frac{7}{12} - \frac{1}{4}$ **c** $\frac{1}{2} + \frac{3}{7} - \frac{5}{8}$

3 Find 42 ÷ 9, giving your answer as a mixed number.

4 Evaluate 1.5 + 6

5 Find   **a** $3\frac{1}{4} + 2\frac{2}{5}$ **b** $7\frac{3}{5} + 2\frac{7}{10}$

6 Find   **a**   7.34 + 2.18   **b**   0.54 + 0.049

7 Find   **a**   10 − 3.98   **b**   4.2 − 0.972

8 Subtract 6.02 from the sum of 1.27 and 18.59

9 In a class the weight of $\frac{1}{3}$ of the students is less than 50 kg and the weight of $\frac{5}{6}$ of the students is less than 60 kg. No student is exactly 50 kg. What fraction of the students weigh between 50 kg and 60 kg?

Exercise 7m

1 Find **a** $\frac{1}{6} + \frac{5}{12}$ **b** $\frac{2}{3} + \frac{1}{5} + \frac{2}{15}$

2 Find **a** $\frac{7}{10} - \frac{1}{2}$ **b** $\frac{13}{21} - \frac{3}{7}$

3 Find the total bill for three books costing £12.79, £15 and £8.99

4 Subtract 14.8 from 16.3

5 The side of an **equilateral triangle** (all three sides are equal) is 14.4 cm. What is the length of the perimeter?

6 Change $5\frac{1}{6}$ into an improper fraction.

7 Find **a** $3\frac{3}{5} + 2\frac{2}{5}$ **b** $9\frac{1}{2} - 3\frac{2}{5}$

8 Find **a** $1.47 + 0.147$ **b** $3.96 + 11.2$

9 Find **a** $53.08 - 16.49$ **b** $0.937 - 0.088$

Consider again

Class 7W collected £252. They decided to give $\frac{1}{4}$ to the NSPCC, $\frac{1}{3}$ to the local hospice and the remainder to OXFAM.

Anna commented, 'That leaves more than half for OXFAM!'
Hasib replied, 'No, it doesn't'. Who is right and why?

Sam joined in the argument with:
'But $\frac{1}{3}$ is more than $\frac{1}{4}$, so the two together must be more than $\frac{1}{2}$.'
Is this a sensible statement?

Give a reason for your answer.

Now try to answer these questions.

🧩 Number puzzles

1
4.33	0.59	2.36	5.608	3.182	0.57	0.649
6.25	1.89	5.81	3.218	1.14	2.98	3.902
3.72	0.9	3.7	5.959	6.27	6.804	0.098
0.13	5.91	3.241	0.68	1.291	2.99	4.2

   a Pair off as many numbers as possible so that all your number pairs add up to a number between 5 and 7. When your time is up your score is the sum of all the remaining numbers. The lower the score the better. (You will probably find it helpful to copy the list and cross out each pair of numbers that satisfies the condition.)
  You have a time limit of 2 minutes for this exercise.

   b Repeat the exercise to try to reduce your score.

   c What is the lowest score possible?

   d Try to write down 12 numbers written as three rows with four numbers in each row so that the rules given in part **a** apply and the lowest possible score is 0. If you think you've succeeded try it on a partner.

   e Using the same list of decimals, pair them off so that the difference between the pairs lies between 0 and 1.

2 If the sum of the numbers in all the rows, columns and diagonals of a square is the same the square is called a *magic square*.

9	8	4
2	7	12
10	6	5

For example, in this magic square the total in every row, column and diagonal is 21.

a
		8.1
5.4	6.3	7.2
	10.8	

Fill in the blanks in this magic square if the total is always 18.9.

b
6.3	5.5	2.8
1.4	4.9	8.5
7.0	4.2	3.5

This magic square contains two wrong numbers. Find these wrong numbers and correct them.

c

15	10	30	60
40	50	16	90
14	11	20	70
10	80	13	12

Insert decimal points so that this is a magic square.

! Investigation

In this investigation all fractions must be less than 1.
Look at the digits 2, 3, 4, 5, 6 and 7.

a Use two of these digits to make
   i the largest fraction possible
   ii the smallest fraction possible.

b Use two of the digits on the top and another two on the bottom to make
   i the largest fraction possible
   ii the smallest fraction possible.

 Note: no digit can be used more than once in the same fraction.

c If possible find two pairs of these digits to make two equivalent fractions.

d Make two fractions so that their difference is
   i the largest possible
   ii the smallest possible.

 Note: Each digit can be used only once. The numerator and denominator must have the same number of digits.

e Investigate what happens if you start with a different selection of six digits.

f What happens if the number of digits on the top and on the bottom can be different?

g What happens if you can have more than six digits to select from?

8 More on decimals

Consider

Zara has £700 to invest in radios costing £30.85 each, which she intends to sell on eBay.
How many can she afford to order?

 Harri needs 36 lengths of timber, each 1.24 m long. The builders'
merchant has a large quantity of this timber at a reduced price,
provided Harri is willing to take 6.1 m lengths.

Harri wonders whether this is the cheapest way of buying what he
wants. Would it be better to buy the exact lengths he needs at the
normal price, which is 20% more per metre than the reduced price?

A chemist finds the easiest way to count tablets is by weighing them. She knows that 30 of a
particular tablet weigh 22.5 g. She needs 100 tablets for a prescription. What weight is needed?

You should be able to solve these problems after you have worked through this chapter.

Class discussion

1   Can you think of any occasion in the last week when you needed
    to multiply or divide decimals?

2   Which of the following people need to be able to multiply and
    divide decimals?
    a   a carpenter   c   a builder   e   a banker
    b   a shopkeeper   d   an engineer   f   a nurse?
    Justify your answers.

3   In which of the following situations is it an advantage to be able
    to multiply and/or divide decimals?
    a   changing pounds into foreign money to go abroad
    b   getting the ingredients together to do some cooking
    c   buying tickets for a group of students to go to a concert

Multiplication by 10, 100, 1000, ...

Consider $32 \times 10 = 320$. Writing 32 and 320 in headed columns gives

hundreds	tens	units
	3	2
3	2	0

Multiplying by 10 has made the number of units become the number of tens, and the
number of tens has become the number of hundreds, so that all the digits have moved one
place to the left.

Consider 0.2 × 10. When multiplied by 10, tenths become units $\left(\frac{1}{10} \times 10 = 1\right)$, so

units	tenths		units
0	. 2	× 10 =	2

Again the digit has moved one place to the left.
Multiplying by 100 means multiplying by 10 and then by 10 again, so the digits move 2 places to the left.

	tens	units		tenths	hundredths	thousandths	
		0	.	4	2	6	× 100
=	4	2	.	6			

Notice that the digits move to the left while the point stays put, but without headings it looks as though the digits stay put and the point moves to the right.
When necessary we fill in an empty space with a zero.

units	tenths		hundreds	tens	units
4	. 2	× 100 =	4	2	0

Exercise 8a

1 Key in 54.2 on your calculator.

  a Multiply it by 10.

  b Multiply your answer by 10.

  c Multiply this answer by 10.

  What happens to the digits 542 each time you multiply by 10?

Worked example

Without using a calculator, find the value of

→ 368 × 100   → 3.68 × 10   → 3.68 × 1000

368 × 100 = 36 800   3.68 × 10 = 36.8   3.68 × 1000 = 3680

Find, without using a calculator

2 72 × 100   **5** 32.78 × 10   **8** 72.81 × 1000

3 8.24 × 10   **6** 0.043 × 100   **9** 0.0063 × 10

4 0.024 × 100   **7** 0.007 × 1000   **10** 3.74 × 100

11 A £1 coin is 2.81 mm thick. How high is a pile of 10 similar coins?

12 Hanwar is cutting pieces off a large ball of string.
Each piece is 14.5 cm long. He cuts off 100 pieces.
Find the total length of the string he cuts off.

Division by 10, 100, 1000, ...

When we divide by 10, the hundreds become tens, and the tens become units.

hundreds	tens	units			tens	units
6	4	0	÷ 10 =		6	4

The digits move one place to the right and the number becomes smaller, but it looks as though the decimal point moves to the left, e.g.

$2.83 \div 10 = 0.283$

To divide by 100 the point is moved two places to the left.
To divide by 1000 the point is moved three places to the left.

Exercise 8b

1 Key in 138.2 on your calculator.

  a Divide it by 10.

  b Divide your answer by 10.

  c Divide this answer by 10.

  d Divide your last answer by 10.

What happens to the decimal point each time you divide by 10?

Worked example

Find, without using a calculator, the value of

➤ $3.2 \div 10$

 The decimal point moves one place to the left.

$3.2 \div 10 = 0.32$

➤ $43 \div 1000$

 The decimal point moves three places to the left, and we need to fill the 'empty' place with a zero.

$43 \div 1000 = 0.043$

Without using a calculator, find the value of

2 $266.8 \div 100$ **5** $27 \div 10$ **8** $426 \div 1000$

3 $76.37 \div 10$ **6** $5.8 \div 100$ **9** $16.8 \div 10$

4 $1.6 \div 100$ **7** $0.44 \div 10$ **10** $0.82 \div 100$

11 A pile of ten 20 p coins is 1.6 cm high. How thick is one 20 p coin?

12 When laid end to end 100 screws stretch a distance of 520 cm. What is the length of 1 screw?

The remaining questions are a mixture of multiplication and division.

Find

13 $1.6 \div 10$

14 1.6×10

15 $0.067 \div 10$

16 0.32×10

17 14.3×100

18 0.068×100

19 $1.63 \div 100$

20 12.3×100

21 $140 \div 1000$

22 7.8×1000

23 $56 \div 100$

24 0.27×1000

25 $8.2 \div 100$

26 $0.078 \div 100$

27 $0.77 \div 100$

28 $0.58 \div 1000$

29 $0.045 \div 1000$

30 0.041×1000

31 Sixty-seven metres of string is shared equally among 10 people. What length of string does each person get?

32 Find the total cost of 100 articles at £1.64 each.

33 Which of the following is the larger, and by how much?

$0.47 \times 100 \quad \text{or} \quad 560 \div 10$

34 Which of the following is the smaller, and by how much?

$1.36 \div 10 \quad \text{or} \quad 0.046 \times 100$

35 Find the cost of 100 programmes at £4.95 each.

36 Multiply 2.7 by 100 and then divide the result by 1000.

37 Divide 740 by 100 and then divide the result by 10.

38 Add 14.9 to 3.45 and then divide the result by 10.

39 Take 3.76 from 10 and then multiply the result by 100.

40 A lorry is carrying 1000 boxes.
If each box weighs 1.34 kg, what load is the lorry carrying?

41 100 cars, each 4.245 m long, are parked nose to tail in a straight line. How far is it from the front of the first car to the tail of the last one?

42 Which of the following is the larger, and by how much?

the difference between 4.6 and 15.9 multiplied by 10

or

the sum of 150.3 and 52 divided by 100

43 A box contains 100 nails, each nail weighing 0.88 g.
Find the weight, in grams, of the nails in
a 1 box
b 100 boxes.

Multiplication by whole numbers

A decimal can be multiplied by a whole number in the same way as one whole number can be multiplied by another. It is easier to keep the decimal point in the correct place when the calculation is set out in columns, e.g.

$1.87 \times 6 = 11.22$

$$
\begin{array}{r}
1.87 \\
\times \quad 6 \\
\hline
11.22 \\
\small 5\ 4
\end{array}
$$

Exercise 8c

Find

1 1.3×4	**5** 2.81×3	**9** 3.9×5
2 2.7×5	**6** 1.95×2	**10** 2.68×3
3 0.8×8	**7** 52.4×4	**11** 0.126×4
4 4.2×3	**8** 812.9×4	**12** 53.72×6

Worked example

→ Find 8.56×300

$$
\begin{aligned}
8.56 \times 300 &= 8.56 \times 3 \times 100 \\
&= 25.68 \times 100 \\
&= 2568
\end{aligned}
$$

First multiply by 3, then by 100.

→ Find 0.63×700

$$
\begin{aligned}
0.63 \times 700 &= 0.63 \times 7 \times 100 \\
&= 4.41 \times 100 \\
&= 441
\end{aligned}
$$

First multiply by 7, then by 100.

13 3.4×30	**16** 5.67×400	**19** 0.86×700
14 0.56×500	**17** 0.083×600	**20** 32.6×90
15 6.40×80	**18** 2.75×50	**21** 0.72×60

Division by whole numbers

We can see that

units	tenths		units	tenths
0 .	6	$\div 2 =$	0 .	3

because 6 tenths $\div 2 = 3$ tenths. So we may divide by a whole number in the usual way as long as we keep the digits in the correct columns and the points are in line.

Exercise 8d

Worked example

➔ Find the value of 6.8 ÷ 2

6.8 ÷ 2 = 3.4

$$2\overline{)6.8}$$
   3.4

 Keep the digits and points in line.

Find the value of

1 0.4 ÷ 2	**5** 0.9 ÷ 9	**9** 42.6 ÷ 2
2 3.2 ÷ 2	**6** 0.95 ÷ 5	**10** 7.53 ÷ 3
3 0.63 ÷ 3	**7** 0.672 ÷ 3	**11** 6.56 ÷ 4
4 7.8 ÷ 3	**8** 26.6 ÷ 7	**12** 0.75 ÷ 5

13 A pile of four 1 p coins is 5.36 mm high. What is the thickness of one coin?

14 Eight boxed exercise benches are stacked one on top of the other and reach a height of 1.152 m. How deep is one box?

Sometimes it is necessary to fill in spaces with zeros.

Worked example

➔ Find 0.000 36 ÷ 3

0.000 36 ÷ 3 = 0.000 12

$$3\overline{)0.00036}$$
   0.00012

➔ Find 0.45 ÷ 5

0.45 ÷ 5 = 0.09

$$5\overline{)0.45}$$
   0.09

➔ Find 6.12 ÷ 3

6.12 ÷ 3 = 2.04

$$3\overline{)6.12}$$
   2.04

Find

15 0.057 ÷ 3	**20** 1.62 ÷ 2	**25** 0.81 ÷ 9
16 0.0065 ÷ 5	**21** 1.232 ÷ 4	**26** 0.5215 ÷ 5
17 0.008 72 ÷ 4	**22** 0.6552 ÷ 6	**27** 6.3 ÷ 7
18 0.012 ÷ 6	**23** 0.0285 ÷ 5	**28** 0.0636 ÷ 6
19 0.036 ÷ 6	**24** 0.0076 ÷ 4	**29** 0.038 ÷ 2

Worked example

➤ Find, without using a calculator, 194.6 ÷ 20

194.6 ÷ 10 = 19.46
19.46 ÷ 2 = 9.73

💡 Divide by 10, then by 2.

Find, without using a calculator.

30 26.4 ÷ 20   **33** 105.6 ÷ 40   **36** 19.5 ÷ 50

31 157.8 ÷ 30   **34** 15.93 ÷ 90   **37** 2.94 ÷ 70

32 40.2 ÷ 600   **35** 1.944 ÷ 800   **38** 59.1 ÷ 300

It may be necessary to add zeros at the end of a number in order to
finish the division.

Worked example

➤ Find   2 ÷ 5

2 ÷ 5 = 0.4

$$5 \overline{)2.0}$$
  0.4

➤ Find   2.9 ÷ 8

2.9 ÷ 8 = 0.3625

$$8 \overline{)2.9000}$$
  0.3625

Find the value of

39 6 ÷ 5   **43** 0.002 ÷ 5   **47** 9.4 ÷ 4

40 7.4 ÷ 4   **44** 7.1 ÷ 8   **48** 0.5 ÷ 4

41 0.83 ÷ 2   **45** 9.1 ÷ 2   **49** 0.31 ÷ 8

42 3.6 ÷ 5   **46** 0.0031 ÷ 2   **50** 7.62 ÷ 4

51 The perimeter (the distance all the way round the edge) of a
square is 14.6 cm.
What is the length of one side?

52 Divide 32.6 into 8 equal parts.

53 Share 14.3 kg equally between 2 people.

54 The perimeter of a regular pentagon (a five-sided figure with all
the sides equal) is 16 cm. What is the length of one side?

Division of decimals by a two-digit whole number

Dividing a decimal by any whole number other than a single digit is best done using a
calculator. Remember to estimate your answer as a check.

Exercise 8e

Worked example

Use a calculator to find the value of

→ $2.56 \div 16$

Estimate: $3 \div 20 = 0.15$

∴ $2.56 \div 16 = 0.16$

To find $2.56 \div 16$ key in: $\boxed{2}\ \boxed{\cdot}\ \boxed{5}\ \boxed{6}\ \boxed{\div}\ \boxed{1}\ \boxed{6}\ \boxed{=}$
The display shows 0.16

→ $4.2 \div 24$

Estimate: $4 \div 20 = 0.2$

∴ $4.2 \div 24 = 0.175$

To find $4.2 \div 24$ key in: $\boxed{4}\ \boxed{\cdot}\ \boxed{2}\ \boxed{\div}\ \boxed{2}\ \boxed{4}\ \boxed{=}$
The display shows 0.175

First write down an estimate, and then use a calculator to find the value of

1 $26.4 \div 24$	6 $85.8 \div 26$	11 $8.96 \div 28$
2 $2.1 \div 14$	7 $8.48 \div 16$	12 $54.4 \div 17$
3 $9.45 \div 21$	8 $5.2 \div 20$	13 $21.93 \div 51$
4 $11.22 \div 22$	9 $25.2 \div 36$	14 $23.4 \div 45$
5 $90 \div 25$	10 $34.54 \div 11$	15 $71.76 \div 23$

16 A carpet with an area of 9 square metres costs £310.50. How much is this a square metre?

17 Divide £18.09 among 27 children so that they each get the same amount.

18 Mr Patel buys 32 DVDs for £159.68. How much each is this?

19 Sixteen screws weigh 19.56 g.
Find the weight of: **a** 1 screw   **b** 7 screws.

Changing fractions to decimals (exact values)

Four friends went for a burger. Together with the tip, the total cost was £25. To find out how much each friend was due to pay we need to divide £25 by 4.

We can write this as £25 ÷ 4 or £$\frac{25}{4}$, but what does £$\frac{25}{4}$ mean? To find out how much each friend pays we work out £25 ÷ 4

$$\begin{array}{r} 6.25 \\ 4\overline{)25.00} \end{array}$$

i.e.   each friend pays £6.25, so £$\frac{25}{4}$ = £6.25,

i.e.   we have changed the fraction $\frac{25}{4}$ to the decimal 6.25.

We know that $\frac{3}{8}$ means 3 ÷ 8, and $8\overline{)3.000}^{\,0.375}$, i.e. $\frac{3}{8}$ = 0.375

To change a fraction to a decimal, divide the bottom number into the top number.

Exercise 8f

Worked example

Express as a decimal

➡ $\dfrac{3}{4}$

$\dfrac{3}{4} = 3 \div 4 = 0.75$

Check: $0.75 = \dfrac{75}{100} = \dfrac{3}{4}$

➡ $1\dfrac{2}{25}$

$1\dfrac{2}{25} = 1 + 2 \div 25$

$= 1 + 0.08$

$= 1.08$

Check: $1.08 = 1\dfrac{8}{100} = 1\dfrac{2}{25}$

Express the following fractions as decimals.

1 $\dfrac{1}{4}$　　　　　　　　5 $\dfrac{1}{25}$

2 $\dfrac{3}{8}$　　　　　　　　6 $2\dfrac{4}{5}$

3 $\dfrac{3}{5}$　　　　　　　　7 $\dfrac{5}{8}$

4 $\dfrac{5}{16}$　　　　　　　8 $1\dfrac{7}{16}$

In questions **9** to **12**, express each fraction as a decimal.

9 Everybody in the class sat a test, and $\dfrac{7}{8}$ of the students passed.

10 A large crowd gathered to watch the opening of the new supermarket; $\dfrac{3}{4}$ of the crowd were women.

11 Hank inspected a delivery of apples. He found that $\dfrac{1}{16}$ of them were bruised.

12 During one cold night last winter, $\dfrac{1}{8}$ of Kim's geraniums were killed by the frost.

Standard decimals and fractions

It is worthwhile knowing a few equivalent fractions, decimals and percentages.

For example

$$\tfrac{1}{2} = 0.5 = 50\% \qquad \tfrac{1}{4} = 0.25 = 25\% \qquad \tfrac{1}{8} = 0.125 = 12.5\%$$

Notice that　　$0.4 = \tfrac{4}{10} = \tfrac{2}{5}$

Exercise 8g

Write the following decimals as fractions in their lowest terms, without any working if possible.

1 0.2	**4** 0.75	**7** 0.9	**10** 0.04
2 0.3	**5** 0.6	**8** 0.05	**11** 0.005
3 0.8	**6** 0.7	**9** 0.375	**12** 0.025

Write the following fractions as decimals.

13 $\frac{9}{10}$	**15** $\frac{4}{5}$	**17** $\frac{3}{100}$	**19** $\frac{5}{8}$
14 $\frac{1}{4}$	**16** $\frac{3}{8}$	**18** $\frac{3}{4}$	**20** $\frac{7}{100}$

Multiplication by a decimal

So far we have multiplied a decimal by a multiple of 10 and by a whole number.

We have also divided a decimal by a multiple of 10, i.e. by 10, 100, 1000, …

Using this knowledge enables us to multiply any two decimals together.

Suppose we wish to find 0.3×0.2

Since $\quad\quad 0.2 = 2 \div 10 \quad\quad 0.3 \times 0.2 = 0.3 \times 2 \div 10$
$$= 0.6 \div 10$$
$$= 0.06$$

Similarly $\quad 0.06 \times 0.08 = 0.06 \times 8 \div 100$
$$= 0.48 \div 100$$
$$= 0.0048$$

Exercise 8h

Worked example

→ Find 0.05×0.7

$0.05 \times 0.7 = 0.05 \times 7 \div 10$
$$= 0.35 \div 10$$
$$= 0.035$$

 $0.7 = 7 \div 10$

Find

1 0.04×0.2	**3** 0.003×6	**5** 0.001×0.3
2 0.1×0.1	**4** 3×0.02	**6** 0.4×0.001

7 Compare the number of decimal places in your answers to questions **1** to **6** with the number of decimal places in the numbers being multiplied. What do you notice?

In the examples above, if we add together the number of digits (including zeros) after the decimal points in the original two decimals, we get the number of digits after the point in the answer.

The number of digits after the point is called the number of **decimal places**. In the example at the start of Exercise 8h, 0.05 has **two** decimal places, 0.7 has **one** decimal place and the answer, 0.035, has **three** decimal places, which is the sum of two and one.

We can use this fact to work out 0.05×0.7 without writing 0.7 as $7 \div 10$. Multiply 5 by 7 ignoring the points; count up the number of decimal places after the points and then put the point in the correct position in the answer, writing in zeros where necessary, i.e. $0.05 \times 0.7 = 0.035$.

Any zeros that come after the point must be included when counting the decimal places.

Exercise 8i

Worked example

Calculate the products

➤ 0.08×0.4

0.08	×	0.4	=	0.032
(2 places)		*(1 place)*		*(3 places)*

 $(8 \times 4 = 32)$

➤ 6×0.002

6	×	0.002	=	0.012
(0 places)		*(3 places)*		*(3 places)*

 $(6 \times 2 = 12)$

Calculate the following products. Do not use a calculator.

1 0.6×0.3	6 0.5×0.07	11 4×0.009
2 0.04×0.06	7 0.08×0.08	12 0.9×9
3 0.009×2	8 3×0.006	13 0.0008×11
4 0.12×0.09	9 0.7×0.06	14 7×0.11
5 0.07×0.003	10 0.07×12	15 0.04×7

16 Zainab saws a length of wood into 7 equal pieces each 23.7 cm long. If each saw cut consumes 0.1 cm, how long was the length of wood before she started sawing?

Zeros appearing in the multiplication, in the middle or at either end, must also be considered when counting the places.

Worked example

→ Find 0.252 × 0.4

0.252	×	0.4	=	0.1008
(3 places)		*(1 place)*		*(4 places)*

$$\begin{array}{r} 252 \\ \times\ \ 4 \\ \hline 1008 \end{array}$$

→ Find 2.5 × 6

2.5	×	6	=	15.0
(1 place)		*(0 places)*		*(1 place)*

$$\begin{array}{r} 25 \\ \times\ \ 6 \\ \hline 150 \end{array}$$

→ Find 300 × 0.02

300	×	0.02	=	6.00
(0 places)		*(2 places)*		*(2 places)*

300 × 2 = 600

Calculate the following products.

17 0.751 × 0.2

18 3.2 × 0.5

19 0.35 × 4

20 400 × 0.6

21 31.5 × 2

22 5.6 × 0.02

23 320 × 0.07

24 0.4 × 0.0055

25 0.5 × 0.006

26 1.6 × 0.4

27 1.6 × 0.5

28 0.16 × 0.005

29 4 × 1.6

30 5 × 0.016

31 16 000 × 0.05

32 0.16 × 4

33 0.0016 × 5

34 310 × 0.04

35 A metal washer is 1.25 mm thick. Six washers are placed on each of the two supports of a gate in order to raise it. By how much is the gate raised?

36 Find the cost of 10 jackets costing £43.50 each.

37 A sheet of paper is 0.065 mm thick.
How thick is a pile of 240 sheets?

38 Find the weight of 34 books if each book weighs 1.35 kg.

Worked example

→ Calculate 0.26 × 1.3

0.26	×	1.3	=	0.338
(2 places)		*(1 place)*		*(3 places)*

$$\begin{array}{r} 26 \\ \times\ 13 \\ \hline 78 \\ 260 \\ \hline 338 \end{array}$$

Calculate the following products.

39 4.2 × 1.6

40 52 × 0.24

41 0.68 × 0.14

42 310 × 1.4

43 1.68 × 0.27

44 13.2 × 2.5

45 0.082 × 0.034

46 0.0016 × 1600

47 0.34 × 0.31

48 A fire engine travels 0.675 miles in each minute.
How far will it travel in
a   4 minutes
b   12 minutes?

49 A taxi, which can travel at 0.6 miles per minute, had a call at
10.22 to pick up a passenger at her home, which was 4.5 miles
away. The passenger wished to be taken to the station to catch a
train due at 10.50. The taxi driver answered the call immediately,
spent 1.5 minutes loading the passenger and her luggage, and
drove the 7.5 miles to the station.
a   How long did the taxi take to get to the passenger?
b   How long did the taxi take to drive the passenger to the
station?
c   At what time did the passenger arrive at the station?
d   If 3.25 minutes were allowed to get from the taxi to the
station platform, did the passenger catch the train?
If so, how much time did she have to spare?

Correcting to a given number of decimal places

Often we need to know only the first few digits of a decimal. For example, if we measure a
length with an ordinary ruler we usually need an answer to the nearest $\frac{1}{10}$ cm and are not
interested, or cannot see, how many $\frac{1}{100}$ cm are involved.

Look at this enlarged view of the end of a line which is being measured. We can see that with
a more accurate measure we might be able to give the length as 4.34 cm. However on the
given ruler, we would probably measure it as 4.3 cm because we can see that the end of the
line is nearer 4.3 than 4.4. We cannot give the exact length of the line but we can say that it
is 4.3 cm long to the nearest $\frac{1}{10}$ cm. We write this as 4.3 cm *correct to one decimal place.*

Consider the numbers 0.62, 0.622, 0.625, 0.627 and 0.63. To compare them we write 0.62
as 0.620 and 0.63 as 0.630 so that each number has three digits after the point, i.e. we are
correcting the numbers to three decimal places.

    0.620
    0.622
    0.625
    0.627
    0.630

When we write them in order in a column we can see that 0.622 is nearer to 0.620 than to 0.630, while 0.627 is nearer to 0.630 so we write

    0.62¦2 = 0.62 (correct to two decimal places)

    0.62¦7 = 0.63 (correct to two decimal places)

> 💡 We can draw a line after the decimal place we want to replace.

It is not so obvious what to do with 0.625 as it is halfway between 0.62 and 0.63. To save arguments, if the figure after the cut-off line is 5 or more we add 1 to the figure before the cut-off line, i.e. we round the number *up*, so we write

    0.62¦5 = 0.63 (correct to two decimal places)

Exercise 8j

Worked example

Give 10.9315 correct to

➡ the nearest whole number

10.¦9315 = 11 (correct to the nearest whole number)

➡ one decimal place

10.9¦315 = 10.9 (correct to one decimal place)

Give, correct to two decimal places

➡ 4.699

4.69¦9 = 4.70 (correct to two decimal places)

Note: The zero in the second decimal place shows that the number *has* been corrected to 2 d.p.

➡ 0.007

0.00¦7 = 0.01 (correct to two decimal places)

Give the following numbers correct to two decimal places.

1 0.328	6 0.6947	11 0.178
2 0.322	7 0.8351	12 1.582
3 1.2671	8 3.927	13 4.995
4 2.345	9 0.0084	14 0.0115
5 0.0416	10 3.9999	15 8.0293

> 💡 Adding a line after the second decimal place helps you to see the next decimal place.

Give the following numbers correct to the nearest whole number.

16 13.9	18 26.5	20 4.45
17 6.34	19 2.78	21 6.783

22 109.7	**25** 3.9999	**28** 15.29
23 6.145	**26** 58.4	**29** 152.9
24 74.09	**27** 0.98	**30** 26.49

Give the following numbers correct to the number of decimal places indicated in the brackets.

31 1.784 (1)	**36** 1.639 (2)
32 42.64 (1)	**37** 1.639 (1)
33 1.0092 (2)	**38** 1.639 (nearest whole number)
34 0.0942 (2)	**39** 343.4984 (2)
35 0.7345 (1)	**40** 3.4984 (1)

If we are asked to give an answer correct to a certain number of decimal places, we work out one more decimal place than is asked for. Then we can find the size of the last figure required.

Exercise 8k

Worked example

→ Find 4.28 ÷ 6, giving your answer correct to two decimal places.

$$6\overline{)4.280...}$$
$$0.713...$$

4.28 ÷ 6 = 0.71⦙3...

= 0.71 (correct to two decimal places)

 We need to give the answer to two decimal places, so we carry on dividing until we know the third decimal place.

→ Calculate 302 ÷ 14 correct to one decimal place.

```
        21.57...
  14)302.00
      28
      ‾‾
       22
       14
       ‾‾
        80
        70
        ‾‾
       100
        98
```

302 ÷ 14 = 21.5⦙7...

= 21.6 (correct to one decimal place)

 We can stop the division when we know the second decimal place.

Calculate, giving your answers correct to two decimal places.

1 0.496 ÷ 3	**4** 25.68 ÷ 9	**7** 5.68 ÷ 24
2 6.49 ÷ 7	**5** 2.35 ÷ 15	**8** 3.89 ÷ 11
3 12.2 ÷ 6	**6** 0.99 ÷ 21	**9** 1.83 ÷ 8

So far, for much of the time we have used pencil and paper methods. However, it is much easier to use a calculator, *provided you make a rough check to see that your answers are sensible.*

Worked example

Use a calculator to find

→ 32.9 ÷ 21 correct to two decimal places

Estimate: 30 ÷ 20 = 3 ÷ 2 = 1.5

32.9 ÷ 21 = 1.57 (correct to two decimal places)

→ 17.89 ÷ 37 correct to one decimal place.

Estimate: 20 ÷ 40 = 2 ÷ 4 = 0.5

17.89 ÷ 37 = 0.5 (correct to one decimal place)

Use a calculator to find each value correct to the number of decimal places indicated in the brackets.

10 32.9 ÷ 8 (1)	**14** 124 ÷ 17 (1)	**18** 213 ÷ 22 (2)
11 402 ÷ 7 (1)	**15** 0.45 ÷ 12 (2)	**19** 519 ÷ 19 (2)
12 9.76 ÷ 11 (1)	**16** 15.1 ÷ 16 (1)	**20** 0.321 ÷ 17 (2)
13 2.3 ÷ 11 (2)	**17** 2.584 ÷ 16 (2)	**21** 54 ÷ 23 (1)

22 Seven brothers and sisters are given £500 to be divided equally among them.

Correct to the nearest penny, how much will each one receive?

If each brother and sister received this amount, would £500 be enough?

Give reasons for your answer.

23 Express each of the fractions $\frac{4}{5}, \frac{6}{7}, \frac{13}{15}$, and $\frac{15}{19}$ as a decimal correct to two decimal places.

Hence write these fractions in order of size with the smallest first.

24 Express $\frac{3}{7}, \frac{5}{12}$, and $\frac{6}{13}$ as decimals correct to two decimal places.

Hence write them in order of size with the smallest first.

25 Write the numbers 0.82, $\frac{9}{11}$, 0.801 and $\frac{19}{23}$ as decimals, correct to three decimal places where necessary, and write them in order of size with the largest first.

26 Look at the numbers 0.7, $\frac{7}{11}, \frac{14}{19}$ and 0.8.

Decide, without using a calculator,

a which is the largest number

b which is the smallest number?

Give reasons for your answers.

27 Four students were asked to put the numbers $\frac{5}{9}$, $\frac{3}{5}$, 0.45 and $\frac{11}{17}$ in order of size, smallest first. Without using a calculator, decide which of the following answers is probably correct.

a Sheena's 0.45, $\frac{5}{9}$, $\frac{3}{5}$, $\frac{11}{17}$ **c** Vicki's 0.45, $\frac{11}{17}$, $\frac{3}{5}$, $\frac{5}{9}$

b Harry's, $\frac{3}{5}$, 0.45, $\frac{5}{9}$, $\frac{11}{17}$ **d** Jamil's 0.45, $\frac{5}{9}$, $\frac{11}{17}$, $\frac{3}{5}$

28 Estimates suggest that the average man uses 12.3 calories per minute when swimming.

How many calories, correct to one decimal place, are used when a man swims for

a 10 minutes   **b** $22\frac{1}{2}$ minutes   **c** $13\frac{1}{4}$ minutes?

Division by decimals

$0.012 \div 0.06$ can be written as $\frac{0.012}{0.06}$. We know how to divide by a whole number so we need to find an equivalent fraction with denominator 6 instead of 0.06.

Now $0.06 \times 100 = 6$. Therefore we multiply the numerator and denominator by 100.

$$\frac{0.012}{0.06} = \frac{0.012 \times 100}{0.06 \times 100}$$
$$= \frac{1.2}{6}$$
$$= 0.2$$

To divide by a decimal, the denominator must be made into a whole number but the numerator need not be. We can write, for short,

$$0.012 \div 0.06 = \frac{0.01 | 2}{0.06} = \frac{1.2}{6} \quad \text{(keeping the points in line)}$$

The broken line indicates where we want the point to be so as to make the denominator a whole number.

Exercise 8l

Worked example

Find the exact value of

→ $0.024 \div 0.6$

$0.024 \div 0.6 = \dfrac{0.0 | 24}{0.6}$

$\qquad\qquad = \dfrac{0.24}{6}$

$\begin{array}{r} 0.04 \\ 6\overline{)0.24} \end{array}$

$\qquad\qquad = 0.04$

Check: $0.04 \times 0.6 = 0.024$

$\rightarrow \quad 64 \div 0.08$

$$64 \div 0.08 \quad = \frac{64.00 \,|}{0.08}$$

$$= \frac{6400}{8}$$

$$= 800$$

$8\overline{)6400}$
800

Check: $800 \times 0.08 = 64$

Find the exact answers to the following questions.

1 $0.04 \div 0.2$	**7** $3.6 \div 0.06$	**13** $0.9 \div 0.009$
2 $4 \div 0.5$	**8** $3 \div 0.6$	**14** $0.92 \div 0.4$
3 $0.8 \div 0.04$	**9** $6.5 \div 0.5$	**15** $0.001\,32 \div 0.11$
4 $90 \div 0.02$	**10** $72 \div 0.9$	**16** $0.000\,068\,4 \div 0.04$
5 $0.48 \div 0.04$	**11** $1.08 \div 0.003$	**17** $20.8 \div 0.0004$
6 $0.032 \div 0.2$	**12** $16.8 \div 0.8$	**18** $4.8 \div 0.08$

 19 How many plastic washers, each 0.4 mm thick, are needed to separate two pieces of metal by 1.6 mm?

 20 The height of one fence post is 1.8 m. The total of the heights of a bundle of fence posts is 39.6 m. How many posts are there in the bundle?

 21 Eddie Davis keeps careful rainfall records. During one period last winter the total rainfall was 29.44 cm which, if the same quantity fell each day, would be 0.32 cm per day. How many days did this period cover?

Worked example

Use a calculator to find the exact value of $0.256 \div 1.6$

$0.256 \div 1.6 = 0.16$

To find $0.256 \div 1.6$ press

$\boxed{0}\ \boxed{\cdot}\ \boxed{2}\ \boxed{5}\ \boxed{6}\ \boxed{\div}\ \boxed{1}\ \boxed{\cdot}\ \boxed{6}\ \boxed{=}$

The displays shows 0.16

Use a calculator to find the exact value of

22 $1.76 \div 2.2$	**25** $34.3 \div 1.4$	**28** $9.8 \div 1.4$
23 $144 \div 0.16$	**26** $10.24 \div 3.2$	**29** $0.168 \div 0.14$
24 $0.496 \div 1.6$	**27** $0.0204 \div 0.017$	**30** $0.192 \div 2.4$

31 How many coins each 0.73 mm thick are there in a pile 8.76 mm high?

32 The product of two numbers is 9.24. One of the numbers is 3.85. What is the other?

33 A company pays a dividend of 13.55 pence per share. Roy Hately receives £203.25. How many shares does Roy have?

34 How many screws, each weighing 1.26 g, have a total weight of 79.38 g?

35 The thickness of a 350 page book (i.e. the book has 175 sheets or leaves) is 12.25 mm.

  a Find the thickness of
    i 1 sheet   **ii** 45 sheets   **iii** a ream (500 sheets).

  b How thick is a book with
    i 120 pages   **ii** 440 pages?

  c How many sheets have a total thickness of
    i 3.5 mm   **ii** 26.25 mm?

  d How many pages are there in a book whose thickness is
    i 12.6 mm   **ii** 8.96 mm?

Exercise 8m

Worked example

Without using a calculator, find the value of $16.9 \div 0.3$ giving your answer correct to one decimal place.

$$16.9 \div 0.3 = \frac{16.9}{0.3}$$
$$= 56.3\,|\,3\ldots$$
$$= 56.3 \quad \text{(correct to 1 decimal place)}$$

$$3)\overline{169.00}$$
$$56.33$$

Without using a calculator, find each value correct to two decimal places.

1 $3.8 \div 0.6$	**5** $0.0024 \div 0.09$	**9** $90 \div 11$
2 $0.59 \div 0.07$	**6** $0.65 \div 0.7$	**10** $0.23 \div 0.007$
3 $15 \div 0.9$	**7** $0.123 \div 6$	**11** $16.2 \div 0.8$
4 $1.25 \div 0.03$	**8** $2.3 \div 0.8$	**12** $85 \div 0.3$

Worked example

Use a calculator to give, correct to two decimal places,

→ $0.52 \div 0.21$

> To find $0.52 \div 0.21$ press
> $\boxed{0}\ \boxed{.}\ \boxed{5}\ \boxed{2}\ \boxed{\div}\ \boxed{0}\ \boxed{.}\ \boxed{2}\ \boxed{1}\ \boxed{=}$
> The displays shows 2.4761904

Estimate: $0.52 \div 0.21 \approx 0.5 \div 0.2 = 5 \div 2 \approx 3$

When we estimate, all we want is a rough idea of the size of the answer, so we can also round the results of calculations when finding an estimate. This is why we give $5 \div 2 \approx 3$.

$\therefore \quad 0.52 \div 0.21 = 2.48$ (correct to two decimal places)

$\longrightarrow$ 56.79 ÷ 1.6

Estimate: 56.79 ÷ 1.6 ≈ 60 ÷ 2 = 30

∴ 56.79 ÷ 1.6 = 35.49 (correct to two decimal places)

To find 56.79 ÷ 1.6 press

5 6 . 7 9 ÷ 1 . 6 =

The displays shows 35.49375

First estimate, and then use a calculator to find the value of each division.

Give each answer correct to   a   one decimal place
                              b   two decimal places.

13 47.3 ÷ 18   **17** 3.65 ÷ 0.92

14 5.33 ÷ 1.08   **18** 64.07 ÷ 12.44

15 0.653 ÷ 1.04   **19** 0.0734 ÷ 0.119

16 0.041 ÷ 0.13   **20** 17.83 ÷ 73.65

Mixed multiplication and division

Exercise 8n

Without using a calculator and giving your answers exactly, calculate

1 0.48 × 0.3   **5** 3.6 ÷ 0.8   **9** 16.8 × 0.4

2 0.48 ÷ 0.3   **6** 9.6 × 0.6   **10** 1.68 ÷ 0.4

3 2.56 × 0.02   **7** 0.0042 × 0.03   **11** 20.4 × 0.6

4 2.56 ÷ 0.02   **8** 0.0042 ÷ 0.03   **12** 5.04 × 0.06

In questions **13** to **21**, use a calculator to find the answers correct to two decimal places.

13 4.87 × 9.04   **16** 15.64 ÷ 8.4   **19** 0.176 × 1.88

14 20.08 ÷ 8.85   **17** 0.074 ÷ 0.22   **20** 31.45 × 0.077

15 67.9 ÷ 126.4   **18** 0.555 × 3.27   **21** 9.004 ÷ 0.435

22 Which is the larger answer?
   a   3.6 × 6   or   36 ÷ 6
   b   0.36 × 6   or   3.6 ÷ 0.6
   c   0.9 × 0.7   or   0.8 × 0.8

23 Fill in the blanks in the following calculations.
   a   5.2 × ☐ = 19.24
   b   17.38 ÷ ☐ = 4.4
   c   0.294 × 0.06 = ☐
   d   ☐ ÷ 0.35 = 1.44
   e   0.93 × 2.72 − ☐ = 0
   f   ☐ × 7.32 = 4.758

Mixed exercises

Do not use a calculator for these exercises except when you are asked to do so.

Exercise 8p

1   Divide 0.082 by 4.
2   Multiply 0.0301 by 100.
3   Express $\frac{7}{8}$ as a decimal.
4   Divide 1.5 by 25.
5   Give the following numbers correct to two decimal places.
    a   3.126   **b**   0.075   **c**   2.999
6   Multiply 3.2 by 1.4.
7   Which is the larger, 6.6 or $6\frac{2}{3}$? Why?
8   Use a calculator to find
    a $50.6 \div 2.2$ **b** 0.683×1.8
9   Last season Jake took 35 wickets for 327 runs.
    How many runs was this for each wicket? Give your answer
    correct to two decimal places.

Exercise 8q

1   Find   **a** 42.64×10 **b** $37.43 \div 100$
2   Find   **a** 6.74×300 **b** $0.81 \div 9$
3   Use a calculator to find
    a $40.8 \div 23$
    b $1.62 \div 36$
4   Find   **a** 0.008×6 **b** 0.5×0.12 **c** 230×1.4
5   Give 17.906 correct to
    a   the nearest whole number
    b   one decimal place
    c   two decimal places.
6   Find   **a** $5.92 \div 7$ **b** $16.4 \div 9$
    giving each answer correct to two decimal places.
7   Find the exact value of   **a** $2.56 \div 3.2$ **b** $0.126 \div 1.8$
8   Use a calculator to decide which is the larger, and by how much.
        0.52×0.6 or 0.55×0.55
9   Sheets of metal, 0.125 cm thick, are piled one on top of the other
    until they reach a height of 36.5 cm.
    Use a calculator to find the number of sheets in the pile.

Consider again

Zara has £700 to invest in radios costing £30.85 each. How many can she afford to order?

Harri needs 36 lengths of timber, each 1.24 m long. The builders' merchant has this timber at a reduced price in 6.1 m lengths. Would it be better to buy the exact lengths at the normal price, which is 20% more per metre than the reduced price?

A chemist counts tablets by weighing them. 30 of a particular tablet weigh 22.5 g. She needs 100 tablets for a prescription. What weight is needed?

Now can you answer these questions?

 Investigation

Recurring decimals

If we divide 2 by 5 we get an exact answer, namely 0.4

However, if we divide 2 by 3 the answer is 0.666 666 6 … forever, i.e. 2 ÷ 3 does not give an exact decimal. We say that the 6 recurs or that this is a **recurring decimal**. Some of the numbers we get when we divide one whole number by another are interesting and are worth investigating.

You should not use a calculator for this work before you have used pencil and paper methods.

a   Find 0.4 ÷ 7. Continue working until you have at least 12 non-zero digits in your answer. Use a calculator to check the first eight non-zero digits of your answer.
   What do you notice about the pattern of digits in your answer?

b   Now try 0.2 ÷ 7. Do you get the same digits in the same order?
   How does this answer differ from the answer you got in part **a**?

c   Can you find any other decimals which, when divided by 7, give the same pattern of digits, but start in a different place in the pattern?

d   Now try any numbers larger than 1 that 7 does not divide into exactly.
   For example, 1.5 ÷ 7 and 2.2 ÷ 7

e   Is it true to say that every decimal, when divided by 7, gives either an exact answer, or a recurring answer that involves the same cycle of digits?

f   Repeat parts **a** to **e** but divide by 9 instead of 7.

g   What happens if you divide by the other odd prime numbers less than 10?

h   What happens if you divide by the even numbers less than 10?

9 Units of length and mass

Consider

To order a new blind for a window, I need to give the width and height of the window. I can give these measurements by saying:

'as wide as my desk and from halfway up the wall to the top of the door' or

'96 centimetres wide and 102 centimetres high'.

What is better about the second way of giving the measurements?

David found instructions in a book for making papier-mâché. Among other things, he needs $1\frac{1}{2}$ lb of flour. He has a 1.5 kg bag of flour and a set of digital scales that weighs in grams and kilograms. Does David have enough flour? What does the reading on his scales need to be to get the correct amount of flour?

You should be able to solve these problems after you have worked through this chapter.

Metric units of length

Metric units are widely used throughout the world, but a few countries still use imperial units. In the UK, most quantities are measured in metric units but long distances are still usually measured in miles.

The basic unit of length is the **metre** (m). (A standard bed is about 2 m long.)

A metre is not a useful unit for measuring either very large things or very small things, so we need larger units and smaller units.

We get the larger unit by multiplying the metre by 1000.

> 1000 metres is called 1 **kilometre** (km)

(It takes about 15 minutes to walk a distance of 1 km.)

We get smaller units by dividing the metre into 100 parts or into 1000 parts.

> $\frac{1}{100}$ of a metre is called 1 **centimetre** (cm)
>
> $\frac{1}{1000}$ of a metre is called 1 **millimetre** (mm)

(You can see centimetres and millimetres on your ruler.)

Class discussion

1 Discuss which metric unit you would use to measure
   a   the length of your classroom
   b   the length of your pencil
   c   the length of a soccer pitch
   d   the distance from London to Beijing
   e   the length of a page in this book
   f   the thickness of your exercise book.

2 You need a new table cloth. You see a cloth that you like.
The label says that it measures 1246 mm by 2560 mm.
You know that your table measures about 1 m by 2 m.
Discuss what you need to know so that you can judge if this cloth
will cover your table.

Estimating lengths

If you are asked how wide a particular book is, can you give a quick estimate of its width
without having to measure it?

If you are told that a poster is 588 mm long, does this mean anything to you?

The skills that enable you to answer 'yes' to these questions come with experience of
measuring and estimating.

Exercise 9a

1 Use your ruler to draw a line of length

a	10 cm	g	15 mm
b	3 cm	h	12 cm
c	15 cm	i	25 mm
d	50 mm	j	16 mm
e	20 mm	k	5 cm
f	20 cm	l	75 mm

2 Estimate the length, in centimetres, of the following lines.

a ▬▬▬▬▬▬▬▬▬▬▬

b ▬▬▬▬▬▬▬▬▬▬▬▬▬▬

c ▬▬▬▬

d ▬▬▬▬▬▬▬▬▬▬▬

e ▬▬▬▬▬▬▬▬▬▬▬▬▬▬▬

Now use your ruler to measure each line.

3 Estimate the length, in millimetres, of the following lines.

a ▬▬▬

b ▬▬

c ▬

d ▬▬▬▬▬

e ▬

Now use your ruler to measure each line.

4 Use a straight edge (not a ruler with a scale) to draw a line that
is approximately

a	10 cm long	c	15 cm long
b	5 cm long	d	20 cm long

Now measure each line to see how good your approximation was.

5 Estimate the length and width of your exercise book in centimetres. Check your estimates by measuring the length and width of your exercise book. Draw a rough sketch of your book with the measurements on it.
Find the **perimeter** (the distance all round the edge) of your book.

6 Each side of a square is 10 cm long.
Draw a rough sketch of the square with the measurements on it.
Calculate the perimeter of the square.

7 A sheet is 200 cm wide and 250 cm long.
   a What is the perimeter of the sheet?
   b Will this sheet cover your bed?
   c Will it cover the table you last sat at?
Explain your answers to parts **b** and **c.**

Questions **8** to **10** are group activities.

8 Estimate the width of your classroom in metres.
Check the estimate by measuring.

9 Estimate the length of your classroom in metres.
Now measure it to check your estimate.

10 a Measure the height of the door into your classroom.
Use this to estimate the height of the room.
   b Discuss how you can use the known height of a person to estimate the heights of some everyday objects, e.g. a street lamp.

Changing from large units to smaller units

Which is longer: a tile 25 cm long or a tile 246 mm long?

It is easier to compare lengths if they are both measured in the same unit.

The metric units of length are the kilometre, the metre, the centimetre and the millimetre.

The relationships between them are

1 km = 1000 m	**1 m = 100 cm**
1 m = 1000 mm	**1 cm = 10 mm**

Exercise 9b

Worked example

⟶ Express 3 km in metres.

$3 \text{ km} = 3 \times 1000 \text{ m}$
$\qquad = 3000 \text{ m}$

⟶ Express 3.5 m in centimetres.

$3.5 \text{ m} = 3.5 \times 100 \text{ cm}$
$\qquad = 350 \text{ cm}$

In questions **1** to **24**, express the given quantity in terms of the unit in brackets.

1 2 m (cm)	**9** 3 m (mm)	**17** 1.9 m (mm)
2 5 km (m)	**10** 2 km (mm)	**18** 3.5 km (m)
3 3 cm (mm)	**11** 5 m (cm)	**19** 2.7 m (cm)
4 4 m (cm)	**12** 7 m (mm)	**20** 1.9 km (cm)
5 12 km (m)	**13** 1.5 m (cm)	**21** 3.8 cm (mm)
6 15 cm (mm)	**14** 2.3 cm (mm)	**22** 9.2 m (mm)
7 6 m (mm)	**15** 4.6 km (m)	**23** 2.3 km (m)
8 1 km (cm)	**16** 3.7 m (mm)	**24** 8.4 m (cm)

25 Which is longer, a piece of wood 24 cm long or a piece 236 mm long?

26 Which piece of tape is longer – one that is 3.5 m long or one that is 1335 mm long?

27 Arrange the following lengths in order of size with the shortest first.

$$25\,\text{m} \qquad 156\,\text{cm} \qquad 2889\,\text{mm} \qquad 3.8\,\text{m} \qquad 0.57\,\text{m}$$

Changing from small units to larger units

Exercise 9c

Worked example

$\rightarrow$ Express 400 cm in metres.

400 cm = 400 ÷ 100 m
       = 4 m

Express the given quantity in terms of the unit in brackets.

1 300 mm (cm)	**6** 72 m (km)
2 6000 m (km)	**7** 12 cm (m)
3 150 cm (m)	**8** 88 mm (cm)
4 250 mm (cm)	**9** 1250 mm (m)
5 1600 m (km)	**10** 2850 m (km)

Imperial units of length

Miles, **yards**, **feet** and **inches** are the imperial units of length that are still used in the United Kingdom and the United States of America. The relationships between them are

12 inches (in) = 1 foot (ft)   3 feet = 1 yard (yd)   1760 yards = 1 mile

Exercise 9d

Worked example

→ Express 2 ft 5 in in inches.

$$2\,\text{ft} = 2 \times 12\,\text{in}$$
$$= 24\,\text{in}$$
$$\therefore\quad 2\,\text{ft}\,5\,\text{in} = 24\,\text{in} + 5\,\text{in}$$
$$= 29\,\text{in}$$

2 feet 5 inches is sometimes written as 2' 5".

Express the given quantity in terms of the unit in brackets.

1 5 ft 8 in (in) **5** 2 ft 11 in (in)

2 4 yd 2 ft (ft) **6** 8 ft 4 in (in)

3 5 yd 2 ft (ft) **7** 9 yd 1 ft (ft)

4 10 ft 3 in (in) **8** 9 ft 10 in (in)

Worked example

→ Express 52" in feet and inches.

$$52" = 52 \div 12\,\text{ft}$$
$$= 4'\,4"$$

 There are 4 twelves in 52 with 4 left over.

Express the given quantity in terms of the units in brackets.

9 36 in (ft) **13** 13 ft (yd and ft)

10 29 in (ft and in) **14** 75 in (ft and in)

11 86 in (ft and in) **15** 100 ft (yd and ft)

12 9 ft (yd) **16** 120 in (ft)

17 How many yards are there in

  a $1\frac{1}{2}$ miles **b** $\frac{1}{4}$ mile **c** $\frac{1}{8}$ mile?

18 Andy walks to school along a main road. At the start of his journey, a road sign tells him it is $\frac{3}{4}$ mile to the junction where his school is. How many yards does he have to walk?

19 Josh has four cork tiles. Each tile is 14 inches square. He arranges them in a row to make a notice board. How long, in feet and inches, is the board?

20 Jane has a liquorice lace that is 2 feet long. She cuts it into 6 equal lengths. How long is each length?

21 Gold-coloured chain is sold in a street market at £1.50 per 4 inches. How much will 2 feet of this chain cost?

22 I passed a sign on a motorway saying 'Road works – 1 mile ahead'. The next sign I passed said 'Road works – 800 yards ahead'. How far apart are the two signs?

23 One lane on a motorway is closed by cones for a distance of 1 mile. The cones are placed 4 feet apart. How many cones are used?

Metric units of mass

The **mass** of an object is the quantity of matter in it; the **weight** of an object is the pull of the Earth on it and this is what we feel. When we put a bag of potatoes on a set of scales, we are measuring its weight but the units on the scales are units of mass. If the reading is 2.5 kg, the mass is 2.5 kg but, in everyday language, we say that the bag of potatoes weighs 2.5 kg, or that the weight is 2.5 kg.

The most familiar units used for weighing are the **kilogram** (kg) and the **gram** (g).

Most groceries that are sold in tins or packets have weights given in grams. For example, the weight of the most common packet of butter is 250 g and one eating apple weighs roughly 100 g. So we see that the gram is a small unit of weight. Kilograms are used to give the weights of sugar and flour; the weight of the most common bag of sugar is 1 kg and the most common bag of flour weighs 1.5 kg.

For weighing large loads (coal or steel, for example) a larger unit of weight is needed, and we use the **tonne** (t). For weighing very small quantities (for example, the weight of a particular drug in one pill) we use the **milligram** (mg).

The relationships between these weights are

$$1\,t\ = 1000\,kg$$
$$1\,kg = 1000\,g$$
$$1\,g\ = 1000\,mg$$

Exercise 9e

Worked example

→ Express 580 g in kilograms.

$$580\,g = 580 \div 1000\,kg$$
$$= 0.58\,kg$$

⟶ Express   2.35 t in grams.

$$2.35\,t = 2.35 \times 1000\,kg$$
$$= 2350\,kg$$
$$= 2350 \times 1000\,g$$
$$= 2\,350\,000\,g$$

 First change tonnes to kilograms, and then change kilograms to grams.

In questions **1** to **34**, express each quantity in terms of the unit given in brackets.

1 12 t (kg)

2 3 kg (g)

3 5 g (mg)

4 1 t (g)

5 1 kg (mg)

6 13 kg (g)

7 6 g (mg)

8 2 t (g)

9 4 kg (g)

10 2 kg (mg)

11 3 t (kg)

12 4 g (mg)

13 1.5 kg (g)

14 2.7 t (kg)

15 1.8 g (mg)

16 0.7 t (kg)

17 5.2 kg (mg)

18 0.6 g (mg)

19 11.3 t (kg)

20 2.5 kg (g)

21 7.3 g (mg)

22 0.3 kg (mg)

23 0.5 t (kg)

24 0.8 g (mg)

25 1500 kg (t)

26 3680 g (kg)

27 1500 mg (g)

28 5020 g (kg)

29 3800 kg (t)

30 86 kg (t)

31 560 g (kg)

32 28 mg (g)

33 190 kg (t)

34 86 g (kg)

35 Which is heavier, a locomotive weighing 86 tonnes or a loaded lorry weighing 39 800 kg?

36 Put these weights in order of size, with the lightest first.

3 t   900 kg   279 000 kg   279 000 g

37 Put these weights in order, with the heaviest first.

7900 mg   2.5 g   0.25 kg   79 g

Imperial units of mass

The imperial units of weight that are still used in everyday life are **stones**, **pounds** and **ounces**. (Most people know their weight in stones and pounds, and know a baby's weight in pounds and ounces.) Other units of weight that you may occasionally see are hundredweights and tons (not to be confused with tonnes).

The relationships between ounces, pounds and stones are

16 ounces (oz) = 1 pound (lb)   **14 pounds = 1 stone**

Exercise 9f

Express the given quantity in terms of the units given in brackets.

1 2 lb 6 oz (oz)

2 1 lb 12 oz (oz)

3 4 lb 3 oz (oz)

4 2 stone 3 lb (lb)

5 7 stone 6 lb (lb)

6 24 oz (lb and oz)

7 18 oz (lb and oz)

8 36 oz (lb and oz)

9 57 lb (stones and lb)

10 106 lb (stones and lb)

11 James went on a diet. Before he started, he weighed 10 stone 6 lb. How much did he weigh after losing 10 lb?

Adding and subtracting quantities

Jane has several items to carry home.
To find out the total weight of these items, she must add their weights.

Before we can add or subtract *any* two quantities, they must both be expressed in the same unit.

Now 250 g = 0.25 kg, and 454 g = 0.454 kg, so Jane has to carry (0.25 + 1.5 + 0.454) kg, i.e. 2.204 kg

Exercise 9g

Worked example

➡ Find   1 kg + 158 g in   **i** grams   **ii** kilograms.

i 1 kg = 1000 g

∴ 1 kg + 158 g = 1000 g + 158 g = 1158 g

ii 158 g = 158 ÷ 1000 kg

= 0.158 kg

∴ 1 kg + 158 g = 1 kg + 0.158 kg = 1.158 kg

➡ Find the sum of 5 m, 4 cm and 97 mm in   **i** metres   **ii** centimetres.

i   4 cm = 4 ÷ 100 m = 0.04 m

97 mm = 97 ÷ 1000 m = 0.097 m

5 m + 4 cm + 97 mm = (5 + 0.04 + 0.097) m

= 5.137 m

ii
$$5\,m = 5 \times 100\,cm = 500\,cm$$
$$97\,mm = 97 \div 10\,cm = 9.7\,cm$$
$$\therefore \quad 5\,m + 4\,cm + 97\,mm = (500 + 4 + 9.7)\,cm$$
$$= 513.7\,cm$$

Find, giving your answer in metres

1 5 m + 86 cm

2 92 cm + 115 mm

3 3 km + 136 cm

4 51 m + 3 km

5 36 cm + 87 mm + 520 cm

6 120 mm + 53 cm + 4 m

Find, giving your answer in millimetres

7 36 cm + 80 mm

8 5 cm + 5 mm

9 1 m + 82 cm

10 2 m + 45 cm + 6 mm

11 3 cm + 5 m + 2.9 cm

12 34 cm + 18 mm + 1 m

Find, giving your answer in grams

13 3 kg + 250 g

14 5 kg + 115 g

15 5.8 kg + 9.3 kg

16 1 kg + 0.9 kg + 750 g

17 116 g + 0.93 kg + 680 mg

18 248 g + 0.06 kg + 730 mg

Find, expressing your answer in kilograms

19 2 t + 580 kg

20 1.8 t + 562 kg

21 390 g+ 1.83 kg

22 1.6 t + 3.9 kg + 2500 g

23 1.03 t + 9.6 kg + 0.05 t

24 5.4 t + 272 kg + 0.3 t

Find, expressing your answer in terms of the unit given in brackets

25 8 m − 52 cm (cm)

26 52 mm + 87 cm (m)

27 1.3 kg − 150 g (g)

28 1.3 m − 564 mm (cm)

29 2.05 t + 592 kg (kg)

30 20 g − 150 mg (mg)

31 36 kg − 580 g (g)

32 1.5 t − 590 kg (kg)

33 3.9 m + 582 mm (cm)

34 0.3 m − 29.5 cm (mm)

Worked example

→ Find, in kilograms, the total weight of a bag of flour weighing 1.5 kg, a jar of jam weighing 450 g, and a packet of rice weighing 500 g.

The jar of jam weighs 450 g = 450 ÷ 1000 kg
$$= 0.45\,kg$$
The packet of rice weighs 500 g = 500 ÷ 1000 kg
$$= 0.5\,kg$$
The total weight = (1.5 + 0.45 + 0.5) kg
$$= 2.45\,kg$$

35 Subtract 52 kg from 0.8 t, giving your answer in kilograms.

36 Find the difference, in grams, between 5 g and 890 mg.

37 Find the total length, in millimetres, of a piece of wood 82 cm long and another piece of wood 260 mm long.

38 Find the total weight, in kilograms, of 500 g of butter, 2 kg of potatoes and 1.5 kg of flour.

39 One tin of baked beans weighs 220 g.
What is the weight, in kilograms, of ten of these tins?

40 One fence post is 150 cm long.
What length of wood, in metres, is needed to make ten such fence posts?

41 A wooden vegetable crate and its contents weigh 6.5 kg.
If the crate weighs 1.2 kg what is the weight of its contents?

For questions **42** to **50**, choose the most suitable unit for your answer.

42 A girl travels to school by walking 450 m to the bus stop and then travelling 1.65 km by bus. The distance she walks after getting off the bus is 130 m.
What distance is her total journey?

43 A man takes three parcels to the Post Office and has them weighed. One parcel weighs 4 kg 37 g, the weight of the second is 3 kg 982 g, and the third one weighs 1 kg 173 g.
What is their total weight?

44 A rectangular field is 947 m long and 581 m wide.
  a What is the perimeter of the field?
  b What length of fencing would be needed to go round the field leaving space for two gates, each 3 m wide?

45 Will these three kitchen units fit along a wall that is 300 cm long?

900 mm   400 mm   1500 mm

46 Janice bought two bags of bait for fishing. One bag weighed 12 oz and the other bag weighed 9 oz.
What is the total weight of this bait in pounds and ounces?

47 Apples are sold from a market at 64 p per lb. What is the cost of one of these apples weighing 3 oz?

48 Daniel has a 56 lb sack of potatoes. He weighs out half of this quantity on his bathroom scales, which measure in stones and pounds. What weight should show on the scales?

49 A freight train has five trucks. Two of them are carrying 15 t 880 kg each. Another has a load of 14 t 700 kg, and the last two are each loaded with 24 t 600 kg.
What is the total weight of the contents of the five trucks?
If the weight of each truck is 5 t 260 kg, what is the combined weight of the trucks and their contents?

50 A boy delivers newspapers by bicycle. The weight of the bicycle is 15.8 kg and the boy weighs 51.3 kg. At the beginning of the round the newspapers weigh 9.9 kg.
What is the total weight of the boy and his bicycle loaded with newspapers?
What is the weight when he has delivered half the newspapers?

51 Newton is 5.62 km from Old Town and Old Town is 3.87 km from Castletown.
If a car goes from Newton to Old Town, then to Castletown, and finally back to Old Town, how many metres has it travelled?
At the beginning of its journey the car had enough petrol to go 27 km. At the end of its journey how much further could it go before running out of petrol?

52 A ream of paper (500 sheets) weighs 2.8 kg.
   a How much does 1 sheet weigh?
   b If a letter weighs more than 100 g, it costs more than one first class stamp to post it. Ten of these sheets are put into an envelope. The envelope weighs 8 g.
   Will one first class stamp be enough to pay for the postage?

53 A damp patch on a wall rises up the wall by 5 cm every night and goes down by 3 cm during the day. The wall is 3.5 m high and the damp patch starts at the bottom of the wall.
If it carries on like this, how many days will it take the damp patch to reach the top of the wall?

54 If a box of bananas weighs 7 kg plus half its own weight, how much does a box and a half of bananas weigh?

Approximate equivalence between metric and imperial units

There are times when we need to convert metric units into imperial units and vice-versa. For example, Nadia needs to replace a $\frac{1}{2}''$ water pipe. Water pipes are now sold with diameters given in millimetres. So that Nadia can decide which is nearest to $\frac{1}{2}''$, it is useful to know that 1 in ≈ 2.5 cm, i.e. 25 mm, so $\frac{1}{2}''$ is about 12.5 mm.

This is easier to remember as

   4 in ≈ 10 cm

Remember: The symbol ≈ means 'is approximately equal to'.

Approximations for other units are

1 m ≈ 39 in	(so 1 m is slightly longer than 1 yard)
5 miles ≈ 8 km	(this means that 1 mile is less than 2 km)
1 kg ≈ 2.2 lb	(so 1 kg is a bit more than 2 lb)
1 lb ≈ 450 g	(so 1 lb is less than $\frac{1}{2}$ kg).

Exercise 9h

In questions **1** to **15**, write the first unit approximately in terms of the unit in brackets. Give answers correct to one decimal place where necessary.

1 3 kg (lb)	**6** 5 m (ft)	**11** 20 ft (m)
2 2 m (ft)	**7** 3.5 kg (lb)	**12** 800 g (lb)
3 4 lb (kg)	**8** 8 ft (m)	**13** 9 lb (kg)
4 9 ft (m)	**9** 250 g (oz)	**14** 50 m (ft)
5 1.5 kg (lb)	**10** 500 g (lb)	**15** 12 kg (lb)

Worked example

→ Use the approximation 5 miles ≈ 8 km to convert 60 miles into an approximate number of kilometres.

If 5 miles ≈ 8 km,
then 60 miles = 5 × 12 miles
$\qquad\qquad$ ≈ 8 × 12 km = 96 km

In questions **16** to **21**, use the approximation 5 miles ≈ 8 km to convert the given number of miles into an approximate number of kilometres.

16 10 miles	**18** 15 miles	**20** 75 miles
17 20 miles	**19** 100 miles	**21** 40 miles

22 I buy a 5 lb bag of potatoes and two 1.5 kg bags of flour.
What weight, approximately, in pounds do I have to carry?

23 A window is 6 ft high.
Roughly, what is its height in metres?

24 I have a picture which measures 2 ft by 1 ft. Wood for framing it is sold by the metre.
Roughly, what length of framing, in metres, should I buy?

25 The distance between London and Dover is about 70 miles.
The distance between Calais and Paris is about 270 km.
Which is the greater distance?

26 A recipe requires 250 g of flour.
Roughly, how many ounces is this?

27 An instruction in an old knitting pattern says knit 6 in.
Mary has a tape measure marked only in centimetres.
How many centimetres should she knit?

28 The instructions for re-potting a plant say that it should go into
a 10 cm pot. The flower pots that Tom has in his shed are marked
3 in, 4 in and 5 in.
Which one should he use?

29 Peter Stuart wishes to extend his central heating which was
installed several years ago using 1 in and $\frac{1}{2}$ in diameter copper
piping. The only new piping he can buy has diameters of 10 mm,
15 mm, 20 mm or 25 mm.
Use the approximation 1 in $\approx$ 2.54 cm to determine which piping
he should buy that would be nearest to
a the 1 in pipes
b the $\frac{1}{2}$ in pipes.

30 A carpenter wishes to replace a 6 in floorboard. The only sizes
available are metric and have widths of 12 cm, 15 cm, 18 cm and
20 cm. Which one should he buy?

31 Eddy knows his height is 4 ft 5 in. He needs to fill in a passport
application form and has to give his height in metres.
What should he enter for his height?

32 Wood is sometimes sold by the 'metric foot'. A metric foot is
30 cm. A man buys a length of wood which is 12 metric feet long.
How long is the piece of wood measured in feet?

33 The doctor tells Mr Brown that he needs to lose 10 kg in weight.
Mr Brown's scales at home show his weight now as 15 stone 6 lb.
What will his scales show when he has lost the required weight?

Mixed exercise

Exercise 9i

Express the given quantity in terms of the unit given in brackets.

1 4 km (m)   **5** 0.03 km (cm)   **9** 65 g (kg)

2 30 g (kg)   **6** 1250 m (km)   **10** $\frac{1}{2}$ a mile (yd)

3 3.5 m (cm)   **7** 1 m 50 cm (m)   **11** $2\frac{1}{4}$ lb (oz)

4 250 g (kg)   **8** 2.8 cm (mm)

12 A tin of meat weighs 429 g. What is the weight, in kilograms, of
ten such tins?

13 One pack of fun-size chocolate bars costs £3.60; the pack weighs 90 g and contains 15 bars.
   a   How much does each bar cost?
   b   How much does each bar weigh?

14 Estimate the lengths of these lines in metric units.

   a   ━━━━━━━━━━━━━
   b   ━━━━━━━━━━━━━━━━━
   c   ━━━━━━
   d   ━━━━━━━━━━━━━━━━━━━━

   Check your estimates by using your ruler.

15 Arrange these weights in order of size, with the lightest first.

   2 oz, 50 g, 0.04 kg, $\frac{1}{5}$ lb

16 Arrange these lengths in order of size, with the longest first.

   25 cm, 8 in, 25 mm, $1\frac{1}{8}$ in

Consider again

To order a new blind for a window, I need to give the width and height of the window. I can give these measurements by saying:

'as wide as my desk and from halfway up the wall to the top of the door' or

'96 centimetres wide and 102 centimetres high'.

What is better about the second way of giving the measurements?

David needs $1\frac{1}{2}$ lb of flour. He has a 1.5 kg bag of flour and a set of digital scales that weighs in grams and kilograms. Does David have enough flour? What does the reading on his scales need to be to get the correct amount of flour?

Now answer these questions.

Investigation

a This is a map of an island. Explain how you could estimate the length of its coastline.

b This is the same island, drawn to a larger scale. Would you get the same answer for the length of its coastline from this drawing?

c This shows the coastline of part of the island drawn to a much larger scale. If you used a map of the whole island drawn with this scale, how would your estimate of the length of the coastline compare with your first estimate?

d Do you think it is possible to measure the length of the coastline exactly? (Think of a bit of coastline you know and imagine measuring a short length of it.)

e Now suppose that you want to measure the length of the table you are sitting at. You could measure it with a ruler. You could measure it with a tape measure marked in centimetres and millimetres. You could measure it with a precision instrument that will read lengths to tenths of a millimetre, or even hundredths of a millimetre. You could measure the length in several different places.
Write down, with reasons, whether it is possible to find the length exactly.
Do you think it is possible to give any measurement exactly?

Summary 2

Sets

A set is a collection of objects that have something in common.

The objects are called members or elements. The members are listed inside curly brackets and separated by commas. For example, the set of even numbers from 0 to 9 is written as {2, 4, 6, 8}.

Venn diagrams

Venn diagrams represent sets by circles inside a rectangle.

This Venn diagram represents the sets A and B. The rectangle represents the universal set. This is a set that includes the members of A and B and possibly other members that are not in A or in B.

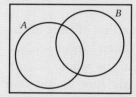

The intersection of the sets A and B is the set containing the members that are in both A and B and is written $A \cap B$. This is represented by the shaded region in the Venn diagram below.

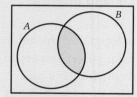

The union of the sets A and B is the set containing the members of A and the members of B. The union of A and B is written $A \cup B$ and is represented by the shaded region in the Venn diagram below.

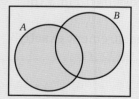

Fractions

The bottom number (denominator) of a fraction tells you how many equal-sized parts the whole quantity is divided into. The top number (numerator) tells you how many of these parts are being considered. For example, $\frac{2}{5}$ of a bar of chocolate means 2 out of the 5 equal-sized parts of the bar of chocolate.

Equivalent fractions are formed by multiplying or by dividing the top and the bottom of a fraction by the same number, for example

$$\frac{1}{2} = \frac{3}{6} \quad \text{and} \quad \frac{5}{10} = \frac{1}{2}$$

Percentages

A percentage of a quantity describes how many of the 100 equal-sized parts of the quantity are being considered, for example

20% of an apple means 20 out of the 100 equal-sized parts of the apple.

i.e. $20\% = \dfrac{20}{100}$

Decimals

In decimal notation, numbers to the right of the decimal point represent tenths, hundredths, thousandths, ...

e.g. $0.534 = \dfrac{5}{10} + \dfrac{3}{100} + \dfrac{4}{1000}$

Changing decimals to fractions

A decimal can be changed to a fraction by using the number after the decimal point as the numerator and 10, 100, 1000, ... as the denominator, for example

$$0.56 = \dfrac{56}{100} = \dfrac{14}{25} \qquad 0.025 = \dfrac{25}{1000} = \dfrac{1}{40}$$

Addition and subtraction of fractions

Fractions can be added or subtracted when they have the same denominator. For example, to add $\frac{1}{2}$ to $\frac{1}{3}$ we must first change them into equivalent fractions with the same denominators:

$$\dfrac{1}{2} + \dfrac{1}{3} = \dfrac{1}{2} \times \dfrac{3}{3} + \dfrac{1}{3} \times \dfrac{2}{2} = \dfrac{3}{6} + \dfrac{2}{6} = \dfrac{5}{6}$$

Addition and subtraction of decimals

Decimals can be added or subtracted using the same methods as for whole numbers, provided the decimal points are placed in line. For example, to add 12.56 and 7.9, we can write them as

$$\begin{array}{r} 12.56 \\ +\ \ 7.9 \\ \hline 20.46 \end{array}$$

Multiplying and dividing decimals by 10, 100, 1000, ...

To multiply a decimal by 10, 100, 1000, ... we move the point 1, 2, 3, ... places to the right,

e.g. $2.56 \times 10 = 25.6$ and $2.56 \times 1000 = 2560(.0)$

To divide a decimal by 10, 100, 1000, ... we move the point 1, 2, 3, ... places to the left,

e.g. $2.56 \div 10 = 0.256$ and $2.56 \div 1000 = 0.002\,56$

Multiplying decimals

To multiply decimals without using a calculator, first ignore the decimal point and multiply the numbers. Then add together the number of decimal places in each of the decimals being multiplied; this gives the number of decimal places in the answer,

e.g. $2.5 \times 0.4 = 1.00 = 1$ $(25 \times 4 = 100)$

   $[(1) + (1) = (2)]$

Dividing by a decimal

To divide by a decimal, move the point in *both* numbers to the right until the number we are dividing by is a whole number,

e.g. $2.56 \div 0.4 = 25.6 \div 4$

Now we can use ordinary division, keeping the decimal point in the same place,

e.g. $25.6 \div 4 = 6.4$ $4\overline{)25.6}^{\,6.4}$

Correcting decimals

To round (i.e. to correct) a number to a specified number of decimal places, look at the figure in the next decimal place: if it is 5 or more, add 1 to the previous figure, otherwise leave the previous figure as it is. For example, to write 2.564 correct to two decimal places, we have

$2.56 | 4 = 2.56$ (correct to two decimal places),

and to write 2.564 correct to one decimal place, we have

$2.5 | 64 = 2.6$ (correct to one decimal place).

Changing a fraction to a decimal

Fractions can be changed to decimal notation by dividing the bottom number into the top number,

e.g. $\frac{3}{8} = 3 \div 8 = 0.375$

Metric units

The metric units of length in common use are the kilometre, the metre, the centimetre and the millimetre, where

$1\,km = 1000\,m, \quad 1\,m = 100\,cm, \quad 1\,cm = 10\,mm$

The metric units of weight are the tonne, the kilogram, the gram and the milligram, where

$1\,tonne = 1000\,kg, \quad 1\,kg = 1000\,g, \quad 1\,g = 1000\,mg$

Imperial units

The imperial units of length in common use are the mile, the yard, the foot and the inch, where

$$1 \text{ mile} = 1760 \text{ yards}, \quad 1 \text{ yard} = 3 \text{ ft}, \quad 1 \text{ ft} = 12 \text{ in}$$

The imperial units of weight still in common use are the stone, the pound and the ounce, where

$$1 \text{ stone} = 14 \text{ lb}, \quad 1 \text{ lb} = 16 \text{ oz}$$

Equivalence between metric and imperial units

For a rough conversion between the two sets of units, use

$$\tfrac{1}{2} \text{ mile} \approx 1 \text{ km}, \quad 1 \text{ yard} \approx 1 \text{ m}, \quad 1 \text{ kg} \approx 2 \text{ lb},$$

For a better approximation, use

$$5 \text{ miles} \approx 8 \text{ km}, \quad 1 \text{ inch} \approx 2.5 \text{ cm}, \quad 1 \text{ kg} \approx 2.2 \text{ lb}$$

REVISION EXERCISE 2.1 (Chapters 5 to 7)

1 Change each fraction into an equivalent fraction with a denominator of 24.

  a $\frac{1}{3}$ **b** $\frac{3}{4}$ **c** $\frac{1}{6}$ **d** $\frac{7}{12}$ **e** $\frac{7}{8}$

2 Express as a decimal

  a $\frac{7}{10}$ **b** $\frac{7}{100}$ **c** $\frac{90}{100}$ **d** $\frac{31}{100}$

3 In a golf club $\frac{4}{5}$ of the members are men.

  a What percentage is this?

  b If there are 450 members, how many of them are men?

4 Express as a fraction in its lowest terms

  a 0.75   **b** 0.2   **c** 0.05   **d** 0.15

5 Due to a reduction in orders the workforce at a factory was reduced by 12%. What fraction is this?

6 Find

  a $\frac{1}{5} + \frac{1}{10}$ **b** $\frac{2}{3} + \frac{1}{7}$ **c** $1\frac{1}{3} + \frac{3}{4}$ **d** $4\frac{7}{12} - 2\frac{1}{6}$

7 Evaluate

  a $0.05 + 2.17$ **b** $31.7 + 5.34$ **c** $3.02 + 0.9$

8 Find

  a $\frac{2}{3} - \frac{1}{5}$ **b** $1\frac{1}{4} - \frac{1}{2}$ **c** $9\frac{1}{3} + 4\frac{5}{6}$

9 Find

  a $7.8 - 0.36$ **b** $3.59 - 1.2$

10 In 1970, about 3 households in every 10 did not have a car. What percentage of households

  a did not have a car   **b** had a car?

11 Draw a Venn diagram to illustrate the sets A = {prime numbers less than twenty}, B = {multiples of 3 less than twenty} with U = {positive whole numbers less than twenty}. Hence write down the set of numbers in U but not in either A or in B.

REVISION EXERCISE 2.2 (Chapters 8 and 9)

1 Find, without using a calculator,

    a 0.25×1.2 **c** $8.4 \div 0.02$

    b 12.03×0.5 **d** $45.6 \div 20$

2 a Estimate the value of $13.23 \div 21$, and then use a calculator to find its exact value.

   b Use a calculator to find $53.4 \div 9$ correct to two decimal places.

3 One box of biscuits costs £5.49. Find the cost of 10 of these boxes.

4 Express the given quantity in terms of the unit in brackets.

    a   480 cm (m)   **b**   2.5 kg (g)   **c**   0.05 g (mg)

5 Express the given quantity in terms of the unit in brackets.

    a   2 feet (inches)   **b**   2 stone (lb)   **c** $1\frac{1}{2}$ lb (oz)

6 How many inches, roughly, are equivalent to 60 cm?

7 Place these lengths in order of size with the smallest first.

     45 in,   573 mm,   0.78 km,   500 yd

8 Measure this line in millimetres.

What is the length of one quarter of this line?

9 Use this drawing to estimate the height, in millimetres, of the back of the lectern. The man is about 190 cm tall.

10 How far, roughly, is

    a   48 miles in kilometres

    b   100 kilometres in miles?

REVISION EXERCISE 2.3 (Chapters 5 to 9)

1 a Simplify the fractions.

    i $\frac{36}{48}$ **ii** $\frac{15}{25}$ **iii** $\frac{54}{90}$

  b Find

    i $\frac{4}{5} + \frac{3}{4}$ **ii** $1\frac{1}{2} - \frac{2}{3}$ **iii** $1\frac{1}{2} + \frac{2}{3}$

2 Express
  a 41 centimetres in millimetres
  b 3516 millimetres in metres
  c 7526 kg in tonnes

3 An alloy is 65% copper and the rest is tin.
  a What fraction of the alloy is copper?
  b Express the part that is tin as
    i a percentage
    ii a decimal
    iii a fraction in its lowest terms.

4 $U = \{\text{whole numbers from 1 to 10}\}$
$A = \{2, 4, 6, 8\}, B = \{3, 4, 5, 6\}$
  a Illustrate these sets on a Venn diagram.
  b Find **i** $A \cap B$ **ii** $A \cup B$

5 The diagram shows part of the display on a voltmeter.
What is the reading?

6 Place these weights in order of size, with the smallest first.

    2 lb,   3 kg, $\frac{1}{2}$ stone,   500 g,   40 oz

7 a Use your calculator to find
    i 8.76×5.2 **ii** 9.37×8.04
  b Use your calculator to find, correct to two decimal places
    i $4.37 \div 7.7$ **ii** $2193 \div 52$ **iii** $4.56 \div 6$

8 A piece of material is $2\frac{1}{8}$ yards long.
Carl cuts off a piece $1\frac{1}{3}$ yards long. What length is left?

9 One paving stone is 382 mm long. Estimate, in metres, the length of 37 of these paving stones placed end to end.

10 This piece of wood is 3.5 m long.
Liam cuts off a piece 1465 mm long.
How much is left?

REVISION EXERCISE 2.4 (Chapters 1 to 9)

1 What is the difference between 173 and 294?

2 Find, without using a calculator, the value of
    a 145×20
    b 803×40
    c $210 \div 30$

3 Which is the heavier, a 2 lb bag of apples or a 1 kg bag of oranges?

4 Pete writes down his height as 131 cm. Joanne writes down her height as 4 ft 5 in. Who is the taller and by how much?

5

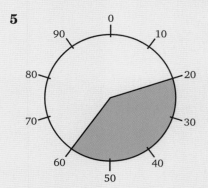

Express the part of the circle that is shaded as
    a   a percentage
    b   a decimal
    c   a fraction in its lowest terms.

6 To 0.74 add the sum of 4.089 and 0.77

7 The height of a pile of twenty 20 p coins is 34 mm. How thick is one coin?

8 Find, without using a calculator,
    a $\frac{3}{4} + \frac{5}{12}$
    b $\frac{9}{10} - \frac{2}{15}$

9 Express the given quantity in terms of the unit in brackets.
    a   4 ft 7 in (in)
    b   7 yd 1 ft (ft)

10 Eve wants to buy some 6 inch plant pots. At the garden centre she sees pots marked 10 cm, 15 cm, 20 cm and 25 cm. Which size should she buy?

11 a   Find the HCF of 30 and 100
     b   Find the LCM of 36 and 42

REVISION EXERCISE 2.5 (Chapters 1 to 9)

1 a Sally uses 3 kg of potatoes a day. How many days will a 50 kg bag last?

b Jean loads a ream of paper (500 sheets) into the tray of her photocopier. She has 23 sheets to copy and needs 20 copies of each sheet.
How many sheets of paper remain unused?

2 a Find, giving the remainder if there is one,

    i $429 \div 37$ **ii** $2193 \div 53$

b Find

    i $3\frac{7}{12} + 1\frac{1}{4}$ **ii** $5\frac{1}{4} - 2\frac{5}{8}$ **iii** $3 \times 5 - 4 \times 2 - 16 \div 4$

3 Find the sum of 3.07 and 0.76, and subtract the result from 7.56.

4 A rectangular table top, measuring 96 cm by 66 cm, is to be tiled with square ceramic tiles.
Find the size of the largest tile that can be used if there is to be no cutting.

5 Jim cleared 2.50 m in a high-jump competition.
Find the height of the bar in feet and inches given that
1 inch ≈ 2.54 cm.

6 Amy measured the length of a screw with a ruler. The reading was $1\frac{1}{4}$ inches. Write this measurement in decimal form.

7 Which is the larger
  a   10 in or 20 cm   **b**   3 yards or 3 metres?

8 Find the difference between
  a   8 g and 650 mg   **b**   0.5 tonnes and 64 kg
(Give each answer in the smaller unit.)

9 A piece of wood is 9 ft 4 in long. It is cut into 8 equal lengths.
How long is each piece?

10 The bar chart shows the number of £5, £10, £20 and £50 notes paid into a bank account by a businessman on a visit to the bank.

  a   How many £5 notes were paid in?

  b   What was the value of all the £10 notes paid in?

  c   How many notes did the bank teller have to count?

  d   What was the total value of the notes that were paid in?

163

Mental arithmetic practice 2

1 What is the simplest fraction equivalent to $\frac{18}{27}$?

2 Subtract 26 from 150.

3 Write 18 as the sum of two prime numbers.

4 Write 7 hundredths as a decimal.

5 Find 4 squared divided by 2.

6 Express 0.66 as a percentage.

7 Simplify $\frac{12}{18}$

8 Which is the larger: $\frac{4}{5}$ or $\frac{3}{4}$?

9 Find $7 + 3 \times 3$

10 Find 30% of 300.

11 What is the smallest whole number that 3 and 8 will divide into exactly?

12 What is 50% of 120?

13 Write 20 as the sum of two prime numbers.

14 Convert $\frac{4}{5}$ to a decimal.

15 What is the remainder when 48 is divided by 9?

16 Write twenty thousand and eight in figures.

17 Express 0.25 as a fraction in its lowest terms.

18 Which is the larger: 5.49 or 7.46?

19 Write $\frac{5}{8}$ as an equivalent fraction with 40 as the denominator.

20 What is the next prime number after 19?

21 Add 0.7 to 1.43

22 Change $5\frac{1}{3}$ to an improper fraction.

23 Add $\frac{3}{5}$ and $\frac{4}{5}$, giving your answer as a mixed number.

24 Find $6 - 0.04$

25 Write 19 hundredths as a decimal.

26 What is $\frac{1}{4} - \frac{1}{5}$?

27 Add 7, 11 and 6

28 What is $2.3 + 5$?

29 Which is smaller: $\frac{3}{16}$ or $\frac{3}{8}$?

30 Subtract 38 from 120

31 Add 0.005 to 2.1

32 Estimate 3954×312

33 Change $\frac{23}{5}$ to a mixed number.

34 Find $10 - 5.97$

35 What needs to be added to 16 to make 30?

36 Find the cost of 10 boxes of cereal at £1.27 each.

37 Divide 0.12 by 4.

38 John pays for a magazine costing £3.65 with a £5 note. How much change does he get?

39 How much is treble 17?

40 Which is larger: $\frac{1}{3}$ or 0.3?

41 Find $7.36 \div 100$

42 What is the prime number immediately before 29?

43 What needs to be added to 5.43 to make 8?

44 Express $\frac{3}{5}$ as an equivalent fraction with 15 as the numerator.

45 Which is larger: $\frac{3}{10}$ or 35%?

46 Give 5.357 correct to two decimal places.

47 Subtract 84 from 123

48 30% of the cars in a garage are red. What percentage are not red?

49 Find 0.08×0.03

50 Estimate 18.87×10.44

51 Find 1.8×100

52 What is 0.4×0.5?

53 What is the value of 3 cubed?

54 Find $0.36 \div 9$

55 A pile of six 1 p coins is 8.04 mm high. How thick is one coin?

56 Find 339×200

57 Express 7 km in metres.

58 Write down the multiples of 7 between 25 and 50.

59 Change $3\frac{3}{5}$ into an improper fraction.

60 Find $8 \times 3 - 9 \times 2$

Consider

Anna is planning the layout of her garden.
Below is her plan for a vegetable patch.

Give two reasons why this design will not work.

Opposite is Anna's revised plan.

Find the size of the missing angle.

You should be able to solve this problem after you have worked through this chapter.

Class discussion

1 How does the pilot of an aeroplane flying from London to Los Angeles measure the direction of the aircraft?

2 When the Channel Tunnel was built, it was necessary to measure direction very accurately. Discuss the consequences of poor measurements.

Can you think of other situations where we have to measure directions accurately?

To describe a direction we measure the amount of turning from some fixed direction. This fixed direction could be the main street in a town, the direction of true north or the position of the minute hand of a clock at a particular time. Having decided on the fixed direction, we measure the amount of turn needed to give the direction we want.

Fractions of a revolution

When the seconds hand of a clock starts at 12 and moves round until it stops at 12 again, it has gone through one complete turn.

One complete turn is called a **revolution**.

When the seconds hand starts at 12 and stops at 3, it has turned through $\frac{1}{4}$ of a revolution.

Exercise 10a

Worked example

What fraction of a revolution does the seconds hand of a clock turn through when

⟶ it starts at 3 and stops at 12

If the seconds hand starts at 3 and stops at 12, it turns through $\frac{3}{4}$ of a revolution.

⟶ it starts at 4 and stops at 8?

If the seconds hand starts at 4 and stops at 8, it turns through $\frac{1}{3}$ of a revolution.

What fraction of a revolution does the seconds hand of a clock turn through when it

1   starts at 12 and stops at 9
2   starts at 12 and stops at 6
3   starts at 6 and stops at 9
4   starts at 3 and stops at 9
5   starts at 9 and stops at 12
6   starts at 1 and stops at 7
7   starts at 5 and stops at 11

8   starts at 10 and stops at 4
9   starts at 8 and stops at 8
10 starts at 8 and stops at 11
11 starts at 10 and stops at 2
12 starts at 12 and stops at 4
13 starts at 8 and stops at 5
14 starts at 5 and stops at 2?

167

Worked example

→ Where does the hand stop if it starts at 12 and turns through $\frac{1}{4}$ of a revolution?

It stops at 3.

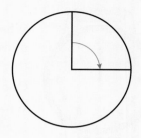

Where does the hand stop if

15 it starts at 12 and turns through $\frac{1}{2}$ a complete turn

16 it starts at 12 and turns through $\frac{3}{4}$ of a complete turn

17 it starts at 6 and turns through $\frac{1}{4}$ of a complete turn

18 it starts at 9 and turns through $\frac{1}{2}$ a complete turn

19 it starts at 6 and turns through a revolution

20 it starts at 9 and turns through $\frac{3}{4}$ of a revolution

21 it starts at 12 and turns through $\frac{1}{3}$ of a revolution

22 it starts at 12 and turns through $\frac{2}{3}$ of a revolution

23 it starts at 9 and turns through a revolution?

Compass directions

The four main **compass directions** are North, South, East and West.

If you stand facing North and turn clockwise through $\frac{1}{2}$ a revolution, you are then facing South.

Exercise 10b

1 If you stand facing West and turn anticlockwise through $\frac{3}{4}$ of a revolution, in which direction are you facing?

2 If you stand facing South and turn clockwise through $\frac{1}{4}$ of a revolution, in which direction are you facing?

3 If you stand facing North and turn, in either direction, through a complete revolution, in which direction are you facing?

4   If you stand facing West and turn through $\frac{1}{2}$ a revolution, in which direction are you facing? Does it matter if you turn clockwise or anticlockwise?

5   If you stand facing South and turn through $1\frac{1}{2}$ revolutions, in which direction are you facing?

6   If you stand facing West and turn clockwise to face South, what part of a revolution have you turned through?

7   If you stand facing East and turn to face West, what part of a revolution have you turned through?

Angles

When the hand of a clock moves from one position to another it has turned through an **angle**.

A quarter of a revolution is called a **right angle**.

Half a revolution is two right angles.

Exercise 10c

Worked example

→   How many right angles does the seconds hand of a clock turn through when it starts at 3 and stops at 12?

It turns through three right angles.

How many right angles does the seconds hand of a clock turn through when it

1   starts at 6 and stops at 9

2   starts at 3 and stops at 9

3   starts at 12 and stops at 9

4   starts at 3 and stops at 6

5   starts at 12 and stops at 12

6   starts at 8 and stops at 2

7   starts at 9 and stops at 6

8   starts at 7 and stops at 7?

How many right angles do you turn through if you

9 face North and turn clockwise to face South

10 face West and turn clockwise to face North

11 face South and turn clockwise to face West

12 face North and turn anticlockwise to face East

13 face North and turn to face North again?

Acute, obtuse and reflex angles

Any angle that is smaller than a right angle is called an **acute angle**.

Any angle that is greater than one right angle and less than two right angles is called an **obtuse angle**.

Any angle that is greater than two right angles is called a **reflex angle**.

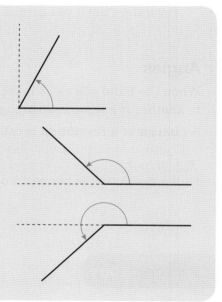

Exercise 10d

What type is each of the following angles?

1

2

3

4

5

6

7

8

9

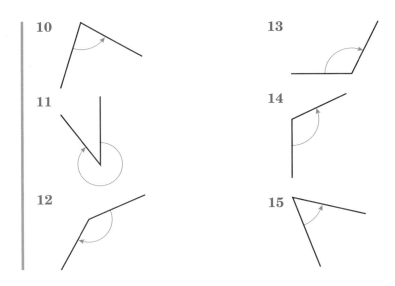

Degrees

One complete revolution is divided into 360 parts. Each part is called a *degree*. 360 degrees is written as 360°.

360 seems a strange number of parts to have in a revolution, but it is a good number because so many whole numbers divide into it exactly. This means that there are many fractions of a revolution that can be expressed as an exact number of degrees.

It is possible that the number 360 was chosen because thousands of years ago the Babylonians believed that the Sun took 360 days to complete one circuit of the Earth, i.e. to make a complete revolution.

Exercise 10e

1 How many degrees are there in half a revolution?

2 How many degrees are there in one right angle?

3 How many degrees are there in three right angles?

Worked example

→ How many degrees has the seconds hand of a clock turned through when it moves from 6 to 9?

It has turned through 90°.

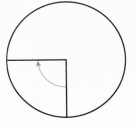

How many degrees has the seconds hand of a clock turned through when it moves from

4 12 to 6

5 3 to 6

6 6 to 3

7 9 to 3

8 9 to 6

9 2 to 5

10 7 to 10

11 1 to 10

12 8 to 5

13 4 to 10

14 5 to 8

15 6 to 12?

Worked example

$\rightarrow$ How many degrees has the seconds hand of a clock turned through when it moves from 6 to 8?

 When the hand moves from 6 to 8 it turns through $\frac{2}{12}$ revolution.

The hand turns through $\frac{2}{12}$ of 360°, i.e. 60°.

In questions **16** to **35**, how many degrees has the seconds hand of a clock turned through when it moves from

16 8 to 9

17 10 to halfway between 11 and 12

18 6 to 10

19 1 to 3

20 3 to halfway between 4 and 5

21 4 to 5

22 7 to 11

23 5 to 6

24 7 to 9

25 11 to 3

26 3 to 10

27 2 to 8

28 10 to 8

29 12 to 11

30 9 to 2

31 8 to 3

32 7 to 5

33 10 to 5

34 11 to 4

35 2 to 9?

36 You wish to divide a complete turn into an exact number of parts.
Is 360 a good number?
Try dividing 360 by each of the whole numbers from 1 to 12.
Now do the same for 100.
Which is the better number of degrees to have in one complete turn, 100 or 360?
Give reasons for your choice.

Using a protractor to measure angles

A **protractor** looks like this:

It has a straight line at or near the straight edge. This line is called the *base line*. The *centre* of the base line is marked.

The protractor has two scales, an inside one and an outside one.

To measure the size of this angle, first decide whether it is acute or obtuse.

This is an acute angle because it is *less* than 90°.

Next place the protractor on the angle as shown.

One arm of the angle is on the base line.

The vertex (point) of the angle is at the centre of the base line.

Choose the scale that starts at 0° on the arm on the base line. Read off the number where the other arm cuts this scale.

Check: Look at your earlier decision about the size of the angle to make sure that you have chosen the right scale.

Exercise 10f

Measure the following angles. (If necessary, turn the page to a convenient position.)

1

2

3

6

7

4

5

8

9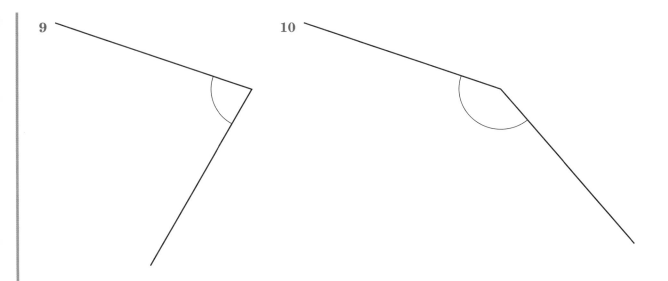

10

Worked example

→ Find the size of the angle marked *p*.

Angle *p* and 40° together make 360°.
So angle *p* is 360° − 40° = 320°.

In questions **11** to **15**, write down the size of the angle marked with a letter.

11

14

12

15

13

Worked example

 Measure the following angle.

This is a reflex angle and it is bigger than 3 right angles, i.e. it is greater than 270°.

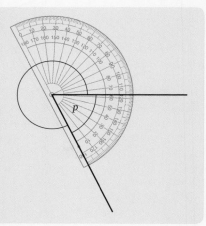

To find this angle, we need to measure the smaller angle, marked p.

Angle p is 64°, so the reflex angle is $360° - 64° = 296°$.

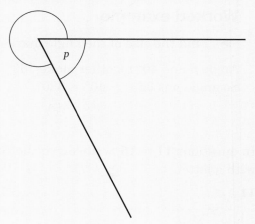

Measure the following angles.

16

18

17

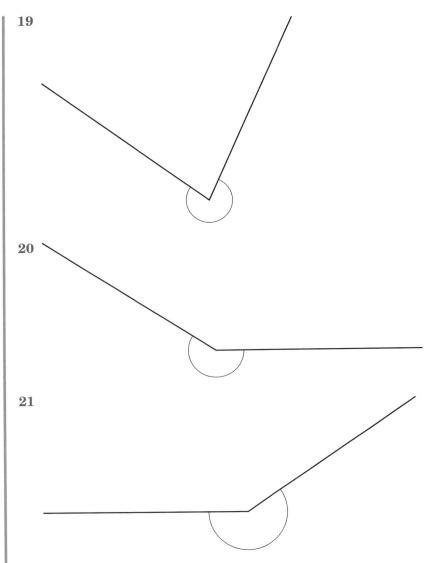

19

20

21

22 Draw a reflex angle. Now find its size.
Swap books with your neighbour and check each other's measurement.

Exercise 10g

This exercise contains mixed questions on angles.
Use a clock diagram to draw the angle that the *minute* hand of a clock turns through in the following times. In each question, write down the size of the angle in degrees.

1	5 minutes	3	15 minutes	5	25 minutes
2	10 minutes	4	20 minutes	6	30 minutes

The seconds hand of a clock starts at 12. Which number is it pointing
to when it has turned through an angle of

7 90°	**11** 150°	**15** 420°	**19** 540°
8 60°	**12** 270°	**16** 180°	**20** 240°
9 120°	**13** 30°	**17** 450°	**21** 390°
10 360°	**14** 300°	**18** 210°	**22** 720°?

Worked example

If you stand facing North and turn clockwise, draw a sketch
to show roughly the direction in which you are facing if you
turn through 60°.

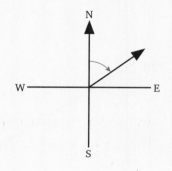

If you start by facing North and turn clockwise, draw a sketch to show roughly
the direction in which you are facing if you turn through the following angles.

23 45°	**26** 50°	**29** 20°	**32** 10°
24 70°	**27** 200°	**30** 100°	**33** 80°
25 120°	**28** 300°	**31** 270°	**34** 250°

Estimate the size, in degrees, of each of the following angles.

35   **38**   **41**   **44**

36   **39**   **42**   **45**

37   **40**   **43**   **46**

Draw the following angles as well as you can by estimating, i.e. without using a protractor. Use a clockface if it helps. Then measure your angles with a protractor.

47 45°	**52** 10°	**57** 5°
48 90°	**53** 150°	**58** 170°
49 120°	**54** 200°	**59** 330°
50 30°	**55** 290°	**60** 95°
51 60°	**56** 20°	**61** 250°

Drawing angles using a protractor

To draw an angle of 120°, start by drawing one arm and mark the corner of your angle.

The corner, or point, of an angle is called the **vertex**.

Place your protractor as shown in the diagram. Make sure that the vertex is at the centre of the base line.

Choose the scale that starts at 0° on your drawn line, and mark the paper next to the 120° mark on the scale.

Remove the protractor and join your mark to the vertex.

Now look at your angle: does it look the right size?

Exercise 10h

Use your protractor to draw the following angles accurately.

1 25°	**6** 15°	**11** 175°
2 37°	**7** 110°	**12** 72°
3 55°	**8** 49°	**13** 105°
4 160°	**9** 65°	**14** 136°
5 83°	**10** 125°	**15** 85°

Swap books with your neighbour and measure each other's angles as a check on accuracy.

Exercise 10i

In questions **1** and **2**, first measure the angle marked r.
Then estimate the size of the angle marked s.
Check your estimate by measuring angle s.

1

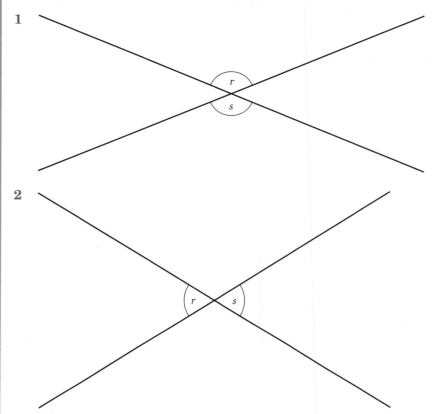

2

3 Draw some more similar diagrams, and repeat questions **1** and **2**.

In questions **4** to **9**, write down the size of the angle marked t, without measuring it.

4

150°

6

65°

8

140°

5

35°

7

20°

9

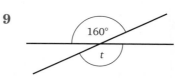
160°

Vertically opposite angles

When two straight lines cross, four angles are formed.

The two angles that are opposite each other are called **vertically opposite angles**. After working through the last exercise you should now be convinced that

Vertically opposite angles are equal.

i.e. $p = r$ and $s = q$

Angles on a straight line

The seconds hand of a clock starts at 9 and stops at 11 and then starts again and finally stops at 3.

Altogether the seconds hand has turned through half a revolution, so $p + q = 180°$.

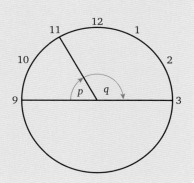

Exercise 10j

1. Draw a diagram showing the two angles that you turn through if you start by facing North and then turn clockwise through 60°, stop for a moment and then continue turning until you are facing South. What is the sum of these two angles?

2. Draw a clock diagram to show the two angles turned through by the seconds hand if it is started at 2, stopped at 6, started again and finally stopped at 8. What is the sum of these two angles?

3. Draw an angle of 180°, without using your protractor.

4. Angelo asks you what an angle of 180° is. Write down how you would answer Angelo.

Supplementary angles

Angles on a straight line add up to 180°.

Two angles that add up to 180° are called supplementary angles.

181

Exercise 10k

Worked example

→ Find the size of the angle marked with a letter.

$d + 150° = 180°$
$\therefore \qquad d = 30°$

In questions **1** to **12,** calculate the size of the angle marked with a letter.

1

5

2

6

3

7

4

8

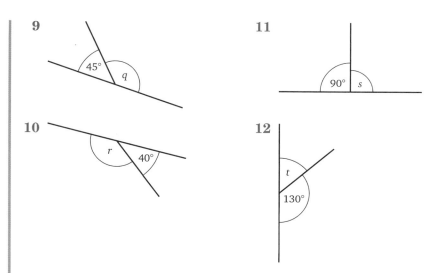

9 45° q

11 90° s

10 r 40°

12 t 130°

In questions **13** to **18**, write down the pairs of angles that are supplementary.

13 d e f

16 e d f g

14 n g f e k j m d

17 f g e d

15 d g f e

18 g h f e m p n d i j k l

Worked example

$\rightarrow$ Calculate the size of each angle marked with a letter.

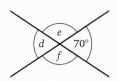

d and 70° are equal
They are vertically opposite.
$\therefore$ $d = 70°$
e and 70° add up 180°
They are angles on a straight line.
$\therefore$ $e = 110°$
f and *e* are equal
They are vertically opposite.
$\therefore$ $f = 110°$
Note: Reasons are given for statements made about angles.

In questions **19** to **24**, calculate the sizes of the angles marked with a letter.

19

20

21

22

23

24

Angles at a point

When several angles make a complete revolution they are called **angles at a point**.

Angles at a point add up to 360°.

Exercise 10l

Worked example

→ Calculate the size of the angle marked with a letter.

The three given angles add up to 250°.

∴ $d = 360° - 250°$
      $d = 110°$

$$
\begin{array}{r}
30 \\
200 \\
+\ 20 \\
\hline
250
\end{array}
$$

Find the size of the angle marked with a letter. Show your working and give reasons.

1

6

2

7

3

8

4

9

5

10

11 Find each of the equal angles marked *s*.

12 Find each of the equal angles marked *d*.

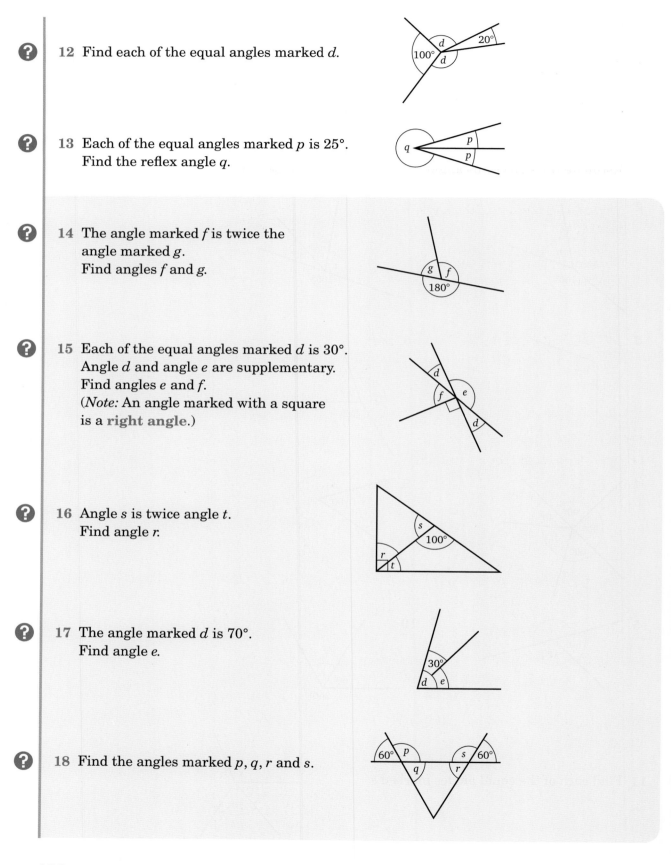

13 Each of the equal angles marked *p* is 25°.
Find the reflex angle *q*.

14 The angle marked *f* is twice the
angle marked *g*.
Find angles *f* and *g*.

15 Each of the equal angles marked *d* is 30°.
Angle *d* and angle *e* are supplementary.
Find angles *e* and *f*.
(*Note:* An angle marked with a square
is a **right angle**.)

16 Angle *s* is twice angle *t*.
Find angle *r*.

17 The angle marked *d* is 70°.
Find angle *e*.

18 Find the angles marked *p*, *q*, *r* and *s*.

Mixed exercise

Exercise 10m

1   What angle does the minute hand of a clock turn through when it moves from 1 to 9?

2   Draw an angle of 50°.

3   Estimate the size of this angle.

4   Write down the size of the angle marked p.

5   Write down the size of the angle marked s.

6   Find each of the equal angles marked e.

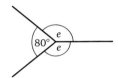

Consider again

Below is Anna's plan for a vegetable patch.

Now can you give two reasons why this design will not work?

Opposite is Anna's revised plan.

Now can you find the size of the missing angle?

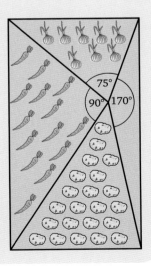

! Investigation

a   How do you find the angle turned through by the
    hour hand of a clock in a given time?

    Start by finding the angle turned through in
    12 hours, then the angle for any other complete
    number of hours.

    Next find the angle turned through for any
    fraction of an hour and, lastly, through a number
    of minutes.

b   Extend your investigation to the minute hand and
    the seconds hand.

c   How do you find the angle between the hands of a
    clock at any time?

    Start with times that give you the angles that are easiest to find.
    Remember that at 4.30 the minute hand will point to the 6, and
    the hour hand will be exactly halfway between 4 and 5.

d   Find out how many times there are in a day when the angle
    between the hour hand and the minute hand has a particular
    value – say 90°, 180° or 120°.

e   What happens if the clock loses 10 minutes each hour?

    How many degrees would the minute hand turn through in
    1 hour, or 15 minutes, or any other time?

f   What happens if the clock gains 5 minutes every hour?

11 Symmetry

Consider

How many different ways are there of describing the shape of this figure?

Can you draw this figure using just a written description of it?

You should be able to solve this problem after you have worked through this chapter.

To most people symmetrical shapes are pleasing to the eye.

These shapes are all around us, whether they are shapes that occur in nature such as a snowflake or an open flower, or human-made things like an aircraft or a suspension bridge.

Class discussion

Name some everyday objects that are symmetrical.

Line symmetry

The four shapes above are **symmetrical**. If they were folded along the broken line, one half of the drawing would fit exactly over the other half.

Fold a piece of paper in half and cut a shape from the folded edge. When unfolded, the resulting shape is symmetrical. The fold line is the **axis of symmetry**.

Exercise 11a

Some of the shapes below have one axis of symmetry and some have none. State which of the drawings **1** to **6** have an axis of symmetry.

1

4

2

5

3

6

Copy the following drawings on squared paper and complete them so that the broken line is the axis of symmetry.

7

8

9

10 **11** **12**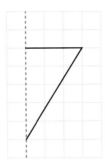

13 Copy and complete each letter so that the dashed lines are lines of symmetry.

Two axes of symmetry

In these shapes there are two lines along which it is possible to fold the paper so that one half fits exactly over the other half.

Fold a piece of paper twice, cut a shape as shown and unfold it.
The resulting shape has two axes of symmetry.

Exercise 11b

How many axes of symmetry are there in each of the following shapes?

1 **2** **3**

191

4   **5**   **6**

Copy the following drawings on squared paper and complete them so that the two broken lines are the two axes of symmetry.

7

10

8

11

9

12

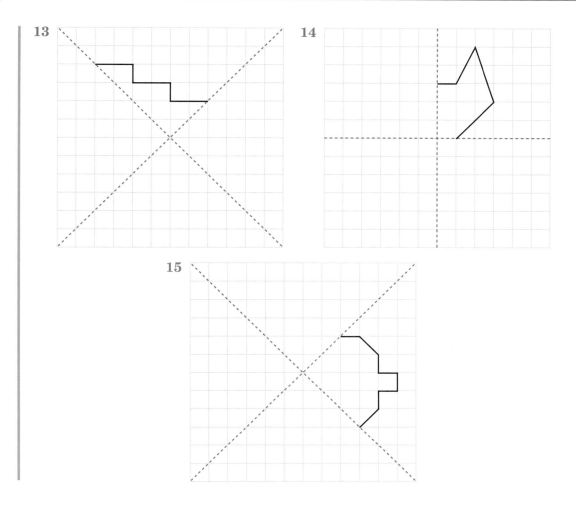

Three or more axes of symmetry

It is possible to have more than two axes of symmetry.

3 axes

4 axes

5 axes

Exercise 11c

How many axes of symmetry are there for each of the shapes in questions **1** to **4**?

1

3

2

4

5 Fold a square piece of paper twice, then fold it a third time along the broken line. Cut a shape, simple or complicated, and unfold the paper. How many axes of symmetry does it have?

6 Copy the triangle on squared paper and mark in the axis of symmetry.

A triangle with an axis of symmetry is called an **isosceles triangle**.

7 Copy the quadrilateral on squared paper and mark in the two axes of symmetry.

This quadrilateral (which has four equal sides) is called a **rhombus**.

8 Trace the triangle. Draw its axes of symmetry. Measure its three sides.

This triangle is called an **equilateral triangle**.

Rotational symmetry

These shapes have a different type of symmetry. They cannot be folded in half but can be turned or rotated about a centre point (marked with ×) and still look the same.

This is called **rotational symmetry**.

Exercise 11d

1   Lay a piece of tracing paper over any one of the shapes above, trace it and turn it about the cross until it fits over the shape again.

Which of the following shapes have rotational symmetry?

2

5

3

6

4

7

Some shapes have both **line symmetry** and rotational symmetry:

8 Sketch the capital letters of the alphabet.
  Mark any axes of symmetry and the centre of
  rotation if it exists.
  For example, draw H.

9 Which of the shapes in Exercise 11c have
  rotational symmetry?

10 Use the letters I, M, W, S and S to form a five-letter word that
   has rotational symmetry – i.e. it reads exactly the same upside
   down.

Congruence

The diagram below was drawn on a computer. Triangle A was drawn first. The other
triangles were obtained by copying A in various ways, including turning it over and round.
All the triangles are exactly the same shape and size. If they were cut out, they would fit
exactly over each other.

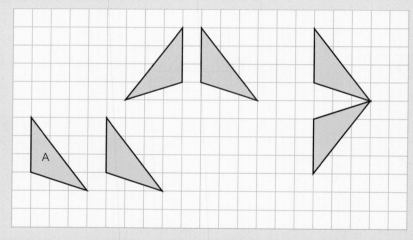

Any two figures that are exactly the same shape and size are called **congruent** figures.

Exercise 11e

In questions **1** to **11**, state whether or not the two figures are
congruent. If you are not sure, trace one figure and see if the tracing
will fit over the other figure. If necessary, turn the tracing over.

1

2

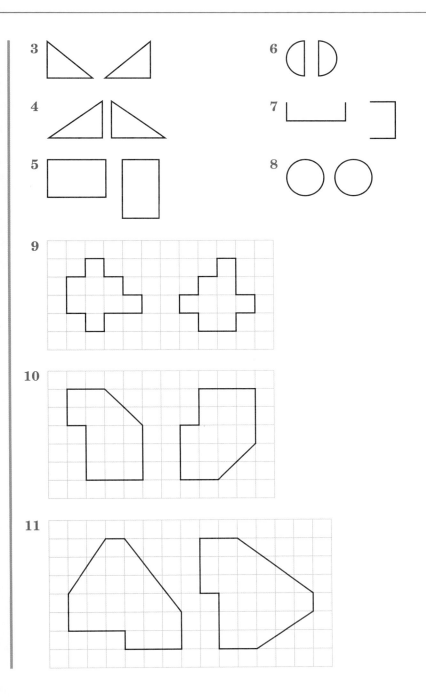

3

4

5

6

7

8

9

10

11

Consider again

Now can you give some different ways of describing the shape of this figure?

Can you draw this figure using just a written description of it?

Investigation

1 In this investigation, squares must meet along complete edges.

Two squares can be put together to give just one shape that has at least one line of symmetry.

There are two ways in which three squares can be arranged to give shapes that have at least one line of symmetry.

Investigate how many different shapes can be made that have at least one line of symmetry, when 4, 5, 6, … squares are used to make a shape.

Is there any connection between the number of squares used and the number of different shapes that satisfy the given condition?

2 Draw a clockface without hands, like this one. Although there are no numbers on the clockface, assume that the 12 is at the top, in its normal position.

a How many axes of symmetry does this face have?

b How many axes of symmetry would it have if the position of the 12 was marked with a double line?

c Repeat parts **a** and **b** if the numbers 1 to 12 are added to the face.

d The time on this clockface is 6 o'clock. What we see is symmetrical about a vertical line drawn through the centre of the clock.

Can you find any other time when the position of the hands is symmetrical about this vertical line through the centre?

Would your answer be the same if the hour hand and minute hand were the same length?

Illustrate your answers with sketches.

e The sketch shows that the time is 2.25. Make a copy and mark the position of the hour hand and the position of the minute hand when they are reflected in the broken line. (It is probably better to do this in a different colour.) Do the reflected hands give an acceptable time? If so, what time is it?

f

Actual time	'Reflected' time
1.55	
2.50	
3.45	
4.40	
5.35	
6.30	
7.25	
8.20	
9.15	
10.10	
11.05	

Copy this table and for each time shown

  i draw this clockface and mark in the time

 ii mark (in a different colour) the position of the hands if they are reflected in the broken line

iii complete the corresponding 'reflected' time in the table.

Can you see a connection between the actual times and the 'reflected' times?

g Draw the horizontal broken line through the centre.

Mark the time 1.10.

Draw the position of the hands if they are reflected in the broken line.

Is the 'reflected' time an acceptable time? Justify your answer.

h In part **a** you found several axes of symmetry for the clockface without hands. Do any of your lines of symmetry give possible 'reflected' times for actual times of your own choice?

12 Triangles and quadrilaterals

Consider

The pictures show a roof truss for a house and part of a railway bridge. After these have been designed they need to be drawn accurately before they can be made.

What information do you need to be able to draw the roof truss accurately on paper?

How can an accurate drawing of one side of the bridge be made?

You should be able to solve these problems after you have worked through this chapter.

To make accurate drawings of simple shapes on paper you need
- a sharp pencil
- a ruler
- a pair of compasses
- a protractor.

Using a pair of compasses

We use a pair of compasses to draw a **circle** or an arc of a circle.

The length of the edge of a circle is called the **circumference**.

Part of the circumference of the circle is called an **arc**.

All points on the circle are the same distance from the centre.

A straight line drawn from the centre of a circle to the circumference is a **radius**.

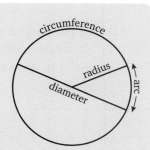

A straight line drawn through the centre of a circle from edge to edge is a **diameter**.

Using a pair of compasses needs practice.
- Draw several circles.

Make some of them small and some large.

You should not be able to see the place where you start and finish.

- Draw a circle of radius 7 cm.
- Draw a diameter of the circle and measure it.

Is it the correct length?

- Now try drawing the daisy pattern below.

Draw a circle of radius 5 cm. Keeping the radius the same, put the point of the compasses at A and draw an arc to meet the circle in two places, one of which is B. Move the point to B and repeat. Carry on moving the point of your compasses round the circle until the pattern is complete.

- Repeat the daisy pattern, but this time draw complete circles instead of arcs.

There are some more patterns using compasses on page 223.

Drawing straight lines of a given length

To draw a straight line that is 5 cm long, start by using your ruler to draw a line that is *longer* than 5 cm.

Then mark a point on this line near one end as shown. Label it A.

Next set your compasses to measure 5 cm on your ruler.

Then put the point of the compasses on the line at A and draw an arc to cut the line as shown.

The length of line between A and B should be 5 cm. Measure it with your ruler.

Exercise 12a

Draw, as accurately as you can, straight lines of the following lengths.

1	6 cm	**5**	8.5 cm
2	2 cm	**6**	3.5 cm
3	12 cm	**7**	4.5 cm
4	9 cm	**8**	6.8 cm

Triangles

A triangle has three sides and three angles.

The corners of the triangle are called **vertices**. (One corner is called a **vertex**.) So that we can refer to one particular side, or to one particular angle, we label the vertices using capital letters.

In the diagram above we used the letters A, B and C so we can now talk about 'the triangle ABC' or '△ABC'.

- The side between A and B is called 'the side AB' or AB.
- The side between A and C is called 'the side AC' or AC.
- The side between B and C is called 'the side BC' or BC.

The angle at the corner A is called 'angle A' or $\hat{A}$ for short.

We can also describe the angle at A using the three letters on the arms that enclose it, with A in the middle, i.e. $C\hat{A}B$ or $B\hat{A}C$.

Exercise 12b

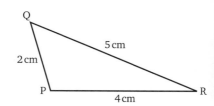

1 Write down the name of the side which is 4 cm long.
Write down the name of the side which is 2 cm long.

2 Write down the name of

   a the side which is 2.5 cm long

   b the side which is 2 cm long

   c the angle which is 70°.

In questions **3** to **6**, draw a freehand copy of the triangle and mark the given measurements on your drawing.

3 In △ABC, AB = 4 cm, $\widehat{B}$ = 60°, $\widehat{C}$ = 50°.

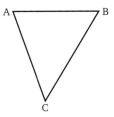

4 In △DEF, $\widehat{E}$ = 90°, $\widehat{F}$ = 70°, EF = 3 cm.

5 In △LMN, $\widehat{L}$ = 100°, $\widehat{N}$ = 30°, NL = 2.5 cm.

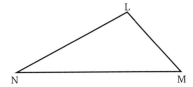

6 In △FGH, FG = 3.5 cm, GH = 3 cm, $\widehat{H}$ = 35°.

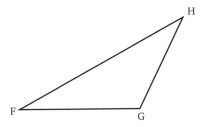

Make a freehand drawing of the triangles in questions **7** to **10**. Label each one and mark the measurements given.

7 △ABC in which AB = 10 cm, BC = 8 cm and $\widehat{B}$ = 60°

8 △PQR in which $\widehat{P}$ = 90°, $\widehat{Q}$ = 30° and PQ = 6 cm

9 △DEF in which DE = 8 cm, $\widehat{D}$ = 50° and DF = 6 cm

10 △XYZ in which XY = 10 cm, $\widehat{X}$ = 30° and $\widehat{Y}$ = 80°

Angles of a triangle

Draw a large triangle of any shape. Use a straight edge to draw the sides. Measure each angle in this triangle, turning your page to a convenient position when necessary. Add up the sizes of the three angles.

Draw another triangle of a different shape. Again measure each angle and then add up their sizes.

Now try this: on a piece of paper draw a triangle of any shape and cut it out. Next tear off each corner and place the three corners together.

They should look like this:

The three angles of a triangle add up to 180°.

Exercise 12c

Worked example

➤ Find the size of angle A.

$\widehat{A} + 57° + 42° = 180°$ (*angles of △ add up to 180°*)

$\therefore \quad \widehat{A} = 180° - 99°$
$\qquad = 81°$

$$\begin{array}{r} 57 \\ + \ 42 \\ \hline 99 \\ \hline \end{array}$$

Find the size of angle A. (An angle marked with a square is a **right angle**.)

1

2

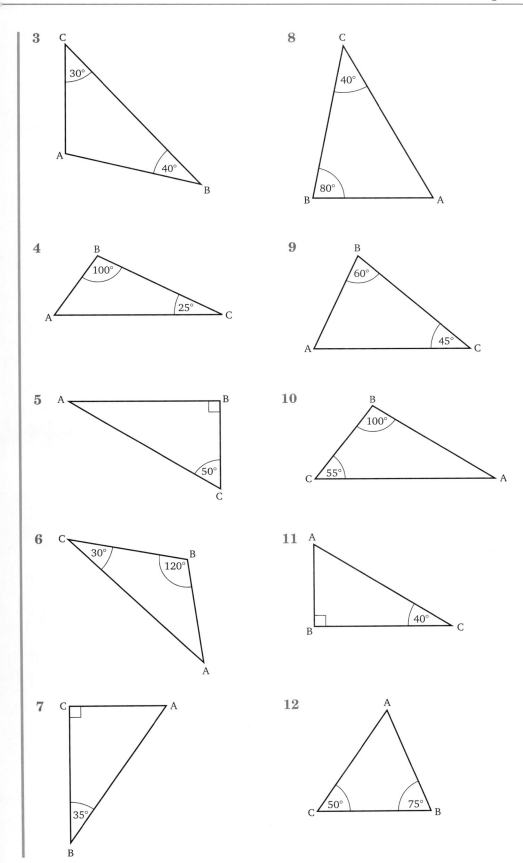

3

C 30°

A

40° B

4

B 100°

A

25° C

5

A B

50°

C

6

C 30°

B 120°

A

7

C

A

35°

B

8

C 40°

B 80°

A

9

B 60°

A

45° C

10

B 100°

C 55°

A

11

A

B

40° C

12

A

C 50°

75° B

13

15

14

Remember these facts which are needed for the remaining questions in this exercise:

Vertically opposite angles **are equal.**

Angles on a straight line add up to 180°.

In questions **16** to **25**, make a rough copy of the diagram, and mark the sizes of the angles that you are asked to find.

16 Find angles d and f.

17 Find angles s and t.

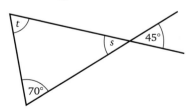

18 Find each of the equal angles x.

19 Find angles *p* and *q*.

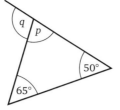

20 Find each of the equal angles *g*.

21 Find each of the equal angles *x*.

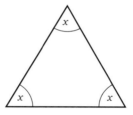

22 Find angles *s* and *t*.

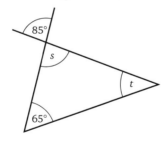

23 Angle *h* is twice angle *j*. Find angles *h* and *j*.

24 Find each of the equal angles *q* and angle *p*.

25

This section of a roof is symmetrical about the vertical line through its highest point. Find the angles marked p, q, r and s.

Constructing triangles given one side and two angles

If we are given enough information about a triangle, we can make an accurate drawing of that triangle. The mathematical word for 'make an accurate drawing of' is **construct**.

For example: construct $\triangle ABC$ in which $AB = 7\,\text{cm}$, $\widehat{A} = 30°$ and $\widehat{B} = 40°$.

First make a rough sketch of $\triangle ABC$ and put all the given measurements in your sketch.

Next draw the line AB making it 7 cm long. Label the ends.

Then use your protractor to make an angle of 30° at A.

Next make an angle of 40° at B. If necessary, extend the arms of the angles until they cross; this is the point C.

We can calculate $A\widehat{C}B$ because all three angles add up to $180°$, so $A\widehat{C}B = 110°$.

Now as a check we can measure $A\widehat{C}B$ in our construction.

Exercise 12d

Construct the following triangles.
Calculate the third angle in each triangle and then measure this angle to check the accuracy of your construction.

1

2

3

4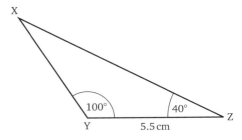

5 △UVW in which $\widehat{V} = 35°$, VW = 5.5 cm, $\widehat{W} = 75°$

6 △FGH in which $\widehat{F} = 55°$, $\widehat{G} = 70°$, FG = 4.5 cm

7 △KLM in which KM = 10 cm, $\widehat{K} = 45°$, $\widehat{M} = 45°$

Constructing triangles given two sides and the angle between the two sides

To construct △PQR in which PQ = 4.5 cm, PR = 5.5 cm and $\widehat{P}$ = 35°, first draw a rough sketch of △PQR and put in all the measurements that you are given.

Draw one of the sides whose length you know; we will draw PQ.

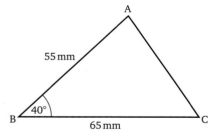

Now use your protractor to make an angle of 35° at P. Make the arm of the angle quite long.

Next use your compasses to measure the length of PR on your ruler.

Then with the point of your compasses at P, draw an arc to cut the arm of the angle.

This is the point R.

Now join R and Q.

Exercise 12e

Construct each of the following triangles, and measure the third side.

1

2

3

4

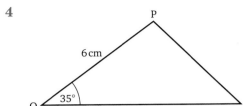

5 △HJK in which HK = 4.2 cm, $\widehat{H}$ = 45°, HJ = 5.3 cm

6 △ABC in which AC = 6.3 cm, $\widehat{C}$ = 48°, CB = 5.1 cm

7 △XYZ in which $\widehat{Y}$ = 65°, XY = 3.8 cm, YZ = 4.2 cm

Constructing triangles given the lengths of the three sides

To construct △XYZ in which XY = 5.5 cm, XZ = 3.5 cm and YZ = 6.5 cm, first draw a rough sketch of the triangle and put in all the given measurements.

Next draw one side; we will draw XY.

Then with your compasses measure the length of XZ from your ruler. With the point of your compasses at X draw a wide arc.

Next use your compasses to measure the length of YZ from your ruler. Then with the point of your compasses at Y draw another large arc to cut the first arc. Where the two arcs cross is the point Z. Join ZX and ZY.

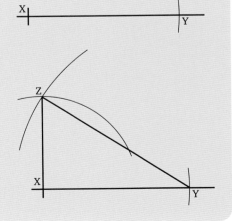

Exercise 12f

Construct the following triangles.

1

2

3

4

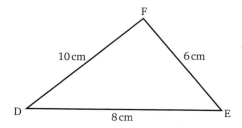

5 △ABC in which AB = 7.3 cm, BC = 6.1 cm, AC = 4.7 cm

6 △DEF in which DE = 10.4 cm, EF = 7.4 cm, DF = 8.2 cm

7 △PQR in which PQ = 8.8 cm, QR = 6.6 cm, PR = 11 cm

Exercise 12g

Construct the following triangles. Remember to draw a rough sketch of the triangle first and then decide which method you need to use.

1 △ABC in which AB = 7 cm, $\widehat{A}$ = 30°, $\widehat{B}$ = 50°

2 △PQR in which PQ = 50 mm, QR = 40 mm, RP = 70 mm

3 △BCD in which $\widehat{B}$ = 60°, BC = 5 cm, BD = 4 cm

4 △WXY in which WX = 5 cm, XY = 6 cm, $\widehat{X}$ = 90°

5 △KLM in which KL = 64 mm, LM = 82 mm, KM = 126 mm

6 △ABC in which $\widehat{A}$ = 45°, AC = 8 cm, $\widehat{C}$ = 110°

7 △CDE in which CD = DE = 60 mm, $\widehat{D}$ = 60°

8 Try to construct a triangle ABC in which $\widehat{A}$ = 30°, AB = 5 cm, BC = 3 cm.

9 Construct two triangles which fit the following measurements:
△PQR in which $\widehat{P}$ = 60°, PQ = 6 cm, QR = 5.5 cm.

10 Construct △ABC in which $\widehat{A}$ = 120°, AB = 4 cm, BC = 6 cm. Can you construct more than one triangle that fits these measurements?

11 You can cut a triangle into 4 smaller triangles using just three cuts.
Here is one way of doing it.
Can you find other ways?

12 Find a way of cutting an equilateral triangle into four pieces so that the pieces fit together to form a square.

Quadrilaterals

A **quadrilateral** has four straight sides. These shapes are examples of quadrilaterals:

The following diagrams are also quadrilaterals, but each one is a 'special' quadrilateral with its own name:

| Square | Rectangle | Parallelogram | Rhombus | Trapezium |

Draw yourself a large quadrilateral, but do not make it one of the special types. Measure each angle and then add up the sizes of the four angles.

Do this again with another three quadrilaterals.

Now try this: on a piece of paper draw a quadrilateral. Tear off each corner and place the vertices together. It should look like this:

The sum of the four angles of a quadrilateral is 360°.

This is true of any quadrilateral whatever its shape or size.

Exercise 12h

Make a rough copy of the following diagrams, and mark on your diagrams the sizes of the required angles. You can also write in the sizes of any other angles that you may need to find.

In questions **1** to **10**, find the size of the angle marked d.

5

8

6

9

7

10

11 Find each of the equal angles d.

a

b

12 Angle *e* is twice angle *d*. Find angles *d* and *e*.

13 Find angles *d* and *e*.

14 Find each of the equal angles *e*.

15 Angles *d* and *e* are supplementary.
Find each of the equal angles *e*.

Equilateral and isosceles triangles

A triangle in which all three sides are the same length is called an **equilateral triangle**.

Note: When lines are marked ⟶╫⟶, it means they are the same length.

Construct an equilateral triangle in which the sides are each of length 6 cm. Label the vertices A, B and C.

On a separate piece of paper construct a triangle of the same size and cut it out.
Label the angles A, B and C inside the triangle.

Place it on your first triangle. Now turn it round and it should still fit exactly.
What do you think this means about the three angles?
Measure each angle in the triangle.

> **In an equilateral triangle all three sides are the
> same length, and each of the three angles is 60°.**

A triangle in which two sides are equal is called an **isosceles triangle**.

On a piece of paper construct an isosceles triangle PQR in which PQ = 8 cm, PR = 8 cm
and $\widehat{P} = 80°$. Cut it out and fold the triangle through P so that the vertices at Q and R
meet. You should find that $\widehat{Q} = \widehat{R}$. (The fold line is a line of symmetry.)

> **In an isosceles triangle, two sides are equal, and the
> two angles at the base of the equal sides are equal.**

Exercise 12i

In questions **1** to **10**, make a rough sketch of the triangle and mark
angles that are equal.

1

2

3

7

4

8

5

9

6

10

In questions **11** to **22**, find angle d. Give reasons for your working.

11

12

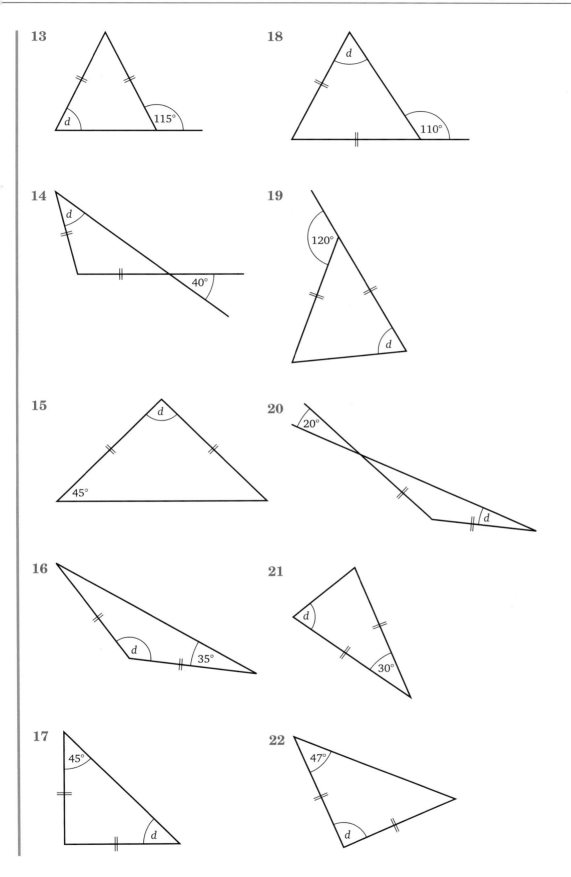

13

d 115°

14

d 40°

15

d 45°

16

d 35°

17

45° d

18

d 110°

19

120° d

20

20° d

21

d 30°

22

47° d

In questions **23** to **26**, make a rough sketch of the triangle and mark the equal sides.

23

24

25

26

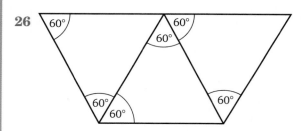

In questions **27** to **32**, find angles d and e.

27

28

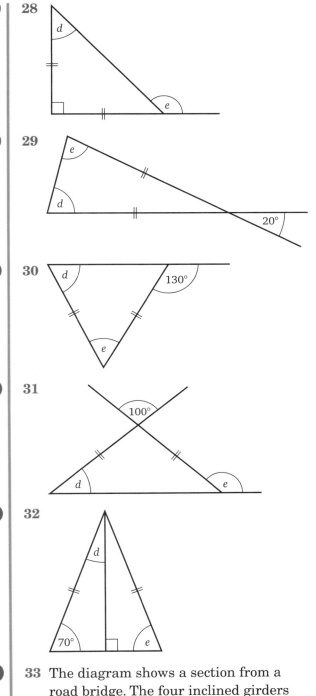

29

30

31

32

33 The diagram shows a section from a road bridge. The four inclined girders are the same length.

Angles *d* and *e* are **supplementary**.

Find the angles marked *d, e, f* and *g*.

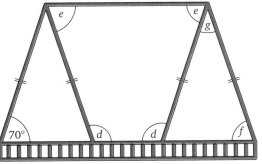

Mixed exercise

Exercise 12j

1 Find the size of the angle marked x.

2 Find the size of the angle marked t.

3 Find the size of the angle marked y.

4 Construct $\triangle ABC$ in which $AB = 6\,cm$, $BC = 4\,cm$ and $\widehat{B} = 40°$. Measure AC.

5 Construct $\triangle ABC$ in which $BC = 10\,cm$, $AB = 6\,cm$, $AC = 8\,cm$. Measure $\widehat{A}$.

Consider again

After a roof truss and a railway bridge have been designed they need to be drawn accurately before they can be made.

Now can you give the information needed to be able to draw them accurately on paper?

Practical work

The patterns below are made using a pair of compasses. Try copying them. Some instructions are given which should help.

1
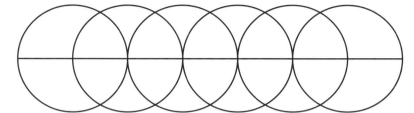

Draw a straight line. Open your compasses to a radius of 3 cm and draw a circle with its centre on the line. Move the point of the compasses 3 cm along the line and draw another circle. Repeat as many times as you can.

2 Draw a square of side 4 cm. Open your compasses to a radius of 4 cm and with the point on one corner of the square draw an arc across the square. Repeat on the other three corners.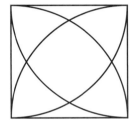

Try the same pattern, but leave out the sides of the square; just mark the corners. A block of four of these looks good.

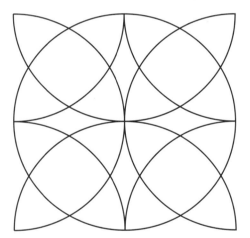

3 On a piece of paper construct an equilateral triangle of side 4 cm. Construct an equilateral triangle, again of side 4 cm, on each of the three sides of the first triangle. Add tabs as shown.

Cut out the complete diagram.
Fold the outer triangles up so that the corners meet. Stick the edges together using the tabs. You have made a tetrahedron.

(These make good Christmas tree decorations if made out of foil-covered paper.)

4

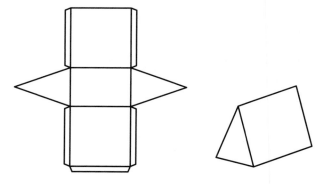

On a sheet of paper, draw a rectangle measuring 6 cm by 4 cm. On each of the shorter sides construct an isosceles triangle with sloping sides of length 6 cm. On each of the longer sides of the rectangle draw a square of side 6 cm. Draw tabs on the sides as shown. Cut out the complete figure. Fold up the squares so that their outer edges meet and fold up the triangles to make the ends.

Use the tabs to stick the edges together.

You have made a triangular prism.

Puzzles

1 This cross can be divided into 4 identical pieces in at least three different ways.
Draw diagrams to show how this is possible.

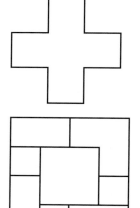

2 Eight serviettes are placed flat but overlapping on a table and give the outlines shown in the diagram. In which order must they be removed if the top one is always taken off next?

! Investigation

1   Five different triangles can be drawn on a 2 × 2 grid.

Two of them are shown. Sketch the other three.

Remember that is the same as

Investigate the number of different triangles that can be drawn on a 3 × 3 grid.

Extend your investigation to a 4 × 4 grid and then to a 5 × 5 grid. Can you find a connection between the number of different triangles that can be drawn and the length of the side of the grid?

2   The diagram shows three rectangles which have been formed by shading some of the squares in this 4 × 4 square. How many different rectangles can you find?

Remember that a square is a special kind of rectangle.

Investigate the number of rectangles there are in other squares. Can you find a connection, expressed in words, between the length of the side of the square and the number of different rectangles that can be found in it?

a Start with the simplest possible square.
b Increase the lengths of the sides of the square 1 unit at a time.
c Try to count up the number of different rectangles in an orderly way.
d When you think you have found a connection, test it to see if it gives the correct answers for squares you have already investigated and for a square you have not yet investigated.

Consider

A fairground game involves choosing four numbers from the numbers 1 to 30 inclusive.

The numbers are written on balls which are in a bag. Four balls are removed at random, one at a time out of the bag.

- If you choose four numbers, what is the probability that one of the chosen numbers comes out first?
- If you choose four numbers that are all even numbers, what is the probability that one of these numbers comes out first?
- If you pick just one of the 30 numbers available, can you measure the chance that it is the first ball that appears?

You should be able to solve this problem after you have worked through this chapter.

Chance

Questions such as
- Will it rain on my way home from school this afternoon?
- Will Manchester United win their next home game?
- Will the next bus to arrive at this stop take me to school?
- If I toss this coin will it land heads up?

have answers that can range from 'No', through 'Maybe', to 'Yes'.

The answer is 'No' when the event described is impossible, 'Yes' when the event is certain, and 'Maybe' when there is chance involved.

If we know something about the event described, we may describe the chance that it will happen using words such as 'improbable', 'evens', 'fairly likely'.

For example, we know that a coin can land either head up or tail up. Unless the coin is faulty, each possibility is equally likely, so the fourth question might be answered 'It is as likely as not.'

To answer the third question, we need 'local' knowledge, such as the number of bus routes that pass the school, how often the buses run, and so on.

Class discussion

Decide first if each event 'Is impossible', 'May happen', or 'Is certain'.

For the events that may happen, use your own words, where you can, to describe the chances that they will happen. Where you cannot, discuss what information is needed to be in a position to quantify the chance.

1 A buttered slice of bread will land butter-side down when dropped.
2 You will go to the cinema next Saturday.
3 If you throw an ordinary six-sided dice, it will score 7.
4 The next sweet in a tube of fruit pastilles is red.
5 It will be dark at midnight tonight.
6 The next vehicle to pass the school gate will be a 46-seater coach.

Outcomes of experiments

Before we can start to quantify chance, we need to know all the possibilities.

If you throw an ordinary dice, there are six possible scores that you can get. These are

1, 2, 3, 4, 5, 6

The act of throwing the dice is called an **experiment**.

The score that you get is called an **outcome** or an **event**.

The list 1, 2, 3, 4, 5, 6 is called the set of *all possible outcomes.*

Exercise 13a

How many possible outcomes are there for each of the following experiments? In each case, write down the list of all possible outcomes.

1 Tossing a 10 p coin. (Assume that it lands flat.)
2 Taking one disc from a bag containing 1 red, 1 blue and 1 yellow disc.
3 Choosing one number from the first ten positive integers.

Remember: An **integer** is a whole number.

4 Taking one crayon from a box containing 1 red, 1 yellow, 1 blue, 1 brown, 1 black and 1 green crayon.

5 Taking one item from a bag containing 1 packet of chewing gum, 1 packet of boiled sweets and 1 bar of chocolate.

6 Taking one coin from a bag containing one 1 p coin, one 10 p coin, one 20 p coin, and one 50 p coin.

7 Choosing one card from part of a pile of ordinary playing cards containing just the suit of clubs.

8 Choosing one letter from the vowels of the alphabet.

9 Choosing one number from the first 5 prime numbers.

10 Choosing an even number from the first 20 positive integers.

Probability

If you throw an ordinary dice, what are the chances of getting a four? If you throw it fairly, it is reasonable to assume that you are as likely to throw any one score as any other, i.e. all outcomes are equally likely. As throwing a four is only 1 of the 6 equally likely outcomes, you have a 1 in 6 chance of throwing a four.

'Odds' is another word that is used in everyday language to describe chances. In mathematical language, we use the word **probability** to describe chances.

We say that the probability of throwing a four is $\frac{1}{6}$.

This can be written more briefly as

$$P(\text{throwing a four}) = \frac{1}{6}$$

We will now define exactly what we mean by 'the probability that something will happen'.

If A stands for a particular event, the probability of A happening is written P(A) where

$$P(A) = \frac{\text{the number of ways in which } A \text{ can occur}}{\text{the total number of equally likely outcomes}}$$

We can use this definition to work out, for example, the probability that if one card is drawn at random from a full pack of ordinary playing cards, it is the ace of spades.

Note: The phrase 'at **random**' means that any one card is as likely to be picked as any other.

There are 52 cards in a full pack, so there are 52 equally likely outcomes. There is only one ace of spades, so there is only one way of drawing that card, i.e.

$$P(\text{ace of spades}) = \frac{1}{52}$$

Exercise 13b

In the following questions, assume that all possible outcomes are equally likely.

1 One letter is chosen at random from the letters in the word SALE. What is the probability that it is A?

2 What is the probability that a red pencil is chosen from a box containing 10 different coloured pencils including a red one?

3 What is the probability of choosing a prime number from the numbers 6, 7, 8, 9, 10?

4 What is the probability of picking the most expensive car from a range of six new cars in a showroom?

5 What is the probability of choosing an integer that is exactly divisible by 5 from the list 6, 7, 8, 9, 10, 11, 12?

6 In a raffle 200 tickets are sold.
If you have bought one ticket, what is the probability that you will win first prize?

7 One card is chosen at random from a pack of 52 ordinary playing cards.
What is the probability that it is the ace of hearts?

8 What is the probability of choosing the colour blue from the colours of the rainbow?

9 A whole number is chosen from the first 15 positive whole numbers. What is the probability that it is exactly divisible by both 3 and 4?

10 Charlie keeps his socks in a drawer. They are all either brown or grey. One night, in the dark, due to an electricity cut, he pulls out some socks to put on. What is the smallest number of socks he must pull out to be certain of having a pair of the same colour?

Experiments in which an event can happen more than once

If a card is picked at random from an ordinary pack of 52 playing cards, what is the probability that it is a 'five'?

There are 4 fives in the pack: the five of spades, the five of hearts, the five of diamonds and the five of clubs.

So there are 4 ways in which a five can be picked.

Altogether there are 52 cards that are equally likely to be picked, therefore

$$P(\text{picking a five}) = \frac{4}{52} = \frac{1}{13}$$

Now consider a bag containing 3 white discs and 2 black discs.

If one disc is taken from the bag it can be black or white. But these are not equally likely events: there are three ways of choosing a white disc and two ways of choosing a black disc, so

$$P(\text{choosing a white disc}) = \frac{3}{5}$$

and

$$P(\text{choosing a black disc}) = \frac{2}{5}$$

Exercise 13c

Worked example

→ A letter is chosen at random from the letters of the word DIFFICULT.

What is the probability that the letter I will be chosen?

$P(\text{choosing I}) = \dfrac{2}{9}$

 There are 2 ways of choosing the letter I and there are 9 letters in DIFFICULT, so the letter I can be chosen in 2 out of 9 equally likely choices.

1 How many ways are there of choosing an even number from the first 10 positive whole numbers?

2 A prime number is picked at random from the list

4, 5, 6, 7, 8, 9, 10, 11

How many ways are there of doing this?

3 A card is taken at random from an ordinary pack of 52 playing cards. How many ways are there of taking a black card?

4 An ordinary six-sided dice is thrown. How many ways are there of getting a score that is greater than 4?

5 A lucky dip contains 50 boxes, only 10 of which contain a prize, the rest being empty. What is the probability of choosing a box that contains a prize?

6 A number is chosen at random from the first 10 positive integers. What is the probability that it is

  a an even number   **c** a prime number
  b an odd number   **d** exactly divisible by 3?

7 One card is drawn at random from an ordinary pack of 52 playing cards. What is the probability that it is

  a an ace   **c** a heart
  b a red card   **d** a picture card (include the aces)?

8 One letter is chosen at random from the word INNINGS. What is the probability that it is

  a the letter N
  b the letter I
  c a vowel
  d one of the first five letters of the alphabet?

9 An ordinary six-sided dice is thrown. What is the probability that the score is

  a greater than 3   **b** at least 5   **c** less than 3?

10 A book of 150 pages has a picture on each of 20 pages. If one page is chosen at random, what is the probability that it has a picture on it?

11 One counter is picked at random from a bag containing 15 red counters, 5 white counters and 5 yellow counters. What is the probability that the counter removed is

  a   red   **b**   yellow   **c**   not red?

12 If you bought 10 raffle tickets and a total of 400 were sold, what is the probability that you win first prize?

13 A roulette wheel is spun.

What is the probability that when it stops it will be pointing to

  a   an even number

  b   an odd number

  c   a number less than 10, excluding zero?

Note: The numbers on a roulette wheel go from 0 to 35, and zero is neither an even number nor an odd number.

14 One letter is chosen at random from the letters of the alphabet. What is the probability that it is a consonant?

15 A number is chosen at random from the set of two-digit numbers (i.e. the numbers from 10 to 99). What is the probability that it is exactly divisible both by 3 and by 4?

16 A bag of sweets contains 4 caramels, 3 fruit centres, 5 mints and 4 cola bottles. If one sweet is taken out, what is the probability that it is

  a   a mint   **c**   not a fruit centre?

  b   a caramel

Finding probability from relative frequency

We have assumed that if you toss a coin it is equally likely to land head up or tail up so that

$$\text{P(a head)} = \frac{1}{2}$$

Coins like this are called **fair** or **unbiased**.

Most coins are likely to be unbiased, but it is not necessarily true of all coins. A particular coin may be slightly bent or even deliberately biased so that there is not an equal chance of getting a head or a tail.

The only way to find out if a particular coin is unbiased is to collect some information about how it behaves when it is tossed. We can do this by tossing it several times and recording the results.

Tossing a bent coin gave these results.

For this coin we have 30 heads out of 110 tosses.

We say that the **relative frequency** of heads with this coin is $\frac{30}{110}$.

We can use the relative frequency of heads as an estimate for the probability of a head with this coin, i.e.

$$P(\text{a head}) \approx \frac{\text{number of heads}}{\text{total number of tosses}} = \frac{30}{110} = \frac{3}{11}$$

The approximation gets more reliable as the number of tosses gets larger, but on this evidence it looks as though this coin is more likely to give a tail than a head.

Consider again

The numbers 1 to 30 inclusive are written on balls which are in a bag. Four balls are removed at random, one at a time out of the bag.

- If you choose four numbers, what is the probability that one of the chosen numbers comes out first?

- If you choose four numbers that are all even numbers, what is the probability that one of these numbers comes out first?

- If you pick just one of the 30 numbers available, can you measure the chance that it is the first ball that appears?

Now answer these questions.

Practical work

Work with a partner or collect information from the whole class.
Use an ordinary six-sided dice.

1 a Throw the dice 25 times and keep a tally of the number of sixes.
       Use your results to find the relative frequency of sixes.
   b Now throw the dice another 25 times and add the results to the
       last set. Use these to find again the relative frequency of sixes.
       Now do another 25 throws and add the results to the last two
       sets to find another value for the relative frequency.
   c Carry on doing this in groups of 25 throws until you have done
       200 throws altogether.

You know that the probability of getting a six is $\frac{1}{6}$. Now look at the
sequence of results obtained from your experiment. What do you notice?
(It is easier to compare your results if you use your calculator to change
the fractions into decimals correct to 2 d.p.)

2 a A dice is to be thrown 60 times and the numbers that appear
       are to be recorded. Roughly how many times do you expect each
       of the numbers 1 to 6 to appear?
   b Now throw a dice 60 times. Record the results on a tally chart
       and draw a bar chart.
       Has it come out as you expected?
   c Combine your information with that of several other people, so
       that you have the results of, say, 180 or 240 throws.
       Draw a bar chart. Comment on its shape.
   d Throw the dice 10 times and record the numbers. Would it make
       sense to make a judgement about the fairness of this dice using
       the relative frequencies of each score from just these 10 results?
   e Throw the dice again 10 times. Has the same set of numbers
       been thrown as in part **d**?
   f Imagine that the dice is thrown 10 more times. Can you rely on
       getting the same numbers again as in parts **d** and **e**?
       What extreme case might you get?

3 *This question should be done as a
   class exercise.*
   A company runs the following
   promotional offer with tubes of sweets.
   What are the chances of getting four
   numbers the same if you just buy four
   tubes?
   What is the most likely number of
   tubes that you need to buy to collect
   enough lids?

Each lid has a
number 1, 2, 3, 4, 5 or 6
printed inside.

Collect 4 lids with
the same number and
get a free T-shirt.

a We could answer the questions by collecting evidence, i.e. buying tubes of these sweets until we have four lids with the same number on them, and repeating this until we think we have reliable results. What are the disadvantages of this?

b We can avoid the disadvantages of having to buy tubes of these sweets by simulating the situation as follows:

First assume that any one of the numbers **1** to **6** is equally likely to be inside a lid.

Now throw a dice to simulate the number you would get if you bought a tube, and carry on throwing it until you get four numbers the same. You will need several tally charts to keep a record of the number of throws needed on each occasion.

This shows the start of the simulation.

Score	Tally
1	/
2	///
3	/
4	//
5	////
6	/
Total	12

Number of throws needed to get 4 numbers the same	4	5	6	7	8	9	10	11	12	13	14	15	16	...
Tally									/					

4 Make two three-sided spinners using card and a pencil.

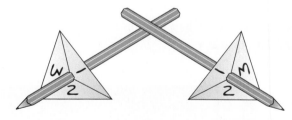

a Write down the list of possible outcomes for the sum of the scores when both spinners are spun.

b Estimate the probability of getting a total score of 3 when both spinners are used. Comment on how reliable your estimate is. Remember to show all your working and explain your reasoning.

Summary 3

Angles

One complete revolution = 4 right angles = 360°.

One right angle = 90°.

An acute angle is less than one right angle.

An obtuse angle is larger than one right angle but less than two right angles.

A reflex angle is larger than two right angles.

Vertically opposite angles are equal.

Angles on a straight line add up to 180°.

Two angles that add up to 180° are called supplementary angles.

Angles at a point add up to 360°.

Symmetry

A figure has line symmetry when it can be folded along the line so that one half fits exactly over the other half.

A figure has rotational symmetry when it can be turned through less than 360° about a point so that it looks the same.

Congruence

Two figures are congruent when they are exactly the same shape and size, even if one is turned over compared with the other.

Triangles

The three angles in a triangle add up to 180°. An equilateral triangle has all three sides equal and each angle is 60°.

An isosceles triangle has two sides equal and the angles at the base of these sides are equal.

Quadrilaterals

A quadrilateral has four straight sides.
The four angles in a quadrilateral add up to 360°.

Probability

The probability that an event A happens is given by

$$\frac{\text{the number of ways in which } A \text{ can occur}}{\text{the total number of equally likely outcomes}}$$

When we perform experiments to find out how often an event occurs, the relative frequency of the event is given by

$$\frac{\text{the number of times the event occurs}}{\text{the number of times the experiment is performed}}$$

Relative frequency is used to give an approximate value for probability.

REVISION EXERCISE 3.1 (Chapters 10 and 11)

1 How many degrees does a hand of a clock turn through when it moves
  a from 7 to 12   **b** from 9 to 3   **c** from 2 to 5?

2 If you stand facing East and turn clockwise through $\frac{1}{4}$ of a turn, in which direction are you facing?

3 Which of these statements are true and which are false?
  a The difference between an obtuse angle and an acute angle is always less than 90°.
  b 190° is an example of an obtuse angle.
  c Every reflex angle is bigger than every obtuse angle.
  d The difference between a reflex angle and an obtuse angle is sometimes less than 90°.

4 Estimate the size of each of the following angles.

a   **b**   **c**

5 Find the size of each angle marked with a letter.

a   **b**

6 Find the size of each angle marked with a letter.

a

b

Angle *r* is twice angle *t*.

7 Copy the drawing onto squared paper, and complete it so that the broken line is the axis of symmetry.

8 Copy the following drawings onto squared paper, and complete them so that the broken lines are the two axes of symmetry.

a

b

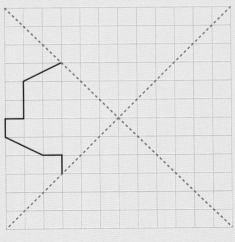

9 Which of these shapes has both line and rotational symmetry?

a b c d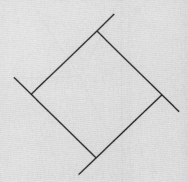

REVISION EXERCISE 3.2 (Chapters 12 and 13)

1 Find the size of the angle at A.

a

b

2 Find the size of the angles marked d and e.

3 Construct a triangle ABC in which AB = 6.5 cm, $\widehat{A}$ = 55°, $\widehat{B}$ = 65°.

4 Construct a triangle XYZ in which XY = 75 mm, YZ = 95 mm, XZ = 80 mm.

5 Find the size of the angle marked with a letter.

6 How many possible outcomes are there of
   a choosing one number from the first six positive whole numbers
   b choosing one number from the first ten prime numbers?

7 One letter is chosen at random from the letters in the word
   TELEVISION.
   What is the probability that the letter is
   a E   **b** a vowel   **c** a consonant?

8 What is the probability of choosing a prime number from the
   numbers 10, 11, 12, 13, 14, 15?

9 A card is chosen at random from a pack of 52 ordinary playing
   cards. What is the probability that it is
   a the ace of spades   **c** a black card
   b the 2 of spades   **d** a club?

10 Which event do you think is the more likely to happen: score 6
   when you roll a dice, or draw a heart when you select a card at
   random from a pack of 52 ordinary playing cards? Give reasons for
   your answer.

REVISION EXERCISE 3.3 (Chapters 10 to 13)

1 Find the size of each of the angles marked with a letter.

a   **b**   **c**

2 Find the size of each angle marked with a letter.

a

b

3 Find the size of each angle marked with a letter.

a

b

4 State whether or not these pairs of figures are congruent.

a   **b**   **c**

5 Find the angles marked p and q.

6 Construct triangle ABC in which AB = 45 mm, BC = 55 mm, $\widehat{B}$ = 50°.

7 Construct a triangle PQR in which PQ = 9.5 cm, $\widehat{P}$ = 63°, $\widehat{Q}$ = 72°.

8 One letter is chosen at random from the letters in the word PSST.
What is the probability that the letter is

   a   a vowel   **b**   a consonant?

9 What is the probability of randomly choosing an integer that is exactly divisible by 6 from the following list?

6, 8, 10, 12, 14, 16, 18, 20

10 A coin is tossed 100 times. It lands heads up 60 times. What is the relative frequency of a tail when this coin is tossed?

REVISION EXERCISE 3.4 (Chapters 1 to 13)

1 a Find   **i** $\frac{7}{12} + \frac{2}{3} + \frac{1}{6}$ **ii** $10\frac{3}{4} - 4\frac{5}{8}$

  b Express 44% as **i** a decimal **ii** a fraction in its lowest terms.

  c Split 184 p equally among four sisters.

2 a Find $3 \times 4 \times 5 + 28 \div 2$

  b Find $5429 \div 42$, giving the remainder if there is one.

  c Use a calculator to find, correct to two decimal places
    i 4.09×1.08 **ii** $5.92 \div 0.87$

3 John bought a loaf of bread costing 87 p and a fruit cake costing £1.95. He paid with a £5 note. How much change did he get?

4 Find the set of prime numbers that are factors of 90, and the set of prime numbers that are factors of 70. Illustrate these sets in a Venn diagram.

5 Two girls set off walking together and are in step for their first pace. One girl has a pace of 90 cm, and the other has a pace of 75 cm. How far will they walk before they are in step together again? Give your answer in **a** centimetres **b** metres.

6 a Fifty cars, each 4165 mm long, are parked nose to tail in a straight line.
How far is it from the front of the first car to the tail of the last car? Give your answer in
    i   millimetres
    ii metres
    iii metres correct to the nearest metre.

  b How many of these cars would be needed, parked nose to tail in a line, to stretch a distance of 1 km?
Give your answer to the nearest whole number.

7
  35   45

The diagram shows a glass tube that is to be scaled to show temperature between 35 °C and 45 °C. The distance between the mark for 35 and the mark for 45 is 12 cm.

  a How far apart should the marks be for the temperatures 35 °C and 36 °C?

  b This distance is then divided to show tenths of a degree. How far apart should these marks be?

8 Find the difference between
  a 0.55 m and 136 cm   **b** 24.6 cm and 565 mm.
  Give each answer in the smaller unit.

9 Which of the shapes are congruent with the coloured shape?

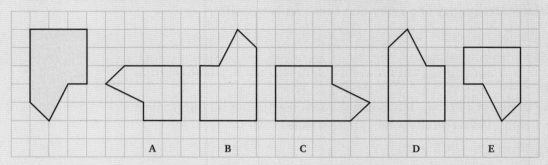

10 Angle *d* is twice angle *e*. Find the angles *d* and *e*.

11 One letter is chosen at random from the letters in the word
  ASSESS. What is the probability that the letter is
  a E   **b** S   **c** not S?

REVISION EXERCISE 3.5 (Chapters 1 to 13)

1 A car travelling at 50 miles per hour took 4 hours to travel from
  Manchester to Cardiff.
  How many miles did the car travel?

2 500 eggs are packed on trays, 36 to a tray. How many trays are
  required?

3 The list shows the marks out of 10 obtained by a group of pupils in
  a test.

8	7	9	4	8	5	6	8	5
4	8	10	8	5	7	3	8	9
7	4	7	6	8	7	5	9	7

  a Make a frequency table for this list.
  b How many pupils were tested?
  c Draw a bar chart to show the information in the frequency
       table.

4 a Add $1\frac{3}{4}$ to $2\frac{5}{12}$ and subtract the total from $5\frac{5}{6}$.

 b To 1.08 add the difference between 7.92 and 6.34.

5

 a How many grams of fat are there in this pot of *fromage frais*?

 b What fraction of the weight in this pot is fat?

6 Express the given quantity in terms of the units in brackets.

 a 124 in (ft and in) **b** 50 ft (yd and ft) **c** 34 yd (ft)

7 Find the size of each angle marked with a letter.

 a

 b

8 Which of the following shapes have rotational symmetry?

 a

 b

 c

9 Construct triangle XYZ in which XY = 10.5 cm, $\widehat{X}$ = 65°, $\widehat{Y}$ = 60°.

10 An ordinary six-sided dice is rolled. What is the probability that the score is

 a 6 **b** greater than 4 **c** less than 4?

Mental arithmetic practice 3

1 Express 645 mm in centimetres.

2 Find 0.007×6

3 What is $1\,\text{m} - 65\,\text{cm}$?

4 Give three numbers which, when multiplied together, give 42.

5 Sally is paid £265 for a 5-day working week. How much is this per day?

6 Find the smallest number that 6 and 8 divide into exactly.

7 Change $\frac{27}{8}$ into a mixed number.

8 Write 19 as the sum of two prime numbers.

9 Express 1200 g in kilograms.

10 Which is the longer: a piece of wood 35 cm long or a piece 339 mm long?

11 Which is the larger: 9000 g or 10 kg?

12 What do you divide 72 by to get 6?

13 Express 0.85 as a fraction in its lowest terms.

14 Give 0.0864 correct to two decimal places.

15 Divide 0.084 by 4

16 Write down all the different factors of 30.

17 Express 1.4 m in millimetres.

18 Which is the larger: 6.97 or 6.79?

19 Find $12 - 3.42$

20 Is 528 divisible by 3?

21 Find 0.1^2

22 Find $12.5 \div 0.5$

23 About how long is your pencil?

24 Give 23 km in metres.

25 Find $5 \times 7 \times 2$

26 Find $240 \div 300$

27 Express $2\frac{3}{5}$ as an improper fraction

28 What is the largest number that will divide exactly into 24 and 36?

29 What is the value of 5 cubed?

30 Write 23% as a decimal.

31 Find 0.35×200

32 About how many inches is 20 cm?

33 Find $72 \div 9$

34 Find $\frac{1}{2} + \frac{1}{3}$

35 What is 25% of £80?

36 What is the change when you pay for 3 cartons of milk costing 94 p each with a £5 note?

37 A 42 cm length is sawn off a 1 m long plank. What length remains?

38 When two straight lines cross, what do you know about the sizes of a pair of angles that are opposite each other?

39 Two angles of a triangle add up to 140°. What is the size of the third angle?

40 What is the remainder when 880 is divided by 50?

For each of statements **41** to **45**, state if it is true or false.

41 Two angles in an isosceles triangle are equal.

42 Any two-digit whole number ending with 5 cannot be prime.

43 Any two squares are congruent.

44 The cost of three peaches at 48 p each is £1.54.

45 $2 \times 2 \times 2 = 16$

46 Find $4 \times 9 \times 5$

47 Find 0.1 cubed.

48 Find 75% of 160 m.

49 Three angles of a quadrilateral are each 90°. What is the quadrilateral called?

50 Give 2.5 cm in millimetres.

51 About how many miles is 100 km?

52 Find $1\frac{1}{3} - \frac{1}{2}$

53 What is 12 squared?

54 The sum of three of the interior angles of a quadrilateral is 240°. What is the size of the fourth interior angle?

55 What number must be multiplied by 0.1 to give 3?

For each of statements **56** to **60**, state if it is true or false.

56 One angle of a triangle can be a reflex angle.

57 A prime number cannot be an even number.

58 A square number cannot be odd.

59 An equilateral triangle has three equal length sides.

60 $9 \div 8 = 11.5$

14 Area

Consider

Which of these rugs takes up more floor space?

How can floor space be measured?

Does it matter that one rug has measurements in inches and the other rug has measurements in millimetres?

You should be able to solve this problem after you have worked through this chapter.

Area

The amount of surface covered by a shape is called its **area**.

The usual way of measuring area is to find the number of squares that give the same amount of surface.

Class discussion

1   John and Hasib each traced the outline of a different leaf on squared paper. They used paper with different sized squares.

John's leaf

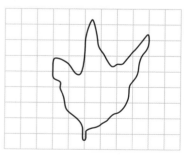

Hasib's leaf

John said that his leaf was bigger because it covered more squares than Hasib's leaf.

Discuss John's claim.

2 Beth traced the outline of a leaf on a piece of paper she found in her mother's drawer.

Discuss whether this can be used to estimate the area of the leaf.

Beth's leaf

3 Discuss how you would compare the areas of two different leaves.

Counting squares to find area

The letter L covers 7 squares. The letter C also covers 7 squares. The squares are all the same size, so we can say these two letters have the same area.

Squares are a convenient way of describing area, but there is nothing special about the size of the square we have used. If other people are going to understand what we are talking about when we say that the area of a certain shape is 12 squares, we must have a square, or unit of area, which everybody understands and which is always the same.

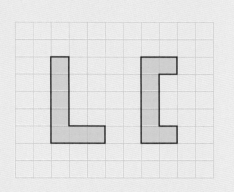

Units of area

A centimetre is a standard length and a square with sides 1 cm long is said to have an area of one **square centimetre**. We write one square centimetre as $1\,cm^2$.

Other agreed lengths such as millimetres, metres and kilometres, can also be used for the sides of squares to measure area.

A square millimetre (mm^2) is a small unit of area. $1\,mm^2 = \square$

A square metre (m^2) is a fairly large unit of area. A standard single bed covers an area of about $2\,m^2$.

The unit of area used depends on what we are measuring.

We could measure the area of a small coin in square millimetres, the area of the page of a book in square centimetres, the area of a roof in square metres, and the area of a town in square kilometres (km^2), or square miles if we want to use imperial units.

We can use a square grid on a flat surface and count the squares inside the surface to estimate its area.

Sometimes the squares do not fit exactly inside the area we are finding. When this is the case, we count a square if at least half of it is within the area we are finding, but exclude it if more than half of it is outside.

This is the outline of Hasib's leaf. It is now drawn on 1 cm squared paper.

We have ticked 20 squares, so the area of this leaf is about 20 cm².

Exercise 14a

This set of diagrams shows the outlines of three leaves that were drawn on 1 cm squared paper. The diagram has been reduced in size to fit this page.

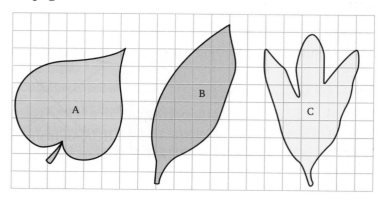

1 By counting squares, find the approximate area of
   a   the leaf outline marked A
   b   the leaf outline marked B
   c   the leaf outline marked C.

2 Which leaf has
   a   the largest area   b   the smallest area?

3 Why are your answers to question **1** only approximate?

4 For each part of question **1**, decide if your answer is larger or smaller than the true area.

Which unit of area would you use to find the area of

5 this page

6 the top of a 20 p coin

7 a tennis court

8 Cape Town?

In questions **9** to **16**, the figures were drawn on 1 cm squares, then the diagrams were reduced in size; so each square represents 1 cm^2. Find the area of the figures by counting squares.

9

13

10

14

11

15

12

16

17 Which do you think is larger, $1\,km^2$ or 1 square mile?
Give a reason for your answer.

18 This diagram is a map of the Isle of Wight.

a Find, roughly, the area of the Isle of Wight as a number of grid squares.

b Each square represents 2.43 square miles. Use this to find an estimate of the area of the Isle of Wight in square miles.

19 This shows the outline of a design for a company logo drawn on 5 mm squared paper.

a Find the number of 5 millimetre squares covered by green.

b How many of these 5 millimetre squares make one square with an area of $1\,cm^2$?

c Find, roughly, the area of green in cm^2.

d Find, roughly, the area of grey in cm^2.

Area of a square

The square is the simplest figure of which to find the area. If we have a square whose side is 4 cm long, it is easy to see that we must have 16 squares, each of side 1 cm, to cover the square, i.e. the area of a square of side 4 cm is 16 cm^2.

In general,

area of a square = (length of side)^2

Area of a rectangle

If we have a rectangle measuring 6 cm by 4 cm, we require 4 rows each containing 6 squares of side 1 cm to cover this rectangle.

i.e.   the area of the rectangle = 6×4 cm^2

$\qquad\qquad\qquad\qquad = 24$ cm^2

A similar result can then be found for a rectangle of any size. For example, a rectangle of length 4 cm and breadth $2\frac{1}{2}$ cm has an area of

$\qquad 4 \times 2\frac{1}{2}$ cm$^2 = 10$ cm^2

In general,

area of a rectangle = length × breadth

Exercise 14b

In questions **1** to **12**, find the area of each of the shapes, clearly stating the units involved.

1   a square of side 2 cm

2   a square of side 8 cm

3   a square of side 5 cm

4   a square of side 1.5 cm

5   a square of side 0.7 m

6   a square of side 0.5 m

7   a rectangle measuring 5 cm by 6 cm

8   a rectangle measuring 6 cm by 8 cm

9   a rectangle measuring 3 m by 9 m

10 a rectangle measuring 1.8 mm by 2.2 mm

11 a rectangle measuring 35 km by 42 km

12 a rectangle measuring 1.5 m by 1.9 m

13 A rectangular table mat measures 24 cm by 15 cm.
What is its area?

14 Find the area of
  a a soccer field measuring 110 m by 75 m
  b a rugby pitch measuring 100 m by 70 m
  c a tennis court measuring 26 m by 12 m.

15 A roll of wallpaper is 10 m long and 50 cm wide.
  a What is the width of the paper in metres?
  b Find the area, in square metres, of the wallpaper in the roll.
  c Is there enough paper in this roll to paper a wall measuring
  2.4 m by 1.9 m?
  Give reasons for your answer.

Compound figures

It is often possible to find the area of a figure by dividing it into two or more rectangles.

Exercise 14c

Worked example

→ Find the area of this tile which has been cut to shape to fit an awkward corner.

 There are two ways to divide this shape into two rectangles. We could draw a line across instead of down as shown.

Area of A = $6 \times 4 \, \text{cm}^2 = 24 \, \text{cm}^2$
Area of B = $6 \times 2 \, \text{cm}^2 = 12 \, \text{cm}^2$
Therefore area of whole figure = $24 \, \text{cm}^2 + 12 \, \text{cm}^2 = 36 \, \text{cm}^2$

Find the areas of the figures in questions **1** to **10** by dividing them into rectangles.

1

12 cm
8 cm
6 cm
4 cm

6

8 mm
8 mm
16 mm
16 mm
12 mm
8 mm

2
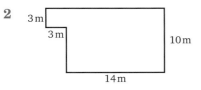
3 m
3 m
10 m
14 m

7

8 cm
3 cm
3 cm
5 cm
3 cm

3

2 m
10 m
8 m
2 m

8
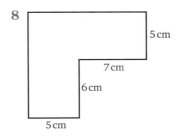
5 cm
7 cm
6 cm
5 cm

4

8 mm
24 mm
4 mm
14 mm

9
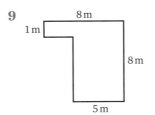
8 m
1 m
8 m
5 m

5

2 m
5 m
6 m
6 m
3 m

10

10 cm
18 cm
24 cm
8 cm

11 The diagram shows the pieces in a puzzle. Find the area of each piece.

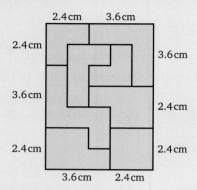

Find the area of the complete puzzle and use this to check your answers.

Perimeter

The **perimeter** of a shape is the total distance round the edge of the shape.

The perimeter of this square is

$$4\,\text{cm} + 4\,\text{cm} + 4\,\text{cm} + 4\,\text{cm} = 16\,\text{cm}$$

If we are given a rectangle whose perimeter is 22 cm and told that the length of the rectangle is 6 cm, it is possible to find its breadth and its area.

The lengths of the two longer sides add up to 12 cm, so the lengths of the two shorter sides add up to $(22 - 12)\,\text{cm} = 10\,\text{cm}$

Therefore the breadth is 5 cm.

The area of this rectangle $= 6 \times 5\,\text{cm}^2$
$$= 30\,\text{cm}^2$$

Exercise 14d

Find the perimeter of each of the shapes in questions **1** to **4**.

1

2.5 cm
2.5 cm

3

2 mm
3 mm
4 mm
3 mm

2

5.2 m
3.4 m

4

1.6 cm
0.2 cm
0.9 cm
0.4 cm
1.3 cm

The following table gives some of the measurements of various rectangles. Fill in the values that are missing.

	Length	Breadth	Perimeter	Area
5	4 cm		12 cm	
6	5 cm		14 cm	
7		3 m	16 m	
8		6 mm	30 mm	
9	6 cm			30 cm^2
10	12 m			120 m^2
11		4 km		36 km^2
12		7 mm		63 mm^2
13		5 cm	60 cm	
14	80 cm			1680 cm^2

Worked example

→ Find the perimeter and the area of this metal plate.

X
8 cm
2 cm
A
2 cm
3 cm
3 cm
5 cm
B
5 cm
3 cm
3 cm
3 cm
C
3 cm
8 cm

To make sure we do not miss any sides, mark one corner X.

Starting at X, the distance all round the plate and back to X is

$(8 + 2 + 3 + 5 + 3 + 3 + 8 + 3 + 3 + 5 + 3 + 2)\,cm = 48\,cm$

Therefore the perimeter is 48 cm.

The area of A = $8 \times 2\,cm^2 = 16\,cm^2$,
the area of B = $5 \times 2\,cm^2 = 10\,cm^2$
and the area of C = $8 \times 3\,cm^2 = 24\,cm^2$

Therefore the total area = $(16 + 10 + 24)\,cm^2 = 50\,cm^2$

Divide the plate into three rectangles, A, B and C.

In questions **15** to **19**, the shapes are metal plates used to strengthen joints in wooden structures.

For each shape find   **a** the perimeter   **b** the area.

15

18

16

19

17

In questions **20** to **24**, find the area that is shaded.

20

21

You will find it easiest to do these by subtracting the area of the missing sections from the complete area.

22

24

23

Worked example

→ Draw a square of side 6 cm.
How many squares of side 2 cm are required to cover it?

We see that 9 squares of side 2 cm are required to cover the larger square.

25 Draw a square of side 4 cm.
How many squares of side 2 cm are required to cover it?

26 Draw a square of side 9 cm.
How many squares of side 3 cm are required to cover it?

27 Draw a rectangle measuring 6 cm by 4 cm.
How many squares of side 2 cm are required to cover it?

28 Draw a rectangle measuring 9 cm by 6 cm.
How many squares of side 3 cm are required to cover it?

29 How many squares of side 5 cm are required to cover a rectangle measuring 45 cm by 25 cm?

30 How many squares of side 4 cm are required to cover a rectangle measuring 1 m by 80 cm?

31 How many squares of side 1 mm are required to cover a square of side 1 cm?

Changing units of area

A square of side 1 cm may be divided into 100 squares of side 1 mm,

1 cm
1 cm

10 mm
10 mm

i.e. $\mathbf{1\,cm^2 = 100\,mm^2}$

Similarly, since   1 m = 100 cm,

1 square metre = 100×100 square centimetres,

i.e. $\mathbf{1\,m^2 = 10\,000\,cm^2}$

and, as   1 km = 1000 m,

1 square kilometre = 1000×1000 square metres,

i.e. $\mathbf{1\,km^2 = 1\,000\,000\,m^2}$

When we convert from a unit of area that is large to a unit of area that is smaller, we must remember that the *number* of units will be bigger,

e.g. $2\,km^2 = 2 \times 1\,000\,000\,m^2$
$$= 2\,000\,000\,m^2$$

but if we convert from a unit of area that is small into a larger unit of area, the number of units will be smaller,

e.g. $500\,mm^2 = 500 \div 100\,cm^2$
$$= 5\,cm^2$$

Exercise 14e

Worked example

$\rightarrow$ Express 5 m² in cm².

As $1\,m^2 = 10\,000\,cm^2$,

$5\,m^2 = 5 \times 10\,000\,cm^2$
$$= 50\,000\,cm^2$$

1 Express in cm²
    a 3 m²   **c** 7.5 m²   **e** 0.5 m²
    b 12 m²   **d** 82 m²

2 Express in mm²
    a 14 cm²   **c** 7.5 cm²   **e** 3.2 cm²
    b 3 cm²   **d** 26 cm²

3 Express 0.056 m² in cm².

4 Express in cm²
  - **a** 400 mm²
  - **b** 2500 mm²
  - **c** 50 mm²
  - **d** 25 mm²
  - **e** 734 mm²
  - **f** 1220 mm²

5 Express in m²
  - **a** 5500 cm²
  - **b** 140 000 cm²
  - **c** 760 cm²
  - **d** 18 600 cm²
  - **e** 29 700 cm²
  - **f** 192 000 cm²

6 Express in km²
  - **a** 7 500 000 m²
  - **b** 430 000 m²
  - **c** 50 000 m²
  - **d** 245 000 m²
  - **e** 176 m²
  - **f** 750 000 m²

7 Use 5 miles $\approx$ 8 km to find an approximate conversion from square miles to square kilometres.

In many problems involving finding the area of a rectangle, the length and breadth are given in different units. When this is the case, we must change the units so that all the measurements are in the same units.

Worked example

$\rightarrow$ A floorboard is 2 m long and 15 cm wide.
Find the area of the top of this floorboard, in cm².

15 cm
2 m

Since the answer is to be given in square centimetres, we express the length in centimetres.

Length = 2 m = 2 $\times$ 100 cm
= 200 cm

Therefore area of rectangle = 200 $\times$ 15 cm²
= 3000 cm²

Find the area of each of rectangles **8** to **15**, giving your answer in the unit in brackets.

	Length	Breadth	
8	10 m	50 cm	(cm²)
9	6 cm	30 mm	(mm²)
10	50 m	35 cm	(cm²)
11	140 cm	1 m	(cm²)
12	400 cm	200 cm	(m²)
13	3 m	$\frac{1}{2}$ m	(cm²)
14	1.2 cm	5 mm	(mm²)
15	0.4 km	0.05 km	(m²)

16 The top of my desk is 1.5 m long and 60 cm wide. Find its area in square centimetres.

17 A roll of wallpaper is 10 m long and 50 cm wide. Find its area in square metres.

18 A school hall measuring 20 m by 15 m is to be covered with square floor tiles of side 50 cm. How many tiles are required?

19 A rectangular carpet measures 4 m by 3 m. Find its area.
What is the cost of cleaning this carpet at £3.45 per square metre?

20 How many square linen serviettes, of side 50 cm, may be cut from a roll of linen 25 m long and 1 m wide?

21 How many square concrete paving slabs, each of side 0.5 m, are required to pave a rectangular yard measuring 9 m by 6 m?

22 A patio that is 9 m square is to be covered with 450 mm square paving stones and edged, all the way round, with 250 mm long bricks. How many paving stones are needed?
What extra information do you need in order to find the number of bricks needed?

23 A rectangular field measuring 40 m by 25 m is to be sown with grass seed so that 90 g of seed is used to cover each square metre. Each box of seed holds 5 kg.
How many boxes are needed?

24 A rectangular lawn measuring 3 m by 4 m has a 1 m wide path round the outside edge.
Find the area of this path.

25 Diana is tiling a wall with two different sized square tiles.
The smaller tile has sides 64 mm long. Four of these smaller tiles cover the same area as one larger tile.
What is the length of a side of a larger tile?

Consider again

Now can you answer these?
Which of these rugs takes up more floor space?

← 16 in →

36 in

← 450 mm →

500 mm

How can floor space be measured?

Does it matter that one rug has measurements in inches and the other rug has measurements in millimetres?

! Investigation

a   This shape has a perimeter of 10 cm.
    What is its area?

b   Find other shapes made from 1 cm squares that also have a
    perimeter of 10 cm.
    Which one has the largest area?

c   Find other shapes that have the same area as the shape above.
    Which shape has the shortest perimeter?

d   Investigate different shapes with a perimeter of 16 cm. Find the
    shape with the largest possible area.

e   Investigate different shapes with an area of 6 cm². Which shape has
    the shortest perimeter?

f   For a given area, what shape has the shortest perimeter?

g   A rectangle has the same number of square
    centimetres of area as it has centimetres of
    perimeter. Find possible whole number values
    for the length and breadth of this rectangle.

 There are two different
rectangles with this property.

15 Parallel lines

Consider

How can you find the size of the angle marked d?

You should be able to solve this problem after you have worked through this chapter.

Parallel lines

Two straight lines that are always the same distance apart, however far they are drawn, are called **parallel lines**.

The lines in your exercise books are parallel. You can probably find many other examples of parallel lines; for example, the edges on many buildings.

Class discussion

1   Discuss with your group examples of parallel lines that

    a   are horizontal and you can see them in the room

    b   are vertical and you can see them in the room

    c   do not look parallel.

2   Using the lines in your exercise book, draw three lines that are parallel. Do not make them all the same distance apart. For example

We use arrows to mark lines that are parallel.

3 Using the lines in your exercise book, draw two parallel lines. Make them fairly far apart. Now draw a slanting line across them. For example

Mark the angles in your drawing that are in the same positions as those in the diagram.

Are they acute or obtuse angles?

Measure your angles marked *p* and *q*.

4 Draw a grid of parallel lines like the diagram below. Use the lines in your book for one set of parallels and use the two sides of your ruler to draw the slanting parallels.

Mark your drawing like the diagram.

Are your angles *p* and *q* acute or obtuse?

Measure your angles *p* and *q*.

5 Repeat question **4**, but change the direction of your slanting lines.

6 Draw three slanting parallel lines like the diagram below. Use the two sides of your ruler and move it along to draw the third parallel line. Draw a horizontal line crossing your parallel lines.

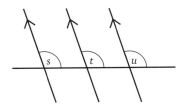

Mark your drawing like the diagram.

Decide whether angles *s*, *t* and *u* are acute or obtuse, and then measure them.

7 Repeat question **6**, but change the slope of your slanting lines.

8 Discuss what you notice about your results in questions **3** to **7**.

Corresponding angles

In the class discussion, lines were drawn that crossed a set of parallel lines.

A straight line that crosses a set of parallel lines is called a **transversal**.

When you have drawn several parallel lines, you should notice that two parallel lines on the same flat surface will never meet, however far they are drawn.

If you draw the diagram above by moving your ruler along, you can see that all the shaded angles are equal. These angles are all in corresponding positions: they are all above the transversal and to the left of the parallel lines. Angles like these are called **corresponding angles**.

When two parallel lines are cut by a transversal, the corresponding angles are equal.

Exercise 15a

For the diagrams in questions **1** to **10**, write down the angle that corresponds to the shaded angle.

1

5

2

6

3

7

4

8

9

10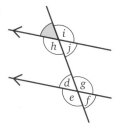

Drawing parallel lines (using a protractor)

The fact that the corresponding angles are equal gives us a method for drawing parallel lines.

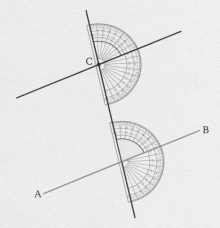

If you need to draw a line through the point C that is parallel to the line AB, first draw a line through C to cut AB.

Use your protractor to measure the shaded angle. Place your protractor at C as shown in the diagram. Make an angle at C the same size as the shaded angle and in the corresponding position.

You can now extend the arm of your angle both ways, to give the parallel line.

Exercise 15b

1   Using your protractor, draw a grid of parallel lines like the one in the diagram. (It does not have to be an exact copy.)

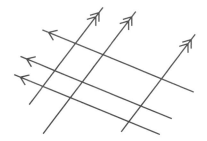

2   Trace the diagram below.

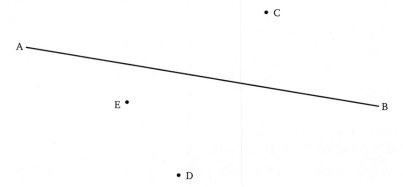

Now draw three lines through the points C, D and E so that each line is parallel to AB.

3   Draw a sloping line in your exercise book. Mark a point C above the line. Use your protractor to draw a line through C parallel to your first line.

4   Trace the diagram below.

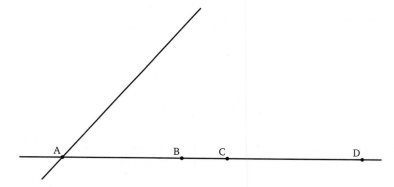

Measure the acute angle at A. Draw the corresponding angles at B, C and D. Extend the arms of your angles so that you have a set of four parallel lines.

In questions **5** to **8**, remember to draw a rough sketch before doing the accurate drawing.

5   Draw an equilateral triangle with sides each 8 cm long. Label the corners A, B and C. Draw a line through C that is parallel to the side AB.

6   Draw an isosceles triangle ABC with base AB which is 10 cm long and base angles at A and B which are each 30°. Draw a line through C that is parallel to AB.

7   Draw the triangle as given in question **6** again, and this time draw a line through A that is parallel to the side BC.

8 Make an accurate drawing of the figure below, where the side AB
is 7 cm, the side AD is 4 cm and $\angle A = 60°$.

Remember: A figure like this is called a **parallelogram**.

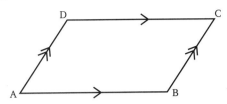

Problems involving corresponding angles

The simplest diagram for a pair of corresponding angles is an F shape.

Looking for an F shape may help you to recognise the corresponding angles.

Exercise 15c

Worked example

➤ Write down the size of the angle marked d.

 d and the angle of 60° are
corresponding angles.

$d = 60°$

In each of the following diagrams, write down the size of the angle
marked d.

1

2

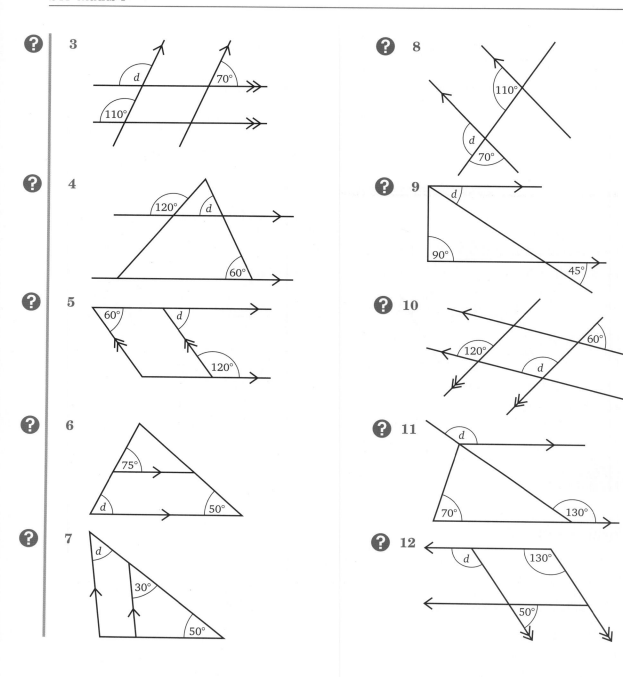

3

d 70° 110°

4

120° *d* 60°

5

60° *d* 120°

6

75° *d* 50°

7

d 30° 50°

8

110° *d* 70°

9

d 90° 45°

10

120° 60° *d*

11

d 70° 130°

12

d 130° 50°

Remember:

Vertically opposite angles are equal.

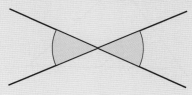

Angles at a point add up to 360°.

Angles on a straight line add up to 180°.

The angles of a triangle add up to 180°.

You will need these facts in the next exercise.

Exercise 15d

Worked example

→ Find the size of each marked angle.

$p = 75°$ (angles of $\triangle$ add up to 180°)

$q = 65°$ (corresponding angles)

$r = 40°$ (corresponding angles)

$s = 115°$ (s and 65° add up to 180°)

$t = 140°$ (t and 40° add up to 180°)

Find the size of each marked angle in questions **1** to **16**.
Give reasons for any statements that you make.

1

2

3

4

5

6

7

8

9

10

11

12

90°
d
e
f
40°

13

60°
40°
d
e

14

e
d
70°
150°

Find the size of angle d in questions **17** to **24**.

17

d
70°

18

d
45°

19

135°
d

20

d
125°

15

125°
p
65°

16

d
40°
80°

21

55°
d

22

d

23

d

24

d

Alternate angles

Draw a large letter Z. Use the lines of your exercise book to make sure that the outer arms of the Z are parallel.

This letter has rotational symmetry about the point marked with a cross. This means that the two shaded angles are equal. Measure them to make sure.

Draw a large N and make sure that the outer arms are parallel.

This letter also has rotational symmetry about the point marked with a cross, so once again the shaded angles are equal. Measure them to make sure.

The pairs of shaded angles like those in Z and N are between the parallel lines and on alternate sides of the transversal. Angles like these are called **alternate angles**.

When two parallel lines are cut by a transversal, the alternate angles are equal.

The simplest diagram for a pair of alternate angles is a Z shape.

Looking for a Z shape may help you to recognise the alternate angles.

Exercise 15e

Write down the angle which is alternate to the shaded angle in the following diagrams.

1

2

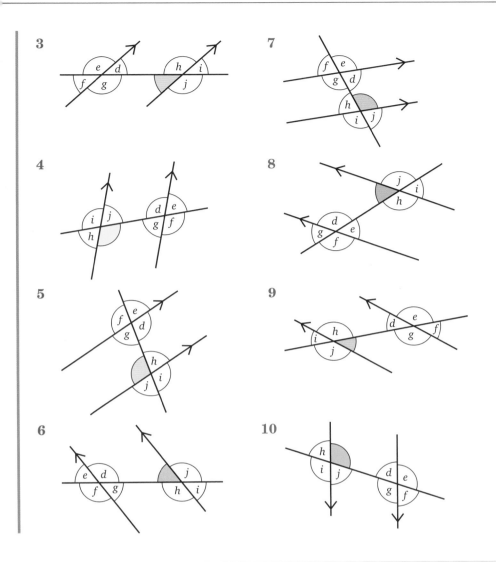

3

4

5

6

7

8

9

10

Problems involving alternate angles

Without doing any measuring, we can show that alternate angles are equal by using the facts that we already know.

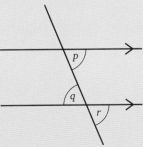

$p = r$ because they are corresponding angles.
$q = r$ because they are vertically opposite angles.
$\therefore p = q$ and these are alternate angles.

Exercise 15f

Find the size of each marked angle.

1

2

3

4

5

6

7

8

9

10

11

12

Interior angles

In the diagram above, f and g are on the same side of the transversal and 'inside' the parallel lines. Pairs of angles like f and g are called **interior angles**.

Exercise 15g

In questions **1** to **6**, two of the marked angles are a pair of interior angles. Name them.

1

4

2

5

3

6

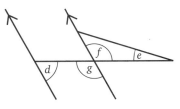

In questions **7** to **10**, use the information given to find the size of p and of q. Then find the sum of p and q.

7

8

9   **10**

11 Make a large copy of the diagram below. Use the lines of your book to make sure that the outer arms of the 'U' are parallel.

Measure each of the interior angles p and q. Add them together.

Pairs of interior angles

The sum of a pair of interior angles is 180°.

You will probably have realised this fact by now. We can show that it is true from the following diagram.

$d + f = 180°$ because they are angles on a straight line.

$d = e$ because they are alternate angles.

So $e + f = 180°$

The simplest diagram for a pair of interior angles is a U shape.

Looking for a U shape may help you to recognise a pair of interior angles.

Exercise **15h**

Find the size of each marked angle.

1

6

2

7

3

8

4

9

5

10
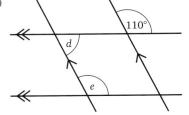

Mixed exercises

You now know that when a transversal cuts a pair of parallel lines

the corresponding (F) angles are equal,
the alternate (Z) angles are equal,
the interior (U) angles add up to 180°.

You can use any of these facts, together with the other angle facts you know, to answer the questions in the following exercises.

Exercise 15i

In questions **1** to **8**, find the size of each marked angle.

1

2

3

4

5

6

7

8
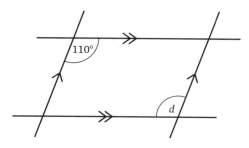

9 Construct a triangle ABC in which AB = 12 cm, BC = 8 cm and
 AC = 10 cm.

 Find the midpoint of AB and mark it D.

 Find the midpoint of AC and mark it E.

 Join ED.

 Measure ∠ADE and ∠ABC.
 (∠ADE means the angle at D formed by the lines AD and DE.)

 What can you say about the lines DE and BC?

Exercise 15j

In questions **1** to **7**, find the size of each marked angle.

1

5

2

6

3

7

4

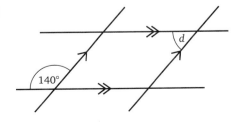

8   Construct this parallelogram, making it full size.

Consider again

Now can you find the size of angle d?

! Investigation

This diagram represents a child's billiards table.

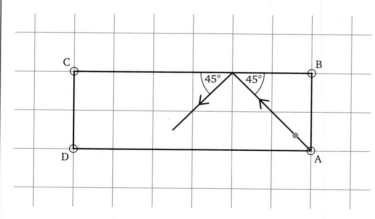

There is a pocket at each corner.

The ball is projected from the corner A at 45° to the sides of the table.
It carries on bouncing off the sides at 45° until it goes down a pocket.
(*Note:* This is a very superior toy – the ball does not lose speed
however many times it bounces!)

a How many bounces are there before the ball goes down a pocket?

b Which pocket does it go down?

c What happens if the table is 2 squares by 8 squares?

d Can you predict what happens for a 2 by 20 table?

e Now try a 2 by 3 table.

f Investigate for other sizes of tables. Start by keeping the width at 2 squares. Then try other widths. Copy this table and fill in the results.

Size of table	Number of bounces	Pocket
2 × 6		
2 × 8		
2 × 3		
2 × 5		

g Can you predict what happens with a 3 × 12 table?

 Number puzzles

Copy this grid.

How many different-shaped parallelograms can you draw on this grid? Each vertex must be on a dot. One has been drawn for you. Do not include squares and rectangles.

Now try the problem with a grid of 4 dots by 4 dots.

16 Coordinates

Consider

1   Your parents tell you that they are going to
    Valletta to see some relatives. You have no idea
    where Valletta is, but you can find out by using
    an atlas.

    In the index you find

    Valletta   23, 38

    This is a short description of where to find
    Valletta on the map.
    Do you know what it means?

2   What special name is given to this quadrilateral?
    How can you justify your answer?

You should be able to solve these problems after you have worked through this chapter.

Class discussion

1   Discuss different ways in which you can give the position of a
    place on a map so that another person can find it.

2   Look up the index in several different atlases. How many
    different ways are there of helping you to find the position of a
    place on a map?

3   A friend rings you up to ask in what ways the pieces can move in
    a game of chess.
    Discuss how you can describe the ways in which the different
    chess pieces can move.

4   Can you think of other situations where you need a short way of
    describing the position of a place?

Plotting points using positive coordinates

There are many occasions when you need to describe the position of an object. For example, you may want to tell a friend how to find your house, or you might want to find a square in the game of battleships. An air traffic controller may have to describe the position of an aeroplane showing up on a radar screen. In mathematics, we need a quick way to describe the position of a point.

We do this by using squared paper and marking a point O at the corner of one square. We then draw a line through O across the page. This line is called Ox. Next we draw a line through O up the page. This line is called Oy. Starting from O we then mark numbered scales on each line.

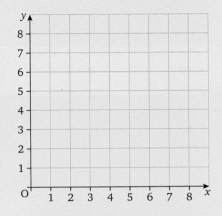

O is called the origin.

Ox is called the x-axis.

Oy is called the y-axis.

We can now describe the position of a point A as follows:

start from O and move 3 squares along Ox, then move 5 squares up from Ox.

We always use the same method to describe the position of a point:

Start from O, *first* move *along* and *then* up.

We can now shorten the description of the position of the point A to the number pair (3, 5).

The number pair (3, 5) gives the coordinates of A.

The first number, 3, is called the x-coordinate of A.

The second number, 5, is called the y-coordinate of A.

Now consider another point B whose x-coordinate is 8 and whose y-coordinate is 3.

If we simply refer to the point B (8, 3), this tells us all that we need to know about the position of B.

Note: The origin is the point (0, 0).

Exercise 16a

1 Write down the coordinates of the points A, B, C, D, E, F, G and H.

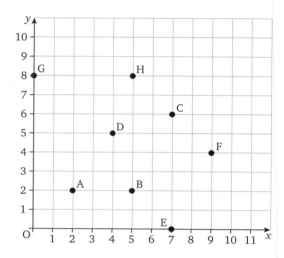

Use this map for questions **2** and **3**.

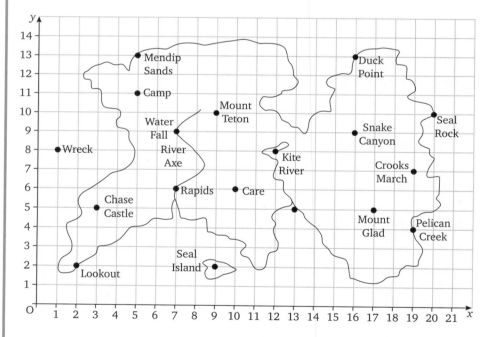

2 Which places on the map have the following pairs of coordinates?

  a (2, 2)   **c** (16, 13)   **e** (9, 10)

  b (19, 4)   **d** (3, 5)   **f** (7, 6)

3 Give the pair of coordinates for each of the following places.

  a Seal Island   **c** Snake Canyon

  b Pelican Creek   **d** Mendip Sands

e Mount Glad   **g** The point where the Kite River enters the sea

f The source of the Kite River   **h** Water Fall

4 Draw a set of axes of your own.
   Give them scales from 0 to 10.
   Mark the following points and label each point with its own
   letter.
   A (2, 8)   B (4, 9)   C (7, 9)   D (8, 7)   E (7, 7)
   F (9, 4)   G (8, 4)   H (7, 3)   I (5, 3)   J (7, 2)
   K (7, 1)   L (4, 2)   M (2, 0)   N (0, 2)

   Now join your points together in alphabetical order and join
   A to N.

5 Draw a set of axes and give them scales from 0 to 10.
   Mark the following points.

   A (2, 5)   B (7, 5)   C (7, 4)   D (8, 4)   E (8, 3)   F (9, 3)
   G (9, 2)   H (6, 2)   I (6, 1)   J (7, 1)   K (7, 0)   L (5, 0)
   M (5, 2)   N (4, 2)   P (4, 0)   Q (2,0)   R (2,1)   S (3,1)
   T (3, 2)   U (0, 2)   V (0, 3)   W (1, 3)   X (1, 4)   Y (2, 4)

   Now join your points together in alphabetical order and join
   A to Y.

6 Mark the following points on your own set of axes.
   A (2, 7)   B (8, 7)   C (8, 1)   D (2, 1)

   Join A to B, B to C, C to D and D to A.
   What is the name of the figure ABCD?

7 Mark the following points on your own set of axes.
   A (2, 2)   B (8, 2)   C (5, 5)

   Join A to B, B to C and C to A.
   What is the name of the figure ABC?

8 Mark the following points on your own set of axes.
   A (5, 2)   B (8, 5)   C (5, 8)   D (2, 5)

   Joint the points to make the figure ABCD.
   What is ABCD?

9 Draw a simple pattern of your own on squared paper, but do not
   show it to anyone.
   Write down the coordinates of each point and give this set of
   coordinates to your partner.
   See if your partner can now draw your diagram.

Questions **10** to **12** use the map opposite.

10 Which places on the map opposite are given by the following pairs of coordinates?

    a (27, 36)   **c** (25, 39)

    b (29, 37)   **d** (28, 34)

Instead of using a pair of coordinates, a place can be described by a six-figure grid reference. The first three figures give the position across the grid, and the second three figures give the position up the grid. For example, the grid reference of Manor Farm is 255 352.

Worked example

→ Find the grid reference of the pumping station, near the tunnel.

The grid reference of the pumping station is 254 360.

We can use the divisions of the squares to give the position of the pumping station. It is between the vertical grid lines marked 25 and 26 and is $\frac{4}{10}$ of the side of the square from the line marked 25, so the horizontal reference is 254. It is on the grid line marked 36, so its vertical grid reference is 360.

11 Give the pair of coordinates and the grid references that fix the position of

    a Sands Court

    b Long Barrow

    c Abbey Gate.

12 Give the grid reference of

    a the church with the tower on the B442 ()

    b Horse Bridge

    c the church with a spire (●)

    d Horton Hall.

Questions **13** to **18** refer to the points A (1, 7), B (5, 0) and C (0, 14).

13 Write down the x-coordinate of the point B.

14 Write down the y-coordinate of the point A.

15 Write down the x-coordinate of the point C.

16 Write down the x-coordinate of the point A.

17 Write down the y-coordinate of the point C.

18 Write down the y-coordinate of the point B.

Questions **19** to **24** refer to points in the following diagram.

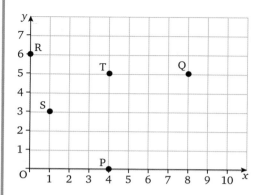

19 Write down the y-coordinate of the point T.

20 Write down the x-coordinate of the point P.

21 Write down the x-coordinate of the point S.

22 Write down the y-coordinate of the point R.

23 Write down the y-coordinate of the point Q.

24 Write down the x-coordinate of the point R.

For each of the following questions you will need to draw your own set of axes.

25 The points A (2, 1), B (6, 1) and C (6, 5) are three **vertices** of a square ABCD.

Mark the points A, B and C.

Find the point D and write down the coordinates of D.

26 The points A (2, 1), B (2, 3) and C (7, 3) are three vertices of a rectangle ABCD.

Mark the points and find the point D.

Write down the coordinates of D.

27 The points A (1, 4), B (4, 7) and C (7, 4) are three vertices of a square ABCD.

Mark the points A, B and C, and find D.

Write down the coordinates of D.

Questions **28** to **31** refer to the following diagram.

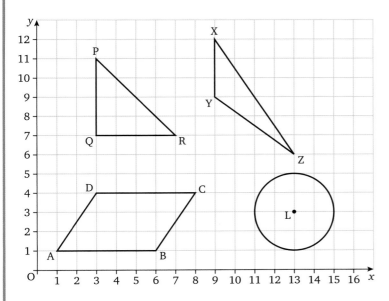

28 Write down the coordinates of the vertices X, Y and Z of triangle XYZ.

29 Write down the coordinates of the vertices of the isosceles triangle PQR.

Write down the lengths of the two equal sides as a number of sides of squares.

30 Write down the coordinates of the vertices of the parallelogram ABCD.

How long is AB?

How long is DC?

31 Write down the coordinates of the centre, L, of the circle.
What is the diameter of this circle?

You will need to draw your own set of axes for questions **32** to **34**.

32 Mark the points A (2, 4) and B (8, 4).

Join A to B, and find the point C which is the midpoint (the exact middle) of the line AB.

Write down the coordinates of C.

33 Mark the points P (3, 5) and Q (3, 9).

Join P and Q, and mark the point R which is the midpoint of PQ.

Write down the coordinates of R.

34 Mark the points A (0, 5) and B (4, 1).
Find the coordinates of the midpoint of AB.

Quadrilaterals

A **quadrilateral** has four sides.

No two of the sides need be equal and no two of the sides need be parallel.

There are, however, some special quadrilaterals, such as a square, which have some sides parallel and/or some sides equal.

The questions in the next exercise investigate the properties of these special quadrilaterals.

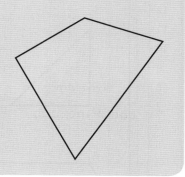

Exercise 16b

If you are not sure whether two lines are equal, *measure them*.
If you are not sure whether two lines are parallel, *measure a pair of corresponding angles*.

1   **The square**

A (3, 2), B (11, 2), C (11, 10) and D (3, 10) are the four corners of a square.

Using squared paper, mark these points on your own set of axes and then draw the square ABCD.

a   Write down, as a number of sides of squares, the lengths of the sides AB, BC, CD and DA.

b   Which side is parallel to AB?
Are BC and AD parallel?

c   What is the size of each angle of the square?

2   **The rectangle**

A (2, 2), B (2, 7), C (14, 7) and D (14, 2) are the vertices of a rectangle ABCD.

Draw the rectangle ABCD on your own set of axes.

a   Write down the sides which are equal in length.

b   Write down the pairs of sides which are parallel.

c   What is the size of each angle of the rectangle?

3   **The rhombus**

A (8, 1), B (11, 7), C (8, 13) and D (5, 7) are the vertices of a rhombus ABCD.

Draw the rhombus on your own set of axes.

a   Write down the sides which are equal in length.

b   Write down the pairs of sides which are parallel.

c   Measure the angles of the rhombus.
Are any of the angles equal?

4 **The parallelogram**

A (2, 2), B (14, 2), C (17, 7) and D (5, 7) are the vertices of a parallelogram.

Draw the parallelogram on your own set of axes.

a Write down which sides are equal in length.

b Write down which sides are parallel.

c Measure the angles of the parallelogram.
Write down which, if any, of the angles are equal.

5 **The trapezium**

A (1, 1), B (12, 1), C (10, 5) and D (5, 5) are the vertices of a trapezium.

Draw the trapezium on your own set of axes.

a Write down which, if any, of the sides are the same length.

b Write down which, if any, of the sides are parallel.

c Write down which, if any, of the angles are equal.

Properties of the sides and angles of the special quadrilaterals

We can summarise our investigations in the last exercise as follows:

In a square
- all four sides are the same length
- both pairs of opposite sides are parallel
- all four angles are right angles.

In a rectangle
- both pairs of opposite sides are the same length
- both pairs of opposite sides are parallel
- all four angles are right angles.

In a rhombus
- all four sides are the same length
- both pairs of opposite sides are parallel
- the opposite angles are equal.

In a parallelogram
- both pairs of opposite sides are the same length
- both pairs of opposite sides are parallel
- the opposite angles are equal.

In a trapezium
- just one pair of opposite sides are parallel.

Exercise 16c

In questions 1 to 10, the points A, B, C and D are the vertices of a quadrilateral. Draw the figure ABCD on your own set of axes, and write down which type of quadrilateral it is.

1 A (2, 4) B (7, 4) C (8, 7) D (3, 7)

2 A (2, 2) B (6, 0) C (7, 2) D (3, 4)

3 A (2, 2)   B (7, 2)   C (5, 5)   D (3, 5)

4 A (2, 0)   B (6, 0)   C (6, 4)   D (2, 4)

5 A (1, 1)   B (4, 0)   C (4, 6)   D (1, 3)

6 A (3, 1)   B (6, 3)   C (3, 5)   D (0, 3)

7 A (1, 3)   B (4, 1)   C (6, 4)   D (3, 6)

8 A (2, 4)   B (3, 7)   C (9, 5)   D (8, 2)

9 A (3, 1)   B (5, 1)   C (3, 5)   D (1, 5)

10 A (0, 0)   B (5, 0)   C (8, 4)   D (3, 4)

Negative coordinates

If A (2, 0), B (4, 2) and C (6, 0) are three vertices of a square ABCD, we can see that the fourth vertex, D, is two squares below the x-axis.

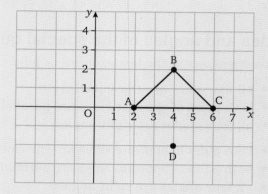

To describe the position of D, we need to extend the scale on the y-axis below zero.
To do this we use the numbers $-1, -2, -3, -4, \ldots$

These are called **negative numbers**.

In the same way, we can use the negative numbers $-1, -2, -3, \ldots$ to extend the scale on the x-axis to the left of zero.

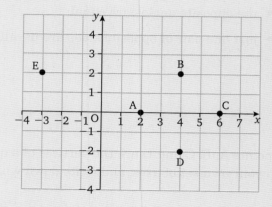

The y-coordinate of the point D is written -2 and is called 'negative 2'.

Some people write the negative sign higher up, e.g. ⁻2, to distinguish 'negative 2' from 'take away 2'.

The x-coordinate of the point E is written -3 and is called 'negative 3'.

The numbers 1, 2, 3, 4, … are called positive numbers. They could be written as $+1$, $+2$, $+3$, $+4$, …, but we do not usually put the $+$ sign in.

Now   D is 4 squares to the right of O so its x-coordinate is 4
           and 2 squares down from O so its y-coordinate is -2,

so   D is the point $(4, -2)$.

         E is 3 squares to the left of O so its x-coordinate is -3
         and 2 squares up from O so its y-coordinate is 2,

so   E is the point $(-3, 2)$.

Exercise 16d

Use this diagram for questions **1** and **2**.

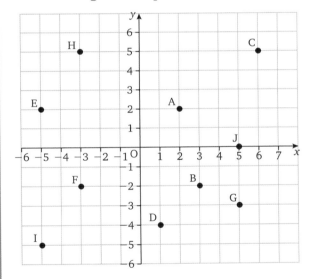

1   Write down the x-coordinate of each of the points A, B, C, D, E, F, G, H, I, J and O (the origin).

2   Write down the y-coordinate of each of the points A, B, C, D, E, H, I and J.

Worked example

→   The point Q has a y-coordinate of -10.
     How many squares above or below the x-axis is the point Q?

Q is 10 squares below the x-axis.

How many squares above or below the x-axis is each of the following points?

3 P: the y-coordinate is -5

4 L: the y-coordinate is $+3$

5 B: the y-coordinate is 10

6 A: the y-coordinate is 0

How many squares to the left or to the right of the y-axis is each of the following points?

7 Q: the x-coordinate is 3

8 R: the x-coordinate is -5

9 S: the x-coordinate is -7

10 V: the x-coordinate is 0

Worked example

Write down the coordinates of the point A.

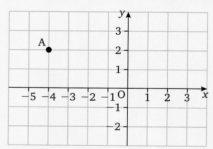

A is the point $(-4, 2)$.

11 Write down the coordinates of the points A, B, C, D, E, F, G, H, I and J.

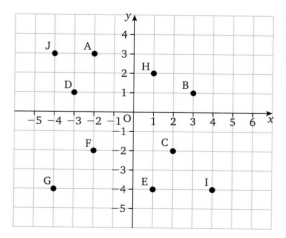

In questions **12** to **16**, draw your own set of axes and mark a scale on each one from −5 to 5.

12 Mark the points A (−3, 4), B (−1, 4), C (1, 3), D (1, 2), E (−1, 1), F (1, 0), G (1, −1), H (1, −2), I (−3, −2).
Join the points in alphabetical order, and join I to A.

13 Mark the points A (2, l), B (−1, 3), C (−3, 0), D (0, −2).
Join the points to make the figure ABCD.
What is the name of the figure?

14 Mark the points A (1, 3), B (−1, −1), C (3, −1).
Join the points to make the figure ABC, and describe ABC.

15 Mark the points A (−2, −1), B (5, −1), C (5, 2), D (2, 2).
Join the points to make the figure ABCD, and describe ABCD.

16 Mark the points A (−3, 0), B (1, 3), C (0, −4).
What kind of triangle is ABC?

Exercise 16e

Use graph paper and draw your own sets of axes.

Mark a scale on each axis from −8 to +8 using 1 cm for each unit.

In questions **1** to **6**, mark the points A and B and then measure the length of the line AB.

1 A (2, 2) B (−4, 2)

2 A (−2, −2) B (6, −1)

3 A (4, −4) B (−4, 2)

4 A (5, −1) B (5, 6)

5 A (−2, 4) B (−7, 4)

6 A (−1, 2) B (−8, −2)

In questions **7** to **11**, the points A, B and C are three vertices of a square ABCD.

Mark the points, and find the point D. Give the coordinates of D.

7 A (1, 1) B (1, −1) C (−1, −1)

8 A (1, 3) B (6, 3) C (6, −2)

9 A (−3, −1) B (−3, 2) C (0, 2)

10 A (−2, −1) B (2, −2) C (3, 2)

11 A (−3, −2) B (−5, 2) C (−1, 4)

In questions **12** to **17**, mark the points A and B and the point C, the midpoint of the line AB.

Give the coordinates of C.

12 A (2, 2) B (6, 2)

13 A (2, 3) B (2, −5)

14 A (−1, −2) B (−9, −2)

15 A (2, 1) B (6, 2)

16 A (2, 1) B (−4, 5)

17 A (−7, −3) B (5, 3)

Questions **12** to **17** show that you can find the coordinates of the midpoint of a line as follows

the x-coordinate is the 'average' of the x-coordinates of the ends of the line, the y-coordinate is the 'average' of the y-coordinates of the ends of the line.

For example, the coordinates of the midpoint of the line joining

A $(2, 5)$ and B $(4, 3)$ are $\left(\dfrac{2+4}{2}, \dfrac{5+3}{2}\right)$, i.e. $(3, 4)$.

Write down the coordinates of the midpoint of AB where A and B are

18 A $(3, 5)$ B $(7, 9)$

19 A $(1, 6)$ B $(0, 2)$

20 A $(1, 3)$ B $(2, 5)$

21 A $(0, 4)$ B $(-4, 0)$

Mixed exercise

Exercise 16f

Questions **1** to **3** refer to the following diagram.

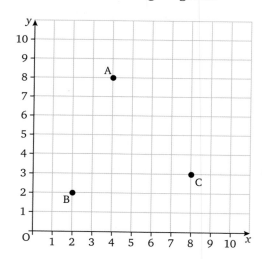

1 Write down
   a the x-coordinate of A
   b the y-coordinate of B
   c the coordinates of C.

2 Write down the coordinates of a fourth point D such that ABCD is a parallelogram.

3 **a** Write down the coordinates of the midpoint of AC.
   b Write down the coordinates of the midpoint of BD.
   c What do you notice?

Questions **4** to **6** refer to the following diagram.

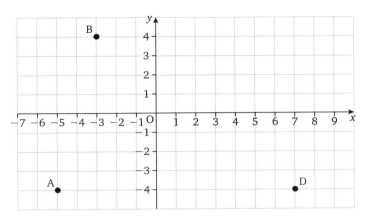

4 Write down
   a the *x*-coordinate of B
   b the *y*-coordinate of D
   c the coordinates of A.

5 **a** Write down the coordinates of C such that the *x*-coordinate of C is 3 and BC is parallel to AD.
   b What name do you give to the shape ABCD?

6 Find the coordinates of E such that BCDE is a parallelogram. (*Note:* The letters should go round the quadrilateral in the order given. BCED is not a parallelogram.)

Consider again

1 This is a short description of where to find Valletta on the map.

   Valletta   23, 38

   Now do you know what it means?

2 What special name is given to this quadrilateral?

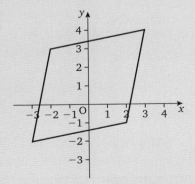

   Now can you justify your answer?

Investigation

Study the number chain 2, 8, 32, 11, 5, ...

The next number in the chain is found by multiplying the number of units by 4 and adding the number of tens – if there are any.

For example,

the number after 32 is $4 \times 2 + 3 = 11$ and
the number after 11 is $4 \times 1 + 1 = 5$

a Write down the next four terms.
What do you notice?

b Write down the first number in the chain, then write each of the following numbers in the chain four times. Bracket these numbers off to give a sequence of ordered pairs. The ordered pairs at the beginning of the sequence are

$(2, 8)$, $(8, 8)$, $(8, 32)$, $(32, 32)$, $(32, 11)$, $(11, 11)$, $(11, 5)$.

Continue the ordered pairs until you find a good reason to stop!
When you stop, state your reason.

c On 2 mm graph paper, draw x- and y-axes and mark a scale on each axis from 0 to 40.
Mark both axes in multiples of 5.
Plot the points that represent the ordered pairs you found in part **b**.
Join each point to the next one with a straight line.
What do you notice when you come to plot the thirteenth pair?

d In part **a** the chain began with 2.
Repeat the investigation starting with 3.
How does the shape you get compare with the shape you got in the previous investigation?

e Repeat the whole investigation starting with
  i 5
  ii 8
Compare the four shapes you have so far.

f Repeat the investigation starting with each of the whole numbers from 1 to 9 that you have not used so far.
How do the shapes you get for these compare with the previous four shapes?

g Do any of the shapes have line or rotational symmetry?
How many different numbers are there in each chain before the chain starts to repeat?
Compare the sums of the different numbers in each chain.

❗ Practical work

1   **a**   At Newtown Comprehensive School important examinations always take place in the school hall. The hall is rectangular and has sufficient space for 8 rows with 16 desks in each row. It is important that each student sits at a particular desk.

How can the desks be described so that a particular student can be directed to a particular desk?

Your system could be all numbers, such as (1, 1), (1, 2), ... or all letters, for example Aa, Ab, ... or a mixture of the two, for example A1, A2, ...

Which system is the best for students to understand easily and quickly where their place is?

b   What system is used when large numbers of people are to be seated, for example in a sports stadium or concert hall?

c   How can you remember where your car is parked in an airport car-park where there may be thousands of cars?

17 Formulas

Class discussion

What instruction in words can be given to answer each of the following questions?

1   If local time in mainland Europe is 1 hour ahead of local time in the United Kingdom, how do I find the time in the UK in terms of the time in mainland Europe?

2   How do we find the distance around a rectangular field in terms of the lengths of the four sides?

3   How can the motor club organiser work out how many boxes of mints he needs to buy for the annual dinner, if he assumes that every person present will eat two?

The instruction for finding a quantity from other quantities is called a **formula**.

Exercise 17a

1   For each of parts **a** to **c**, write in words a formula that will enable you to find

a   the number of drawing pins needed to put up posters advertising the school musical, if four pins are needed for each poster

b the amount of hardcore delivered in a day to a motorway construction site, if all the lorries carry the same amount

c the total number of legs on all the four-legged dining chairs in a furniture store.

2 You are told the number of county cricket games taking place each Saturday of the season.

Write a formula in words that will give you the number of

a wickets   **c** bails

b stumps   **d** bats

being used at any one time when all the matches are in progress.

(*Note:* In a cricket match each of the two wickets has three stumps and two bails. During play there are always two batsmen.)

Expressing formulas in words and symbols

There is a rule for changing the numbers in the top row of this table to the numbers in the bottom row.

1	3	5	9	15
7	9	11	15	21

The rule is:

'The bottom number is equal to the top number plus six.'

We know and use symbols for 'is equal to' ($=$) and 'plus' ($+$) so we can shorten the rule to

bottom number = top number + 6

Exercise 17b

In each of questions **1** to **6**, write in words and symbols the rule that tells you how to get the bottom number from the top number.

1

1	2	3	4	5
6	7	8	9	10

2

2	4	6	7	12
4	8	12	14	24

3

5	8	16	21	34
2	5	13	18	31

5

1	2	3	4	5
4	6	8	10	12

4

8	12	22	34	46
4	6	11	17	23

6

2	4	5	7	9	12
4	16	25	49	81	144

Worked example

→ Local time in Miami is found by subtracting 5 hours from the time in London. What time is it in Miami when it is 3 p.m. in London?

Local time in Miami = time in London − 5 h
                    = 3 p.m. − 5 h
                    = 10 a.m.

7 The Dobsons leave London Heathrow at 11.30 a.m. to fly to Vancouver. The flight takes 9 hours. The time in Vancouver is 8 hours behind the time in London.

  a Write a formula, in words, linking the time in London with the time in Vancouver?

  b What will be the time in London when they arrive in Vancouver?

  c What time, local time, will they arrive in Vancouver?

8 The profit made by a company is equal to its income minus its costs. Last year John Smith inc had an income of £4 m and costs of £3.2 m.

 £4 m means £4 million, i.e. £4 000 000.

  a Write in words and symbols, a formula to show the connection between income, costs and profit.

  b Use your formula to find the profit made by John Smith inc last year.

9 The perimeter of a rectangle is found by doubling the length of a longer side and adding it to double the length of a shorter side.

  a Write a formula connecting the perimeter and the sides.

  b Use your formula to find the perimeter of a rectangle measuring 12 m by 7 m.

10 The capacity of an engine is found by multiplying the capacity of one cylinder by the number of cylinders.

Write a suitable formula connecting these quantities, and use it to find the capacity of an engine that has 4 cylinders, each with a capacity of 498 cubic centimetres.

11 The number of cans of cola on a supermarket shelf is found by counting the number of packs and multiplying by 4.

a What formula connects the number of cans with the number of packs?

b At the end of a day an assistant counts 23 packs on the shelves.
How many cans are there?

c She wants to put another 60 cans on the shelves.
How many packs is this?

12 First class stamps cost 60 p each and are sold in books of 12.
In parts **a** to **c** write a formula that gives

a the number of stamps in terms of the number of books

b the cost, in pence, of the stamps in terms of the number of books

c the cost, in pounds, of the stamps in terms of the number of books.

d Find the number of complete books that can be bought with two £20 notes.

Formulas using letters for unknown numbers

We are always looking for shorter ways of giving the same amount of information.

On a score sheet you sometimes see o.g. which is short for 'own goal'; we use p to stand for pence, EU for European Union and PO for Post Office.

Things are no different in mathematics: we use a letter for *an unknown number* so that we can write a formula in a shorter way.

To give the number of biscuits each pupil in a class gets when a box containing 60 biscuits is shared out among them, we could use the formula

number of biscuits each pupil gets = 60 ÷ number of pupils in the class

Using n for the number of biscuits each pupil gets and x for the number of pupils in the class, we can write the formula as

$$n = 60 \div x \quad \text{or} \quad n = \frac{60}{x}$$

This is a simple example of a formula using letters.

Note: $2 \times w$ or $w \times 2$ can be written $2w$.

To find the value of $2w$ when $w = 5$ we find 2×5
i.e. when $w = 5$, the value of $2w$ is 10.

Exercise 17c

1   Write each of the following formulas in a shorter form.

   a $P = 4 \times a$

   b $Q = p \times 3$

   c $w = \dfrac{3}{4} \times m$

   d $M = 2 \times y \div 3$

2   Write each of the following formulas in an alternative form using $\times$ and/or $\div$ signs.

   a $X = 5y$

   b $A = \dfrac{v}{5}$

   c $P = \dfrac{4q}{7}$

   d $H = \dfrac{2x}{3}$

In each of questions **3** to **7**, write a formula, in letters and symbols, that connects the two given letters.

3   The number of stones (s) that a person weighs is the number of pounds (w) the person weighs divided by 14.

4   The number of inches (P) round the edge of a square is four times the number of inches (x) along the length of one side.

5   The number of kilometres (k) in the distance between two villages, measured in miles, is the number of miles (m) multiplied by 1.61.

6   The number of eggs (n) in a box is the number of trays (t) in the box multiplied by 48.

7   The number of components (N) taken out of stock is 10 more than the number of units to be assembled (n).

Worked example

Pearl is 8 years older than Carol.

→   Write a formula that expresses Pearl's age (p years) in terms of Carol's age (q years).

In words, Pearl's age is equal to Carol's age plus 8.
As a formula, using the letters given in the question, this becomes

   $p = q + 8$

→   Use your formula to find Pearl's age when Carol is 30.

If Carol is 30, we replace q by 30 in the formula and so

   $p = 30 + 8 = 38$

i.e. Pearl is 38 when Carol is 30.

8 Omar is 5 years older than Linda.

   a   If Omar is T years old and Linda is x years old, write a formula connecting their ages.

   b   How old is Linda if Omar is 12?

   c   How old will each person be in 5 years' time?

   d   Will the same formula be valid in 5 years' time? Justify your answer.

9 A number y is always 13 less than a number x.

   a   Write the formula connecting x and y.

   b   Find y when x is
      i   4
      ii 16

10 Richard is 28 years younger than his father. Write a formula for Richard's age (N years) in terms of his father's age (m years).

   a   Richard's father is 38 now. How old is Richard?

   b   How old will Richard be when his father is 60?

11 The charge to send a parcel by courier is £6 per kilogram plus a fixed fee of £5.50.
   Construct a formula that connects the total cost with the weight of the parcel.
   Choose your own letters for this question, but remember to give the exact meaning of each one.

12 A father is three times as old as his son.

   a   If the father's age is H years when the son's age is x years, write down a formula connecting H and x.

   b   Use your formula to find the father's age if the son is 12.

   c   Will the same formula be valid in 12 years' time? If not, suggest what the formula will be in 12 years' time.

13 One packet of crisps costs 55 p.
   Construct a formula that gives the cost of a number of packets of crisps.
   Choose your own letters for the unknown numbers and give the meaning of each one.

When a formula is given that connects two related quantities, we can find the value of one quantity for any given value of the other. Often the letters that represent the unknown quantities are given. Sometimes we have to choose the letters ourselves.

Exercise 17d

Worked example

→ The total number of plastic extrusions produced by a machine is found by multiplying the number of hours for which the machine is operating by 15. Choose your own letters to represent the unknown numbers and use the letters to write a formula connecting them.

Let the total number of extrusions be N when the machine is operating for t hours.

Total number of extrusions = number of hours $\times$ 15

$$N = t \times 15$$
$$N = 15t$$

In this exercise, choose your own letters to represent the unknown numbers that can vary. State clearly the meaning you give to each letter. Write the resulting formula.

1   The profit made by a business is equal to its income minus its costs.

2   The perimeter of a rectangle is found by doubling the length of the longer side and adding to it twice the length of the shorter side.

3   The displacement of an engine is found by multiplying the capacity of one cylinder by the number of cylinders.

4   The number of cans of lemonade delivered to a store is found by multiplying the number of boxes delivered by the number of cans in each box.

Exercise 17e

Worked example

→ Copy the table and use the formula $P = a + 6$ to complete it.

a	3	8	12	16	30
P					

a	3	8	12	16	30
P	9	14	18	22	36

 When $a = 3$, $P = 3 + 6 = 9$
In each case the value of P is 6 more than the value of a.

In each of questions **1** to **8**, copy the table and use the given formula to complete it.

1 $a = b + 7$

b	1	2	3	4	5	6
a						

2 $P = 6a$

a	1	3	6	8	10	12
P						

💡 Remember that $6a$ means $6 \times a$.

3 $M = m - 4$

m	6	8	10	13	17
M					

4 $c = 10 - a$

a	1	2	3	4	5	6
c						

5 $b = 2.5 + c$

c	2	5	5.6	5.8	6.3
b					

6 $p = 12.5 - q$

q	3	5	6.5	7.2	8.9
p					

7 $y = 3.5x$

x	2	4	5	5.6	7.2
y					

8 $p = \dfrac{36}{v}$

v	1	2	3	4	5	8
p						

9 With the formula $t = 50w$, we can work out how long it takes to bake a loaf of bread, where w is the number of kilograms that the uncooked loaf weighs and t is the number of minutes it takes to bake.
  a How many minutes are needed to bake a loaf weighing 1 kg?
  b How long should a loaf weighing 1.5 kg take to bake?
  c If a loaf weighs 750 g how long will it take to bake?

10 When tyres are bought for a car assembly line the formula $t = 5c$ is used, where c is the number of cars to be assembled and t is the number of tyres needed.
  a How many tyres do they need to assemble one car?
  b They plan to assemble 2500 cars next week. How many tyres are needed?
  c The last delivery of tyres was an order for 2500. How many cars will this supply?

Formulas with two operations

A printer quotes a fixed cost of £5000 plus £5 per copy to print a local history book. To work out the cost he uses the formula

$C = 5000 + 5n$

where C is the number of £s it costs to print n books.

To find the value of C when $n = 2000$, two operations are necessary. First we must multiply 5 by 2000, and secondly we must add the result to 5000.

If $n = 5000$, $C = 5000 + 5 \times 2000$

$= 5000 + 10\,000$

$= 15\,000$

Using this formula, the cost for printing 2000 books is £15 000.

Exercise 17f

Worked example

$\rightarrow$ The number of drawing pins (N) needed to pin up q pictures is given by the formula $N = 2q + 2$
How many pins are needed to pin up 5 pictures?

$N = 2q + 2$

If $q = 5$, $N = 2 \times 5 + 2$

$= 10 + 2$

$= 12$

$\therefore$ 12 pins are needed to pin up 5 pictures.

 $2q$ is short for $2 \times q$

Use the formula $N = 2q + 2$, which gives the number of pins needed to pin up q pictures, to answer questions **1** to **5**.

1   How many pins are needed to pin up 8 pictures ?

2   If 13 pictures are pinned up, how many pins are used?

3   How many pins are used to pin up a single picture?

4   If $q = 6$, what is N?

5   What is N when $q = 11$?

Sari is making a matchstick pattern. If she completes n squares she needs M matchsticks, where $M = 4n + 1$.
Use this formula to answer questions **6** to **9**.

6   How many matchsticks does Sari need to complete 6 squares?

7 She completes 9 squares. How many matchsticks does she use?

8 Find M if $n = 4$.

9 When $n = 12$, what is M?

10 The formula for C in terms of n is $C = 3n + 4$.
Copy the table and complete it.

n	1	4	9	12
C				

11 p and q are connected by the formula $q = 5p - 4$.
Copy the table and complete it.

p	2	5	7	11	15
q					

12 A bicycle manufacturer buys in tyres and uses the formula
$N = 2a + 10$
to calculate the number of tyres to order when a is the number of bicycles to be assembled.
a How many tyres should be ordered if 50 bicycles are to be assembled?
b Why do you think 10 has been added to $2a$ in the formula?

Formulas with two substitutions

In the previous exercise we had to substitute a value for one letter on the right-hand side to find the value of the letter on the left-hand side. In the next exercise two substitutions are required on the right-hand side.

Exercise 17g

Worked example

→ Use the formula $A = l \times b$, where A cm^2 is the area of a rectangle of length l cm and breadth b cm, to find the area of a rectangle that is 8 cm long and 5 cm wide.

$$A = l \times b$$
If $l = 8$ and $b = 5$, $A = 8 \times 5$
$$= 40$$

The area of the rectangle is 40 cm^2.

Use the formula $A = l \times b$ to find A when

1 $l = 5$ and $b = 3$ 3 $l = 8$ and $b = 3.5$

2 $l = 8$ and $b = 6$ 4 $l = 4.4$ and $b = 2.7$

5 A rectangle is 12 cm long and 6 cm wide. Find its area.

6 Find the area of a rectangle measuring 20 mm by 15 mm.

Worked example

→ If $c = 5a - 2b$, find c when $a = 3$ and $b = 4$.

If $a = 3$ and $b = 4$,
$$c = 5 \times 3 - 2 \times 4$$
$$= 15 - 8$$
$$= 7$$

Remember, do multiplication first.

7 If $P = 2l + 2b$, find P when
   a $l = 7.5$ and $b = 2.4$ **b** $l = 5.6$ and $b = 2.8$

8 Given that $I = m \times v$, find I when
   a $m = 2.5$ and $v = 4$ **b** $m = 1.8$ and $v = 6.5$

9 Use the formula $v = u + 10t$ to find v when
   a $u = 3$ and $t = 8$ **b** $u = 8$ and $t = 3$

10 If $p = \dfrac{48}{v}$, find p when
   a $v = 4$ **b** $v = 12$ **c** $v = 16$

11 A printer uses the formula $P = a + 6b$ to work out the cost (£P) of printing b books when the set-up costs are £a.
   a   What do you think the '6' means in the formula?
   b   Find the cost of printing 1500 books if the set-up costs are £1800.
   c   Find the value of P when $a = 3750$ and $b = 2500$.

Directed numbers

In the last chapter we came across negative numbers for the first time. Sometimes negative numbers are used in formulas, so we need to become more familiar with working with them. Positive and negative numbers together are called **directed numbers**.

Directed numbers can be used to describe any quantity that can be measured above or below a natural zero. For example, a distance of 50 m above sea level and a distance of 50 m below sea level could be written as +50 m and −50 m.

They can also be used to describe time before and after a particular event. For example, 5 seconds before the start of a race and 5 seconds after the start of a race could be written as −5 s and +5 s.

Directed numbers can also be used to describe quantities that involve one of two possible directions. For example, if a car is travelling north at 70 km/h and another car is travelling south at 70 km/h they can be described as going at +70 km/h and −70 km/h.

A familiar use of negative numbers is to describe temperatures. The freezing point of water is 0° Celsius and a temperature of 5 °C below freezing point is written −5 °C.

Most people would call −5 °C 'minus 5 °C' but we will call it 'negative 5 °C' and there are good reasons for doing so, because in mathematics 'minus' often means 'take away'.

A temperature of 5 °C above freezing point is called 'positive 5 °C' and can be written as +5 °C. Most people would just call it 5 °C and write it without the positive symbol.

A number without any symbol in front of it is a positive number,
i.e. 2 means +2
and +3 can be written as 3.

Exercise 17h

Use the drawing to write the following temperatures as positive or negative numbers.

1 10° above freezing point   4 5° above zero

2 7° below freezing point   5 8° below zero

3 3° below zero   6 freezing point

Write down, in words, the meaning of the following temperatures.

7 −2 °C   9 4 °C   11 +8 °C

8 +3 °C   10 −10 °C   12 0 °C

Which temperature is higher?

13 +8° or +10°   17 −8° or 2°   21 −7° or −10°

14 12° or 3°   18 −2° or −5°   22 −2° or −9°

15 −2° or +4°   19 1° or −1°

16 −3° or −5°   20 +3° or −5°

23 The contour lines on the map below show distances above sea-level as positive numbers and distances below sea-level as negative numbers.

Write down in words the position relative to sea-level of the points A, B, C, D, E, F, G and H.

Worked example

→ Use positive or negative numbers to describe the height of a ball thrown up a distance of 5 m.

+5 m

In questions **24** to **34**, use positive or negative numbers to describe the quantities.

24 5 seconds before blast-off of a rocket

25 5 seconds after blast-off of a rocket

26 50 p in your purse

27 50 p owed

28 1 minute before the train leaves the station

29 a win of £50 on premium bonds

30 a debt of £5

31 walking forwards five paces

32 walking backwards five paces

33 the top of a hill which is 200 m above sea-level

34 a ball thrown vertically down a distance of 5 m.

35 At midnight the temperature was −2 °C. One hour later it was 1° colder.
What was the temperature then?

36 At midday the temperature was 18 °C. Two hours later it was 3° warmer.
What was the temperature then?

37 A rock-climber started at 200 m above sea-level and came a vertical distance of 50 m down the rock face.
How far above sea-level was he then?

38 At midnight the temperature was −5 °C. One hour later it was 2° warmer.
What was the temperature then?

39 At the end of the week, my financial state could be described as −75 p. I was later given £2. How could I then describe my financial state?

40 Positive numbers are used to describe a number of paces forwards and negative numbers are used to describe a number of paces backwards. Describe where you are in relation to your starting point if you walk +10 paces followed by −4 paces.

Extending the number line

If a **number line** is extended beyond zero, negative numbers can be used to describe points to the left of zero and positive numbers can be used to describe points to the right of zero.

On this number line, and we say that
5 is to the *right* of 3
5 is *greater* than 3

or
5 > 3

Also
and we say that
−2 is to the *right* of −4
−2 is *greater* than −4

or
−2 > −4

 A temperature of −2 °C is higher than a temperature of −4 °C.

'Greater' means 'higher up the scale'.

Now
and we say that
2 is to the *left* of 6
2 is *less* than 6

or
2 < 6

Also
and we say that
−3 is to the *left* of −1
−3 is *less* than −1

or
−3 < −1

'Less' means 'lower down the scale'.

Exercise 17i

Draw a number line to help you answer these questions.
In questions **1** to **12**, write either > or < between the two numbers.

1	3	2		**7**	3	−2
2	5	1		**8**	5	−10
3	−1	−4		**9**	−3	−9
4	−3	−1		**10**	−7	3
5	1	−2		**11**	−1	0
6	−4	1		**12**	1	−1

In questions **13** to **24**, write down the next two numbers in the sequence.

13	4, 6, 8		**19**	5, 1, −3
14	−4, −6, −8		**20**	2, 4, 8
15	4, 2, 0		**21**	36, 31, 26
16	−4, −2, 0		**22**	−10, −8, −6
17	9, 6, 3		**23**	−1, −2, −4
18	−4, −1, 2		**24**	1, 0, −1

Addition and subtraction of positive numbers

If you were asked to work out $5 - 7$ you would probably say that it cannot be done. But if you were asked to work out where you would be if you walked 5 steps forwards and then 7 steps backwards, you would say that you were two steps behind your starting point.

On the number line, $5 - 7$ means

> Start at 0 and go 5 places to the right
> and then go 7 places to the left.
> So $5 - 7 = -2$

i.e. 'minus' a positive number means *move to the left*
and 'plus' a positive number means *move to the right*.

In this way, $3 + 2 - 8 + 1$ can be shown on the number line as follows:

Therefore $3 + 2 - 8 + 1 = -2$

Exercise 17j

Find, using a number line if it helps

1 $3 - 6$	**3** $4 - 6$	**5** $4 - 2$	**7** $-2 + 3$	**9** $-5 - 7$
2 $5 - 2$	**4** $5 - 7$	**6** $5 + 2$	**8** $-3 + 5$	**10** $-3 + 2$

Worked example

→ Find $(+4) + (+3)$

$$(+4) + (+3) = 4 + 3$$
$$= 7$$

→ Find $(+4) - (+3)$

$$(+4) - (+3) = 4 - 3$$
$$= 1$$

Find

11 $(+3) + (+2)$	21 $(+3) + (+4) - (+1)$
12 $(+2) - (+4)$	22 $(+2) - (+5) + (+6)$
13 $(+5) - (+7)$	23 $-(+5) + (+4) - (+8)$
14 $-(+3) + (+2)$	24 $-3 - 4 + 2$
15 $-(+1) - (+5)$	25 $-2 - 3 + 9$
16 $5 - 2 + 3$	26 $-4 + 2 + 5$
17 $7 - 9 + 4$	27 $-3 + 1 - 4$
18 $5 - 11 + 3$	28 $(+9) - (+7) - (+2)$
19 $10 - 4 - 9$	29 $-(+3) + (+5) - (+5)$
20 $3 + 6 - 10$	30 $-(+8) - (+4) + (+7)$

Addition and subtraction of negative numbers

In a quiz, 3 points are awarded for a correct answer and 2 points are deducted for an incorrect answer.

Frank answered the first question correctly so gained 3 points, but he gave incorrect answers to the next three questions.

What was his score after each question?

After 1 question he had 3 points.

After 2 questions the number of points he had was $3 - 2$, i.e. 1.

Now, each wrong answer can be thought of as adding -2 to the score. This means that adding a negative number is the same as subtracting a positive number,

i.e. $3 + (-2) = 3 - 2 = 1$

After 3 questions, the number of points he had was

$1 + (-2) = 1 - 2 = -1$

After 4 questions, his score was $(-1) + (-2) = -1 - 2 = -3$.

Another situation where positive and negative numbers are used regularly is in the bank.

Eve is £100 overdrawn.

This could be shown on a statement as -100.

We know that to get the amount she has in the bank back to 0 she must take away -100, which is another way of saying that she must add 100 to her present balance, i.e. if, from her balance of -100, she takes away -100 the result is 0.

In a shorter form we can write

$$-100 - (-100) = 0$$

But we know that $\quad -100 + 100 = 0$

So $\quad\quad\quad\quad\quad -(-100) = +100$

You can confirm this by using your calculator.

There is a key to change the sign of a number; it is usually $(-)$,
i.e. to get -100 in the display press $(-)$ 1 0 0
To work out $-100 - (-100)$ key in
$(-)$ 1 0 0 $-$ $(-)$ 1 0 0 $=$
The display shows 0.

Find out how to use your calculator to change the sign of a number.

We can now use the following rules:

$$+ (+a) = +a \quad \text{and} \quad - (+a) = -a$$
$$+ (-a) = -a \quad \text{and} \quad - (-a) = +a$$

i.e. when two signs meet

signs that are the same make plus; signs that are different make minus.

Exercise 17k

Worked example

Use a calculator to find

$\rightarrow$ $5 + (-7)$

5 $+$ $(-)$ 7 $=$ -2

$\rightarrow$ $3 - (-7)$

3 $-$ $(-)$ 7 $=$ 10

$\rightarrow$ $-4 + (-8)$

$(-)$ 4 $+$ $(-)$ 8 $=$ -12

Use a calculator to answer questions **1** to **9**.

1 $3 + (-1)$	**4** $-1 - (-4)$	**7** $5 + (-7)$
2 $5 + (-8)$	**5** $-2 + (-7)$	**8** $-3 - (-9)$
3 $4 - (-3)$	**6** $-2 - (-5)$	**9** $-4 + (-10)$

Worked example

$\rightarrow$ Find $3 + (-4)$

$3 + (-4) = 3 - 4 = -1$ *Check:* $(-1) - (-4) = 3$

$\rightarrow$ Find $-3 - (-5)$

$-3 - (-5) = -3 + 5 = 2$ *Check:* $2 + (-5) = -3$

Do not use a calculator in questions **10** to **21**.

Find

10 $2 - (-8)$

11 $-7 + (-7)$

12 $-3 - (-3)$

13 $+4 + (-4)$

14 $+2 - (-4)$

15 $-3 + (-3)$

16 $3 + (-2)$

17 $-3 - (+2)$

18 $6 - (-3)$

19 $4 + (+4)$

20 $-5 + (-7)$

21 $9 - (+2)$

 Remember that when two signs meet, the same signs make plus, different signs make minus.

Worked example

$\Rightarrow$ Find $2 + (-1) - (-4)$

$2 + (-1) - (-4) = 2 - 1 + 4$
$= 5$

Find, without using a calculator

22 $5 + (-1) - (-3)$

23 $(-1) + (-1) + (-1)$

24 $4 - (-2) + (-4)$

25 $-2 - (-2) + (-4)$

26 $6 - (-7) + (-8)$

27 $9 + (-5) - (-9)$

28 $8 - (-7) + (-2)$

29 $10 + (-9) + (-7)$

30 $12 + (-8) - (-4)$

31 $9 + (-12) - (-4)$

32 $7 + (-3) - (+5)$

33 $2 - (-4) + (-6)$

34 $5 + (-2) - (+1)$

35 $8 - (-3) + (+5)$

36 $7 + (-4) - (-2)$

37 $8 - (-2) - (-1)$

38 Use a calculator to check your answers to questions **22** to **37**.

Worked example

$\Rightarrow$ Find $-8 - (4 - 7)$

$-8 - (4 - 7) = -8 - (-3)$
$= -8 + 3$
$= -5$

Find, without using a calculator

39 $3 - (4 - 3)$

40 $5 + (7 - 9)$

41 $4 + (8 - 12)$

42 $-3 - (7 - 10)$

43 $6 + (8 - 15)$

44 $(3 - 5) + 2$

45 $5 - (6 - 10)$

46 $(4 - 9) - 2$

47 $(3 - 8) - (9 - 4)$

48 $(3 - 1) + (5 - 10)$

49 $(7 + 4) - 15$

50 $8 + (3 - 8)$

51 $(7 - 12) - (6 - 9)$

52 $(4 - 8) - (10 - 15)$

 Brackets first

53 Add $+7$ to -5.

54 Subtract 7 from -5.

55 Subtract -2 from 1.

56 Find the value of '8 take away -10'.

57 Add -5 to $+3$.

58 Find the sum of -3 and $+4$.

59 Find the sum of -8 and $+10$.

60 Subtract positive 8 from negative 7.

61 Find the sum of -3 and -3 and -3.

62 Find the value of twice negative 3.

63 Find the value of four times -2.

64 At the start of the last round in a competition the scores stand at

     Alf 37,   Tanita 24,   Colin 35,   Jean 42

Each competitor gains points for correct answers but loses them for wrong answers.

During the last round
- Alf gained 24 points and lost 15
- Tanita gained 16 and lost 21
- Colin gained 8 and lost 29
- Jean gained 26 and lost 14.

Who won the competition? Who came second, third and last?

65 Newton is 5 miles from Menton and p miles from Leek.
All three villages lie on one road.
How far is it from Menton to Leek if
  a they are on opposite sides of Newton
  b they are on the same side of Newton but
     i Leek is furthest away
     ii Menton is furthest away?

Multiplying and dividing with directed numbers

We know that $\qquad\qquad 2a = a + a$

therefore, if $a = -4$, $\qquad 2a = (-4) + (-4)$

$$= -4 - 4$$
$$= -8$$

But $\qquad\qquad\qquad 2a = 2 \times a$

so $\qquad\qquad 2 \times (-4) = -8$

A negative number multiplied by a positive number gives a negative number.

We can rewrite $\quad 2 \times (-4) = -8$
as $\qquad\qquad (-8) = 2 \times (-4)$
i.e. $\qquad\qquad (-8) \div 2 = -4$, dividing both sides by 2
or $\qquad\qquad \dfrac{(-8)}{2} = -4$

A negative number divided by a positive number gives a negative number.

Exercise 171

Worked example

→ Find the value of $\quad 5 \times (-6)$

$5 \times (-6) = -30 \qquad Check: (-30) \div (-6) = 5$

→ Find the value of $\quad (-3) \times 7$

$(-3) \times 7 = -21$

 $(-3) \times 7$ is the same as $7 \times (-3)$.

→ Find the value of $\quad \dfrac{(-14)}{7}$

$\dfrac{(-14)}{7} = -2 \qquad Check: (-2) \times (7) = -14$

Find the value of

1 $\quad 3 \times (-5)$ $\qquad$ 5 $\quad (-5) \times 4$ $\qquad$ 9 $\quad \dfrac{(-6)}{3}$ $\qquad$ 13 $\quad \dfrac{(-26)}{2}$

2 $\quad 6 \times (-8)$ $\qquad$ 6 $\quad (-8) \times 3$ $\qquad$ 10 $\quad \dfrac{(-18)}{9}$ $\qquad$ 14 $\quad \dfrac{(-48)}{8}$

3 $\quad 4 \times (-8)$ $\qquad$ 7 $\quad (-6) \times 6$ $\qquad$ 11 $\quad \dfrac{(-24)}{6}$ $\qquad$ 15 $\quad \dfrac{(-36)}{6}$

4 $\quad (-3) \times 9$ $\qquad$ 8 $\quad 4 \times (-6)$ $\qquad$ 12 $\quad \dfrac{(-24)}{8}$ $\qquad$ 16 $\quad \dfrac{(-36)}{12}$

Formulas that involve directed numbers

Many formulas involve negative numbers.

One of the most important is the formula

$$c = \frac{5}{9}(f - 32)$$

which converts temperature from f degrees Fahrenheit to c degrees Celsius.

Exercise 17m

Worked example

→ Use the formula $c = \frac{5}{9}(f - 32)$ to convert 14 °F to °C.

If $f = 14$, $c = \frac{5}{9}(14 - 32)$

$= \frac{5}{9} \times (-18)$

$= 5 \times (-18) \div 9$

$= -10$

∴ 14° F is equivalent to −10°C

In questions **1** to **8**, use the formula $c = \frac{5}{9}(f - 32)$ to convert the following temperatures into °C.

1 5 °F

2 23 °F

3 32 °F

4 −4 °F

5 −13 °F

6 24.8 °F

7 10.4 °F

8 −12.5 °F

9 If $v = u + 5t$, find v when
  a $u = -10$ and $t = 1$
  b $u = -15$ and $t = 0.5$

10 Given that $P = q + 2r$, find P when
  a $q = -4$ and $r = 3$
  b $q = 6$ and $r = -4$
  c $q = -3$ and $r = -2$
  d $q = 8$ and $r = -4$

11 Given that $S = 2a + 3b$, find S when
  a $a = 4$ and $b = -3$
  b $a = -3$ and $b = 5$

12 If $y = 3x + c$, find y when
  a $x = 6$ and $c = -5$
  b $x = -4$ and $c = 7$
  c $x = -3$ and $c = -1$
  d $x = -7$ and $c = 9$

13 If $y = 5x - c$, find y when
  a $x = 4$ and $c = -5$
  b $x = -3$ and $c = 5$
  c $x = -3$ and $c = -9$
  d $x = 2$ and $c = -10$

14 Given that $A = 5b - 2c$, find A when
  a $b = -3$ and $c = 9$
  b $b = 2$ and $c = -6$
  c $b = -7$ and $c = 4$
  d $b = -0.05$ and $c = -1.5$

15 Given that $P = 3q - 2r$, find P when
  a $q = 0.7$ and $r = -3.5$
  b $q = -0.55$ and $r = 3.4$

Mixed exercises

Exercise 17n

1   Each pack delivered to an electronics company by Modcomp Ltd contains 48 components.
   a   Write down a formula that connects the total number (N) of components delivered with the number (n) of packs delivered.
   b   Use your formula to find the number of components in 12 packs.

2   The formula connecting p, q and r is $r = 5p - 2q$.
   Find the value of r when
   a $p = 4$ and $q = 3$
   b $p = 4.7$ and $q = 1.3$

3   Which is the higher temperature, $-5\,°C$ or $-8\,°C$?

4   Write < or > between
   a -3 2
   b -2 -4

5   Find   a $-4 + 6$ b $3 + 2 - 10$ c $2 + (-4)$

6   Find   a $3 - (-1)$ b $-2 + (-3) - (-5)$ c $4 - (2 - 3)$

7   If $y = 3x + c$, find the value of y when
   a $x = -2$ and $c = 8$
   b $x = 4$ and $c = -7$

Exercise 17p

1   Electric light bulbs are sold in packs of six.
   a   Write a formula that gives the total number of bulbs (N) in terms of the number of packs bought (n).
   b   Anne buys 6 packs. How many bulbs has she bought?

2   Given that $E = Ri$, find E when
   a $R = 8$ and $i = 2$
   b $R = 4.5$ and $i = 0.6$

Ri means $R \times i$.

3   Which is the lower temperature, $0\,°C$ or $-3\,°C$?

4   Write < or > between
   a   3 -4
   b -7 -10

5   Find   a $2 - 8$ b $3 - 9 + 4$ c $(+2) - (-3)$

6   Find   a $(-4) - (-5)$ b $3 + (5 - 8)$ c $-2 - (4 - 9)$

7   Given that $P = 12 - 5q$, find P when
   a $q = 5$
   b $q = -6$

Consider again

Now can you write these instructions without using words?

- When Sam does her accounts she calculates her profits by multiplying the number of items she sells by the price she sells them for.
- She then subtracts from this the cost of raw materials used for the items made.
- She also subtracts a fixed amount for the cost of using the rooms she works in.

! Investigation

1   Try this on a group of students or friends.
    Think of a number between 1 and 10.
    - Add 4.
    - Multiply the result by 5.
    - Double your answer.
    - Divide the result by 10.
    - Take away the number you first thought of.
    - Write down your answer.

    However many times you try this, the answer is 4.

    Investigate what happens when you use numbers other than whole numbers between 1 and 10. Try, for example, larger whole numbers, decimals, negative whole numbers, fractions.

    Is the answer always 4?

    Try to use the algebra you have learned in this chapter to explain your answer.

2   a

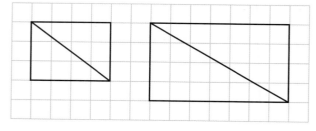

On squared paper mark out several rectangles of different sizes. The length (l) and breadth (b) of each rectangle must be a whole number of squares with a common factor of 1 only. For example, a rectangle with sides 6 squares by 7 squares is acceptable, but 4 squares by 6 squares is not because 4 and 6 also have a common factor of 2.

For each rectangle draw a diagonal and count the number of squares (d) through which the diagonal passes. Two examples are given on the previous page.

Gather all your results together in a table like the one given here. Now find a formula that connects d with l and b. You should collect the data for at least six rectangles before you try to write your formula. When you think you have found the formula, test it on some other rectangles.

l	b	d
4	3	6
7	4	10

b When you are satisfied that you have found the correct formula, draw rectangles that have sides with a highest common factor greater than 1. For example, a rectangle 6 squares by 9 squares will do, or one 8 squares by 12 squares. You will find it helpful to use this table. The letters l, b and d have the same meaning as in part **a**. h is the highest common factor of l and b.

For example, if $l = 6$ and $b = 4$, then $h = 2$.

l	b	h	d
6	4	2	8

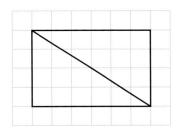

Find a formula that connects l, b, h and d.

18 Straight line graphs

Consider

Consider this graph.

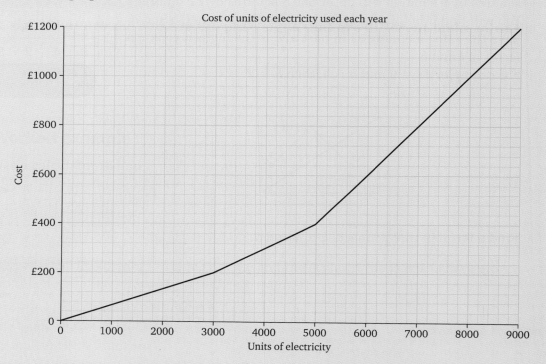

Cost of units of electricity used each year

Mr Wright used 4000 units of electricity one year. How much did it cost him?

Mrs Jones used 2500 units of electricity one year. What did she have to pay for this?

How much would it cost to use 7500 units in a year?

What happens to the cost when more than 3000 units are used? Why do you think this is the case?

Find out the cost per unit of electricity where you live. Does the cost per unit increase, decrease or stay the same when more than a given number of units are used?

You should be able to solve these problems after you have worked through this chapter.

A **graph** is a diagram showing the relationship between two varying quantities.

Line graphs

When Sara went into hospital, her temperature was taken every hour and recorded on this chart. The points representing the temperatures were joined by straight lines. A graph like this is called a **line graph**. The result gives a clear picture of what is happening to her temperature as the hours pass.

To find Sara's temperature at 1 a.m., first find 1 a.m. on the time scale, then go up to the graph and straight across to read the value on the temperature scale.
The value is 38.4 °C.

Any graph like this, where a quantity is measured at different times, is called a **time series**.

Class discussion

Use the graph above to answer these questions.

a   What was Sara's highest recorded temperature and when did it occur?

b   What was her lowest recorded temperature?

c   By 6 a.m. her temperature had returned to normal.
    What is her normal temperature?

d   How long was she in hospital before her temperature returned to normal?

e   Can you say what her highest temperature was while she was in hospital?

Exercise 18a

1

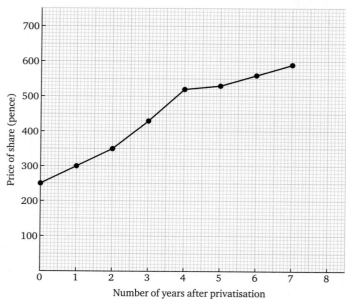

The graph shows the total monthly sales at Benshaw plc.

a In which month were the sales
   i greatest   **ii** least?
b Does the graph suggest gradually increasing sales?
c Does it look as though the sales improve around Christmas?
d Assuming that the sales graph has looked like this every year for the last five years, can you think of a business that could have this sales pattern?

2 The line graph shows the price of a share in a privatised company at yearly intervals after privatisation.

a What was the price of the share when issued?

b Copy and complete the following table.

Time after privatisation (years)	Price of share (pence)
1	
2	
3	
4	
5	
6	

c In which year after privatisation did the price of the share rise most?

d What trend do you notice in the price of the share?

3 **a** Use the graph given in question **2** to estimate the price of the share, 8 years after privatisation.

b Do you think that, 8 years after privatisation, the share price will be the same as your estimate?
Give a reason for your answer.

4 Use the graph for question **1** for these questions.

a Can the graph be used to find the half-monthly sales figures for the year? Explain your answer.

b Looking at this graph, the managing director asked why the sales had fallen in the first half of July. The sales director replied that they had not; they had in fact increased for the first two weeks of July. How could the sales director justify this statement and, assuming it is correct, describe what happened to the sales in the second half of July.

Conversion graphs

In a line graph, the lines between the points on the graphs show the general shape only. We cannot find values between points.

For example, in the temperature chart at the beginning of this chapter, Sara's temperature was taken at 3 a.m. and at 4 a.m. It was not taken between these times so we have no way of knowing what Sara's temperature was at, say, 3.30 a.m. We certainly cannot use the line between the points on the graph to find this.

In the graphs that follow, the lines have meaning along the whole of their length.

Exercise 18b

1 **Conversion graphs** are very useful for changing from one system of units to another. The graph on page 328 can be used to convert between pints and litres.
For example, to find the rough equivalent of 15 pints in litres, we find 15 on the horizontal (pints) axis, go up to the line and then across to the vertical (litres) axis. The reading here is about 9 litres, i.e. 15 pints ≈ 9 litres.

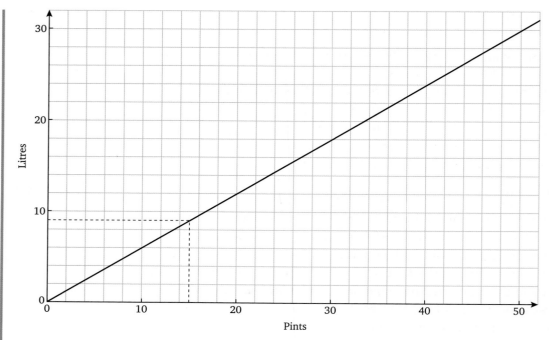

a   Use the conversion graph to find the rough equivalent in
    litres of
      i   10 pints
     ii   24 pints
    iii   44 pints

b   Find the rough equivalent in pints of
      i   10 litres
     ii   24 litres
    iii   13 litres

2

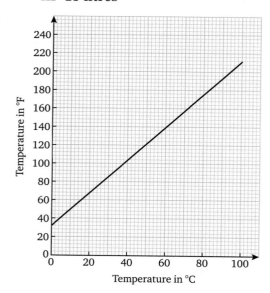

This graph converts between temperature in degrees Celsius and
in degrees Fahrenheit. Use the graph to answer these questions.

a Convert
  i 40 °C to °F   ii 140 °F to °C
b On a warm sunny day the temperature was 25 °C.
  What is this in °F?
c On a cold day last winter the temperature was 40 °F.
  What is this in °C?
d Water freezes at 0 °C and boils at 100 °C.
  Give these temperatures in °F.
e Normal body temperature is about 98 °F.
  What is this in °C?

3 The freezing point of water is 0 °C, but temperatures can fall below this
  value. We can describe a temperature below freezing using negative
  numbers, for example 2 °C below freezing can be written −2 °C.
  a Copy the graph used in question 2 on to squared paper so that
    there is space to the left and below. Extend the axes to the left and
    down, and extend the sloping line backwards.
  b Use your graph to convert
    i −2 °C to °F   ii 5 °F to °C
  c The temperature in New York on a cold February day in 2012 was
    −2 °F. What is this in °C?
  d The temperature in Moscow on a cold day last winter was −1 °C.
    What was this in °F?
  e When an explorer reached the North Pole, the temperature was
    −35 °C. Convert this temperature into °F.

Coordinates and straight lines

Exercise 18c

1 The points A, B, C, D and E are all on the same straight line.

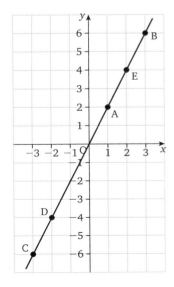

a Copy and complete this table for the coordinates of the points A, B, C, D and E.

	A	B	C	D	E
x					
y					

b F is another point on the same line.
The x-coordinate of F is 5.
Write down the y-coordinate of F, and add F to the table.

c What is the connection between the y-coordinate and the x-coordinate of points on this line?

d G, H, I, J, K, L and M are also points on this line.
Write down the missing coordinates.
G (8, ☐)   H (10, ☐)   I (−4, ☐)   J (☐, 12)   K (☐, 18)
L (☐, −10)   M (a, ☐)

All the lines we have met so far have ends, so they have a length that we can measure; lines like these are called **line segments**. In question 1, we can extend the line in both directions as far as we wish so the line has no ends; this is correctly called a line, not a line segment.

2 The points A, B, C, D and E are all on the same straight line.

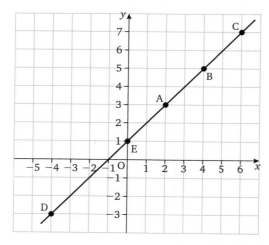

a Write down the coordinates of the points A, B, C, D, E, placing them in a table like the one given for question **1**.

b H is another point on this line.
Its x-coordinate is 8; what is its y-coordinate?

c How is the y-coordinate of each point related to its x-coordinate?

d I, J, K, L, M, and N are further points on this line.
Write down the missing coordinates.
I (12, ☐)   J (20, ☐)   K (30, ☐)   L (−12, ☐)   M (☐, 9)   N (a, ☐).

3

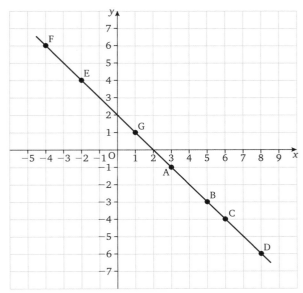

The points A, B, C, D, E, F and G are all on the same straight line.

a   Write down the coordinates of the points A, B, C, D, E, F and G.

b   H, I, J, K, L, M, N, P and Q are further points on the same line.
Write down the missing coordinates.

H (7, ☐)   I (10, ☐)   J (12, ☐)   K (20, ☐)   L (−7, ☐)
M (−9, ☐)   N (☐, 10)   P (☐, −8)   Q (☐, 12)

c   How is the y-coordinate related to the x-coordinate?

Consider again

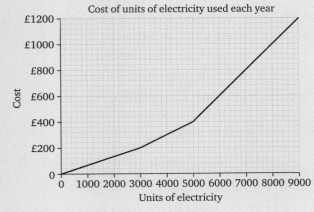

Now answer these questions.

Mr Wright used 4000 units of electricity one year. How much did it cost him?

Mrs Jones used 2500 units of electricity one year. What did she have to pay for this?

How much would it cost to use 7500 units in a year?

What happens to the cost when more than 3000 units are used? Why do you think this is the case?

Find out the cost per unit of electricity where you live. Does the cost per unit increase, decrease or stay the same when more than a given number of units are used?

Practical work

1 Collect examples of graphs from newspapers and magazines or from school textbooks in other subjects.

   a Which of your graphs are like question 1 of Exercise 18a, i.e. graphs where the lines have little or no meaning between the points that they join?

   b In which graphs do the lines have meaning along the whole of their lengths?

2 What data could you collect that gives a straight line graph that has meaning along the whole of its length?

   Gather such data and plot it on a graph.

   Explain how you can use your graph to give information that was not available to you before you drew the graph.

Summary 4

Perimeter

The perimeter is the distance all round the edge of a shape.

Area

Area is measured in standard sized squares.

A square with side 1 cm long is called one square centimetre and written $1\,cm^2$.

$$1\,cm^2 = 10 \times 10\,mm^2 = 100\,mm^2$$
$$1\,m^2 = 100 \times 100\,cm^2 = 10\,000\,cm^2$$
$$1\,km^2 = 1000 \times 1000\,m^2 = 1\,000\,000\,m^2$$

The area of a square $=$ (length of a side)^2

The area of a rectangle $=$ length $\times$ breadth

Special quadrilaterals

In a square

- all four sides are the same length
- both pairs of opposite sides are parallel
- all four angles are right angles.

In a rectangle

- both pairs of opposite sides are the same length
- both pairs of opposite sides are parallel
- all four angles are right angles.

In a rhombus

- all four sides are the same length
- both pairs of opposite sides are parallel
- the opposite angles are equal.

In a parallelogram

- both pairs of opposite sides are the same length
- both pairs of opposite sides are parallel
- the opposite angles are equal.

In a trapezium

- just one pair of opposite sides are parallel.

Parallel lines

When two parallel lines are cut by a transversal

- the corresponding angles are equal

- the alternate angles are equal

- the interior angles add up to 180°.

Coordinates

Coordinates give the position of a point as an ordered pair of numbers, e.g. (2, 4).

The first number gives the distance from O in the direction of the x-axis, and is called the x-coordinate.

The second number gives the distance from O in the direction of the y-axis, and is called the y-coordinate.

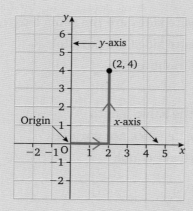

Directed numbers

Positive and negative numbers are collectively known as directed numbers. They can be represented on a number line.

The rules for adding and subtracting directed numbers are

$$+(+a) = +a \qquad -(+a) = -a$$
$$+(-a) = -a \qquad -(-a) = +a$$

Formulas

A formula is a general rule for finding one quantity in terms of other quantities, e.g. the formula for finding the area of a rectangle is given by

Area = length × breadth

When letters are used for unknown numbers, the formula can be written more concisely, i.e. the area, A cm^2, of a rectangle measuring l cm by b cm, is given by the formula

$A = l \times b$

REVISION EXERCISE 4.1 (Chapters 14 and 15)

1

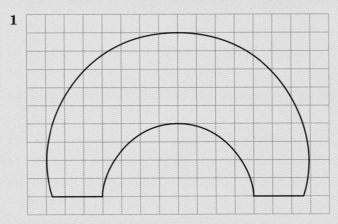

Each square represents 1 cm^2.
By counting squares find, approximately, the area of the shape.

2 Find the area of each shape.

a

b

3 The table gives some measurements of two rectangles.
Copy the table and fill in the missing values.

Rectangle	Length	Breadth	Perimeter	Area
A	6 cm		18 cm	
B		5 cm		50 cm^2

4 Change
  a $5.6\,\text{cm}^2$ into mm^2
  b $5\,000\,000\,\text{m}^2$ into km^2.

5 A rectangular carpet measures $3\,\text{m}$ by $4.5\,\text{m}$.
Find
  a   its area
  b   the cost of cleaning it at £3.80 per square metre.

6 Find the area of the cork (shown shaded) in this gasket.

7 Find the size of the angle marked d.

8 Find the size of each of the marked angles.

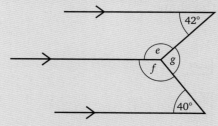

9 Copy these statements and fill in the blanks.
  a   The _____ of the three angles of a triangle is 180°.
  b   Corresponding angles are _____.
  c   56° and _____ are supplementary angles.

10

Use the letters marked in the diagram to give

a   two angles that are corresponding angles, one of which is *d*

b   two angles that are interior angles, one of which is *e*

c   two angles that are supplementary angles, one of which is *d*

d   two angles that are alternate angles, one of which is *e*.

REVISION EXERCISE 4.2 (Chapters 16 to 18)

Copy this diagram and use your copy to answer questions **1** to **4**.

1 Write down the coordinates of

   a   A

   b   D

2 Join the points ABCDA in order.
   What name do you give to this shape?

3 Mark a point E so that ABED is a parallelogram.
   Write down the coordinates of E.

4 Write down the coordinates of M, the midpoint of AD.
   Join MC.
   How is CM related to ED?

5 Which is the higher temperature, $-3\,°C$ or $-5\,°C$?

6 The formula connecting p, q and r is $r = 3p - 2q$.
   Find the value of r when

   a $p = 4$ and $q = 5$

   b $p = -3$ and $q = 4$

7 Subtract 4 from the sum of -5 and 8.

Questions **8** to **10** refer to the diagram given below.

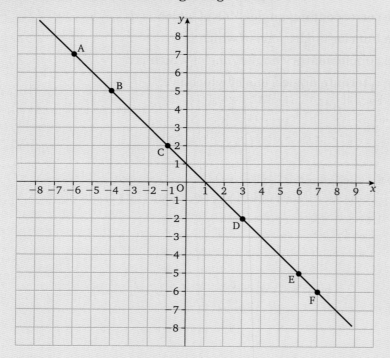

8 The points A, B, C, D, E and F are all on the same straight line.
Write down the coordinates of each point.

9 G, H, I, J, K and L are further points on the line.
Fill in the missing coordinates.
G (−2, ☐), H (5, ☐), I (☐, 6) J (☐, −1), K (−5, ☐),
L (☐, −7)

10 Use your answers to questions **8** and **9** to decide how the
x-coordinate is related to the y-coordinate for any point that lies on
the given line.

REVISION EXERCISE 4.3 (Chapters 14 to 18)

1 Change
  a $4400\,\text{cm}^2$ into m^2 **b** $790\,000\,\text{mm}^2$ into m^2

2 Five squares, each of side 4 cm, are arranged to form a cross as
shown in the diagram.
  a Find
    i its perimeter
    ii its area.
  b Suppose the squares are rearranged in a row.
    How does the length of the perimeter compare with the
    perimeter of the cross in part **a**?

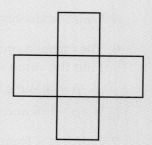

3 Find the value of three times negative three.

4 Write $<$ or $>$ between each pair of numbers.

   a -4 6

   b -7 -3

   c -5 -9

5 The temperature when I got up at 6 a.m. yesterday was $-4\,°C$. By noon it had increased by $6\,°C$. From noon to 6 p.m. the temperature dropped by $10\,°C$.

   a What was the temperature at 6 p.m.?

   b How much did the temperature fall between 6 p.m. and midnight if the temperature at midnight was $-11\,°C$?

6 Use the formula $f = \dfrac{9c}{5} + 32$ to find the value of f when

   a $c = 40$

   b $c = 0$

   c $c = -10$

Draw your own set of axes and mark a scale on each one from -10 to 10.

Use them to answer questions **7** and **8**.

7 Plot the points P $(-8, -3)$, Q $(-4, 2)$, R $(0, -3)$ and S $(-4, -8)$. What name do you give to the shape PQRS?

8 a Write down the coordinates of T if its y-coordinate is the same as the y-coordinate of Q and its x-coordinate is minus the x-coordinate of Q.

   b Find the coordinates of U if its x-coordinate is the same as the x-coordinate of T and its y-coordinate is the same as the y-coordinate of R.
       What name do we give to the shape QTUR?

9 Find each angle marked with a letter.

10

The points A, B, C and D are all on the same straight line.

a Write down the coordinates of these four points.

b F is another point on this line. The *x*-coordinate of F is 4.
Write down the *y*-coordinate of F.

c G is another point on this line. The *y*-coordinate of G is −1.
What is the *x*-coordinate of G?

REVISION EXERCISE 4.4 (Chapters 1 to 18)

1 Subtract one thousand eight hundred and seventy-nine from three
thousand two hundred and forty-eight.

2 Find the value of

   a 3^4

   b 7^3

   c $2^2 \times 5^3$

3 a Estimate the value of $647 \div 19$

   b Use a calculator to find $647 \div 19$ correct to two decimal places.

   c Find $36 \div 9 - 2 + 15 \times 7 \div 3$

4 a Which is the larger: $\frac{8}{9}$ or $\frac{9}{10}$?

   b Which is longer: a pipe 322 mm long or one 300 cm long?

5 Find, giving your answer in the unit in brackets

   a 4.5 m + 85 cm (cm)

   b 3 m + 165 cm + 40 mm (cm)

6 At the beginning of term, a teacher has 12 packs of exercise books, each pack containing 20 books.

   a How many exercise books does she have altogether?

   b She has 27 pupils in her form.
What is the largest number of exercise books she can give out so that every pupil has the same number of books?

7 Construct a triangle ABC in which the length of the side AB is 9.7 cm, the length of the side AC is 10.6 cm and the length of the side BC is 8.3 cm.

8 Which is heavier, a 5 lb bag of potatoes or a 2 kg bag of sugar?

9 One letter is chosen at random from the letters in the word EFFORT. What is the probability that the letter is

   a R   **b** F   **c** a consonant?

10 Use the formula $R = p \times q$ to find the value of R when

   a $p = 3.5$ and $q = 3$

   b $p = 2.4$ and $q = 5.5$

   c $p = 4$ and $q = -1.5$

   d $p = -3$ and $q = 2.5$

REVISION EXERCISE 4.5 (Chapters 1 to 18)

1 In an election there were three candidates. 1273 voted for Bullen, 942 for Wilson and 372 for Chan.

   a How many people voted?

   b If 7261 people were entitled to vote, how many people did not vote?

2 a Find $18 \div 6 \times 3 + 15 \times 2 - 42 \div 7$

   b Find

      i $2\frac{7}{13} + 1\frac{1}{2}$ **ii** $11\frac{4}{7} - 5\frac{1}{3}$

   c Express $\frac{12}{30}$ as

      i a decimal   **ii** a percentage.

3 Find, without using a calculator

   a $0.42 + 1.37 - 2.45$ **c** $0.059 \div 100$

   b 0.043×10 **d** $5.727 - 2.9$

4 a Estimate the value of $169.4 \div 52$, and then use a calculator to find its value correct to two decimal places.

   b Express 0.48 as

      i a percentage

      ii a fraction in its lowest terms.

   c Express $\frac{4}{13}$ as a decimal correct to two decimal places.

5 Find the value of the angle marked with a letter.

a
         b

6 Arrange the following lengths in order of size with the smallest first.

0.75 m,   693 mm,   73 cm,   2.4 m,   610 cm

7 The diagram shows the floor plan of Sean's bedroom.

Find

a   the length of skirting board used if the door is 80 cm wide

b   the area of the floor in square metres.

8 The coordinates of three vertices of a square ABCD are
A $(-3, -4)$, B $(-2, 3)$, C $(5, 2)$.
Find the coordinates of D.

9 a   Write down two angles that are supplementary.

   b   Draw a diagram to show an example of

      i corresponding angles

      ii alternate angles

      iii vertically opposite angles.

10 Find

    a $4 + (7 - 5)$ **b** $9 - (7 - 4)$ **c** $(5 - 7) + (2 - 7)$

Mental arithmetic practice 4

1 Find the area of a square of side 4 cm.

2 Find 0.08×9

3 Express 5.4 km in metres.

4 What is the largest number that will divide exactly into 45 and 60?

5 Give 0.095 correct to two decimal places.

6 Find 0.8^2

7 Express 732 mm in centimetres.

8 A rectangle measures 60 cm by 20 cm. Find its area.

9 Express 0.15 as a fraction in its lowest terms.

10 Write 12 as the sum of two prime numbers.

11 Write 0.36 as a percentage.

12 Is it true or false that the cost of 4 loaves at 57 p each is £2.18?

13 The area of a square is 36 cm². What is the length of a side?

14 Write thirteen thousand and seventy in figures.

15 Find 70% of £70.

16 Give 15.926 correct to two decimal places.

17 How many square millimetres are there in 12 cm²?

18 What is the probability of choosing a multiple of 3 from the numbers 1 to 11?

19 Change $5\frac{4}{5}$ into an improper fraction.

20 A rectangle is 2 m long and 50 cm wide. Find its area in m².

21 Find $5 \times 7 \times 4$

22 What word completes the statement: corresponding angles are __?

23 Is it true or false that the radius of a circle is half the length of its diameter?

24 Express 1500 mm² in cm².

25 How many possible outcomes are there when a six-sided dice is rolled?

26 Find $5 \times 5 + 5$

27 Subtract 36 from 95.

28 Is '5 take away −5' zero?

29 A is the point (8, 0) and B is the point (4, 0). How long is AB?

30 What is the difference between 5.89 and 7.21?

31 Add 0.05 to 2.05

32 P is the point $(-3, 0)$ and Q is the point $(7, 0)$. What is the length of PQ?

33 Change 16 cm to millimetres.

34 Is 49 a multiple of 6?

35 How many quarters are there in $2\frac{1}{2}$?

36 What number when multiplied by 7 gives 63?

37 C is the point $(5, 5)$ and D is the point $(5, -4)$. How long is CD?

38 Simplify $\frac{18}{24}$

39 Two angles are supplementary. One angle is 80°. What is the other?

40 Divide 0.048 by 6.

41 Find $3 -(-6)$

42 One of the angles at the base of an isosceles triangle is 70°.
What is the size of the smallest angle in the triangle?

43 Which is the smaller: $\frac{4}{5}$ or $\frac{5}{6}$?

44 What is '5 take away -8'?

45 Write down all the factors of 18.

46 An alloy of copper and tin is 55% copper. What percentage is tin?

47 Find $(-6) \times 6$

48 Which number is the larger: -3 or -5?

49 If $p = 5.5 - q$, find p when $q = 5$.

50 In a triangle, the sum of two of the angles is equal to the third
angle. Find the size of the largest angle in the triangle.

51 Find 0.7×0.04

52 Find $7 - 4 - 8$

53 Express 8% as a decimal.

54 Which temperature is higher: $-3°$ or $-4°$?

55 Roughly, how far is 100 miles in kilometres?

56 Subtract 0.04 from 2.

57 Which number is the smaller: -7 or -9?

58 If $P = a + 2b$, find P when $a = 5$ and $b = 10$.

59 Two angles of a triangle add to 125°.
What is the size of the third angle?

60 Which is the heavier: 500 g or 1 lb?

19 Summarising and comparing

Consider

Aisha collected the following information about the prices of personal music pla____ ____ £80 from two different websites, A and B.

A: £59.99, £11.97, £49.99, £24.99, £16.99, £29.99, £24.99, £72.99, £10.99, £24.99

B: £60.99, £21.97, £45.99, £34.99, £14.99, £25.99, £74.99, £52.99, £11.99, £14.99

In how many ways can Aisha compare these two lists?

If Aisha wants to buy a personal music player, what is likely to be the most useful information from these lists?

You should be able to solve this problem after you have worked through this chapter.

Class discussion

In each of the following situations, discuss whether it would be more useful to you to have detailed figures or some form of summary.

1 You are going on holiday and want to know what weather to expect.

2 You need to buy some soft drinks for an end-of-term party for your class.

3 You want to know if there are more people taller than you than there are shorter than you.

4 You want to know how much you would have to pay for a new smart television.

Range and central tendency

We often need to represent a set of numbers by one representative number which gives an indication of the middle of the set. It is also useful to have an indication of the spread of the numbers.

We can give an indication of the spread of a list of values by giving their **range**.

The range is the difference between the largest and smallest values.

The range of Aisha's prices for personal music players is £74.99 − £10.99 = £64.

Figures which give an indication of the middle of a set are called measures of **central tendency**. There are three of these and we will look at each one in turn.

Mean value

The most commonly used central figure is the arithmetic average or **mean**.

This is the figure that results from sharing out the different values equally.

For example,

Jan   Raj   Sara

Jan, Raj and Sara searched for some pebbles to use for skimming on water.

Jan found 9 pebbles, Raj found 4 and Sara found 5 pebbles.

They decided to put the pebbles into one pile and divide them up equally.

There are 18 pebbles in total to be shared among the three of them, so this gives 6 pebbles each.

The 6 pebbles that each child then has is called the *mean* of the 9, 4 and 5 pebbles that the children found.

To find the mean we add up all the values and divide by the number of values:

$$\textbf{Mean} = \frac{\textbf{sum of all the values}}{\textbf{number of values}}$$

The mean is not always a whole number, or even a quantity that can exist.

For example, if Jan has 2 dogs, Raj has 1 dog and Sara has 1 dog, then this gives 4 dogs in total.

If they could be shared equally, each of the three children would have $\frac{4}{3} = 1\frac{1}{3}$ dogs, and this is clearly impossible!

But $1\frac{1}{3}$ *is* the mean of the *numbers* 2, 1 and 1.

Exercise 19a

Worked example

➡ In five tests, Alan received marks of 7, 8, 7, 9 and 4.
What is his mean mark?

Total marks scored $= 7 + 8 + 7 + 9 + 4$
$\qquad\qquad\qquad = 35$
There are 5 tests.
Mean mark $= 35 \div 5$
$\qquad\qquad = 7$

➡ What is the range of his marks?
The highest mark is 9 and the lowest mark is 4. The range of the marks is $9 - 4 = 5$

1 Six students got the following marks in a test: 5, 7, 8, 4, 8, 4.
What is the mean mark?

2 In three different shops, the price of a can of cola is 49 p, 55 p
and 59 p.

  a What is the mean price?

  b What is the range of the prices?

3 Five students decided to pool their money. They put in the
following amounts:

  £10, £5, £6, £7, £12

  a How much was in the pool?

  b If the five students had contributed equally to this total, how
  much would each have given?

  c What was the mean amount contributed to the pool?

4 The ages of the children in a swimming club are

  9, 10, 8, 10, 11, 8, 12, 9, 10, 11, 10, 12

Find the mean age and the range of ages.

5 Find the mean and range of

  a 2,4, 8,4, 7, 1, 7, 6, 5, 6

  b 12, 15, 13, 10, 24, 16

  c 24, 35, 44, 28, 34

  d 1.2, 1.5, 1.3, 1.2

  e 12.4, 16.5, 27.9, 3.5, 26.1

6 The buses that passed the school gate in four hours were
counted.
From this information it was found that the average number of
buses per hour was 3.
How many buses were counted?

7 The 28 students in Class 7R took a maths test. The average mark
was 15. Carlos was away on the day of the test and took it later.
His mark was 24.

  a Will Carlos's mark increase or decrease the average mark for
  the test?

  b What is the total of the marks for all the students who took
  the test at the proper time?

  c Find the new mean mark when Carlos's mark is added to the
  total.

Finding the mean from a frequency table

This table shows the marks in a maths test.

Mark	Frequency
0	1
1	1
2	8
3	11
4	5
5	4
	Total: 30

From the figures in the table we can guess that the mean mark is about 3. To find the mean mark we first need to add up all the marks.

We could do this by listing each mark, but it is quicker to find the sum of the 0s, 1s, 2s, ... separately and then add these up. We can do this easily direct from the table.

For example, there are eight 2s, so the 2s add up to $8 \times 2 = 16$.

We add another column to the table so that we can keep track of what we are doing.

Mark	Frequency	Frequency × Mark
0	1	0
1	1	1
2	8	16
3	11	33
4	5	20
5	4	20
	Total: 30	*Total: 90*

Now we can see that there are 30 students and their marks add up to 90, so the mean mark is $90 \div 30 = 3$

This agrees with our guess.

Exercise 19b

1 The students in Class 7G gathered this information about themselves.

   a Guess the mean number of children per family.

   b Find the mean number of children per family.

Number of children in each family	Frequency
1	8
2	12
3	4
4	2

2 Joshua tossed three coins several times and recorded the number of heads that showed at each toss.

His results are shown in the table on the next page.

a Guess the value of the mean.
b Find the mean number of heads per toss.
c Is it better to give the answer for the mean as a fraction or as a decimal correct to one decimal place?
Give reasons for your answer.

Number of heads obtained when three coins are tossed	Frequency
0	9
1	7
2	16
3	3

3 Once every five minutes, Debbie counted the number of people queuing at a checkout and gave her results in this table.
a How many times did she count?
b What is the mean number of people queuing?

Number of people queuing at a supermarket checkout	Frequency
0	4
1	6
2	5
3	2
4	2

4 The students in Class 7P were asked to count the number of one pound coins that they had with them. The distribution of these coins is shown in the bar chart.
a How many students took part?
b What is the total value of the one pound coins?
c What is the range of the number of one pound coins?
d If the total sum of money represented here was shared out equally among the students, how much would each student have?
e What is the mean number of one pound coins?

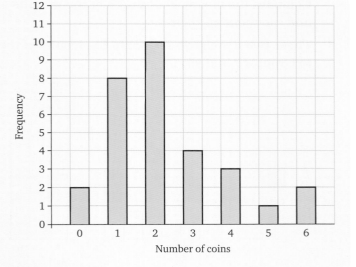

Using mean and range to compare two distributions

So far in this cricket season, Tom Batt has played five innings. His scores were 22, 53, 40, 35 and 25, so his mean score is 35. Reg Wicketaker has also completed five innings of 26, 90, 0, 52 and 17, so his mean score is 37.

There is little difference between the mean scores, but the range of Tom's scores is 53 − 22 = 31, and the range of Reg's scores is 90 − 0 = 90.

Comparing the two batsmen's scores indicates that, although Tom Batt has a slightly lower batting average, his scores are the more consistent of the two.

Exercise 19c

1   In the end-of-term tests, nine subjects were set and each one was marked out of 20. Sandra took eight subjects and her marks were

    12, 16, 14, 9, 8, 20, 15, 10

Karen took only five subjects and scored

    10, 15, 11, 14, 10

   a   On average, which girl did better?
   b   Which girl was more consistent in the standard she achieved?

2   Mr and Mrs Ng each made a batch of raisin cookies for a stall at the school fête. Out of curiosity they weighed each cookie and found that Mr Ng's weighed

    20, 25, 16, 21, 24, 26, 13, 17, 22 and 16 grams

Mrs Ng's weighed

    22, 21, 18, 17, 20, 20, 21, 19, 20 and 22 grams

Compare the means and ranges of the weights of the two batches and comment on them.

3   These two bar charts illustrate the results of the same test given to Group 7P and Group 7B.

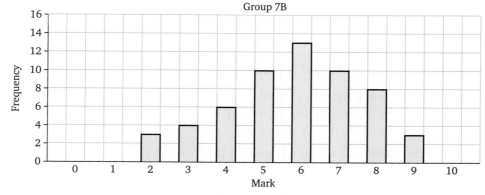

   a   Find the mean and range of each set of marks.
   b   Compare the two sets of marks.

Median

The **median** value of a set of numbers is the value of the middle number when they have been placed in ascending (or descending) order of size.

Imagine nine children arranged in order of their height.

Median value   154 cm

Middle child

The height of the fifth or middle child is 154 cm, i.e. the median height is 154 cm.

Similarly, 24 is the median of 12, 18, 24, 37 and 46; two numbers are smaller than 24 and two are larger.

To find the median of 16, 49, 53, 8, 32, 19 and 62, first rearrange the numbers in ascending order:

     8, 16, 19, 32, 49, 53, 62

Then we can see that the middle number of these is 32, i.e. the median is 32.

If there is an even number of values, the median is found by finding the average or mean of the two middle values after they have been placed in ascending or descending order.

To find the median of 24, 32, 36, 29, 31, 34, 35, 39, rearrange in ascending order:

     24, 29, 31, 32, 34, 35, 36, 39

Then the median is

$$\frac{32 + 34}{2} = \frac{66}{2} = 33$$

i.e. the median is 33.

Exercise 19d

Find the median of each of the following sets of numbers.

1 1, 2, 3, 5, 7, 11, 13

2 26, 33, 39, 42, 64, 87, 90

3 13, 24, 19, 13, 6, 36, 17

4 4, 18, 32, 16, 9, 7, 29

5 1.2, 3.4, 3.2, 6.5, 9.8, 0.4, 1.8

6 5, 7, 11, 13, 17, 19

7 34, 46, 88, 92, 104, 116, 118, 144

8 34, 42, 16, 85, 97, 24, 18, 38

9 1.92, 1.84, 1.89, 1.86, 1.96, 1.98, 1.73, 1.88

Worked example

This table shows the marks of Class 7G in a maths test.

Mark	Frequency
0	1
1	5
2	7
3	8
4	8
5	4
	Total: 33

➡ Find the median mark.

There are 33 marks, so the median mark is the 17th mark.
The median mark is 3.

 We can count down the frequencies until we find the 17th mark. The first six marks are zero and ones, adding on 7 gives 13 marks and takes us to the end of the twos. Adding on 8 gives 21 marks and takes us to the end of the threes. Therefore the 17th mark is in the list of threes, so 3 is the median mark.

➡ Lisa got 4 for this test. Is it true to say that she did better than half the class?

Yes, because Lisa's mark is higher than the median mark.

These distributions come from Exercise 19b. Find the median of each set of values.

10 The students in Class 7G gathered this information about themselves.

Find the median number of children per family.

Number of children in each family	Frequency
1	8
2	12
3	4
4	2

11 Joshua tossed three coins several times and recorded the number of heads that showed at each toss. His results are shown in the table.

Find the median number of heads per toss.

Number of heads obtained when three coins are tossed	Frequency
0	9
1	7
2	16
3	3

12 Once every five minutes Debbie counted the number of people
queuing at a checkout and gave her results in this table.

What is the median number of people queuing?

Number of people queuing at a supermarket checkout	Frequency
0	4
1	6
2	5
3	2
4	2

Mode

The **mode** of a set of numbers is the number that occurs most frequently, e.g. the mode of
the numbers

    6, 4, 6, 8, 10, 6, 3, 8, 4

is 6, since 6 is the only number occurring more than twice.

It would obviously be of use for a firm with a chain of shoe shops to know that the mode or
modal size for men's shoes in one part of the country is 8, whereas in another part of the
country it is 7. Such information would influence the number of pairs of shoes of each size
kept in stock.

If all the figures in a set of figures are different, there cannot be a mode, because no figure
occurs more frequently than all the others. On the other hand, if two figures are equally the
most popular, there will be two modes.

In Chapter 3, we used bar charts to show such things as the spread of shoe sizes in a group
of children, and the favourite
colour of a group of people.
These may be used to
determine the mode of
the group.

This bar chart shows the
colour selected by 35 people
when asked to choose their
favourite colour from a card
showing six colours.

It shows that the most
popular colour, or the modal
colour, is tomato red.

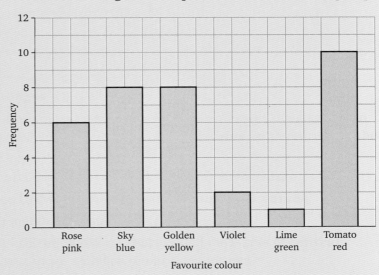

Exercise 19e

What is the mode of each of the following sets of numbers?

1   10, 8, 12, 14, 12, 10, 12, 8, 10, 12, 4

2   3, 9, 7, 9, 5, 4, 8, 2, 4, 3, 5, 9

3   1.2, 1.8, 1.9, 1.2, 1.8, 1.7, 1.4, 1.3, 1.8

4   58, 56, 59, 62, 56, 63, 54, 53

5   5.9, 5.6, 5.8, 5.7, 5.9, 5.9, 5.8, 5.7

6   26.2, 26.8, 26.4, 26.7, 26.5, 26.4, 26.6, 26.5, 26.4

7   The table shows the number of goals scored by a football club last season.

Number of goals	0	1	2	3	4	5	6
Frequency	12	16	7	4	2	0	1

Draw a bar chart to show these results and give the modal score.

8   Given below are the marks out of 10 obtained by 30 girls in a history test.

    8, 6, 5, 7, 8, 9, 10, 10, 3, 7, 3, 5, 4, 8, 7,
    8, 10, 9, 8, 7, 10, 9, 9, 7, 5, 4, 8, 1, 9, 8

Draw a bar chart to show this information and find the mode.

9   The heights of 10 girls, correct to the nearest centimetre, are

    155, 148, 153, 154, 155, 149, 162, 154, 156, 155

What is their modal height?

Which measure of central tendency?

Shaun was given the following information about the prices of trainers.

The prices ranged from £15 to £140. The mean price was £65, the median price was £52 and the mode was £45.

The mean price involves adding up all the prices, so its value takes into account the most expensive trainers and Shaun is probably not interested in those.

The median price shows that half the trainers cost £52 or less. This shows that there is a choice of trainers costing £52 or less.

The mode tells Shaun that more than one pair costs £45, but not how many cost £45. It could be just two pairs.

So the median price is the most useful information.

Exercise 19f

Decide the most useful way of summarising the information for the purpose given. Give a reason for your answer.

1 You have a list of the heights of 100 twelve-year-old girls. You want to know if you are taller or shorter than most of these girls.

2 You have a list giving the numbers sold over the last term of each item stocked by the school tuck shop.
   a You need to buy more stock and do not want to run out of the most popular item.
   b You have to buy the same quantity of each item.

3 You have a list giving the maximum and minimum temperature in Cairo each day in February for the last five years. You need to decide what clothes to take with you for a 10-day trip to Cairo in February.

4 You have a list of all models of inkjet printers that will print colour on A4 paper. You want an idea of the price you would have to pay for one.

5 Which form of summary would be most useful for each situation given in the class discussion on page 345? given in the class discussion on page 345?
   Give a reason for your choice.

Mixed exercise

Exercise 19g

1 In seven rounds of golf, a golfer gets scores of:
      72, 87, 73, 72, 86, 72 and 77
   Find the mean, mode and median of these scores.

2 The heights (correct to the nearest centimetre) of a group of boys are:
      159, 155, 153, 154, 157, 162, 152, 160, 161, 157

   Find   a their mean height   c their median height
          b their modal height   d the range of the heights.

3 The table shows how many students in a form were absent for various numbers of sessions during a certain school week.

Number of sessions absent	0	1	2	3	4	5	6	7	8	9	10
Frequency	20	2	4	0	2	0	1	2	0	0	1

   Find   a the mode   b the median   c the mean.

4   The mean number of words in each sentence on the first page of *The Machine Gunners* is 10 and the lengths of sentences range from 1 word to 25 words. For the first page of *Oliver Twist*, the mean length of the sentences is 68 words and they range from 34 words to 98 words.

Use this information to compare the sentences in the two books.

5   The table shows the marks obtained by a group of children in a quiz.

Mark	1	2	3	4	5	6	7	8	9	10
Frequency	5	10	14	10	9	8	8	6	6	9

a   How many children took part in the quiz?
b   Find the mean, median and modal marks.

Which of the following statements are true?
c   More than half the children got a score of 4 or more.
d   A score of 3 is the most likely score.
e   Jane got a score less than the mean, so more than half the group did better than Jane.

6   These frequency tables show the number of 20 p coins that ten students from two different classes had with them on one day.

Class 7T	
Number of 20 p coins	**Frequency**
0	2
1	6
2	0
3	2
4	0
5	0
6	0

Class 7R	
Number of 20 p coins	**Frequency**
0	0
1	4
2	3
3	2
4	0
5	0
6	1

a   Find the mean number of coins that each group had with them.
b   Is the mean a good representative for each distribution?
c   What would you use if you wanted to compare the two distributions?

Consider again

Here is Aisha's information about the costs of personal music players under £80 from websites A and B:

A: £59.99, £11.97, £49.99, £24.99, £16.99, £29.99, £24.99, £72.99, £10.99, £24.99

B: £60.99, £21.97, £45.99, £34.99, £14.99, £25.99, £74.99, £52.99, £11.99, £14.99

In how many ways can Aisha compare these two lists?

If she wants to buy a personal music player, what is likely to be the most useful information from these lists?

 Practical work

1   If you throw a fair dice 60 times, then *in theory* you should get each score 10 times, i.e. a frequency table would look like this.

Score	1	2	3	4	5	6
Frequency	10	10	10	10	10	10

    a   Find the mean score of this theoretical distribution.

    b   If you throw a dice 60 times, you will be very unlikely indeed to get equal numbers of each score. But, if your dice is unbiased, and if you throw it fairly, you should get a mean score near to the theoretical mean.
Throw a dice 60 times, record your results and find your mean score. How does your mean compare with the theoretical mean?
Can you say whether your dice is likely to be unbiased?

    c   Now repeat part **b** with an obviously biased dice. (You can make one like the one shown on page 362 and stick a bit of Blu-Tack inside one face before you make it up.)

2   Do a search on the Internet to get prices for 500 g of tomatoes from at least ten different suppliers. Write these down as a list and use the information to find
    a   the range of prices
    b   the mean price
    c   the modal price.

20 Solids

Consider

Lee has a bucket that holds two gallons. He fills it up from a tank full of water. The tank is a cuboid measuring 600 mm by 800 mm by 1000 mm. How many times can he fill his bucket from the tank?

You should be able to solve this problem after you have worked through this chapter.

We live in a three-dimensional world among solid objects. Solids have depth as well as length and breadth. Sometimes we have to tell other people what a particular solid looks like. We might, for example, see a bookcase in a shop and want to describe it to someone. We could use words or a drawing or a photograph; we cannot show the bookcase itself unless we buy it or take people to the shop to look at it.

Sometimes there is no object to show, just an idea of one in our heads. Greg is designing a set of building blocks for young children.

To start with, he could
• make a few blocks
• draw his ideas on paper.

Trying out ideas by making blocks is time consuming. It is better to try them out by drawing them on paper first.

Class discussion

1 Work in pairs for this question.
   a One of you should think of a table in your home.
      Try describing it to your partner in words, without using the word 'table'.
   b Now try drawing the table.
      Which method gives most information?
   c Now change roles and repeat parts **a** and **b**.
2 Lydia has an idea for a new desk which she is hoping to be allowed to make for herself.
   Discuss the ways in which she can get her ideas over to her family.

Drawing a three-dimensional object on paper is often the most effective way of showing other people what it looks like.

Drawing cubes and cuboids

A **cube** is a three-dimensional object. Each of its faces is a square. When we draw a cube on a flat sheet of paper, only one of its faces is drawn as a square; the others that can be seen are drawn as parallelograms.

Using a square grid of lines or dots makes it easier to get parallel edges.

Rectangular blocks, called **cuboids**, can be drawn in a similar way.

Exercise 20a

1 Use the diagrams above to answer the following questions.
   a Measure each of the lines on the drawing of the cube.
      Are they all the same length?
   b Measure each of the lines on the drawing of the cuboid.
      Are these the same as the measurements marked on the drawing?

2 Use squared paper to draw a cube of side 3 cm.
   Do you need to put the measurements on the diagram?
   Give a reason for your answer.

3 Use squared paper to draw a picture of a cuboid measuring 4 cm by 2 cm by 1 cm.
   If you do not put the dimensions of the cuboid on your drawing, can someone else tell what the measurements of the cuboid are?

Using isometric paper to draw cubes and cuboids

A cube can be drawn in another way, with a vertical edge right at the front, as shown below.

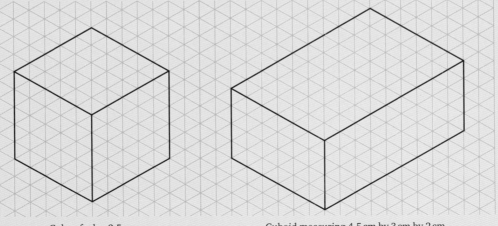

Cube of edge 2.5 cm   Cuboid measuring 4.5 cm by 3 cm by 2 cm

Drawn in this way, each face is a parallelogram. This is not easy to do freehand but there is a grid, called an **isometric grid**, that makes the job simple. (Sometimes the grid is replaced by dots.)

Cuboids can be drawn in a similar way.

Exercise 20b

Use isometric paper for this exercise. Make sure that the paper is the correct way round, i.e. that one set of lines is vertical.

1   Measure each of the lines on the drawings of the cubes on page 359.
What do you notice?

2   Measure each of the lines on the drawings of the cuboids on page 359.
What do you notice?

3   This drawing represents a cuboid measuring 5 cm by 3 cm by 1 cm.

    a   Measure each line on the drawing.
What do you notice?

    b   Draw a picture of a cuboid measuring 6 cm by 4 cm by 3 cm. Measure each of your lines.
What do you notice?

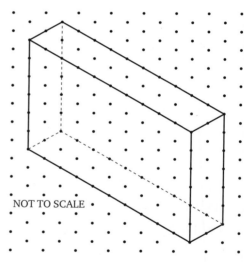

NOT TO SCALE

4   This drawing represents a cube of side 2 cm.

    a   Measure each line in this drawing.
What do you notice?

    b   Draw a picture of a cube of side 4 cm on a 1 cm isometric grid, then measure each of the lines you have drawn.

    c   Do you need to put measurements on your drawing?

    d   What is the disadvantage of using isometric paper to draw a cube?

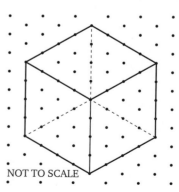

NOT TO SCALE

When cubes and cuboids are drawn on isometric paper, the lengths of the lines representing the edges are the correct length.

5 Draw a picture of each of the following solids on an isometric grid.

    a   a cube of side 5 cm

    b   a cube of side 8 cm

    c   a cuboid 6 cm by 4 cm by 1 cm

    d   a cuboid 3 cm by 5 cm by 3 cm

6 Isometric paper is useful when drawing stacks of cubes.

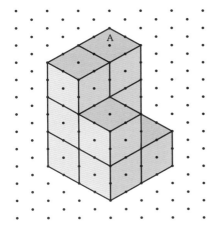

    a   How many loose cubes are needed to make the stack that you can see here?

    b   Explain how your answer to part **a** might be affected if you are told that the cubes are stuck together.

    c   Draw the stack with the cube marked **A** removed.

7 Sixty-four cubes, each with an edge of 1 cm, are arranged to form a large cube with an edge of 4 cm as shown in the diagram.

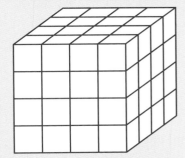

The large cube is painted red.
How many of the sixty-four cubes are unpainted?

Making cubes and cuboids

Any solid with flat faces can be made from a flat sheet.

(*Note:* We are using the word 'solid' for any object that takes up space, i.e. for any three-dimensional object, and such an object can be hollow.)

A cube can be made from six separate squares.

We can avoid a lot of unnecessary sticking if we join some squares together before cutting out.

This is called a **net**.

There are other arrangements of six squares that can be folded up to make a cube. Not all arrangements of six squares will work, however, as we will see in the next exercise.

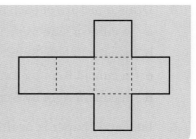

Exercise 20c

1 Below is the net of a cube of edge 4 cm.

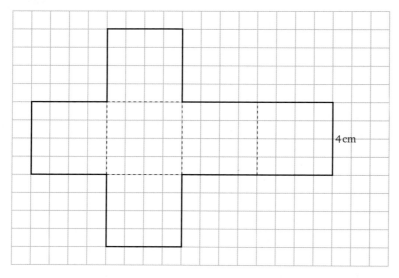

Draw the net on 1 cm squared paper and cut it out.
Fold it along the broken lines.
Fix it together with sticky tape.
If you mark the faces with the numbers 1 to 6, you can make a dice.

2 Draw this net full-size on 1 cm squared paper.

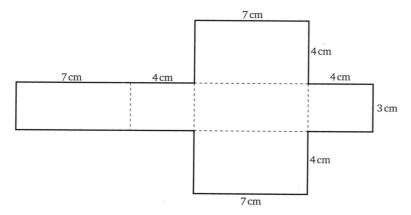

Cut the net out and fold along the dotted lines.
Stick the edges together.

a   **i** How many faces are rectangles measuring 7 cm by 4 cm?
    ii How many faces are rectangles measuring 7 cm by 3 cm?
    iii What are the measurements of the remaining faces?

b Draw another arrangement of the rectangles which will fold
up to make this cuboid.

3 This cuboid is 4 cm long, 2 cm wide and 1 cm high.

  a How many faces does this cuboid have?
  b Sketch the faces, showing their measurements.
  c On 1 cm squared paper, draw a net that will
make this cuboid.

4 This net will make a cuboid.

  a Sketch the cuboid, and show its measurements.
  b Which edge meets HI?
  c Which other corners meet at A?

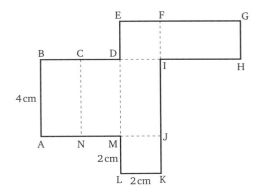

5 This net will make a cube.

  a Which edge meets AB?
  b Which other corners meet at H?

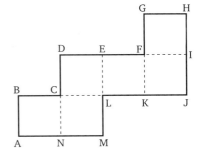

6 This cube is cut along the edges
drawn with a coloured line and
flattened out.
Draw the flattened shape.

7 Here are two arrangements of six squares.

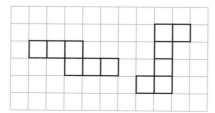

   a Copy these on 1 cm squared paper.

   b Draw as many other arrangements of six squares as you can find.

   c Which of your arrangements, including the two given here, will fold up to make a cube?

     If you cannot tell by looking, cut them out and try to make a cube.

Volume

The **volume** of a solid is the amount of space it occupies.

In a science laboratory you may have seen a container with a spout, similar to the one shown in the diagram.

The container is filled with water to the level of the spout. Any solid which is immersed in the water will force a quantity of water into the measuring cylinder. The volume of this water is equal to the volume of the solid.

Cubic units

As with area, we need a convenient unit for measuring volume. The most suitable unit is a cube.

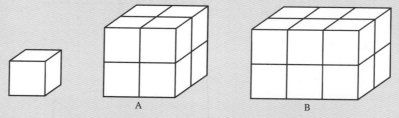

Now we can count how many of the smallest cubes are needed to fill the same space as each of the solids A and B: 8 small cubes fill the same space as solid A and 12 small cubes fill the same space as solid B.

This tells us that solid B occupies $1\frac{1}{2}$ times as much space as solid A, but it does not help if we want to compare the volume of A with the volume of this book, say. To do this we need to measure volume in standard cubic units. These are based on the standard units of length.

A cube with a side of 1 cm has a volume of one **cubic centimetre** which is written $1\,cm^3$. Similarly a cube with a side of 1 mm has a volume of $1\,mm^3$ and a cube with a side of 1 m has a volume of $1\,m^3$.

Volume of a cuboid

The diagram shows a cuboid measuring 4 cm by 3 cm by 2 cm.

To cover the area on which the block stands we need three rows of standard 1 cm cubes with four cubes in each row, i.e. 12 cubes.

A second layer of 12 cubes is needed to give the volume shown, so the volume of the block is 24 standard 1 cm cubes.

Therefore the volume of the solid is $24\,cm^3$.

This is also given when we calculate length × breadth × height, i.e.

Volume of block $= 4 \times 3 \times 2\,cm^3$

Volume of cuboid = length × breadth × height

Exercise 20d

1 Which unit would you use to give the volume of
  a this book
  b the room you are in
  c one vitamin pill
  d a lorry load of rubble
  e a packet of cornflakes
  f a 2 p coin
  g a concrete building block?

Worked example

→ Find the volume of a cuboid measuring 12 cm by 10 cm by 5 cm.

Volume of cuboid = length × breadth × height
$$= 12 \times 10 \times 5\,cm^3$$
i.e.   Volume $= 600\,cm^3$

Find the volume of each of the following cuboids.

	Length	Breadth	Height
2	4 cm	4 cm	3 cm
3	20 mm	10 mm	8 mm
4	6.1 m	4 m	1.3 m
5	3.5 cm	2.5 cm	1.2 cm
6	4 m	3 m	2 m
7	8 m	5 m	4 m
8	8 cm	3 cm	$\frac{1}{2}$ cm
9	12 cm	1.2 cm	0.5 cm
10	4.5 m	1.2 m	0.8 m

When the lengths of the edges of a cuboid are given in different units, we must change some of them so that all measurements are given in the same unit.

11 A rectangular block of concrete is 1 m long, 20 cm wide and 25 cm deep.
Find the volume of the block in cubic centimetres.

12 A rectangular piece of aluminium measures 25 cm by 15 mm by 5 mm.
Find its volume in cubic millimetres.

13 The shape of an outdoor aviary is a cuboid with measurements 2 m by 90 cm by 90 cm.
Find the volume of the aviary, giving your answer in the most appropriate unit.

Worked example

→ Find the volume of a cube with side 6 cm.

Volume of cube = length × breadth × height
$$= 6 \times 6 \times 6 \text{ cm}^3$$
i.e.   Volume = 216 cm³

Find the volume of a cube with the given side.

14 4 cm

15 5 cm

16 2 m

17 $\frac{1}{2}$ cm

18 2.5 cm

19 3 km

20 8 cm

21 $\frac{1}{2}$ m

22 3.4 m

Worked example

→ Draw a cube of side 8 cm.
How many cubes of side 2 cm would be needed to fill the same space?

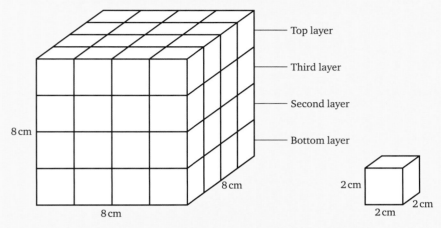

The bottom layer needs 4 × 4, i.e. 16 cubes of side 2 cm, and there are four layers altogether.
64 cubes are required.

23 Draw a cube of side 4 cm.
How many cubes of side 2 cm would be needed to fill the same space?

24 Draw a cuboid measuring 6 cm by 4 cm by 2 cm.
How many cubes of side 2 cm would be needed to fill the same space?

25 Draw a cube of side 6 cm.
How many cubes of side 3 cm would be needed to fill the same space?

26 Draw a cuboid measuring 8 cm by 6 cm by 2 cm.
How many cubes of side 2 cm would be needed to fill the same space?

27 A cuboid measures 4 cm by 8 cm by 4 cm. The same space is to be filled with smaller cubes.
How many cubes are needed if their sides are
a   1 cm
b   2 cm
c   4 cm?

28 Find the volume of air in a room measuring 4 m by 5 m which is 3 m high.

29 Find the volume, in cm³, of a concrete block measuring 36 cm by 18 cm by 12 cm.

30 Find the volume of a school hall which is 30 m long and 24 m wide if the ceiling is 9 m high.

31 An electric light bulb is sold in a box measuring 10 cm by 6 cm by 6 cm.
If the shopkeeper receives them in a carton measuring 50 cm by 30 cm by 30 cm, how many bulbs are packed in a carton?

32 A classroom is 10 m long, 8 m wide and 3 m high.
How many students should it be used for if each student requires 5 m^3 of air space?

33 How many rectangular packets, measuring 8 cm by 6 cm by 4 cm, can be packed in a rectangular cardboard box measuring 30 cm by 24 cm by 16 cm?

34 A kitchen worktop is 2 m long, 60 cm deep and 90 cm above the floor. What is the volume of the space below the worktop?

35 Rectangular blocks of stone measure 30 cm by 20 cm by 35 mm. How many of these blocks can be laid flat in a cube-shaped crate whose edge is 1 m?

Changing units of volume

Consider a cube of side 1 cm. If each edge is divided into 10 mm, the cube can be divided into 10 layers, each layer with 10 × 10 cubes of side 1 mm,

100 cubes, each with a volume of 1 mm^3, in every one of these layers

i.e. $1\,cm^3 = 10 \times 10 \times 10\,mm^3$
              $= 1000\,mm^3$

Similarly,   since 1 m = 100 cm

1 cubic metre (m^3) = 100 × 100 × 100 cm^3
                  = 1 000 000 cm^3

Exercise 20e

Worked example

→ Express $2.4\,\text{m}^3$ in cm^3

Since $1\,\text{m}^3 = 100 \times 100 \times 100\,\text{cm}^3$
$2.4\,\text{m}^3 = 2.4 \times 100 \times 100 \times 100\,\text{cm}^3$
$= 2\,400\,000\,\text{cm}^3$

→ Express $0.0025\,\text{cm}^3$ in mm^3

As $1\,\text{cm}^3 = 10 \times 10 \times 10\,\text{mm}^3$
$0.0025\,\text{cm}^3 = 0.0025 \times 10 \times 10 \times 10\,\text{mm}^3$
$= 2.5\,\text{mm}^3$

→ Express $126\,\text{cm}^3$ in m^3

$1\,\text{m}^3 = 1\,000\,000\,\text{cm}^3$ so $1\,\text{cm}^3 = \frac{1}{1\,000\,000}\,\text{m}^3$
$\therefore \quad 126\,\text{cm}^3 = 126 \div 1\,000\,000\,\text{m}^3$
$= 0.000\,126\,\text{m}^3$

Express in mm^3

1 $8\,\text{cm}^3$	**3** $6.2\,\text{cm}^3$	**5** $0.0092\,\text{m}^3$
2 $14\,\text{cm}^3$	**4** $0.43\,\text{cm}^3$	**6** $0.0004\,\text{cm}^3$

Express in cm^3

7 $3\,\text{m}^3$	**10** $0.0063\,\text{m}^3$	**13** $29\,300\,\text{mm}^3$
8 $2.5\,\text{m}^3$	**11** $22\,\text{mm}^3$	**14** $2.5\,\text{mm}^3$
9 $0.42\,\text{m}^3$	**12** $731\,\text{mm}^3$	**15** $1000\,\text{mm}^3$

Capacity

When we buy a carton of milk or a can of engine oil we are not usually interested in the external measurements or volume of the container. What really concerns us is how much milk is inside the carton, or how much engine oil is inside the can, i.e. the **capacity** of the container.

The most common unit of capacity in the metric system is the **litre**.

(*Note:* A litre is roughly equivalent to a full carton of milk.) A litre is much larger than a cubic centimetre but much smaller than a cubic metre. The relationship between these quantities is:

$1000\,\text{cm}^3$ = 1 litre

i.e. a litre is the volume of a cube of side 10 cm.

1000 litres = $1\,\text{m}^3$

When the amount of liquid is small, such as dosages of medicines, the **millilitre** (ml) is used. A millilitre is a thousandth part of a litre, i.e.

1000 ml = 1 litre or 1 ml = $1\,\text{cm}^3$

Exercise 20f

Worked example

→ Express   5.6 litres in cm³

1 litre = 1000 cm³

5.6 litres = 5.6 × 1000 cm³
      = 5600 cm³

Express in cm³

1   2.5 litres

2   1.76 litres

3   0.54 litres

4   0.0075 litres

5   35 litres

6   0.028 litres

Express in litres

7   7000 cm³

8   4000 cm³

9   2400 cm³

10   5 m³

11   12 m³

12   4.6 cm³

Worked example

→ Find the capacity, in litres, of a water tank whose internal measurements are 2 m by 70 cm by 30 cm.

70 cm

30 cm

2 m

 We need to find the volume of the tank in cm³. To do this, all the measurements must be in centimetres, so first convert 2 m into centimetres.

Length of cuboid = 2 m = 2 × 100 cm = 200 cm

Volume of cuboid = length × breadth × height
      = 200 × 70 × 30 cm³
      = 420 000 cm³

Capacity of tank = 420 000 ÷ 1000 litres
      = 420 litres

 1000 cm³ = 1 litre, so to convert cubic centimetres to litres, we divide by 1000.

13 Find the capacity, in litres, of these cuboids.

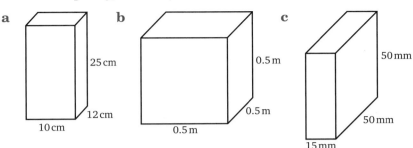

a   25 cm   12 cm   10 cm

b   0.5 m   0.5 m   0.5 m

c   50 mm   50 mm   15 mm

14 How many litres will it take to fill a rectangular petrol can measuring 30 cm by 20 cm by 10 cm?

15 A metal block, measuring 50 cm by 12 cm by 12 cm, is melted. How many litres of liquid metal are there?

16 A rectangular water storage tank is 3 m long, 2 m wide and 1 m deep. How many litres of water will it hold?

17 How many cubic metres of water are required to fill a rectangular swimming bath 15 m long and 10 m wide, which is 2 m deep throughout?
How many litres is this?

18 Find the capacity, in litres, of a rectangular carton measuring 20 cm by 15 cm by 30 mm.

19 A rectangular fish tank is 1 m long, 30 cm deep and 20 cm high. How many litres of water will it hold?

20 A rectangular carton of concentrated orange juice measures 5 cm by 10 cm by 4 cm. To make one glass of juice, 5 ml of this concentrate are needed. How many glasses of juice can be made from one full carton?

21 How many lead cubes, of side 2 cm, can be cast from 5 litres of liquid lead?

22

When the lump of metal has been lowered into the water, the reading on the small container is 250 ml.

Find the volume of the lump in cubic centimetres.

Imperial units of capacity

Imperial units of capacity are still in use, and the common ones are the **pint** and **gallon**.

Some drinks are sold over the counter in pints. Many cars give the capacity of the fuel tank in gallons. The relationship between pints and gallons is

1 gallon = 8 pints

Approximate conversions between metric and imperial units of capacity can be made using

1 litre ≈ 1.75 pints   and   1 gallon ≈ 4.5 litres

Exercise 20g

1   Give, roughly, the number of pints equivalent to

   a 20 litres   **b** 12 litres   **c** 1.5 litres

2   Roughly, how many gallons is

   a 50 litres   **b** 30 litres   **c** 25 litres?

3   Give the approximate number of litres equivalent to

   a 4 pints   **b** $2\frac{1}{2}$ gallons   **c** 10 gallons

4   Arrange these containers in order of capacity, with the largest first.

5 gallons   2 litres   2.5 gallons   4 pints

750 millilitres   2 pints

5   Liz fills her car up with petrol. The reading on the pump is 38 litres. How many gallons is that?

6   A recipe needs 100 ml of cream.
   Will half a pint be enough?

7   A rectangular fish tank measures 300 mm by 250 mm by 500 mm. Roughly, how many gallons of water will it hold when full?

8   Petrol costs 140 p a litre. How much, roughly, will it cost to fill a tank whose capacity is 1.5 gallons?

Mixed exercises

Exercise 20h

1. Express $3.2\,\text{m}^3$ in   **a** cm^3 **b** mm^3.

2. Express 1.6 litres in cm^3.

3. Find the volume of a cube of side $4\,\text{cm}$.

4. Find the volume, in cm^3, of a cuboid measuring $2\,\text{m}$ by $25\,\text{cm}$ by $10\,\text{cm}$.

5. Find the volume, in mm^3, of a cuboid measuring $5\,\text{cm}$ by $3\,\text{cm}$ by $9\,\text{mm}$.

6. Find, roughly, the capacity in pints of a carton designed to hold 1.5 litres.

7. The diagram shows a stack of loose $2\,\text{cm}$ cubes. What is the volume of the stack?

Exercise 20i

1. Express $8\,\text{cm}^3$ in   **a** mm^3 **b** m^3.

2. Express $3500\,\text{cm}^3$ in litres.

3. Find the volume of a cuboid measuring $10\,\text{cm}$ by $5\,\text{cm}$ by $6\,\text{cm}$.

4. Find, in cm^3, the volume of a cube of side $8\,\text{mm}$.

5. Find the volume, in cm^3, of a cuboid measuring $50\,\text{cm}$ by $1.2\,\text{m}$ by $20\,\text{cm}$.

6. Which holds more water, a rectangular carton measuring $20\,\text{cm}$ by $20\,\text{cm}$ by $10\,\text{cm}$, or a bottle whose capacity is $750\,\text{ml}$?

7. Which holds more liquid, a plastic carton whose capacity is 1 pint or a plastic bottle whose capacity is $500\,\text{ml}$?

8. Find the volume of this stack of $1\,\text{cm}$ cubes.

Consider again

Lee fills his two-gallon bucket from a tank full of water.

The tank is a cuboid measuring 600 mm by 800 mm by 1000 mm.

Now find how many times he can fill his bucket from the tank.

 Number puzzles

Which two of these shapes will fit together to make a cube?

A   B   C   D

Practical work

This pattern is drawn on isometric dots.

It can be continued in the same way to fill the grid.

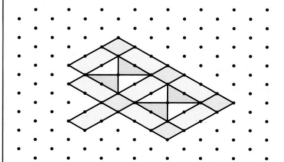

Draw some different patterns on isometric paper.

! Investigation

A rectangular piece of card measuring 12 cm by 9 cm is to be used to make a small open rectangular box. The diagram shows one way of doing this.

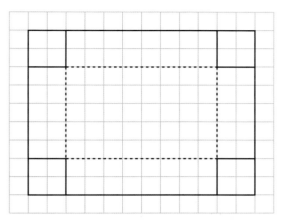

a How many different open boxes can be made from this piece of card, if the length and breadth of the base is to be a whole number of centimetres?
Draw each possibility on squared paper.

b For each different box in part **a**, find
  i its dimensions
  ii its total external surface area
  iii its capacity.

c Use the information you have found in part **b** to state whether each of these statements is true (T) or false (F).
  A The box with the largest base has the greatest capacity.
  B The box with the smallest total external surface area has the smallest capacity.
  C The box with the greatest capacity is as deep as it is wide.

d Find the dimensions of the open cubic box with the largest capacity that can be made from a rectangular card measuring 12 cm by 9 cm.
How much card is wasted?

e Investigate other sizes of card to find the dimensions of the box with the largest volume that can be made from each size.

21 Equations

Equations

Jo went into a shop and bought some chocolate for Karl and some boiled sweets for herself. Together they cost £2.13.

When Karl asked Jo how much he owed her for his chocolate, all she could remember was that it cost 15 p more than her boiled sweets. They could find out how much each had to pay by

- guessing until they found two amounts that have a total of 213 p and a difference of 15 p, or
- writing down the information using mathematical symbols.

To do this we can write

$$\text{(amount Karl owed)} + \text{(amount Jo owed)} = 213\,\text{p}$$

But (amount Jo owed) = (amount Karl owed − 15 p)

So   (amount Karl owed) + (amount Karl owed − 15 p) = 213 p

This is called an **equation**.

Now we can see that twice the amount Karl owed = 228 p

so Karl owed Jo 114 p. i.e £1.14

Class discussion

Discuss how you might solve the problems that arise in the following situations.

1   Chris and Grace have been given £50 between them and must divide it so that Chris has £1 more than Grace.

2   Yasmin and Dan go for a meal. The total cost comes to £34.60. Dan's meal costs £1.70 more than Yasmin's and Yasmin is unwilling to split the bill down the middle. She wants each of them to pay the cost of their own meal.

3   Miss Goodard had a full box of 100 drawing pins. She gave 4 to each student to pin a painting on the wall. She came across 3 faulty pins and still had 5 pins left over when all the students had taken the pins they needed. Miss Goodard wondered how many students had come to her to put their paintings up.

4   Can you think of other situations where it should be easier to form an equation and use it, rather than guess and then have to check to see if the chosen solution works?

The idea of equations

I think of a number, add seven and get twenty-one. This sentence could be rewritten

The number I think of $+ 7 = 21$

from which we can see that the number I think of is 14.

If we use a letter (we shall use x) to stand for the number I think of, the sentence could be rewritten

$x + 7 = 21$

Then, if we take away 7 from each side:

$x = 21 - 7$
$ = 14$

so the number I first thought of was 14.

Exercise 21a

Worked example

⟶ I think of a number, add 4, and the result is 10.
   If x stands for the unknown number, form an equation in x and solve it to find the number I thought of.

The equation is $\quad x + 4 = 10$
The number is 6 $\qquad$ *Check:* $6 + 4 = 10$

In each of questions **1** to **15**, let the letter x stand for the unknown number. Use the given statement to form an equation in x and solve the equation to find the unknown number.

1 I think of a number, subtract 3 and get 4.
2 I think of a number, add 1 and the result is 3.
3 If a number is added to 3 we get 9.
4 If 5 is subtracted from a number we get 2.
5 I think of a number, add 8 and get 21.
6 If 7 is subtracted from a number we get 19.

Worked example

⟶ I think of a number, multiply it by 3 and the result is 12.
   What is the number?

The equation is $\quad 3x = 12$
The number is 4 $\qquad$ *Check:* $3 \times 4 = 12$

 $3x$ means $3 \times x$

7 I think of a number, double it and get 8.

8 If a number is multiplied by 7 the result is 14.

9 When we multiply a number by 3 we get 15.

10 6 times an unknown number gives 24.

11 I think of a number, multiply it by 4 and get 24.

12 I think of a number, divide it by 6 and get 5.

13 When a number is divided by 3 we get 7.

14 If a number is divided by 7 the answer is 7.

15 I think of a number, divide it by 8 and get 32.

Worked example

→ Write a sentence to show the meaning of the equation $4x = 20$.

$4x = 20$ means '4 times an unknown number gives 20' or
'I think of a number, multiply it by 4 and the result is 20'.

Write sentences to show the meaning of the following equations.

16 $3x = 18$

17 $x + 6 = 7$

18 $x - 2 = 9$

19 $5x = 20$

20 $5 + x = 7$

21 $x - 4 = 1$

22 $4x = 8$

23 $x + 1 = 4$

Solving equations

Some equations need an organised approach, rather than guesswork.

Imagine a balance:

On this side there is a bag containing an unknown number of marbles, say x marbles, and 4 loose marbles.

On this side there are 9 separate marbles, balancing the marbles on the other side.

$$x + 4 = 9$$

Take 4 loose marbles from each side, so that the two sides still balance.

$$x = 5$$

We write: $\qquad\qquad x + 4 = 9$

Take 4 from both sides $\qquad x = 5$

When we have found the value of x we have *solved the equation.*

As a second example suppose that:

On this side there is a bag that originally held x marbles but now 2 are missing.

On this side there are 5 loose marbles.

$$x - 2 = 5$$

We can make the bag complete by putting back 2 marbles but, to keep the balance, we must add 2 marbles to the right-hand side also.

So we write $\qquad\qquad x - 2 = 5$

Add 2 to each side $\qquad\quad x = 7$

Whatever you do to one side of an equation you must also do to the other side.

Use the equations in the following exercise to practise this idea. It is easy enough to 'see' the solutions, so you should have no difficulty in checking your answers.

Exercise 21b

Worked example

→ Solve the equation $\quad y + 4 = 6$

$\qquad\qquad\qquad\qquad y + 4 = 6$

Take 4 from both sides $\quad y = 2$ $\qquad$ *Check:* $2 + 4 = 6$

Solve

1 $x + 7 = 15$	**5** $a + 3 = 7$	**9** $a + 1 = 6$
2 $x + 9 = 18$	**6** $x + 4 = 9$	**10** $a + 8 = 15$
3 $10 + y = 12$	**7** $a + 5 = 11$	**11** $7 + c = 10$
4 $2 + c = 9$	**8** $9 + a = 15$	**12** $c + 2 = 3$

13 Kim is n years old and Toni is 2 years older than Kim.
If Toni is 14, we can form the equation

$$n + 2 = 14$$

How old is Kim?

14 A cup of coffee costs 15 pence more than a cup of tea. If a cup of
tea costs x pence and a cup of coffee costs 215 pence, we can form
the equation

$$x + 15 = 215$$

How much is a cup of tea?

15 Adam has c marbles and Una has 8. Altogether they have
21 marbles between them.
Use this information to form an equation.
How many marbles does Adam have?

16 A concert hall has two car-parks and 364 cars are parked in them.
There are 193 cars in the East car-park and n cars in the
North car-park.
Use this information to form an equation in n.
How many cars are parked in the North car-park?

Some equations may have negative answers.
For example, if we know the temperature fell last night by 3 °C to
-9 °C, we can find the temperature before it got colder by forming
the equation

$$x - 3 = -9$$

where x °C was the temperature before it fell.
Then adding 3 to both sides gives

$$x = -9 + 3 = -6$$

Worked example

→ Solve $x + 8 = 6$

$$x + 8 = 6$$

Take 8 from both sides $\quad x = -2 \quad$ *Check:* $-2 + 8 = 6$

Solve

17 $x + 4 = 2$	**19** $3 + a = 2$	**21** $4 + w = 2$
18 $x + 6 = 1$	**20** $s + 3 = 2$	**22** $c + 6 = 2$

Worked example

→ Solve $x - 6 = 2$

$$x - 6 = 2$$

Add 6 to both sides $\quad x = 8$ $\qquad$ *Check:* $8 - 6 = 2$

Solve

23 $x - 6 = 4$	**27** $c - 8 = 1$	**31** $a - 4 = 8$
24 $a - 2 = 1$	**28** $x - 5 = 7$	**32** $x - 3 = 0$
25 $y - 3 = 5$	**29** $s - 4 = 1$	**33** $c - 1 = 1$
26 $x - 4 = 6$	**30** $x - 9 = 3$	**34** $y - 7 = 2$

35 A Chelsea bun costs 16 pence less than a jam doughnut. If a jam doughnut costs n pence and a Chelsea bun costs 82 pence, we can form the equation

$$n - 16 = 82$$

What is the cost of a jam doughnut?

36 A small loaf weighs 450 grams less than a large loaf. If a large loaf weighs x grams and a small loaf weighs 500 grams, we can form the equation

$$x - 450 = 500$$

How heavy is a large loaf?

37 A cup of tea cost 80 pence less than a sandwich. Together they cost 420 pence.

Use this information to form an equation.

How much is a sandwich?

38 The temperature early this morning was t °C. Since then it has increased by 3 °C and is now 2 °C. From this information we can form the equation

$$t + 3 = 2$$

Solve this equation to find the temperature early this morning.

39 Seth paid his gas bill for £240 using a debit card. Before Seth paid the bill he had a credit of £155. After the bill had been paid he was £x overdrawn.

Form an equation in x and solve it.

How much overdrawn was he after the gas bill had been paid?

40 Simon Weinmann lives just outside Jerusalem. His house is 510 m above sea-level. He also has a weekend flat near the Dead Sea which is 220 m below sea-level. The vertical distance through which he descends when he travels from his Jerusalem home to his flat is x m. Form an equation in x and solve it.

What vertical distance does he descend when he goes to his flat for the weekend?

Exercise 21c

Sometimes the letter term is on the right-hand side instead of the left.

Worked example

⟶ Solve $3 = x - 4$

Add 4 to both sides

$$3 = x - 4$$
$$7 = x$$
$$x = 7 \qquad \text{Check: } 3 = 7 - 4$$

 $7 = x$ is the same as $x = 7$

Solve

1 $4 = x + 2$	7 $x + 3 = 10$	13 $7 = x + 3$
2 $6 = x - 3$	8 $9 + x = 4$	14 $x + 1 = 9$
3 $7 = a + 4$	9 $c + 4 = 4$	15 $x - 6 = 5$
4 $6 = x - 7$	10 $3 = b + 2$	16 $x + 3 = 15$
5 $1 = c - 2$	11 $6 + c = 10$	17 $y - 6 = 4$
6 $5 = s + 2$	12 $d + 4 = 1$	18 $x - 7 = 4$

Worked example

⟶ Solve $7.5 = x - 2.8$

$$7.5 = x - 2.8$$
Add 2.8 to both sides
$$7.5 + 2.8 = x$$
$$10.3 = x$$
Check: $7.5 = 10.3 - 2.8$
$$x = 10.3$$

Solve the equations.

19 $x - 1.5 = 6$	28 $x - 4 = 2$	37 $y - 9 = 14$
20 $6 = x - 4$	29 $3 = x - 5.6$	38 $2 = z - 2$
21 $x - \frac{1}{2} = 5$	30 $4 + x = 5\frac{1}{4}$	39 $d - 3 = 1$
22 $x - 3.2 = 5.6$	31 $9 = x - 7$	40 $x + 1 = 8$
23 $10 = a - 1$	32 $x + 4.7 = 11.2$	41 $x - 1 = 8$
24 $x + \frac{1}{2} = 4$	33 $\frac{3}{4} + x = 1\frac{1}{2}$	42 $1 = c + 3$
25 $x - 4.1 = 7.8$	34 $c - 7 = 10$	43 $x + 8 = 1$
26 $x - 3 = 6$	35 $6.6 = x - 3.9$	44 $x - 8 = 1$
27 $\frac{2}{3} = x - 1\frac{2}{3}$	36 $x - 1\frac{3}{4} = \frac{1}{2}$	45 $z + 3 = 5$

46 Tania cuts a piece of wood 1.75 m long from a piece that is 2.64 m long.
The piece she has left is x m long.
Form an equation in x and solve it.

47 A lorry weighs 5.25 tonnes and is loaded with 5.75 tonnes of steel. The total weight of the loaded lorry is N tonnes.
Form an equation in N and solve it to find the weight of the loaded lorry.

Multiples of x

Imagine that on this side of the scales there are 3 bags, each containing an equal unknown number of marbles, say x in each.

On this side there are 12 loose marbles.

$$3 \times x = 12$$
$$3x = 12$$

We can keep the balance if we divide the contents of each scale pan by 3.

$$x = 4$$

Exercise 21d

Worked example

→ Solve $\quad 6x = 12$

$$6x = 12$$
Divide both sides by 6 $\quad x = 2$

→ Solve $\quad 3x = 7$

$$3x = 7$$
Divide both sides by 3 $\quad x = \frac{7}{3}$
$$x = 2\frac{1}{3}$$

Solve the following equations.

1 $5x = 10$	**9** $5p = 7$	**17** $5z = 9$
2 $3x = 9$	**10** $2x = 40$	**18** $2y = 7$
3 $2x = 5$	**11** $7y = 14$	**19** $3x = 27$
4 $7x = 21$	**12** $6a = 3$	**20** $8x = 16$
5 $4b = 16$	**13** $6x = 36$	**21** $4y = 3$
6 $4c = 9$	**14** $6x = 6$	**22** $5x = 6$
7 $3a = 1$	**15** $6x = 1$	**23** $2z = 10$
8 $6z = 18$	**16** $5z = 10$	**24** $7x = 1$

25 Charlie is n years old now. Her father is 48 and is four times as old as Charlie. From this information, we get the equation $4 \times n = 48$ or more simply $4n = 48$.
How old is Charlie?

26 A light bulb costs x pence and a pack of 6 light bulbs costs 960 pence. We can form the equation $6x = 960$.
How much does 1 bulb cost?

27 A plank of wood 3.4 m long is cut into 4 equal pieces, each x m long. Form an equation in x and solve it. How long is each piece?

28 Salman has $3\frac{1}{2}$ lb of potatoes. They are divided equally among 7 diners.
If each diner receives x lb, form an equation in x and solve it.
What weight of potatoes does each diner receive?

Mixed operations

Exercise 21e

Solve the following equations.

1 $x + 4 = 8$	**7** $2x = 11$	**13** $7y = 2$
2 $x - 4 = 8$	**8** $x - 2 = 11$	**14** $3x = 8$
3 $4x = 8$	**9** $x - 12 = 4$	**15** $x + 6 = 1$
4 $5y = 6$	**10** $8 = c + 2$	**16** $3 = a - 4$
5 $4x = 12$	**11** $20 = 4x$	**17** $3x = 5$
6 $x - 4 = 12$	**12** $2 + x = 4$	**18** $z - 5 = 6$

19 The temperature at mid-day was $T\,°C$. By 6 p.m. it had fallen by $6\,°C$ to $12.5\,°C$.
From this information we can form the equation $T - 6 = 12.5$.
Solve this equation.
What was the temperature at mid-day?
Now that you think you know what the temperature was, read through the given information again to see that it fits.

20 A glass of squash costs 95 pence and a chocolate éclair costs x pence more than a glass of squash. Together they cost 450 pence. As a chocolate éclair costs $(95 + x)$ pence we can form the equation

$$95 + 95 + x = 450$$

Solve this equation.

How much does an éclair cost?

21 Helen is x years old now. Her mother, who is 35 years old, is five times as old as Helen.

Form an equation in x and solve it. How old is Helen now?

Two operations

One of the problems in the class discussion on page 376 concerned Yasmin and Dan sharing the cost of a meal. If we suppose that Yasmin's meal cost £x, then the cost of Dan's meal was £x + £1.70. The total cost of the two meals was £34.60, so we can form the equation

$$x + x + 1.70 = 34.60$$

i.e. $\qquad 2x + 1.70 = 34.60$

To solve this equation requires two operations.

First, subtract 1.70 from both sides

$$2x = 34.60 - 1.70$$
$$2x = 32.90$$

Secondly, divide both sides by 2

$$x = 16.45$$

The cost of Yasmin's meal was £16.45 and the cost of Dan's meal was £16.45 + £1.70 = £18.15.

(*Check*: Cost of Yasmin's meal + cost of Dan's meal = £16.45 + £18.15 = £34.60, which agrees with the information given in the question.)

Exercise 21f

Worked example

→ Solve the equation $\quad 7 = 3x - 5$

$$7 = 3x - 5$$

Add 5 to both sides $\qquad 12 = 3x$

Divide both sides by 3 $\qquad 4 = x$

i.e. $\qquad\qquad\qquad x = 4$

 To solve an equation, our aim is to get the letter on its own.

→ Solve the equation $2x + 3 = 5$

$$2x + 3 = 5$$

Take 3 from both sides $2x = 2$
Divide both sides by 2 $x = 1$
Check: If $x = 1$, left-hand side $= 2 \times 1 + 3 = 5$
Right-hand side $= 5$, so $x = 1$ fits the equation.

 It is possible to check whether your answer is correct. We can put $x = 1$ in the left-hand side of the equation and see if we get the same value as on the right-hand side.

Solve the following equations.

1 $6x + 2 = 26$	**13** $20 = 12x - 4$	**25** $2x + 6 = 6$
2 $4x + 7 = 19$	**14** $9x + 1 = 28$	**26** $3x + 1 = 11$
3 $17 = 7x + 3$	**15** $9 = 8x - 15$	**27** $2x + 4 = 14$
4 $4x - 5 = 19$	**16** $8 = 8 + 3z$	**28** $16 = 7x - 1$
5 $3a + 12 = 12$	**17** $5x - 4 = 5$	**29** $2.4 = 3x - 1.2$
6 $10 = 10x - 50$	**18** $15 = 1 + 7x$	**30** $10x - 6 = 24$
7 $6 = 2x - 4$	**19** $9x - 4 = 14$	**31** $5x - 7 = 4$
8 $5z + 9 = 4$	**20** $3x - 2 = 3$	**32** $9 = 6a - 27$
9 $3x - 4 = 4$	**21** $7 = 2z + 6$	**33** $7 = 1 - 2x$
10 $3x + 4 = 25$	**22** $6x + 1 = -5$	**34** $10 + 2x = -2$
11 $13 = 3x + 4$	**23** $5x + 1 = 4.5$	**35** $2 + 3x = 7.4$
12 $5z - 9 = 16$	**24** $3a + 4 = 1$	

Worked example

→ I think of a number, double it and add 3. The result is 15. What is the number?

Let the number be x $2x + 3 = 15$
Take 3 from both sides $2x = 12$
Divide both sides by 2 $x = 6$
The number is 6.

In the remaining problems in this exercise, form an equation and solve it.

36 I think of a number, multiply it by 4 and subtract 8.
The result is 20.
What is the number?

37 I think of a number, multiply it by 3 and add 6. The result is 21.
What is the number?

38 I think of a number, multiply it by 3 and add the result to 7.
The total is 28.
What is the number?

39 The sides of a rectangle are x cm and 3 cm. The perimeter is 24 cm.
    Find x.

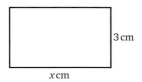

3 cm

x cm

40 The lengths of the three sides of a triangle are x cm, x cm and
    6 cm. The perimeter is 20 cm.
    Find x.

41 Marit and Jo each have x sweets and Samira has 10 sweets.
    They have 24 sweets altogether.
    What is x?

42 Three boys had x sweets each. They gave 9 sweets to a fourth
    boy and then found that they were left with 18 sweets among the
    three of them.
    Find x.

43 I have two pieces of ribbon each x cm long and a third piece 9 cm
    long. Altogether there are 31 cm of ribbon.
    What is the length of each of the first two pieces?

44 Jen is y years old and her mother is 27 years older. Together their
    ages total 45 years.
    a   In terms of Jen's age, how old is her mother now?
    b   Form an equation in y and solve it to find Jen's age and her
         mother's age now.

45 A fishing rod is 27 ft long and consists of three parts. The first
    part is x ft long, the second part is 1 ft longer than the first, and
    the third part is 1 ft longer than the second part.
    Form an equation in x, and solve it to find the length of each part.

46 Sonia is n years old now and Wendy, her sister, is 2 years older.
    In 5 years' time the sum of their ages will be 20.
    How old is Sonia now?
    How old will Wendy be in 5 years' time?

Simplifying expressions

Worked example

We can shorten, i.e. simplify, $2x + x$ to $3x$
because $2x$ means $x + x$,
i.e. $2x + x = x + x + x$
                $= 3x$

Like terms

Consider $3x + 5x - 4x + 2x$

This is called an **expression** and can be simplified to $6x$.

$3x$, $5x$, $4x$ and $2x$ are all **terms** in this expression. Each term contains x.

They are of the same type and are called **like terms**.

Like terms can be simplified using the ordinary rules of addition and subtraction.

Worked example

→ Simplify $4h - 6h + 7h - h$

$$4h - 6h + 7h - h = 4h + 7h - 6h - h$$
$$= 11h - 7h$$
$$= 4h$$
$$4h - 6h + 7h - h = 4h$$

 Remember, the sign in front of a term tells you what to do with just that term.

Simplify

1   $3x + x + 4x + 2x$

2   $3x - x + 4x - 2x$

3   $-6x + 8x$

4   $6 - 1 + 4 - 7$

5   $-8x + 6x$

6   $9y - 3y + 2y$

7   $2 - 3 + 9 - 1$

8   $-16 - 3 - 4$

9   $-3 + 5 - 1$

10   $-2x - x + 3x$

Unlike terms

$3x + 2x - 7$ can be simplified to $5x - 7$, and $5x - 2y + 4x - 3y$ can be simplified to $9x - 5y$.

Terms containing x are different from terms without an x.

They are called **unlike terms** and cannot be collected together.

Similarly $9x$ and $5y$ are unlike terms; therefore $9x - 5y$ cannot be simplified.

Worked example

→ Simplify $3x + 4 - 7 - 2x + 4x$

$$3x + 4 - 7 - 2x + 4x = 3x - 2x + 4x + 4 - 7$$
$$= 5x - 3$$

 $5x$ and 3 are unlike terms, so $5x - 3$ cannot be simplified.

→ Simplify $2x + 4y - x - 5y$

$$2x + 4y - x - 5y = x - y$$

x and y are unlike terms, so $x - y$ cannot be simplified.

Simplify

1   $2x + 4 + 3 + 5x$

2   $2x - 4 + 3x + 9$

3   $5x - 2 - 3 - x$

4   $4a + 5c - 6a$

5   $6x - 5y + 2x + 3y$

6   $6x + 5y + 2x + 3y$

7   $6x + 5y + 2x - 3y$

8   $6x + 5y - 2x + 3y$

9 $4x + 1 + 3x + 2 + x$

10 $6x - 9 + 2x + 1$

11 $7x - 3 - 9 - 4x$

12 $9x + 3y - 10x$

13 $2x - 6y - 8x$

14 $7 - x - 6 - 3x$

15 $8 - 1 - 7x + 2x$

16 $9x - 1 + 4 - 11x$

17 $6x - 5y + 2x + 3y + 2x$

18 $6x - 5y - 2x - 3y + 7x - y$

19 $30x + 2 - 15x - 6 + 4$

20 $-2z + 3x - 4y + 6z + x - 3y$

21 $4x + 3y - 4 + 6x - 2y - 7 - x$

22 $7x + 3 - 9 - 9x + 2x - 6 + 11$

Equations with letter terms on both sides

Some equations have letter terms on both sides. Consider the equation

$$5x + 1 = 2x + 9$$

We want to have a letter term on one side only, so we need to take $2x$ from both sides. This gives

$$3x + 1 = 9$$

and we can go on to solve the equation as before.

Notice that we want the letter term on the side which has the greater number of x s to start with.

If we look at the equation

$$9 - 4x = 2x + 4$$

we can see that x s have been taken away on the left-hand side, so there are more x s on the right-hand side.

Add $4x$ to both sides and then the equation becomes

$$9 = 6x + 4$$

and we can go on as before.

Exercise 21i

Deal with the letters first, then the numbers.

Worked example

$\rightarrow$ Solve $5x + 2 = 2x + 9$

Take $2x$ from both sides $3x + 2 = 9$

Take 2 from both sides $3x = 7$

Divide both sides by 3 $x = \dfrac{7}{3} = 2\dfrac{1}{3}$

 Deal with the x terms first.

Solve the equations.

1 $3x + 4 = 2x + 8$

2 $x + 7 = 4x + 4$

3 $2x + 5 = 5x - 4$

4 $3x - 1 = 5x - 11$

5 $7x + 3 = 3x + 31$

6 $6z + 4 = 2z + 1$

7 $7x - 25 = 3x - 1$

8 $11x - 6 = 8x + 9$

Worked example

➡ Solve $9 + x = 4 - 4x$

$$9 + x = 4 - 4x$$

Add $4x$ to both sides $9 + 5x = 4$

Take 9 from both sides $5x = -5$

Divide both sides by 5 $x = -1$

Check: If $x = -1$, left-hand side $= 9 + (-1)$

$$= 8$$

right-hand side $= 4 - (-4)$

$$= 8$$

So $x = -1$ is the solution.

 The left-hand side contains the greater number of x s, so we add $4x$ to both sides to remove the x s from the right-hand side.

Solve the equations.

9 $4x - 3 = 39 - 2x$

10 $5 + x = 17 - 5x$

11 $7 - 2x = 4 + x$

12 $24 - 2x = 5x + 3$

13 $5x - 6 = 3 - 4x$

14 $12 + 2x = 24 - 4x$

15 $32 - 6x = 8 + 2x$

16 $9 - 3x = -5 + 4x$

Equations containing like terms

If there are a lot of terms in an equation, first collect the like terms on each side separately.

Exercise 21j

Worked example

➡ Solve $2x + 3 - x + 5 = 3x + 4x - 6$

$$2x + 3 - x + 5 = 3x + 4x - 6$$

$$x + 8 = 7x - 6$$

Take x from both sides $8 = 6x - 6$

Add 6 to both sides $14 = 6x$

Divide both sides by 6 $\frac{14}{6} = x$

$$x = \frac{7}{3} = 2\frac{1}{3}$$

 Simplify each side.

Solve the following equations.

1 $3x + 2 + 2x = 7$

2 $7 + 3x - 6 = 4$

3 $6 = 5x + 2 - 4x$

4 $9 + 4 = 3x + 4x$

5 $3x + 8 - 5x = 2$

6 $3x + 2x - 4x = 6$

7 $7 = 2 - 3 + 4x$

8 $5x + x - 6x + 2x = 9$

9 $5 + x - 4x + x = 1$

10 $6x = x + 2 - 7 - 1$

11 $5x + 6 + 3x = 10$

12 $8 = 7 - 11 + 6x$

13 $7 + 2x = 12x - 7x + 2$

14 $1 - 4 - 3 + 2x = 3x$

15 $3x - 4x - x = x - 6$

16 $2 - 4x - x = x + 8$

Worked example

➡ Solve $9 - 3x = 15 - 4x$

Add $4x$ to both sides $\qquad 9 + x = 15$

Take 9 from both sides $\qquad x = 6$

 Notice that $-3x$ is greater than $-4x$, so add $4x$ to both sides.

Solve the equations.

17 $5 - 3x = 1 - x$

18 $16 - 2x = 19 - 5x$

19 $6 - x = 12 - 2x$

20 $-2 - 4x = 6 - 2x$

21 $16 - 6x = 1 - x$

22 $4 - 3x = 1 - 4x$

23 $4 - 2x = 8 - 5x$

24 $3 - x = 5 - 3x$

25 $6 - 3x = 4x - 1$

26 $4z + 1 = 6z - 3$

27 $3 - 6x = 6x - 3$

28 $8 - 4x = 14 - 7x$

29 $13 - 4x = 4x - 3$

30 $7x + 6 = x - 6$

31 $6 - 2x = 9 - 5x$

32 $3 - 2x = 3 + x$

Worked example

➡ Solve $3 - 2x = 5$

Add $2x$ to both sides $\qquad 3 = 5 + 2x$

Take 5 from both sides $\qquad -2 = 2x$

Divide both sides by 2 $\qquad x = -1$

 $-2x$ is smaller than "no xs" so we add $2x$ to both sides.

33 $13 - 4x = 5$

34 $6 = 2 - 2x$

35 $6 = 8 - 3x$

36 $0 = 6 - 2x$

37 $9x + 4 = 3x + 1$

38 $2x + 3 = 12x$

39 $7 - 2x = 3 - 6x$

40 $3x - 6 = 6 - x$

41 $-4x - 5 = -2x - 10$

42 $5 - 3x = 2$

43 $6 + 3x = 7 - x$

44 $5 - 2x = 4x - 7$

45 $5x + 3 = -7 - x$

46 $4 - 3x = 0$

47 $-2x + x = 3x - 12$

48 $-4 + x - 2 - x = x$

49 $3x + 1 + 2x = 6$

50 $4x - 2 + 6x - 4 = 64$

51 $2x + 7 - x + 3 = 6x$

52 $6 - 2x - 4 + 5x = 17$

53 $9x - 6 - x - 2 = 0$

54 $4 - x - 2 - x = x$

55 $4 - x - 2 + x = x$

56 $2x + 7 - 4x + 1 = 4$

57 $6 - 3x - 5x - 1 = 10$

58 $6x + 3 + 6 = x - 4 - 2$

59 $x - 3 + 7x + 9 = 10$

60 $15x + 2x - 6x - 9x = 20$

61 Jill is an operator on a production line in a car assembly plant. She is given a box containing n windscreen wipers. Jill uses 3 to a car until all that remain are 2 faulty wipers. A check shows that she has fitted the wipers on 58 cars.
Form an equation in n and solve it.
How many wipers were in the box to start with?

62 Nia weighs 4 kg less than Maggie who weighs 3 kg less than Pedro. Altogether they weigh 137 kg.
If Maggie weighs x kg, what is the weight of each of Pedro and Nia in terms of x?
How much does Maggie weigh?

63 Laura goes to a shop that sells two models of radio. One costs three times as much as the other and the two together cost £72. Laura's mother wants to know the cost of the cheaper one.
If the cheaper radio costs £x, form an equation in x.
What should Laura's answer be?

64 Kurt and Sarita go into a cafe because they want a hot drink. Kurt has a cup of tea and a cake, while Sarita has a cup of coffee and 2 cakes. Coffee costs 15 pence more than tea, and each cake is 35 pence more than a cup of coffee.

a If a cup of tea costs x pence write down, in terms of x, the cost of
  i a cup of coffee   **ii** a cake   **iii** 2 cakes.

b The total cost of the tea, coffee and cakes is £7.65.
Form an equation in x and solve it.
Hence write down the cost of
  i a cup of tea   **ii** a cup of coffee   **iii** a cake.

65 Divide 45 into two parts, so that if 4 is subtracted from the larger number the result is 7 more than the smaller number.

66 Four brothers play in a cricket team. In their last match Jack scored 15 more runs than Toby, Dylan scored 5 times as many as Toby and 16 more than Pete. In total they scored 107 runs. How many did each brother score?

67 Two sisters, Janet and Nora, each have a box holding 20 chocolates. Janet eats 5 and gives some away to her friends. Nora gives 1 away and eats 3 times as many as Janet has given away. When they compare boxes, each sister still has the same number of chocolates left as the other.
If Janet gave x chocolates away, form an equation in x and solve it. How many chocolates did Nora eat?

68 In three years' time, I shall be three times as old as I was three years ago. How old am I?

Mixed exercises

Exercise 21k

1 A cola costs 10 pence more than an orange squash.
If the orange squash costs x pence and the cola costs 75 pence, form an equation in x and solve it.
How much does an orange squash cost?

2 Solve $5y = 45$

3 Solve the equation $5x - 0.7 = 2.8$

4 Solve the equation $3x + 2 = 4$

5 I think of a number, add 4 and the result is 10.
Form an equation and solve it to find the number I thought of.

6 Solve the equation $6x + 2 = 3x + 8$

7 Solve the equation $4x - 2 = -6$

8 Simplify $4x - 3y + 5x + 2y$

9 Solve the equation $4x + 2 - x = 6$

10 Solve the equation $14 - 3x = 5$

Exercise 21l

1 An iced slice costs 14 pence less than a cream doughnut.
If a cream doughnut costs n pence and an iced slice costs 67 pence, form an equation in n and solve it.
How much does a cream doughnut cost?

2 Solve $5x = 1$

3 Solve the equation $4x = 0.5$

4 Solve the equation $4x - 5 = 3$

5 Simplify $3c - 5c + 9c$

6 Solve the equation $3x - 2 - 4 = x$

7 When I think of a number, double it and add three, I get 11. What number did I think of?

8 Solve the equation $x + 2x - 4 = 9$

9 Simplify $2a + 4 - 3 + 5a - a$

10 Solve the equation $12 - x = 6 - 2x$

Consider again

In the quiz, Kate scored 12 more than Tareq. Mona scored 5 times as many as Tareq and 15 more than Lim. Together they scored a total of 105.

Now can you find the score of each friend?

! Investigation

Meg wanted to find out Malcolm's age without asking him directly what it was. The following conversation took place.

Meg: Think of your age but don't tell me what it is.

Malcolm: OK.

Meg: Multiply it by 5, add 4 and take away your age.

Malcolm: Yes.

Meg: Divide the result by 4 and tell me your answer.

Malcolm: 15

Meg: That means you are 14.

Malcolm: Correct. How do you know that?

However many times Meg tried this on her friends and relations, she found their age by taking 1 away from the number they gave.

Does it always work?

Can you use simple algebra to prove that it always gives the correct answer?

22 Grouping data

Consider

Saskia uses the number 24 bus to get to school. The number of people waiting at the bus stop varied from just herself to several people. Saskia collected the following information.

The number of people waiting at a bus stop for the number 24 bus when it first arrives after 8 a.m. on 30 days														
5	7	15	20	25	14	12	8	3	1	11	15	7	9	4
9	12	18	21	25	17	6	9	13	4	10	13	17	23	1

a How can this information be illustrated so that it shows
  i the frequency of days when the numbers of people waiting fall into various groups
  ii the proportion of days when the numbers of people waiting fall into various groups?

b Draw the two illustrations for part **a**.

You should be able to solve this problem after you have worked through this chapter.

Grouping information

This list shows how much, in pence, each student in Class 7H spent in the school canteen one day.

45	47	48	52	62	63	80	95	97	97
101	103	108	115	132	132	134	139	142	146
150	151	154	163	170	179	185	194	210	217

Any number from 0 to about 250 could appear in a list like this one.

In this list, a couple of numbers appear twice, but most of the possible numbers do not appear at all.

* If this information has been collected to find the total amount spent, then each individual amount is needed. If we attempted to collect amounts like these on a tally chart, we would have to list every number from 0 to about 250. Doing this would take a long time, so collecting them as a simple list and putting them in order later would be sensible.

* On the other hand, if we want some idea of the spending pattern, the detail given by having each individual amount is not important; a clearer picture of the pattern can be obtained by collecting the amounts in groups of, say, less than 50 p, 50 p to less than £1, and so on. We can then collect the figures on a tally chart like the one on the next page.

Amount in pence	Frequency
0 to 49	///
50 to 99	//// //
100 to 149	//// ////
150 to 199	//// ///
200 to 249	//

Notice that, without the detail of the exact figures, we would not know whether anyone had spent exactly £1, for instance.

Class discussion

1 The following questions need answering about the marks in last summer's maths exam for Year 7 students.

   a How many students got between 50% and 59%?

   b Did anyone get exactly 50%?

   c To the nearest 10, what was the commonest mark?

   d How many students got less than 25%?

   There is some information available. For each of these questions, discuss whether you need to know
   • the range of the marks
   • the number of possible marks
   • each individual mark
   • grouped marks.

2 As in question 1, discuss which information you would need to answer these questions, which refer to the numbers of people queuing at a supermarket checkout.

   a How often was the queue less than five people?

   b How many times were there two people in the queue?

   c What was the largest number recorded?

3 As in question 1, discuss which information you would need to answer these questions, which refer to the prices of personal music players.

   a I have £25 to spend. Can I buy a player for this?

   b How many different models are available for between £20 and £30?

   c What proportion of the models cost less than about £40?

   d In what price range is there the largest choice of models?

Displaying grouped data in a bar chart

When information has been collected using a grouped tally chart, we can illustrate it using a bar chart. The data, given opposite, about the amounts of money spent in the school canteen can be shown in this bar chart.

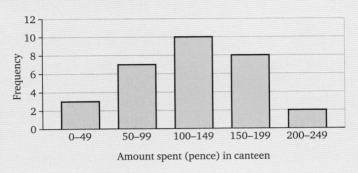

Exercise 22a

1 For an English project, students were asked to investigate the number of letters per word from a paragraph of the book *Tom's Midnight Garden*. This is the list of the number of letters per word.

```
4   3   3   5   3   12   4   6   4   3   9   2   4   4   1   4
6   4   3   6   4   6   3   7   4   1   6   4   5   3   4   3
6   4   3   4   6   6   5   3   3   2   7   3   4   10   11
```

a How many words were there in the paragraph?
b Copy and complete this frequency table.

Number of letters	Tally	Frequency
1–3		
4–6		
7–9		
10–12		
	Total:	

c Draw a bar chart to illustrate the information in this frequency table.

2 A group of ten-year-olds were asked how much pocket money they were given each week. This frequency table was made from the information.

Weekly pocket money in pence	0–99	100–199	200–249	300–399	400–499
Number of children	10	15	42	68	18

a How many children were asked how much pocket money they received?

b How many children received more than 199 p each week?

c How many children did not receive any pocket money?

3 This frequency table is based on the journey times of the employees of Able Engineering Co.

Journey time in minutes	0–14	15–29	30–44	45–59
Number of employees	3	8	6	2

a How many employees took part in this survey?

b How many employees had a journey time of less than half an hour?

c How many employees had a journey time of quarter of an hour or more?

d Is it possible to tell from the table how many had a journey time of five minutes?

4 Make your own survey of the pocket money given to your friends and classmates.

a Start by preparing a frequency table like the one in question **2**, but leave the numbers of children blank. You may have to add further groups: 500–599, and so on.

b Ask about 10 students to put a tally mark in the appropriate column of your table. (Some of your friends may not want to tell you how much money they are given, and asking them to draw the tally mark avoids possible embarrassment. Do not press anyone who is reluctant to give the information.)

c Illustrate your survey with a bar chart.

d Compare your bar chart with those produced by other members of your class.

5 Investigate the number of letters per word in question **4**.

a Make a list of the number of letters per word. (Do not count the numbers in the question as words.)

b Make a frequency table for this list using the groups 1–3 letters, 4–6 letters, 7–9 letters, 10–12 letters, more than 12 letters.

c Draw a bar chart to illustrate the information in your frequency table.

6 This bar chart illustrates a survey into the number of books (not counting school books) read each week by some sixteen-year-olds.

a How many read less than two books each week?

b How many read four or more books each week?

c Why is it not possible to tell how many read four books each week?

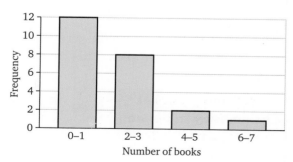

Pie charts

Pie charts are used to show the fraction that each category or group is of the whole.

This is the frequency table showing the amounts of money spent in the school canteen at break by 30 students.

Amount in pence	Frequency
0 to 49	3
50 to 99	7
100 to 149	10
150 to 199	8
200 to 249	2
	Total: 30

If we are interested in the fraction that the number in each group is of the 30 students, we can write these fractions down from the information in the table

i.e. $\frac{3}{30}$ of the group spent 0 to 49 p,

$\frac{7}{30}$ of the group spent 50 p to 99 p, and so on.

We can illustrate these proportions with a pie chart; a pie chart is a circle that is divided into 'slices'. The size of each slice represents the fraction that each group is of the whole.

Pie charts do not usually come with the circumference of the circle divided into a convenient number of parts. Each slice is usually labelled with what it represents and its percentage of the whole quantity.

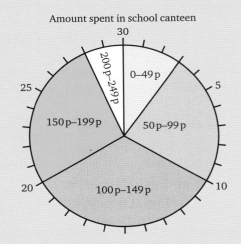

Amount spent in school canteen

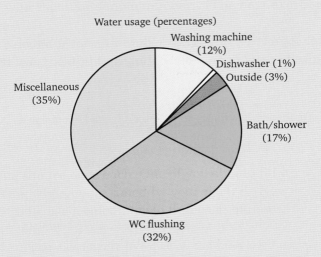

Water usage (percentages)

Without looking at the percentages, we can see that the proportion of water used for WC flushing is about $\frac{1}{3}$ of the total used and the water used for washing machines is about $\frac{1}{3}$ of that used for WC flushing, i.e. about $\frac{1}{9}$ of the total water used.

Exercise 22b

1 This pie chart shows the uses made of personal computers.

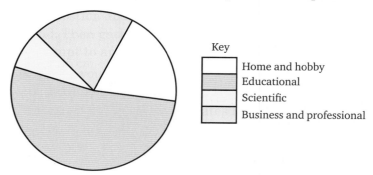

Key

Home and hobby
Educational
Scientific
Business and professional

   a For which purpose were computers used most?

   b Estimate the fraction of the total number used for
     i scientific purposes   **ii** home and hobbies.

2 The pie chart shows how fuel is used for different purposes in the average house.

   a For which purpose is most fuel used?

   b How does the amount of fuel used for cooking compare with the amount used for hot water?

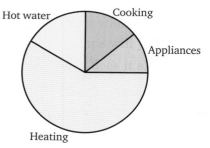

3 These pie charts show the age distribution of the population of the UK in years, in 1988 and in 2011.

   a For each year, estimate the size of the fraction of the population in the age groups
     i under 10 years   **ii** 60–79 years.

   b State which groups are of roughly the same size.

   c Describe briefly how the distribution of the ages in the population has changed between 1988 and 2011.

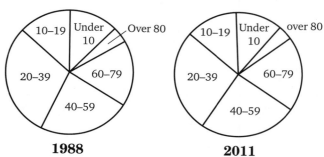

Drawing pie charts

The easiest way to draw a pie chart is to get a computer program to do it for you. This table shows the numbers of people with eyes of certain colours.

Eye colour	Brown	Hazel	Blue	Grey
Frequency	22	6	12	20

Entering the last four columns into a spreadsheet program, and then asking it to draw a pie chart, produced this diagram – it even works out the percentages for each slice.

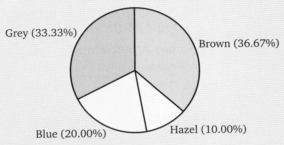

To draw it ourselves, we have to work out the size of each pie slice; this is given by the size of the angle at the 'point', i.e. at the centre. Therefore we need to calculate the sizes of the angles.

The number of people is 60, and $\frac{1}{60}$ of 360° is 6°.

As there are 12 blue-eyed people, they form $\frac{12}{60}$ of the whole group and are therefore represented by that fraction of the circle.

Blue: $\frac{12}{60}$ of 360° = 72°

Grey: $\frac{20}{60}$ of 360° = 120°

Hazel: $\frac{6}{60}$ of 360° = 36°

Brown: $\frac{22}{60}$ of 360° = 132°

           (*Check:* Total of the angles is 360°)

Now draw a circle of radius about 5 cm (or whatever is suitable). Draw one radius as shown and complete the diagram using a protractor, turning your page into the easiest position for drawing each new angle. Label each 'slice'.

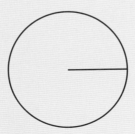

Exercise 22c

Draw pie charts to represent the following information, first working out the angles.

1   A box of 60 coloured balloons contains the following numbers of balloons of each colour.

Colour	Red	Yellow	Green	Blue	White
Number of balloons	16	22	10	7	5

2   Ninety people were asked how they travelled to work and the following information was recorded.

Transport	Car	Bus	Train	Motorcycle	Bicycle
Number of people	32	38	12	6	2

3   On a cornflakes packet the composition of 120 g of cornflakes is given in grams as follows.

Protein	Fat	Carbohydrate	Other
101	1	10	8

4   Of 90 cars passing a survey point it was recorded that 21 had two doors, 51 had four doors, 12 had three (two side doors and a hatchback) and 6 had five doors.

5   A large flower arrangement contained 18 dark red roses, 6 pale pink roses, 10 white roses and 11 deep pink roses.

6   The children in a class were asked what pets they owned and the following information was recorded.

Animal	Dog	Cat	Bird	Small animal	Fish
Frequency	8	10	3	6	3

Sometimes the total number involved does not work as conveniently as in the previous problems. In this case we find the angle correct to the nearest degree.

Worked example

→   The eye colour of 54 people is recorded in the table. Draw a pie chart to show the proportions of this group with each different eye colour.

Eye colour	Blue	Grey	Hazel	Brown	
Frequency	10	19	5	20	Total: 54

Angles: Blue: $\frac{10}{54}$ of 360° = 66.6...°
= 67° to the nearest degree

Grey: $\frac{19}{54}$ of 360° = 126.6...°
= 127° to the nearest degree

Hazel: $\frac{5}{54}$ of 360° = 33.3...°
= 33° to the nearest degree

Brown: $\frac{20}{54}$ of 360° = 133.3...°
= 133° to the nearest degree

 Use your calculator to find $(360 \div 54) \times 10$

Check: 67 + 127 + 33 + 133 = 360

 In this case, adding up the angles gives 360°.
Sometimes, because of rounding, the sum of the calculated angles comes to one or two degrees more or less than 360°. If the sum is more than 360°, find the rounded-up angle that is nearest to half way between two values, and round it down. If the sum is less than 360°, find the rounded-down angle that is nearest to half way between two values and round it up.

Draw pie charts to represent the following information. Work out the angles first and, where necessary, give the angles to the nearest degree. Try using a chart drawing package for some of these.

7   300 people were asked whether they lived in a flat, a house, a bedsit, a bungalow or in some other type of accommodation and the following information was recorded.

Type of accommodation	Flat	House	Bedsit	Bungalow	Other
Frequency	90	150	33	15	12

8   In a street in which 80 people live the numbers in various age groups are as follows.

Age group (years)	0–15	16–21	22–34	35–49	50–64	65 and over
Number of people	16	3	19	21	12	9

9 A group of people were asked to select their favourite colour from a card showing 6 colours and the following results were recorded.

Colour	Rose pink	Sky blue	Golden yellow	Violet	Lime green	Tomato red
Number of people (frequency)	6	8	8	2	1	10

10 Peter recorded the types of vehicle moving along a road during one hour and drew up this table.

Vehicle	Cars	Vans	Lorries	Motorcycles	Bicycles
Frequency	62	11	15	10	2

11 This table showing the hours of sunshine per day during June was compiled using information from the school's weather station.

Hours per day	0–2	3–4	5–6	7–8	over 8
Frequency	3	9	11	5	2

12 This table shows the average attendances at football matches in a European country for various years.

	Football division			
	Division A	Division B	Division C	Division D
2004–05	33 900	17 400	7700	4500
2005–06	33 900	17 600	7600	4200
2006–07	34 400	18 200	7500	4100
2007–08	36 100	17 000	8000	4300
2008–09	35 600	17 900	7600	4200
2009–10	34 200	18 000	9100	3900
2010–11	35 300	17 400	7500	4200
2011–12	34 600	17 700	7400	4400
2012–13	35 900	17 500	6400	4400

Figures are rounded to the nearest hundred.

a Draw a pie chart showing the proportions attending each division in 2004–05.

b Draw another pie chart showing the proportions attending each division in 2012–13.

c Have the proportions changed between 2004–05 and 2012–13?

13 This chart shows the percentage of spending money used for various categories of purchases by a group of 12-year-olds.

Show this information in a pie chart.

Consider again

The number of people waiting at the bus stop varied from just Saskia to several people. Saskia collected the following information.

The number of people waiting at a bus stop for the number 24 bus when it first arrives after 8 a.m. on 30 days														
5	7	15	20	25	14	12	8	3	1	11	15	7	9	4
9	12	18	21	25	17	6	9	13	4	10	13	17	23	1

a How can this information be illustrated so that it shows
  i the frequency of days when the numbers of people waiting fall into various groups
  ii the proportion of days when the numbers of people waiting fall into various groups?

b Draw the two illustrations for part **a**.

Now can you answer these questions?

! Practical work

1   This is a group activity for the whole class.

Think of a question about the money that the class-mates in your group spend. Then gather and organise the information so that you can attempt to answer some questions.

Some questions you might like to answer are:
- How much do my class-mates spend on fares each day?
- How much money do my class-mates have each week?
- What do they spend it on?
- How much of that money are they given and how much do they have to earn by doing tasks around the home?
- How does the spending pattern in the school canteen by my group compare with the data given at the beginning of this chapter?

When you have decided what question you want to answer, think about the information that you need to collect and how you are going to collect it.

Will you group the information – if so, what groups will you use?

When you have organised the information, what does it show?

What is the best way to illustrate the information?

2   This is an individual activity.

Choose two different daily newspapers. For each one find the area of the front page used for each of the categories 'Headlines', 'Pictures', 'Text', 'Everything else'.

Illustrate your results with either bar charts or pie charts and give a reason for your choice.

What comparisons can you make between the two front pages?

Summary 5

Summarising data

For a list of values,

- the range is the difference between the largest value and the smallest value
- the mean is the sum of all the values divided by the number of values
- the median is the middle value when they have been arranged in order of size (when the middle of the list is half way between two values, the median is the average of these two values)
- the mode is the value that occurs most frequently.

Pie charts

Pie charts are used to show the fraction that each group or category is of the whole list.

The size of a 'slice' is given by the angle at the centre of the circle. This angle is found by the number of values in the group as a fraction of all the values, and then finding this fraction of 360°.

Volume

Volume is measured using standard sized cubes.

A cube with edges 1 cm long has a volume of 1 cubic centimetre, written $1\,cm^3$.

$$1\,cm^3 = 10 \times 10 \times 10\,mm^3 = 1000\,mm^3$$
$$1\,m^3 = 100 \times 100 \times 100\,cm^3 = 1\,000\,000\,cm^3$$

Capacity

The capacity of a container is the volume of liquid it will hold.

The main metric units of capacity are the litre (1) and the millilitre (ml), where

$$1\,litre = 1000\,ml, \quad 1\,litre = 1000\,cm^3 \quad and \quad 1\,ml = 1\,cm^3$$

The main imperial units of capacity are the gallon and the pint, where

$$1\,gallon = 8\,pints$$

Rough conversions between metric and imperial units of capacity are given by

$$1\,litre \approx 1.75\,pints \text{ and } 1\,gallon \approx 4.5\,litres$$

Algebraic expressions

Terms such as $2x$ and $5x$ mean $\quad 2 \times x$, i.e $\quad x + x$

and $\quad 5 \times x$, i.e. $\quad x + x + x + x + x$

Similarly ab means $a \times b$

$2x + 5x$ can be simplified to $7x$, since

$$2x + 5x = x + x + x + x + x + x + x$$
$$= 7x$$

$2a + 3b$ cannot be simplified.

Solving equations

An equation is a relationship between an unknown number, represented by a letter, and other numbers, e.g. $2x - 3 = 5$

Solving the equation means finding the unknown number, i.e. ending up with $x = $ (a number)

Provided that we do the same to both sides of an equation, we keep the equality; this can be used to solve the equation.

e.g. to solve $\qquad\qquad\qquad 2x - 3 = 5$

First, add 3 to both sides $\qquad 2x - 3 + 3 = 5 + 3$

This gives $\qquad\qquad\qquad\qquad 2x = 8$

Now divide each side by 2 $\qquad\qquad\quad x = 4$

REVISION EXERCISE 5.1 (Chapters 19 and 20)

1 In three different bookshops a particular school textbook costs £12.49, £14.49 and £14.99.

   a What is the mean price?   **b** What is the range of prices?

2 Find the mode and the median of the numbers
5, 4, 7, 4, 5, 9, 8, 7, 4, 3, 5, 4, 8

3 Tim and Meg sold bunches of flowers which they had put together. Out of curiosity they counted the number of flowers in several bunches to see how the numbers that Tim put in a bunch compared with the numbers that Meg put in a bunch. The numbers in Tim's bunches were 12, 17, 11, 15, 20, 11, 16, 19, 21, 8 and the numbers in Meg's bunches were 17, 15, 14, 16, 13, 12, 15, 15, 16, 17

Compare the mean and range of the number of flowers in Tim's bunches with the mean and range of the number of flowers in Meg's bunches.

4 Tara chose four cards at random several times from an ordinary pack of 52 playing cards. Each time, she counted the number of the cards that were red. Her results are given in the table.

Number of red cards	Frequency
0	1
1	5
2	9
3	7
4	3

a How many times did she choose four cards?

b What was the median number of red cards she chose?

c How many red cards did she choose altogether?

d What was the modal number of red cards she chose?

e What was the mean number of red cards she chose?

5 Use isometric paper to draw a cube of side 4.5 cm.

6 This closed presentation box for holding a watch is 6 cm long, 4 cm wide and 2 cm high.

a How many faces does it have?

b Sketch the faces, showing their measurements.

c On 1 cm grid paper, draw a net that will make this box.

7 Express   **a**   9 cm³ in mm³   **b**   2 m³ in cm³

8 Give, roughly

  a the number of pints in 5 litres

  b the number of litres in 20 pints.

9 a Find the volume of a solid wooden cube of side 2 cm.

  b How many cubes of side 2 cm will fit inside a cubical box of side 10 cm?

10 Petrol costs £1.50 a litre. Roughly, how much is this a gallon?

REVISION EXERCISE 5.2 (Chapters 21 and 22)

1 Solve the equations

  a $a + 4 = 11$ **c** $3.5 + x = 8$

  b $b - 3 = 12$ **d** $y - 3.5 = 6$

2 Solve the equations

  a $6z = 24$ **b** $3x + 2 = 17$

3 Simplify

  a $5x - 4x - 7x$ **b** $5a - 4b - 3a + 2b$

4 Solve the equations

   a $5x - 2x = x + 8$ **b** $7x - 6 - 2x - 14 = 0$

5 Pete is p years old now and his sister Carol is 3 years older. In 10 years' time the sum of their ages will be 33. How old is Pete now? How old will Carol be in 10 years' time?

6 I think of a number, add 3 and multiply the answer by 4. The result is 40. What is the number?

7 A hotel group grades its hotels from 1 star (*) up to 5 star (*****) depending on the facilities the hotel offers. The number of hotels in each grade is given in the table.

Grade of hotel	Number of hotels in grade
1 star	2
2 star	6
3 star	11
4 star	12
5 star	5

   a   How many hotels are there in the group?

   b   Draw a bar chart to illustrate the information in this frequency table.

8 This frequency table gives the time taken by the students in a group to solve a puzzle.

Time in minutes	0–4	5–9	10–14	15–19
Number of students	3	10	7	2

   a   How many students were there in the group?

   b   How many students took less than 10 minutes?

   c   How many students took 10 minutes or more?

   d   Can you tell how many students took 10 minutes?

9 The pie chart shows the choice of juices taken for breakfast by the 60 guests in a hotel one morning.

Estimate the sizes of the angles and hence find, approximately, the number who preferred

   a   orange juice

   b   tomato juice

   c   apple juice.

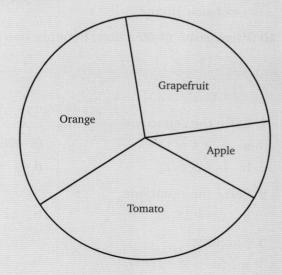

10 A survey of Year 7 students gave the following information about the way they came to school.

Way of coming to school	Bus	Car	Walk	Bicycle
Number of students	43	21	14	12

   a How many students in Year 7 took part in the survey?

   b Draw a pie chart to represent this information after you have calculated the angles corresponding to each slice.

REVISION EXERCISE 5.3 (Chapters 19 to 22)

1 The pie chart shows how 40 chocolates are shared among three sisters.

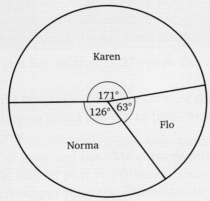

   a Find each angle as a fraction of a revolution.

   b How many chocolates did Karen get?

   c How many did Norma get?

   d How many did Flo get?

2 Use isometric paper to draw a cuboid measuring 3 cm by 5 cm by 4 cm.

3 This net will make a cube.

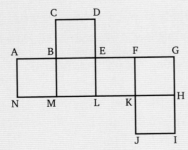

   a Which edge meets
     i AB   **ii** FG?

   b Which other corners meet at
     i J   **ii** G?

4 Find the capacity, in litres, of a rectangular metal tank measuring 40 cm by 30 cm by 1 m.

5 Express

   a $5000 \, \text{mm}^3$ in cm^3

   b $0.5 \, \text{m}^3$ in cm^3

6 Solve the equations

   a $p + 6 = 9$

   b $q - 10 = 12$

7 I think of a number, subtract 4 and multiply by 6. The answer is 48. What is the number?

8 Solve the equation $2x + 7 = 5x - 14$

9 Simplify

   a $5x - 3 + 4x - 1$

   b $3x + 5y - 2x + 4y$

10 Once every 10 minutes, Diana counted the number of people standing at the bus stop outside her home. Her results are given in the table.

Number of people at bus stop	Frequency
0	6
1	2
2	3
3	6
4	2
5	1

   a How many times did she count?

   b How long did she spend gathering the information?

   c What was the mean number of people waiting at the bus stop?

REVISION EXERCISE 5.4 (Chapters 1 to 22)

1 a Find the difference between the value of the 4 in 3408 and the 7 in the number 1079.

   b Estimate the value of $742 + (53 - 37) \times 22$ and then use your calculator to find its exact value.

   c What is the remainder when 659 is divided by 56?

2 a Find

     i $4\frac{5}{8} + 7\frac{4}{5}$

     ii $18\frac{2}{7} - 6\frac{7}{12}$

b Which is the greater: $\frac{7}{21}$ or $\frac{5}{14}$?

c Change

   i 0.86 into a percentage

   ii 34% into a decimal

   iii $\frac{27}{50}$ into a percentage.

3 a Find, without using a calculator

   i 0.043×10

   ii $66 \div 100$

   iii 0.057×30

   iv $1.28 \div 40$

b From 3.74 subtract the difference between 4.53 and 5.27

4 a Estimate the value of

   i 63×382

   ii $6394 \div 278$

   Now use your calculator to find the exact values.

b Use your calculator to change the fractions

$\frac{4}{5}, \frac{19}{25}, \frac{17}{20}, \frac{2}{3}$ and $\frac{5}{8}$ into decimals.

Use these values to put the fractions in order of size with the smallest first.

5 Express

  a 0.46 cm in mm   **d** $0.0008\,\text{m}^3$ in cm^3

  b 0.55 km in m   **e** 7690 kg in tonnes

  c $240\,\text{mm}^2$ in cm^2 **f** $750\,000\,\text{cm}^3$ in m^3

6 Find the size of each angle marked with a letter.

a

b

7 Write down the next three numbers in each sequence.

  a $8, 5, 2, \ldots$ **b** $-12, -9, -6, \ldots$

8 a The formula for finding profit £p when n boxes of chocolates are sold is $p = 2.5n - 30$

Find p when $n = 10$, and explain what you think that answer means.

b I think of a number, double it and then add 15 to the result.

The answer is three times the number I thought of.

If x stands for the number I first thought of, form an equation in x and solve it.

9 One side of a rectangle is 5 cm longer than another. Its perimeter is 50 cm.

What is the length of

a   a long side

b   a short side?

10 Find the mode and median of the following set of numbers.

4.1, 3.8, 4.2, 4.3, 3.9, 3.8, 4.5, 3.7

REVISION EXERCISE 5.5 (Chapters 1 to 22)

1 A sequence is formed by starting with 5 and adding 8 each time.

a   Write down the first eight terms.

b   What is the difference between the sum of the first four terms and the sum of the next four terms in this sequence?

2 Find

a $4\frac{7}{10} + 3\frac{4}{5}$

b $5\frac{1}{6} - 2\frac{2}{3}$

c $6 \times 3 \times 4 - 7 \times 3$

d $18 \div 3 + 3 \times 3 - 4 \div 2$

3 a   Find, giving your answer in metres,   156 cm + 84 mm + 2.1 m

b   Find, giving your answer in grams,   465 g + 0.44 kg + 750 mg

c   Find, giving your answer in inches,   10 inches + 3 feet + 1 yard

4 a $A = \{3, 4, 5, 6, 7, 9\}$ and $B = \{1, 2, 3, 4, 5, 6, 7, 8\}$. Find

   i $A \cap B$ **ii** $A \cup B$.

b   A rectangular box measures 4.78 cm by 3.23 cm by 1.88 cm.

Estimate its capacity.

Use a calculator to find the capacity of the box correct to two decimal places.

How near is your estimate?

5 In a boat race, one crew rows at 30 strokes to the minute while another crew rows at 20 strokes to the minute.

a   How long is it, in seconds, between strokes for

   i   the faster crew

   ii   the slower crew?

b   They start the race with their oars in the water at the same moment. How long will it be before their oars are in the water at the same instant again?

6 a   By choosing a letter to stand for the number of length units of the side of an equilateral triangle, find a formula for the perimeter, P units of the triangle.

b   The formula for changing $x\,°C$ to $y\,°F$ is $y = \frac{9x}{5} + 32$.

Find the temperature in °F when a thermometer reads 20 °C.

7 The bar chart shows how a family's weekly income is spent.

Amount in £'s

a On which item do they spend
   i most   **ii** least?

b How much do they spend on
   i fuel   **ii** leisure?

c How much do they spend altogether?

8 Solve the equations

   a $3x - 4 = 5$ **b** $2 - x = 4 + x$ **c** $0.7 = 0.9 - 4x$

9 The diagram shows a rectangular plot of ground measuring 30 m by 20 m. It is laid out as a rectangular lawn surrounded by a path that is everywhere 1 m wide.

20 m

30 m

Find

   a the measurements of the lawn   **c** the area of the whole plot

   b the area of the lawn   **d** the area of the path.

10 Hank has three pieces of string. The first piece is x cm long, the second piece is 4 cm longer than the first and the third piece is 5 cm longer than the second. Altogether he has 49 cm of string. How long is each piece?

11 The ages (in years) of 20 children attending a swimming class are

   9, 10, 10, 10, 10, 11, 11, 11, 11, 12

   9, 10, 10, 10, 11, 11, 11, 11, 11, 12

The ages (in years) of a different group of 20 children in a trampoline class are

   6, 7, 7, 8, 8, 8, 9, 9, 9, 9, 9, 10, 10, 11, 11, 11, 12, 13, 13, 14

   a Find the mean and range of the ages of each group.

   b Use your answers to part **a** to compare the ages of the two groups.

Mental arithmetic practice 5

1 Change $0.7\,cm^2$ to mm^2

2 Find the mode of 4, 5, 6, 6

3 Is 7.46 nearer to 7 than it is to 8?

4 Estimate 493×307

5 What is the probability of getting an even number when a fair dice is rolled?

6 Divide 0.12 by 0.4

7 Express 0.58 as a percentage.

8 Is it true or false that the difference between 0.84 and 0.084 is 0.756?

9 Express 55% as a fraction in its lowest terms.

10 Is $\frac{8}{9}$ smaller than $\frac{9}{10}$?

11 There are 3 red discs and 2 white discs in a bag. What is the probability that a disc chosen at random is white?

12 Find 0.3^2

13 What is the area of a rectangle in mm^2 measuring 2 cm by 5 mm?

14 Which is larger, -2 or -5?

15 Find 283×60

16 Express $\frac{13}{20}$ as a decimal.

17 Express $\frac{4}{25}$ as a percentage.

18 A can of cola cost 60 p in a supermarket, 76 p in a 24-hour shop and £1.40 in a bar. What was the average cost?

19 Find $\frac{2}{3} + \frac{3}{4}$

20 Find $1.36 \div 20$

21 Find the difference between the value of the figure 4 in 4.3 and the value of the figure 6 in 2.6.

22 Which is larger, 1 litre or 1 pint?

23 Find the area in mm^2 of a rectangle measuring 5 mm by 1.5 cm.

24 Find 20% of £1200.

25 Find the volume of a cuboid measuring 5 cm by 8 cm by 6 cm.

26 Simplify $4 -$ (negative 2)

27 Change $\frac{10}{4}$ to a decimal.

28 What is the sum of the four interior angles of a parallelogram?

29 Which holds more water, a carton measuring 10 cm by 20 cm by 5 cm or a bottle whose capacity is 1.5 litres?

30 Express 12% as a decimal.

31 Find 400×0.38

32 Find $76 \div 100$

33 Change 0.06 into a percentage.

34 Find $1\frac{1}{2} + \frac{3}{4}$

35 Write down the next two numbers in the sequence 10, 6, 2, …

36 Give 0.3 km in metres.

37 Give $\frac{3}{25}$ as a decimal.

38 Find 0.3 cubed.

39 What is the lowest common multiple of 2, 3 and 5?

40 One side of an equilateral triangle is x cm long and the perimeter of the triangle is P cm. Write down a formula for P.

Use these amounts for questions **41** to **45**   £1, £1.10, £1.20, £1.20, £1.50.

41 What is the modal amount?

42 What is the range of these amounts?

43 What is the mean amount?

44 What is the median amount?

45 If £1.05 is added to this list, will the mean amount increase or decrease?

46 A sequence starts with 3 and then each subsequent number is found by multiplying the last term by 6. What are the next two terms?

47 About how many litres is 5 gallons?

48 Simplify $4a - 2a$

49 Simplify $2x - 2 + x + 2$

50 If $13 - x = 7$, what is x?

For questions **51** to **55**, is it true or false that

51 corresponding angles add up to 180°?

52 $289 \div 2.52 = 11.5$?

53 2500 mm is longer than 1 m?

54 the probability of throwing a 6 with a fair six-sided dice is less than the probability of throwing a 2?

55 all four sides of a rhombus are the same length?

56 The angle at the centre of one slice of a pie chart is 90°. The slice represents the proportion of the 28 students in a class who failed to hand in their homework on time. How many students didn't hand in their work on time?

57 Find $1\frac{2}{3} - \frac{5}{6}$

58 What must be added to 58 to give 100?

59 What is the mean of the numbers 1, 2, 2 and 5?

60 Write $x + x + x + x$ in a simpler form.

Key words

acute angle	an angle between 0 and 90 degrees
alternate angles	equal angles that are each side of a line across parallel lines and between the parallel lines; they can be recognised by drawing a Z on the diagram
angle	an amount of turning from a fixed line
angles at a point	the angles between lines that meet at a point; they add up to 36 degrees
arc of a circle	part of the circle
area	amount of surface
arithmetic progression	a sequence of numbers where each number is obtained by adding the same amount to (or subtracting the same amount from) the previous number
axis of symmetry	a line about which a shape can be folded so that one half fits exactly over the other half
bar chart	bars or columns showing information; the height of the bar gives the size
cancelling a fraction	dividing the numerator and denominator of a fraction by the same number to reduce the size of the numerator and the size of the denominator; this does not reduce the size of the fraction
capacity	a measure of volume, usually showing how much a container can hold
centimetre	a metric measure of length, one hundredth of a metre
central tendency	measures representing the centre of a set of figures
circle	a closed curve where every point on the curve is the same distance from one point, called the centre of the circle
circumference	the length round a circle
common denominator	when two or more fractions have the same denominator
common factor	a factor of two or more numbers
common multiple	a multiple of two or more numbers
compass directions	directions based on North, South, East and West
congruent	two or more shapes that are the same shape and size
construct	to make an accurate drawing
conversion graph	a line that can be used to convert between two different units of the same quantity, e.g. converting temperatures between degrees Celsius and degrees Fahrenheit
coordinates	measurements that fix the position of a point with reference to a known position
correcting a number	rounding a number to a given degree of accuracy, e.g. to the nearest ten, or to two decimal places
corresponding angles	equal angles on the same side of a line across parallel lines and in similar positions; they can be recognised by drawing an F on the diagram
cube	a solid with six faces, each of which is a square
cube number	a number that can be written as the product of three equal numbers, e.g. 27 (= 3 × 3 × 3)

cubic centimetre	the volume occupied by a cube whose edges are 1 cm long
cuboid	a solid with six faces, each of which is a rectangle
decimal fraction	a fraction with a denominator that is a power of 10, with just the numerator written after a point, e.g $\frac{47}{100}$ is written as 0.47
decimal place	the position of a digit to the right of the decimal point, e.g. 2 is in the second decimal place in 3.026
denominator	the number underneath the line in a fraction
diameter	a straight line from one side of a circle going through the centre of the circle to the other side
difference	the larger number minus the smaller number
digit	one of the symbols 0, 1, 2, 3, 4, 5, 6, 7, 8, 9
directed numbers	positive and negative numbers
elements of a set	the objects included in the set
equation	the equality between two expressions
equilateral triangle	a triangle with three equal sides and three equal angles
equivalent fractions	fractions of the same size but with different denominators, e.g. $\frac{1}{2}$ and $\frac{2}{4}$
event	what happens when a task is performed
experiment	a task to find out what happens
expression	a collection of numbers and letters without an equals sign
factor	a number that divides exactly into another number
fair	not biased, as likely to give a particular result as any other result
finite set	a set where the number of members is a natural number, e.g. {days of the week}
foot (feet)	an imperial measure of length, 3 feet = 1 yard
formula	an instruction for finding one quantity in terms of other quantities
fraction	part of a quantity, e.g. $\frac{1}{4}$
frequency	the number of times that an event occurs
frequency table	a table giving the number of times different events occur
gallon	an imperial measure of capacity, 1 gallon = 8 pints
gram	a metric measure of mass
graph	a diagram showing the relationship between two varying quantities
highest common factor (HCF)	the highest number that divides exactly into two or more numbers
improper fraction	a fraction whose numerator is greater than its denominator, e.g. $\frac{7}{5}$
inch	an imperial measure of length, 12 inches = 1 foot
index of a number	a superscript giving how many of that number are multiplied together, e.g. 4^3 means $4 \times 4 \times 4$
infinite set	a set whose members cannot be listed because it carries on indefinitely, e.g. {whole numbers}

integer	a positive or negative whole number
interior angles	**i** angles inside a triangle or any closed figure
	ii the pair of angles on the same side of a line across parallel lines and between the parallel lines
intersection of sets	the set of members common to two or more sets
isometric grid	a grid where the gridlines intersect at 60 degrees
isosceles triangle	a triangle with two equal sides
kilogram	a metric measure of mass, $1\,kg = 1000\,g$
kilometre	a metric measure of length, $1\,km = 1000$ m
least common multiple (LCM)	the lowest number that each of two or more numbers divide into exactly
like terms	terms which have the same combination of letters, e.g. $5xy$ and $2xy$
line graph	a graph where lines join separate points
line segment	a line with two ends
line symmetry	where there is a line which can be folded along so that one half of the shape fits exactly over the other half
litre	a metric measure of capacity
mass	the quantity of matter in an object
mean	the mean of n numbers is the sum of the numbers divided by n
median	the middle number when a set of numbers is arranged in order of size
members of a set	the objects included in the set
metre	a metric measure of length
mile	an imperial measure of length
milligram	a metric measure of mass, one thousandth of a gram
millimetre	a metric measure of length, one thousandth of a metre
mixed number	a whole number plus a fraction, e.g. $3\frac{1}{2}$
mode	the item in a set that occurs most often
multiple	a multiple of a number is the product of that number and any other number
negative numbers	numbers that are below a natural zero, e.g. 2 degrees below freezing
net	a flat shape that can be cut out and folded to make a solid
number line	a line where points on the line represent numbers, including decimals and fractions
numerator	the number above the line in a fraction
observation sheet	a sheet designed to record a number of different events
obtuse angle	an angle between 90 and 180 degrees
origin	the fixed point from which the position of another point can be described
ounce	an imperial measure of mass, 16 ounces = 1 pound

outcome	what happens when a task is performed
palindrome	a number that reads the same forwards and backwards, e.g. 1221
parallel lines	lines that are always the same distance apart
parallelogram	a shape bounded by four straight lines where the pairs of opposite sides are parallel
per cent	out of one hundred
perimeter	the distance round the sides of a shape
pie chart	a circle divided into slices, where the sizes of the slices represent the fraction that each category is of all the information
pint	an imperial measure of capacity
pound	an imperial measure of mass
power of a number	another word for index, i.e. a superscript giving how many times that number is multiplied together, e.g. 4^3 means $4 \times 4 \times 4$
prime number	a number that has only two different factors, 1 and itself
probability	a measure of the likelihood that a particular event will happen, given by the number of ways that the event can occur divided by the number of possible outcomes
product	the product of two or more numbers means the numbers are multiplied, e.g. the product of 2, 3 and 4 is $2 \times 3 \times 4$
proper fraction	a fraction whose numerator is smaller than its denominator
protractor	an instrument for measuring angles
quadrilateral	a figure with four straight line sides
radius	a straight line from the centre of a circle to its edge
random	a random event is as likely to happen as any other event
range	the difference between the largest and smallest value in a set of values
rectangular ••• number •••	a number that can be expressed as the product of two different factors excluding 1 and itself, and can be represented by a rectangular array of dots, e.g. $6 = 2 \times 3$
recurring decimal	a decimal where the number or group of numbers after the decimal point repeat indefinitely
reflex angle	an angle between 180 and 360 degrees
relative frequency	the number of times a particular event occurs when an experiment is repeated divided by the number of times the experiment is performed
revolution	a complete turn of 360 degrees
rhombus	a four-sided figure in which all the sides are the same length
right angle	quarter of a revolution, i.e. 90 degrees
rotational symmetry	a figure that has rotational symmetry can be rotated by less than 360 degrees about a point and still look the same
rounding	a way of approximating numbers

sequence	an ordered set of numbers or objects, usually with a rule for continuing the sequence
set	a collection of objects, not in any particular order
simplifying a fraction	dividing the numerator and denominator of a fraction by the same number to reduce the sizes of the numerator and denominator; this does not reduce the size of the fraction
square centimetre	a metric measure of area equivalent to the area covered by a square of side 1 cm
square number	a number that can be expressed as the product of two equal numbers, e.g. $36 = 6 \times 6$
stone	an imperial measure of mass, 1 stone = 14 pounds
supplementary angles	two angles whose sum is 180 degrees
symmetrical	a shape is symmetrical if it can be divided into halves such that each half is exactly the same shape and size, although one half is turned over with respect to the other half
term	a product of numbers and letters, e.g. $7x$
time series	a sequence of values of a quantity measured at intervals of time
tonne	a metric measure of mass, 1 tonne = 1000 kg
transversal	a line that crosses other lines
trapezium	a four-sided figure with just one pair of opposite sides parallel
triangular number	the number of dots in a triangle of dots where each line has one more dot than the line above it, e.g. 10
unbiased	not biased, as likely to give a particular result as any other result
union of sets	the set comprising the members of two or more sets
universal set	a set containing all the members of some given sets, possibly together with other numbers
unlike terms	terms containing different combinations of letters, e.g. $3xy$ and $5x$
Venn diagram	a diagram illustrating sets with circles inside a rectangle for the universal set
vertex (vertices)	a corner of a flat shape or of a solid
vertically opposite angles	the angles formed when two straight lines cross
volume	the space occupied by a solid, measured in cubic units
weight	the pull of the Earth on an object
x-axis	a straight number line through the origin, usually drawn horizontally across the page
yard	an imperial measure of length
y-axis	a straight number line drawn through the origin perpendicular to the x-axis

Index

Note: key words are in **bold** type